BRIGHT, INFINITE FUTURE

ALSO BY MARK GREEN

*Change for America: A Progressive Blueprint for the
44th President* (ed. with Michele Jolin, 2009)

*Losing Our Democracy: How Bush, the Far Right & Big Business
Are Betraying Americans for Power & Profit* (2006)

*Defend Yourself! How to Protect Your Health, Your Money,
and Your Rights in 10 Key Areas of Your Life* (2006)

What We Stand For: A Program for Progressive Patriotism (ed., 2004)

*The Book on Bush: How George W. (Mis)Leads
America* (with Eric Alterman, 2004)

*Selling Out: How Big Corporate Money Buys Elections, Rams
Through Legislation, and Betrays Our Democracy* (2002)

Mark Green's Guide to Coping in New York City (2000)

The Consumer Bible (with Nancy Youman, 1998)

Changing America: Blueprints for the New Administration (ed., 1993)

America's Transition: Blueprints for the 1990s (ed. with Mark Pinsky, 1989)

*Reagan's Reign of Error: The Instant Nostalgia
Edition* (with Gail MacColl, 1987)

*The Challenge of Hidden Profits: Reducing Corporate
Bureaucracy and Waste* (with John Berry, 1985)

Who Runs Congress? (with Michael Waldman, 1984)

Winning Back America (1982)

The Big Business Reader (ed. with Robert Massie Jr., 1980)

Taming the Giant Corporation (with Ralph Nader and Joel Seligman, 1976)

Verdicts on Lawyers (ed. with Ralph Nader, 1976)

The Other Government: The Unseen Power of Washington Lawyers (1975)

Corporate Power in America (ed. with Ralph Nader, 1973)

The Monopoly Makers (ed., 1973)

The Closed Enterprise System (with Beverly C.
Moore Jr. and Bruce Wasserstein, 1972)

With Justice for Some (ed. with Bruce Wasserstein, 1970)

BRIGHT, INFINITE FUTURE

A GENERATIONAL MEMOIR
ON THE PROGRESSIVE RISE

MARK GREEN

St. Martin's Press
New York

www.stmartins.com

Design by Letra Libre, Inc.

Library of Congress Cataloging-in-Publication Data

Names: Green, Mark J., author.

Title: Bright, infinite future : a generational memoir on the progressive rise / Mark Green.

Description: First edition. I New York : St. Martin's Press, 2016.

Identifiers: LCCN 2015049287I ISBN 9781250071576 (hardback) I ISBN 9781466882713 (e-book)

Subjects: LCSH: United States—Politics and government—1945–1989. I United States—Politics and government—1989– I New York (N.Y.)—Politics and government. I Progressivism (United States politics) I Liberalism—United States. I Green, Mark J. I Political activists—United States—Biography. I BISAC: POLITICAL SCIENCE / Government / General. I BIOGRAPHY & AUTOBIOGRAPHY / Political.

Classification: LCC E839.5 .G744 2016 I DDC 320.97309/04—dc23

LC record available at http://lccn.loc.gov/2015049287

Our books may be purchased in bulk for promotional, educational, or business use. Please contact your local bookseller or the Macmillan Corporate and Premium Sales Department at 1-800-221-7945, extension 5442, or by e-mail at MacmillanSpecialMarkets@macmillan.com.

First Edition: May 2016

10   9   8   7   6   5   4   3   2   1

To Ava & Otis

CONTENTS

PREFACE

INTERTWINING ARCS

THE ARC OF MY PUBLIC LIFE—AS A PROGRESSIVE AD-
vocate, politician, lawyer, and author—roughly tracks the political
arc of the country from the 1960s to 2016. So I write this "generational memoir" not because I'm *the* but rather *a* boomer who's trav-
eled this personal and political journey, working with some of the
greatest liberals and against some the most talented conservatives of
this era. I'll occasionally provide profiles of these "forces of nature"
who have moved the needle of history.

The core premise of *Bright, Infinite Future* is that there's a rising
progressive majority and era in this country due to a combination
of demographic and social trends and a Republican lurch from the
mainstream to the extreme.

Political memoirs, however, often disappoint because public figures have an inner press secretary, to use Jonathan Haidt's metaphor
in *The Righteous Mind,* warning them away from risky, vote-losing,
donor-offending Bulworthian candor. But to keep my wife and san-
ity, I'm now done with electoral politics and free to be candid about
politicians of all persuasions—and myself.

Especially myself. I've made law and made mistakes and I've lost
to enough major figures—Michael Bloomberg, Chuck Schumer, Andrew Cuomo, and Bill de Blasio—that I began to think that someone
couldn't rise in New York politics unless they got by me first. But I
learned valuable if expensive lessons about what it's like and what it
takes to succeed in the public arena, lessons I want to share in *Bright,
Infinite Future.*

Books about contentious issues in this very polarized time can easily slip into two genres: either false symmetry passing for thoughtfulness—*well, both sides do it*—or the partisan hysteria seen in big-selling books with titles that are synonyms for *traitor* followed by an exclamation mark. I'm aiming instead for a blend of memoir and manifesto—call it evidence-based advocacy.

People born before 1945 or after 1961 may plausibly wonder about my linkage of the Sixties to today. "Arrgh, yet more boomer hubris?" Well, every affinity group seeks some uniqueness to give their lives special meaning as part of a larger whole. In my view, the Sixties constitutes *the* Consequential Generation. It's pretty remarkable how the creativity and values of that decade—liberally stretching from the sit-ins in Greensboro, North Carolina, and John F. Kennedy's defeat of Richard Nixon in 1960 to Nixon's resignation in August 1974—have gestated so many positive ideas that are becoming public policy. These are now echoing in the 2016 national election and will for years to come. True, short of H. G. Wells, there's no going back to Che T-shirts, but Earth Day connects to the 2015 Paris Climate Summit just as Dr. King connects to *#BlackLivesMatter*.

In my view, if liberal values were a stock, now is the time to buy. Read on to find out why.

Mark Green

BRIGHT, INFINITE FUTURE

INTRODUCTION

THE PROGRESSIVE-CONSERVATIVE CLASH

Progress is our most important product.

—Ronald Reagan, for GE, 1950s

History is like waves lapping at a cliff. For decades nothing happens and then the cliff collapses.

—French historian Henry See

"I'D LIKE TO MEET WITH MR. NADER," SAYS THE SPRY *voice on the phone in June 1972. In the throes of researching* Who Runs Congress?, *I'm awed to be talking with Jeannette Rankin, 92 years old and the first woman ever elected to the United States Congress back in 1916. She explains, "I want to meet another believer in democracy, someone who also made the right enemies."*

She arrives the following month at the offices of Ralph's Center for Study of Responsive Law at 19th and Q Streets NW, a fading Victorian semi-castle that would soon make way for a gleaming Metro subway stop. It's a warren of cluttered desks and earnest students challenging President Nixon and the 91st Congress on a broad array of consumer, worker, and health issues.

With a cane to steady her, Rankin marches to a first-floor conference room. Ralph lifts his lanky six-foot-four frame and greets her with an enthusiastic "Finally!" She smiles broadly, waves off coffee, and, with zero small talk, launches into a mini monologue on how to fix Congress—more women in Congress, far less military spending, voting reform. Though lacking the broad-rimmed hat that made her the Bella of the House nearly six decades before, Rankin wears a cheap wig that's dancing on her head every time she throws it back to make a point emphatically, which is often.

We chat about her unique history as a young pacifist who got elected from Montana in time to be among 49 voting against our entry into World War I—"Hell, Wilson ran on the slogan 'he kept us out of war.'" She was then voted out on a wave of patriotism in 1918 but, after subsequent decades of work as a suffragette and pacifist, got reelected in 1940 . . . in time to be the only member voting against our entry into World War II! She did not—could not due to her notoriety—seek reelection in 1942.

Today she probes Ralph about his ability to recruit so many young activists to do research and organizing. "At ten my father said to me, 'Ralph, today did you learn how to believe or did you learn how to think?' I'm really interested in whether students ask the right questions, whether they can think." Each seems impressed with the other's unusual route to this place and time. When I ask how she was able to persevere for so many years up against near-unanimous public sentiment and such transcendent figures as Woodrow Wilson and Franklin Roosevelt, she stares at me for two beats, then explains: "Son, you can't lose if you never give up—you can't lose if you never give up."

Jeannette Rankin died ten months later. In the Congressional Hall of Statues, where each state gets only two residents to venerate, Montana chose this pioneer whom history has judged to be a far greater advocate than politician.

I'M AN ADVOCATE and politician who loves biographies and dancing; would rather make policy than money; debated Buckley and Buchanan a couple hundred times; advised Hart, both Clintons, and Kerry in their presidential bids; tried to save Air America Radio; spent a third of my life writing books; and suffered the despair of losing to a multi-billionaire in the closest New York City mayoral election in a century.

With that brief, eclectic backstory, I'll be combining the biographical, historical, and political to explain America's Left-Right tug-of-war over the past five decades.

This current history rests on three cornerstones:

Outside/In. Political change requires independent advocates to fearlessly provide ideas, organizers, and moral clarity to professional politicians who in turn can convert proposals into law—think King and Kennedy/Johnson on race. That is, it really takes two to tangle first, *then* tango. Usually, change begins with disruptive outsiders—"unreasonable men," to use George Bernard Shaw's apt phrase.

The skills essential to one are not identical to the other. Pols have a *Janus* gene, the ability to look in two directions at once, while advocates can't take their eyes off the moral high ground. It's hard, actually impossible, to think of activist Lyndon Johnson picketing the powerful or a President Ralph Nader splitting differences based on polling. Both driven, tough, and smart, these men possessed very different approaches consistent with their personalities.

A New Patriotism. America is exceptional because America is optimistic.

While it's difficult to discern national character, America is as much a notion as a nation—and that notion is *progress,* as embodied in the breathtaking first line of the Preamble to the Constitution about forming "a *more* perfect union" (emphasis added). America is not a country stuck in time or determined by monarchical succession but one in which—based on ideas from the Enlightenment—reason, science, the rule of law, free speech, religious tolerance, and democratic voting can keep our progress going for centuries to come.

Hence Albert Einstein wrote that America and its people were "always becoming, never being," while Barack Obama said in his heralded remarks at the fiftieth anniversary of the march from Selma to Birmingham that "America is a constant work in progress." Their focus on the journey rather than the destination reflects a collective optimism that over 240 years has helped us win a revolution against the world's most feared army, survive a Civil War, prevail in two world wars, create the world's strongest economy, and, however imperfectly, advocate for worldwide democracy and human rights.

Many chesty patriots have tried to kidnap this core ethos by confusing nationalism with patriotism or by freezing us in the amber of our original glorious moment. But there's a new patriotism emerging in our third century, based less on the size of our armies or GDP than on the big idea that government is *us*—all of us in a thing called Democracy. This book, therefore, is animated by the democratic exceptionalism of Leonard Bernstein rather than the rearview-mirror exceptionalism of William F. Buckley Jr. Bernstein said in 1953 that "a Liberal is a person who believes in the bright, infinite future," while Buckley in his 1955 mission statement for the *National Review* said, "A Conservative is a fellow who is standing athwart history yelling 'Stop!'"*

A Progressive Majority. Based on this premise of progress rather than stasis, one side recently appears to be prevailing in the ideological battle of "inches," as it was once called by Thomas Jefferson, who anticipated few final victories or irreversible trends.

Some historians, most notably Arthur Schlesinger Sr. and Jr. and Sean Wilentz, argue that there are political cycles in our binary politics that last roughly 30 years before the political pendulum swings back. Where's the pendulum today? Progressives appear to be winning the *culture war* (see women's and gay equality, drug reform), with conservatives starting to lose their traditional advantage on the economic *class war* as liberal Democrats are making a sustained assault on the Bastille of worsening economic inequality.

Indeed, principles from the Sixties—originating in movements for civil rights, peace, women, gays, environmental justice, health care for all, corporate accountability, and consumer justice—are now slowly resurfacing and shifting our politics. After three distinct eras over the past century—the *Progressive Era* (1900–1920), the *New Deal Era* (1933–1968), and the *Backlash Era* (1969–1992)—it appears that we're early in a *New Progressive Era*.

Many political commentators have been over-interpreting low-turnout, mid-term elections as red states turn more red at congressional and local levels, which in part reflects the clustering (i.e., wasting) of Democratic voters in cities, the GOP 2010 blowout win, and the resulting gerrymandering favoring them the entire decade. At the same time, the country is getting more blue in national elections because of an evolving tilt away from the "Party of Lincoln" to the values of

---

* Without picking nits, *progressive* and *liberal* will be used interchangeably in this book, the current difference being largely that the latter polls worse largely because it's been the target of a formidable, decades-long conservative offensive. Also, in the spirit of Kareem Abdul Jabbar, who believes that you get to name yourself, I'll be usually using the term "conservative" to describe the not-progressive. While one could argue that trying to shred the safety net of regulated capitalism isn't very conservative but is closer to "radical reactionary," this book accepts common parlance in an attempt to focus more on analysis than pejoratives.

Lincoln. For values of democracy, tolerance, fairness, and environmentalism—stretching from our sixteenth president to '60s Boomers—are now being increasingly embraced by the rising majority of Millennials and minorities of the twenty-first century. And in 2020, they will help determine congressional redistricting for that decade.

Despite stale rhetoric about "big government" and "traditional values," few thinking conservatives really want to go back to women as subordinate, literacy tests, gay discrimination, senior insecurity, inaccessible health care, the Corvair, Love Canal, and other relics of "smaller government" . . . you know, the good old days when you were "free" to be ejected through windshields, breathe Monsanto's air, sit at whites-only lunch counters if you were the right shade of American. So while the Right continues to energetically condemn the Left, the values of modern liberalism have already been vindicated by America's peristaltic history of progress. In the words of Bill Moyers and Michael Winship: "The progressive agenda is America's story—from ending slavery to ending segregation to establishing a woman's right to vote to Social Security, the right to organize, and the fight for fair pay and against income inequality. Strip those from our history and you might as well contract America out to the U.S. Chamber of Commerce the National Association of Manufacturers, and Karl Rove, Inc."

The perennial struggle for America's future is, as this book will argue, now one presidential win and decennial census away from a more permanent progressive democracy.

OVER MY PUBLIC LIFE I've been "bumping into geniuses," in Ahmet Ertegun's phrase, which has proven an invaluable way to absorb, learn, and navigate the world. These are people whose pilot light is always on, who seem to possess some as-yet-undiscovered hormone that makes them strive for prominence and dominance, who fuse sheer talent with great effort. Some are insiders skilled at ingratiation, compromise, and likability while others are outsiders who are righteous, uncompromising, perhaps abrasive and annoying. But all are forces of nature whose energy and talent have shaped our world.

In my experience, there's Ralph Nader in 1964 leaving behind his only draft of *Unsafe at Any Speed* in a Washington, D.C., cab—and then rewriting it from scratch; Fidel Castro telling me at a dinner in 1987 that he won't allow a Cuban human rights group to publish a newsletter because "why waste the paper?"; Arianna Huffington proofing galleys of her next book not just during breaks on our 2008 weekly radio show *Both Sides Now* but *while I was asking her a question;* an ebullient mayor Rudy Giuliani joining me for an odd-bedfellows endorsement of Democratic governor Mario Cuomo in 1994 and roiling the assembled city hall press by declaring that "if Pataki wins, we'll have a government of, by, and for Al D'Amato"; Bill Clinton calmly regrouping 12 hours after unexpectedly losing the 1992 Connecticut primary to Jerry Brown by hammering Brown for his flat-tax idea over the next two weeks before the decisive New York primary.

I've been fortunate to learn from, and sometimes lose to, some of the best of them—Ralph, Bill and Hillary, Rudy, Bloomberg, Buckley, Huffington, Steinem, both Cuomos, de Blasio, Schumer, Koch, Moynihan, Sharpton, Spitzer, Clark, Abzug. All of them appear in the pages to come.

TODAY'S PROGRESSIVES trace back to Federalists at the Constitutional Convention who abrogated (illegally though happily) the 1783 Articles of Confederation that had put the country in a states-rights straitjacket as the rule of unanimity produced paralysis. Over the next two centuries, the liberal/progressive tradition embraced the tolerance and justice of *democratic government* as the counterweight to the unsentimental efficiency of *free-market capitalism,* each relying on the other for legitimacy.

In the 1930s, liberalism was about "improving people's lives while treating them alike and shielding them from undue power," in the words of Edmund Fawcett in *Liberalism: The Life of an Idea.* Reflecting that wisdom was liberalism's avatar, Franklin Delano Roosevelt, at the 1936 Democratic Convention: "Governments can err. Presidents do make mistakes, but the immortal Dante tells us that justice weighs the sins of the cold-blooded and the sins of the warm-hearted in different scales. Better the occasional faults of a Government that lives in a spirit of charity than the consistent omissions of a Government frozen in the ice of its own indifference."

The conservative tradition traces back to Adam Smith's *The Wealth of Nations* and British philosopher John Locke. The latter's observation that "private vice makes public virtue" finds its modern manifestation in Andrew Mellon's 1924 theory—ardently embraced by Ronald Reagan six decades later—that only low taxes on the wealthiest Americans can provide prosperity for all.

Government here is seen as tyrannically creating dependency and allowing unaccountable bureaucrats to supplant the "magic of the marketplace." A monarchical Washington, D.C., now replaces King George as the enemy, although conservative rhetoric does not distinguish between a government of inbred lords ruling over serfs and a self-governing democracy.

These two great traditions collided in the 1960s as bitterly as during any period in our history since the 1850s and 1860s. The Sixties seemed to comprise two Americas, or at least two zeitgeists—a younger generation saying "Question Authority!" and an older one demanding "Respect Authority!," a struggle between the forces of innovation and tradition. That is, John Kennedy intoning that America has "tossed its cap over the wall of space" versus Richard Nixon embracing big business and the race-based Southern Strategy.

Similar forces with new faces are still at odds in our new century. Witness the post-Charleston massacre debate over the Confederate flag a mere 150 years after the Civil War and 50 years after Jim Crow. But while the "cliff hasn't collapsed," there has been a slow, lurching shift in their comparative political fortunes, a shift largely missed by conventional political Geiger counters which ignore trends that are reshaping America and that frame this book.

WHATEVER THE SLURS de jour against President Barack Obama over eight years—and he's still some 30+ points more popular than the Republican Congress—when it literally counts, he becomes the first Democrat since FDR to win two consecutive national popular majorities. Indeed, Democrats capture the popular vote in five of the past six presidential elections—and appear on track to make it six of seven and perhaps seven of eight as the electorate gets steadily browner and Latinos break 3–1 for them.

It's a huge political problem when one party in a two-party democracy gets a shrinking share of a growing constituency. Beyond the gravity of demography, there are other political, sociological, and philosophic forces weighing conservatism down in twenty-first-century America, discussed at length in chapter 8: a bulge of more-liberal Millennials comparing the failed Bush 43 and successful Clinton and Obama presidencies; a growing number of single, secular moms unhappy with Republican attacks on reproductive rights and equal pay for equal work; a sharp reduction over 30 years in the percentage of Americans belonging to an organized religion; the declining political sway of traditional boogeymen such as communism, crime, gays, and deficits; a GOP apparently in thrall to a reactionary base despite a country with large majorities now in favor of gun safety, science-based climate policies, an increased minimum wage, expanded health-care coverage, and a pathway to citizenship; and perhaps most ominously, there's a "Blue Wall" in the electoral college, in Ron Brownstein's apt phrase, that gets a Democratic nominee to 242 electoral votes based on states that have gone Democratic in six of the last six presidential contests.

A party largely relying on older white men and rich old men can for now win "throw-the-bums-out" mid-term elections, but in the context of generational politics, it's struggling to catch up with an accelerating bus called the Future.

Bright, Infinite Future concludes that a movement on the wrong side of history, demography, reality, science, policy, and polls will be a King Canute shouting at the political tides. It's hard to see how the world's most sophisticated democracy can be governed by a right-wing party whose electoral strategy relies on more money, fewer voters, and stacked elections via secret super PACs, voter suppression, and congressional gerrymandering.

And then? As the conservative party loses altitude, can the progressive party rise?

Democrats are in a position to take advantage of all four of the greatest phenomena of the modern era—greater diversity, worsening inequality, women's rights, and global warming. Now let's imagine a sequence of probable or at least plausible events: a Democratic nominee in 2016 building on these developments wins; POTUS 45 gets re-elected as 42, 43, and 44 did; post-Scalia, she then gets to replace one or two of the five conservative justices, effectively ending the very conservative Roberts Court; and the 2020 Census reallocates congressional seats based on the new minority math. Then by 2022—or even sooner if the Cruz–Tea Party wing of a discombobulated GOP seizes control after years of Barack and Hillary—there could be Democratic control of the White House, Congress, Supreme Court, and federal courts.

All of this, however, starts with the unusual 2016 POTUS and SCOTUS election that will likely serve as a tie-breaker for those thinking we're still a 50-50 country. As in 1932 and 1980, it is likely to be another "hinge of history" and to determine if we're in an expanding progressive era. My public journey tracks the renewal of an optimistic liberalism vying with angry conservatives yelling "Stop!" History, however, is not a stop sign.

"LOOKS LIKE I'LL *be running for mayor." It's September 24, 1999, and I'm sitting in my living room overlooking the East River at 90th Street, breaking some big news gently to my savvy, skeptical, beautiful wife. "But what if you lose?" asks Deni, perennially anxious given my line of work and wary of my irrational overconfidence that critics call arrogance.*

Lose? "Okay, there aren't any guarantees in politics. But I think I'm going to win unless there's some big, unexpected event that changes everything, like that racial killing in Bensonhurst during the Dinkins-Koch campaign in August '89."

So begins two years of glad-handing, fund-raising, and speechifying, as we giddily confide to each other, away from the kids, staff, and journalists, "Can't wait till September 11!" . . . "two months to September 11" . . . "next week is September 11!" That being the long-scheduled date of the 2001 Democratic primary.

Fast-forward to the evening of September 10, 2001. Polls show me ahead in the four-way Democratic primary and trouncing Republican multi-billionaire Michael Bloomberg in a general election matchup. I announce, as any vindicated husband would, "Well, honey, there was no big unexpected event—it has all gone as planned." We hug, kiss, and sit motionless for several moments. "Can't wait till September 11," she says for the last time.

The next morning we walk through a clutch of journalists and exuberant supporters in front of our residence only 100 yards north of Gracie Mansion. I vote and then hurry to PS 41, a grade school at Sixth Avenue and 11th Street, to greet parents and fidgety kids on the first day of class. One couple coaxes a wary child, "Samantha, shake hands with the next mayor of the city." I bellow my final "Don't forget to vote today!" to young couples walking west and, at 8:46 a.m., turn with satisfaction to deputy campaign manager Jeremy Ben-Ami. "That was the last handshake! Primary's over! Let's go back to the apartment." Just then I spot an educator I know, walking south. But instead of saying hello, she blurts out an ominous-sounding "ohhh." On a completely blue, clear, and sunny day, I too look up toward downtown . . .

ONE

THE SIXTIES

Boomers and Backlash

Republicans made a living off the excesses of the Sixties until the 2006 election.

—President Bill Clinton

In a sense, I'm a pure product of that era.

—President Barack Obama

I come from the Sixties. . . . There was a lot of activism on campus and I do appreciate [today] the way young people are standing up and speaking out.

—Hillary Clinton, 2015

WE THINK WE'RE ON THE BRINK OF SOMETHING BIG, *"really really big," as campy icon Ed Sullivan puts it. It's 11:59 p.m., December 31, 1959, in Alan Branfman's backyard at 41 South Drive. Seven of us, all ninth graders at Great Neck South High School, are grabbing for the rebound to make the last shot of the decade.*

"Yes!" I bank one from the left side with 30 seconds to go. Larry, Tony, and Alan are scrambling for the ball. Tony grabs it, dribbles back, and lets fly. CLANG. *It bounces high off the back rim and into the sure hands of Steve Eliot, by far the best shooter of the Magnificent Seven, as we self-reverentially would later call ourselves. He calmly waits until 11:59:57 and releases a jumper from 20 feet.* Swish.

Bring on the Sixties! It's our time.

SCHOOLED IN THE SIXTIES

Unlike 9 p.m. election night when you count votes, social and cultural progress don't have a simple metric. It's only later when a moniker is born that we can figure out what especially bound us together and what made us different from our parents . . . that we were, in fact, a "generation."

"The Greatest Generation" earned its name by surviving a depression and winning a world war. My Uncle Phil regaled us with stories of his landing at Normandy, when as a lieutenant he led 30 men out of their swaying landing craft onto the beach and into withering fire. Later that day he directed flamethrowers into German bunkers and incinerated brazen enemies who knew that morning, looking out at the massive armada offshore, that would be the day they died.

My generation is born when the Phils come home, marry, raise families, start careers, and spend money jump-starting a consumer engine that doesn't really slow down until the 1973 Arab Oil Embargo. But as "the child is father to the man," the Fifties—derided as static, conformist, repressed—are prequel to the tumultuous decade to follow.

The president had been a warrior, but as a politician, Dwight David Eisenhower wants to govern more peacefully. Historians later dub it his "hidden-hand" presidency, reflecting Ike's modest Kansas temperament and infectious grin. On the one hand, knowing war too well, he avoids military entanglements, so there are reportedly no American military deaths abroad in his eight years in the Oval Office (not counting the winding down of the Korean conflict). On the other, he never denounces Senator Joseph McCarthy, assuming that "Tail Gunner Joe" will destroy himself, which happens only after McCarthy rips up much of our social fabric. And Ike's all-white upbringing, wartime staff, and presidential cabinet ill-equip him to understand, much less play an active role in, the ripening civil rights movement.

Other events plant the seeds of the Sixties. The U.S. Civil Rights Commission's report on racial segregation in 1958 meticulously documents the evils of Jim Crow; France's defeat at Dien Bien Phu in 1954 presages how America stupidly stumbles into the same Big Muddy; Sputnik in 1957 awakens the country out of a smug complacency. And assembly lines of housing, food, and cars—in Levittown,

McDonald's, and Detroit—create a mass consumer culture that in turn creates a new generation resenting such homogenization.

The arts also provide a foundation for boomers. The writings and prosecutions of Jack Kerouac, Allen Ginsberg, and D. H. Lawrence inspire a counterculture that becomes the culture itself in the next decade. Holden Caulfield's disgust with "phonies" and Elvis's fusion of soul and country penetrate deeply into the youth psyche. The brooding contempt of Marlon Brando and James Dean depict a generation dissatisfied with its generational dowry.

Adults are often infantilized or frightened. *The Man in the Grey Flannel Suit* and *The Organization Man* are the best of a literature about the conformity required to rise in the new corpocracies. C. Wright Mills, Vance Packard, and John Kenneth Galbraith write huge best-sellers about how the corporate economy allows private pursuits to "crowd out" public needs. *Leave It to Beaver* and *Father Knows Best* are completely at odds tonally with *Modern Family* and *Glee* a half century later. And films like *On the Beach* ensure that people are in a state of perpetual anxiety, especially kids like me cowering under school desks during air raid drills.

Then, BOOM!

From John Kennedy gracefully announcing his presidential candidacy on January 2 in the Senate Caucus Room to a besieged Richard Nixon in the White House ten years later—one rising on a wave of hope, the other on a backlash against anti-war protestors—the intervening years frame the progressive-conservative tension that has divided America ever since.

Demographically, it's not hard to chart what's happening. It starts with, obviously, a baby boom: Todd Gitlin summarizes it best in his monumental 1987 generational biography *The Sixties: Years of Hope, Days of Rage.* The number of births jumps by 19 percent from 1945 to 1946, then another 12 percent the next year . . . and continues to grow into the early Sixties. More babies are born between 1948 and 1953 than in the previous 30 years. By 1964, 77 million Americans make up the largest expansion in our history. By decade's end, the number of students is triple the number of farmers.

This reordering only accelerates when the federal government builds highways and makes home loans to spur suburban development. Millions of families, including mine, move into split-levels from 1948 to 1957, like on the South Shore of Long Island, and then from 1958 to 1973, on the North Shore.

Other political and social upheavals, however, are not as easy to spot as births and homes. No one has uncovered a great, collective *aha* moment that sparks the explosion of creativity and disruption to come. Earlier eras have some obvious triggers, like Black Tuesday, October 29, and the "Day of Infamy." But not the Sixties. They are far too kaleidoscopic for such a singular lens: the Kennedy-Nixon debates, Tet and My Lai, MLK and Malcolm X, Watts and Chicago, assassinations and the Free Speech Movement, *Easy Rider* and *The Green Berets,* the Voting Rights Act and Earth Day, *Unsafe at Any Speed* and speed, Dylan and the Silent Majority, Stonewall and the moon landing.

Critics of this period casually pigeonhole it as merely the "Woodstock Generation," hoping its only memory will be feather-haired acid freaks screwing in muddied tents during a Grateful Dead show. Former GOP congressman Dick Armey once blustered, "To me, all the problems in the country began in the Sixties." Even as astute an observer as author Kurt Anderson asserts that "hippie selfishness" contributed to the greed-is-good ethos of the roaring Eighties.

True, this boomer generation is in part about lifestyle, "doing your own thing" in the phrase of the day. There are also gross excesses as sanctimonious protestors call cops "pigs" and soldiers "baby killers." Little surprise that the initial impact of the decade is to pull the country to the right starting in 1966, since it's way more popular to salute the flag than burn it.

But the Sixties are far larger than that. Serious social movements begin or grow that tap us on the shoulder a half century later. The names Martin Luther King, Gloria Steinem, and Rachel Carson— classic outsiders who radically overturn the status quo—will continue to historically overshadow the Yippie Left. But their very movements inspire a backlash, more like a whiplash, that becomes a living demonstration that in politics, like physics, for every action there is an equal and opposite reaction.

The political divisions start early. In February 1960, "Negro" students sit in at a lunch counter in Greensboro, South Carolina, a heroic nonviolent tactic that spreads throughout the South. In 1962, a meeting of old and new leftists under Tom Hayden's direction draft the Port Huron Statement, which lays down an ideological marker for

how to restore the promise of America: "We are people of this generation . . . looking uncomfortably to the world we inherit."

Port Huron leads directly to the SDS (Students for a Democratic
Society) and a swelling anti-war movement. Senator Barry Goldwater
publishes *The Conscience of a Conservative*, articulating a polar opposite right-wing view of how small government can keep America
great. Which in turn creates the Ripon Society and, ultimately, the
successful Nixon and Reagan candidacies of 1968 and 1980.

Oddly, there is no economic decline or domestic repression of
the kind that has produced revolutions, from 1776 to 1848 to 1917.
Yet despite, or perhaps because of, relative prosperity—real income
is rapidly climbing—a generation of students is able to focus not on
how good America is but how much better it should be. It's a classic
revolution of rising expectations as the deal of affluence for acquies-
cence offends millions of the young. For members of this new generation, a life of organizational obedience is too dispiriting, and John
Kennedy is way more appealing than John Galt.

I'm one.

FROM RUSSIA TO CORNELL

It begins in 1905 when my paternal grandfather flees from Kamian-
ets-Podilskyi on the Ukraine-Russian border, hiding in a wheelbar-
row to escape pogroms that every few decades kill thousands of Jews.
Nathan Greene (at Ellis Island they drop the third *e*) sells buttons
("notions") from a cart on the Lower East Side before settling down
in attached housing off the Grand Concourse in the Bronx. The next-
door neighbors are Morris and Eva Suna—he's a plumber and she a
clerk—who emigrated from Konsk (later Kinsk), Poland, at around
the same time. They are among the 18 million who arrive after the
turn of the century to the "new country," as they come to call it.

Nathan and Fannie Green's son Irving (1907) and Morris and
Eva's daughter Anne (1912) grow up next door to each other and, presumably because of love and not just proximity, marry in 1933. Irv's
a quick-witted kibitzer, the life of the party in a "yesterday I flew to
Europe, boy were my arms tired" kind of way. He is also on the short
side, bald, brusque, almost handsome. Amazingly for a Jew from
the Bronx, then Brooklyn, he attends the University of Virginia as
an undergraduate and then New York Law School. Anne is far more

subdued, shy almost, pretty and petite; she attends Mills College to become a grade school teacher.

Stephen is born in 1938. He proves to be a terrific athlete, a fair student, popular, and 60 years later not only one of the largest influences in my life but also founder of SL Green Realty Corp, the largest owner of commercial buildings in Manhattan. Between 1938 and 1945 there are five miscarriages—*five*—before Anne and Irv make one last attempt. I arrive in this context, regarded almost as a miracle child, on March 15.

In 1948, we move from Bensonhurst to Elmont, literally a stone's throw from Queens if, like me, you recklessly throw rocks over traffic on the Cross Island Parkway. We live in a modest two-story home three long blocks away from the Belmont Race Track, where I hear trumpets announcing races and occasionally sneak in to watch. The community is composed of largely middle-class Jews and, decades later, middle-class Asians. I'm a good but poorly behaved student, a "smart aleck" in my mother's constant refrain. My teacher Vera Fisher writes on my report card, "In his utter disregard for authority and lack of respect, Mark has failed to measure up to our expectations for 4th graders in the development of good citizens." In a newspaper interview 15 years later, she says that she expected big things from me, adding, "The worst thing I can say is that he was a bit of a show-off."

I have a clique of buddies who play lots of touch football and also discover girls (Judi Calflisch, if you're reading this, please call to say hi). I like winning at whatever I'm doing. My default activity is playing stickball with next-door neighbor Carl Shreck, whom I once beat 63–0 in obnoxious overkill, this apparently being before the invention of the Mercy Rule.

Like so many families in this era, Dad's the decider. A small-time lawyer and landlord, he buys a Lincoln Continental every couple of years—not just another Cadillac but a *Lincoln*. I think that's so different and very cool. But it's not cool when I periodically take phone calls from building supers and tenants screaming about various emergencies involving water, fire, you name it. "Oh, you want my father, bye." He also founds a Reform synagogue, Temple B'nai Israel, on Elmont Road just off Hempstead Turnpike, for which he and I occasionally go door to door to raise funds. It's where I'm bar mitzvahed in 1958, presciently discussing in my speech (given my later career) how to keep "Jews honest in their business dealings in the marketplace." Even as I become steeped in the tradition of *tikkun olam* ("repairing the world"), I'm displaying some cha-cha steps at the post-Haftorah party that are the talk of the congregation.

Then, like a Jewish *Jeffersons,* we move on up in 1957 to Great Neck, a North Shore enclave of spacious, upscale homes on rolling hills off the Long Island Sound made famous by *The Great Gatsby*'s fictitious West Egg. There I'm ceaselessly borne forward from seventh to twelfth grades, first at the 1895 brick-covered Great Neck North High School (Frances Ford Coppola, '56) and then the 1958 glassy Great Neck South (Andy Kaufman, '67) on the Phipps Estate right off what soon becomes exit 33 of the Long Island Expressway.

It's a crisis-free adolescence of grades, sports, and girls, in that order. Summers are spent at Camp Oquago in the Catskills, where I'm in athletic heaven nine hours a day. That includes basketball with the best white player I'd ever seen (Gary Goldberg, later creator of *Family Ties*) and with a mediocre but very determined ball-handler (David Stern, later the head of the NBA). The summer of 1960 I play in sanctioned Eastern Lawn Tennis Association tournaments in order to attain a top eastern ranking. But in my last event, I lose in an upset and fall to number 10. The next morning, with no more events to recoup the season, I practice all day in a frenzied attempt to get ready for the next summer.

To this day, with chagrin, I recall my exact grade point average and earned run average as the starting pitcher in high school, my tennis record as first singles from ninth to twelfth grade, as well as the team's 49 straight wins in '62 and '63 that make us Island champions. For years, people only refer to me as Mark Green, *the tennis player.*

That's fine, because the competitive impulse honed on those courts becomes embedded in my approach to politics later. *"Jeez, I'm down one set and 4–1 in the second. But I'm better than this guy! Stay calm, win your serve, get to a third set, think about this point, not the last one, outlast him . . ."* I'm what's called, with disdain by opponents, a "pusher" because I always keep the ball in play and try to wear down the other guy more with willpower than power. One New Year's Eve, I listen to Fontella Bass sing *Rescue Me* 43 straight times, a level of obsession that pretty much sums up my later ability to sit in the same place for hours putting out 80 calls a day every day, every month for two years running for the U.S. Senate and then NYC mayor.

Politics hasn't yet penetrated my consciousness. Indeed, like most kids, I simply mimic my father's politics—he's a Rockefeller Republican who ran for state senate in 1940 in the Lower East Side and campaigned on a platform with, he claims, Wendell Willkie. (When I later ask why he ran, he candidly admits "to boost my law practice," a rationale that does *not* inspire my future campaigns.) So, choosing sides in a mock presidential debate in 1960, I pick Nixon! Experience counts and Ike chose him, right? But, like my guy, I lose the debate. And like Hillary Clinton and Elizabeth Warren decades later, both of whom start out as Goldwater Girls, I sin and, apparently, spend a lifetime atoning.

Strikingly, the sports symbol at Great Neck *South* is the Confederate flag and the football team's name is *the Rebels.* And in case anyone misses the branding, our newspaper is *The Southerner*—even though this is the year of Martin Luther King's "Letter from a Birmingham Jail" and the murder of four black girls at the 16th Street Baptist Church. I don't recall anyone making a fuss in this liberal community in the early Sixties; that happens only in 1980 when the flag is dropped and the Rebels become, in a smart pivot, the "Colonial Rebels."

What were we thinking?

IT'S AUGUST 20, 1963. My dad, mom, and I hook up the U-Haul stuffed with boxes of books, clothing, and other knickknacks to set off for the nearly five-hour drive from Great Neck north up the New York State Thruway and then west on Route 17 to Cornell.

We follow the exact path, month, and year that Jennifer ("Nobody puts Baby in the corner") Grey travels in *Dirty Dancing,* by the same rural Catskills towns, same schlocky motels, same music on our car radio over and over—"Twist and Shout," "Heat Wave," "One Fine Day," "Louie Louie"—plus ads mysteriously saying only "the Beatles are coming" with no indication whether it's a band, movie, or plague. We stop halfway en route at the famous Roscoe Diner where I devour a giant hamburger as my folks try to also stuff me with last-minute wisdom and ease any anxieties.

But I'm not nervous or scared, only eager to test myself on this next stage, scholastically and athletically. Cornell is sort of Great Neck writ large. There are lots of smart, competitive Jewish kids as well as black and Asian students, Chinese food, "mu-sic ev-ry-where," and, again, grades, sports, and girls (still in that order). I major in government, minor in English, and really enjoy classes on industrial economics and Soviet relations. A few times I sit in on a real estate class at the urging of my father though I hate the subject, not then knowing that I'd be subsequently leaving this line of work to my big brother. *(The visiting teacher is a knowledgeable and charming New York City Realtor by the name of Jay Frand, who flies up weekly and whose daughter I'd marry in 1977; I love Deni way more than Jay's course.)*

I also love Cornell, with its sweeping foliage and deep gorges slicing through campus. I'm captain of the tennis team, number 2 on the squash team, and study my brains out to the point (remember Fontella Bass) that I leave a body imprint on a particular chair on the ground floor of the Uris Library where I would sit from 7 to 11 every night. For four years.

But this being the Sixties, politics does arrive on campus, suddenly.

I'm late to Government 101 as I trudge up The Hill, as it's unaffectionately called, that all freshmen have to scale to get to the main campus. On my way, I stop at the dry cleaner's. "Hey," says the kid behind the counter, almost nonchalantly, "did you hear, Kennedy's been shot?" I freeze, unable to process information so outside my experience and realm. I'm too confused to fully understand, too shocked to cry, but armed with darkness I sprint to class where it turns out that the professor, Allen Gothelf, hasn't heard yet. When I tell him, he screams, then launches into a monologue against the right wing, the Republican Party, and Dallas. We hear within the hour that the president is dead. Gothelf—whom I'd periodically bump into four decades later at the West 72nd Street subway as I campaigned for office—bursts into tears and cancels the rest of the class.

The power of that event is magnified three days later when I go home for Thanksgiving. Sitting in my girlfriend's living room and fixated on TV coverage that serves as a kind of national communal fire during the grief, I watch on live TV as suspect Lee Harvey Oswald—a nobody with a beat-up, uneven face—is taken on a perp walk. As he's approaching the cameras, the lens shifts, there's a momentary blur on the screen as a man leaps in front of Oswald, and a loud bang fills my living room, all our living rooms.

Of course everyone my age remembers November 1963. For me, this seismic, psycho-spiritual end of innocence coincides with the literal end of my adolescence. While everyone's horrified by the assassination, we late-teens absorb it on a level deep enough to almost reconfigure strands of DNA. It's now really time to say good-bye to Archie and Veronica, the Rebels, the Lindy. A door opens for me that hasn't and can't be closed.

Increasingly absorbed by public affairs and politics, I stand dumbstruck in October 1964 as Robert Kennedy drives by on Cornell's East Avenue waving from an open white convertible while campaigning for the U.S. Senate. The next year I hear Adlai Stevenson give a speech on nuclear disarmament in the cavernous Barton Hall and get to shake his hand. I also attend a talk at the law school in May 1967 by an Allard Lowenstein, who is starting up what becomes the Dump Johnson movement. Unkempt, passionate, convincing, and formidable, he hangs around afterward with me and others answering question after question. *(Thirteen years later, on March 14, 1980, I'm scheduled to be his 5 p.m. appointment to learn if he'll be seeking the Manhattan House seat I'm running for, but at 4 p.m. in his Rockefeller Plaza office, he's shot to death by a deranged former associate.)*

I settle on the history of birth control in America for my senior government thesis—how Comstockery and the Catholic Church stigmatized and stymied birth control methods, especially among the low-income minority population. So I'm eager to go hear Black Power radical Stokely Carmichael speak at Bailey Hall in February 1967 since he's been quoted saying "Birth control is black genocide." He's a gifted orator who holds the packed audience spellbound about the subjugation of blacks in America. Then comes the Q&A. I gather my nerve to raise my hand, stand up, and ask, "How can you call birth control black genocide given the rate of infant *morality* in America [emphasis added]?" There's then a strange stillness as my brain begins to process my faux pas as 3,000 people inhale before explosively laughing, wave after wave of laughter. My ears grow hot and I sit down, clutching my spiral notepad. Carmichael waits until folks calm down to stick in the stiletto. "Son, I think that's what's called a Freudian slip."

THE SUMMER OF '67

I graduate that spring and head for a Washington, D.C., summer internship in the office of Senator Jacob Javits, who is a "moderate

Republican" (i.e., a political dinosaur that later dies off when the Tea Party comet slams into America). I room in Anacostia with several Long Island friends and a Cornell junior named Tom Jones. But when the owner of the apartment complex a few days into our lease informs us that "Negroes" like Tom aren't welcome there, Sandy Berger, Art Kaminsky, Ken Schanzer, and I tell him to shove it and we overnight move into a different location in D.C. (*As for Tom, a year later he leads the armed takeover of Willard Straight Hall at Cornell and, with two bullet belts strapped across his chest, is the person on the* Newsweek *cover that becomes among the most famous photos of the 1960s. And 20 years after that, he becomes the CFO at TIAA-CREF and sits on the Board of Trustees at Cornell.*)

By the time I start in Senator Javits's office in late June, I have two modest goals for my ten weeks in Washington—be a good intern and end the war in Vietnam. Then, as now, the ideal congressional intern is supposed to be like the ideal hairpiece—effective and unnoticeable. But instead I adopt Andrea del Sarto's credo that "a man's reach should exceed his grasp."

Angered by LBJ's criticism of "cussers and doubters" opposing his Vietnam policy, I organize 20 interns from different congressional offices—a well-scrubbed, quintessentially Ivy League group—who share my anti-war views. We hold several meetings to draft a letter protesting U.S. involvement in Vietnam that we intend to send to President Johnson. My long-winded 15-page version is condensed to two pages of earnest prose: "We sign this statement as a matter of conscience that we can no longer condone this war through our silence . . . [turning] a local struggle into an ideological war in which hundreds of thousands of people have died."

Compared to other events of the Vietnam era—massive street protests, the killings at Kent State—a congressional intern petition is what later would be greeted with *meh*. But in what's evidently a slow news week, I saunter into work on the morning of July 21 and spot an unusual stack of messages on my desk. "You're dead," a secretary sitting nearby deadpans.

It seems that our anti-war rump caucus has been infiltrated by a pro-war intern, who's been ordered by his conservative Republican boss to pilfer the letter. That morning's *Washington Post* carries a story (by a stringer named Richard Blumenthal, who will return to Connecticut and big things) about a speech on the House floor by Illinois Republican congressman Bob Michel (later to be House minority leader) "exposing to public light activities of a group of 20 ringleaders . . . behind closed doors about which you may not be aware." He links us to something called the Washington Spring Mobilization Committee, whose members, he charges, "include Dick Gregory, Muhammad Ali and hippies who work with Hap [sic] Brown's SNCC"—none of whom we've met. Many members of Congress regard us as impertinent if not treasonous. Dixiecrat Mendel Rivers announces, "We must get these pro-Communist agitators off the Hill." Representative Jacob Gilbert of New York remarks to a colleague, "I'd like to beat the shit out of the kid who started this."

Perhaps Michel thinks our letter will be his version of Nixon's "Pumpkin Papers," though it serves largely to boost not him but us, generating a level of attention we never could have attracted on our own. My life speeds up as if someone pushed the forward arrow. A researcher for columnist Drew Pearson asks me for some dirt on Representative Michel; feeling way over my head, I decline comment. The Taiwanese embassy threatens to cancel its annual summer party for congressional interns unless I promise not to circulate my "left-wing petition." A ranking Cornell official urges me to "keep Cornell's name out of this. The alumni will never understand."

Press coverage is generally favorable, focusing on the David and Goliath aspect and on whether interns have the right of free speech. "Are Summer Interns Muzzled?" is the headline in the *Washington Daily News* and, as my mother would not soon forget, the *Chicago Tribune* lists me as one of "the 10 most radical students in America." Late afternoon two days later, several dozen of us spill out into Delaware Park adjoining the Russell Senate Office Building to plan next steps. We reach an easy consensus that we will immediately go door-to-door scouring for signatures. "Guys, look sharp, and girls, wear nice dresses, so we don't play into stereotypes," I suggest, combining Great Neck and Port Huron.

Ultimately, we gather 179 signatures including one from a Robert Reich in Senator Robert Kennedy's office, who becomes a lifelong friend. When I call the White House to ask if we can present our petition to the president, he instead cancels his traditional summer address to all summer interns at the Washington Monument.

No, the Intern Letter doesn't end the war. But it does end the intern program itself when an annoyed House votes that fall to terminate it (reinstating it three years later). This episode does, however, have several spin-offs. My immediate boss, Javits's foreign policy aide Les Gelb, informs me that I escaped firing since, fortunately, I did mention to him that I'd be circulating a petition before Blumenthal's piece; and it turns out that he and the senator are kind of impressed at my chutzpah. *(Les leaves the next year to work on a project with Defense Secretary Robert McNamara that will become the Pentagon Papers and 26 years later is chosen president of the Council on Foreign Relations.)*

It proves to be a big learning experience. But what are the lessons? Professionally, I relish attracting attention by framing a strong argument, standing up to big shots, and organizing allies. What, however, is my *motivation?* There's the chemical rush of the pace and coverage intersecting with the urgent moral issue of the war. I come to realize later in my public life that the spur of both is what drives me, drives almost all public people, and the way to get stuff done is to be sure that neither narcissism nor sanctimony becomes consuming.

THE LAW SCHOOL

On the first day at Harvard Law School in 1967, we gather in Langdell Hall to hear from the legendary Dean Erwin Griswold. As if sent from central casting in 1947 when he first arrives, he now majestically explains in his "Voice of God" how "lucky" we are to be there and how responsible we must be to advance both the law school's tradition as well as that of the larger society. Luck?

Everywhere there's intimidating history. Our professors deploy the Socratic Method (which in the original Latin is probably synonymous with *in terrorem*), calling on one of us for much of an hour class to ensure that *all* of us read all the cases beforehand to avoid potential humiliation. My administrative law course excites my interest in regulatory and consumer law in part because of the brilliance and, well, judicious manner of my professor, Stephen Breyer. Torts is run by the iron intellect of Charles Fried (later to be President Reagan's solicitor general as well as a fierce critic of President George W. Bush's torture policy).

My greatest reverence is reserved for constitutional law professor Paul Freund, always supposedly the next Supreme Court justice. When I visit him in an office piled high with law books, I can't get out of my head that this man was a law clerk in 1932 to Justice Louis Brandeis, probably the greatest progressive lawyer in American history.

My two roommates at 65 Eustis Street include a fellow Cornellian whom I never met while in college. Sandy Berger comes from tiny Millerton, New York, and smokes throughout the day to relieve his tension. He's part of our small "study group" that meets weekly to toughen each other up for end-of-year exams that become the stuff of high drama in Scott Turow's later best-selling book and film, *One L*. It's Sandy who's on the back of my motorcycle en route to our Property exam on June 6, the morning that Bobby Kennedy dies from handgun wounds suffered the night before at the Ambassador Hotel in Los Angeles. Settling in to our seats and struggling to separate our personal grief from the course's only test all year, we watch as many classmates come in openly weeping. And then, a first in the recorded history of the 150-year-old law school: our professor walks to the front of the room and announces, "Due to the death of Senator Kennedy, this exam is canceled and everyone will get the same passing grade." Silence. Gasps. Relief. Sadness.

(Sandy combines brains, a welcoming personality, and real writing skills. Just two years after law school he becomes George McGovern's speechwriter in his 1972 presidential campaign and, 28 years later, President Clinton's national security advisor. On the evening of September 11, 2001, when he can't get out of New York City because the airports are shut down, he stays at our apartment talking about terrorism and security.)

There is no way these student years will be walled off from the larger society. Not with MLK's and then RFK's assassinations and with the military draft hanging over all of us. I bus with friends to the march on the Pentagon in 1969 and join 32 law students signing a public ad in the *Crimson* saying that I would not serve if drafted. Later that year I draw a high number, avoiding selection and what would have been an impossible clash between conscience and career.

I spend my Saturdays at Cambridge Legal Services handling cases of low-income residents, including Abbie Hoffman's wife seeking a divorce. I convince our placement office to send a survey to all law firms coming to conduct interviews so students can easily access information about pro bono work, hours, and diversity before deciding whether to even interview with a firm. I write articles outside of class, including my first for *The Nation* after the renowned editor Carey

McWilliams amazingly takes my cold call and agrees to assign a piece on the new breed of law students. I coedit a book for Beacon Press of 14 essays titled *With Justice for Some: An Indictment of the Law by Young Advocates*. Dean Derek Bok, later to be Harvard's president, calls me into his office to cheerfully say that, while he's impressed by my many activities, could I please remember to be a law student too? "You'll have decades of activities ahead of you but only three years as a law student here."

But really, my passion is the *Harvard Civil Rights–Civil Liberties Law Review*, started only the year before as a progressive alternative to the *Law Review*. I write my initial article, a 62-footnoted piece on racial discrimination in urban renewal, and then barely beat out Bruce Wasserstein to be chosen editor in chief. Bruce becomes the deputy editor in chief and coeditor with me of *With Justice for Some*. Among others, I convince Joe Califano, recently President Johnson's special assistant, and Leon Panetta, who has just resigned from the Nixon White House over its civil rights policy, to write book reviews. Panetta proves to be a personal delight though an unusually poor writer. Putting out a publication with a staff of 60 is my maiden voyage in management.

(Of course, "Bid-'em-Up Bruce"—a phrase he despised—goes on to extraordinary success as a Wall Street Master of the Universe, cofounding Wasserstein, Perella before taking over the investment banking giant Lazard Freres until his untimely death in 2009. At his wedding in Paris in 1996, we have great fun in a roast-toast when I recall our election fight because "if only he had won, perhaps today Deni and I would be living on a 29-acre waterfront estate in Easthampton and he'd be a much-admired assemblyman in Albany.")

Then, a life-altering event. It's snowing heavily in Cambridge in mid-March 1969 a couple of months after the Green-Wasserstein showdown. I'm in my driveway shoveling out my car when a roommate shouts down from the window, "Mark, *Ralph Nader*'s on the phone for you."

Ralph Nader? The guy pictured as a knight-in-shining-armor on the cover of *Newsweek* for his auto safety crusade? In the first of what would be perhaps a few thousand phone calls over the next decades, he pleasantly explains that he's gathering a group of law graduates from Harvard, his alma mater ('58), to research Washington institutions, and he'd like me to be part of his team.

"But Mr. Nader, I've been offered an internship with New York City mayor John Lindsay." "Well, that *is* exciting," he allows. "But let me ask you—this summer, would you rather be a political cog or a participant in changing your country?"

It takes me a week but I can't resist the personal wooing of such a public hero. So I decline the 103rd mayor's offer and throw in with the person who would become among the most influential private citizens in American history, and my mentor.

EIGHT MOVEMENTS: BACK TO OUR FUTURE

Russia, Brooklyn, Tikkun Olam, Great Neck, Cornell, Harvard Law, Nader—I've now picked sides in the skins-shirts political contest. This kickoff of my public life coincides with the rise of eight movements that subpoena the attention of the country. "If one of us does [something], they'll think he's crazy," says Arlo Guthrie, who wrote a '60s anthem of sorts, "Alice's Restaurant." "If two of us do it, they'll think we're funny. If three of us do it, they'll think it's a movement." In the 1960s, millions do it.

As the Thirties set in motion forces that permanently reshaped Americans' relationships to government and business, the Sixties too are still occupying America today across the divide of decades. Tom Hayden has written that Obama's presidential campaign "was a social movement in electoral form, a renewal of sixties energies inside a political system and culture broken open under sixties pressures . . . Without [those movements], there likely would have been no Obama presidency."

Because principles from that period both molded my life and are influencing the 2016 election, let's briefly revisit events that many have either forgotten or disparaged as "going back to the Sixties." Of course, nostalgia should be a thing of the past. But while issues, styles, and politics shift, often values endure to create continuity. It's odd that traditionalists who today embrace the literal Bible, the originalism of the 1789 Constitution, and the Southern Heritage of the 1860s draw the line at the heritage of the 1960s. Conservatives have chosen a convenient time to conserve—one that preserves the power and privilege of a largely all-white elite. To paraphrase Buffalo Springfield, there *was* something happenin' there, and what it was is increasingly clear.

The Civil Rights Movement

For all the obvious civil rights progress since slavery came to America in 1619, racism is still the weed of democracy that hasn't been pulled out.

Still, an army of idealists has been trying—from the earliest abolitionists to the canny Thurgood Marshall litigating in the South in the 1930s to Gunnar Myrdal's epochal *An American Dilemma* in 1944. Then, the great breakthrough—the unanimous 1954 Supreme Court decision in *Brown* v. *Board of Education* declaring that public school segregation creates a "badge of inferiority," which constitutionally violates the Equal Protection Clause of the Fourteenth Amendment.

Though *Brown* provokes the white southern establishment to respond with "massive resistance," the genie is out. Then the immoveable object of tradition collides with the irresistible force of the greatest moral movement in American history. Starting with the lunch-counter sit-ins in February 1960, a tactic as symbolically powerful as Gandhi's salt march to the sea to protest British colonial rule, thousands of small and large protests as well as murderous violence spreads throughout the South. Scores of civil rights heroes—Bob Moses, John Lewis, Bayard Rustin, Ralph Abernathy, Andrew Young—multiply the power of Dr. King's message in his masterful "Letter from a Birmingham Jail" to cautious black ministers:

> You may well ask, "Why direct action?" Why sit-ins, marches and so forth . . . For years now I have heard the word "Wait!" This "Wait" has almost always meant "Never." But when you have seen vicious mobs lynch your mothers and fathers at will . . . when your first name becomes "nigger" and your middle name becomes "boy" . . . when you suddenly find your tongue twisted as you seek to explain to your six year old daughter why she can't go to the amusement park and see tears welling up in her eyes when she is told that Funtown is closed to colored children, then you will understand why we find it difficult to wait.

Senator and presidential candidate John Kennedy is initially reluctant to offend those few southern states like Texas that might give him their electoral votes. Kennedy aide and historian Arthur

Schlesinger Jr. says years later, "The Kennedy civil rights strategy miscalculated the dynamism of a revolutionary movement." But this northern Catholic politician does at the least understand prejudice and power. So late in the presidential campaign, JFK makes a bold move. At Chicago's O'Hare Airport, his brother-in-law Sargent Shriver exhorts him to call a pregnant and very anxious Coretta Scott King to express his sympathy when a local judge in Georgia hauls her husband away in chains for four months of hard labor on some technical ground. "What the hell. That's a decent thing to do. Why not? Get her on the phone." The conversation takes two minutes, but word of it ricochets around black churches and communities contributing to Kennedy's narrow 113,000-vote margin.

When King begins organizing his march on Washington in the spring of 1963, the Kennedys worry that it could erupt in violence, be all-black, and backfire. But the president and attorney general relent in the face of implacable determination by black leaders at a White House meeting, with two enormous results. First, on June 11, 1963, President Kennedy federalizes the Alabama National Guard to escort two admitted students to the University of Alabama who have been blocked by Governor George Wallace because, says Kennedy, they "happen to be born Negroes." That evening, the president addresses the nation from the Oval Office in order to introduce what becomes the 1964 civil rights bill: "We are confronted primarily with a moral issue . . . This nation, for all its hopes and all its boasts, will not be fully free until all its citizens are free."

Two months later on August 28, the march—massive, interracial, peaceful—is a marker on America's journey to justice. And King's mesmerizing cadence and words become as much a part of American history as Lincoln's and Kennedy's inaugural addresses. A year later, President Lyndon Johnson understands that the martyrdom of Kennedy should stand for *something*—and invests that moral and political capital in civil rights. In the ultimate melding of outside and inside, it's Johnson, the president himself, who evokes the movement's mantra of "we *shall* overcome" in his historic address to a joint session of Congress in 1965 on behalf of voting rights legislation. Over the course of a tumultuous year and a half, Johnson signs the 1964 Civil Rights Act, forbidding discrimination in public accommodations, and then the 1965 Voting Rights Act, banning restrictions like literacy tests and poll taxes. By the end of that year,

250,000 additional black voters are registered to vote and black state legislators in the South grow from 3 to 176 by 1985.

On the other side of the Sixties racial ledger, however, are the Watts riots of August 1965, when an arrest from a traffic infraction lights the kindling of housing discrimination, poverty, lack of jobs, and LAPD abuses, which in turn leads to 34 deaths and $40 million in property damage. Polls and votes reflect an enormous backlash to this event, with Democrats suffering the loss of 47 House seats in the 1966 elections. Subsequent riots in Detroit, Newark, and nationally after King's assassination leave scores more dead. The decade's racial timeline concludes in 1968 with the Kerner Commission report that "our nation is moving toward two societies, one black and one white."

The Anti-War Movement

The leaders of the great powers meet at the Quai d'Orsay in January 1919 to decide the fate of Germany and the borders of scores of nations. One thin, small leader, a former teacher and cook from Indochina, can't even get President Wilson to acknowledge his urgent request to recognize his homeland. After returning empty-handed to Vietnam, Nguyen Tat Thanh changes his name to Ho Chi Minh, which means "He who enlightens," and devotes his life to uniting his country. That effort indeed does attract the attention, later, of several American presidents.

In early 1954, the Geneva Accords divide Vietnam temporarily at the 17th parallel into a communist North under Ho Chi Minh and an anti-communist, Catholic South, with promised elections two years later. But the South reneges. Wisely refusing to intervene militarily to save the French at Dien Bien Phu, President Eisenhower then unwisely explains his regional concerns at a press conference: "You have a row of dominoes set up, you knock over the first one, and what will happen to the last one is the certainty that it will go over very quickly."

Using a Cold War lens to view a localized conflict, the United States tragically misses the big picture. The first two American deaths in Vietnam occur on July 8, 1959, when Chester Ovnand and Dale Buis are ambushed at Bien Hoa. Then, after Kennedy's own humiliation at the Bay of Pigs, he decides not to again look weak in the context of another communist insurgency. So he sends in (ultimately)

16,000 "advisors" to make sure that Vietnam doesn't become a "domino"—he adopts Eisenhower's word—that might begin the cascade of Marxist states owing allegiance to China.

When the dovish deputy undersecretary of state, George Ball, tells the president that any commitment of forces would mean that "within five years we'll have 300,000 men in the paddies and jungles and never find them again," Kennedy responds with irritation, "George, you're crazier than hell, it isn't going to happen." Speaking of the South Vietnamese government, he publicly repeats that ultimately it has to be "their war" and privately tells Walt Rostow and Arthur Schlesinger Jr. that after his reelection he'll start drawing American advisors there down.

But there will be no reelection. Looking back after the Gulf of Tonkin, Tet, the secret bombing of Cambodia, My Lai, Kent State, and a fractured America, has there ever been a worse foreign policy mistake than America's political and military elites losing a war and 58,151 servicepeople—and up to 4 million Vietnamese dead—because of an easy-to-grasp though stupid *metaphor?*

Outside pressure on inside politicians begins with some street demonstrations in 1963 and 1964, cresting on October 21, 1969, when upward of a half million protestors march on the Pentagon. I travel there and stay over at a girlfriend's family home in Alexandria, Virginia, much to the displeasure of her father, a crew-cut, no-nonsense Air Force colonel. The march is massive, joyous, raucous, peaceful, and President Nixon says he'll ignore such protestors no matter what their numbers.

Journalist James Fallows (later to be President Carter's speechwriter and coauthor with me of *Who Runs Congress?*), writes a moving and influential piece in the *Washington Monthly* entitled "What Did You Do in the Class War, Daddy?" He explains how, as a Harvard student, he evades the draft only to realize with anguish that lower-class kids from Southie will instead fight and die.

Divisions peak during the last week of August 1968 at the Democratic Convention in Chicago. Protestors and police clash violently in Grant Park while inside the International Amphitheater, Senator Abe Ribicoff (D-CT) denounces "gestapo tactics" and hometown mayor Richard Daley in the audience shouts, "Fuck you, you Jew son of a bitch." It's at that moment that Vice President Hubert Humphrey essentially loses the presidential election—although it is Humphrey who aches for peace while Richard Nixon is purposefully ambiguous—as protests ironically elevate the Republican backlash into a governing majority.

The Sixties peace movement contains two big takeaways. First, outside activists can move inside politicians. Second, as revolutionaries from George Washington to Ho Chi Minh have shown, the record of an external power trying to suppress local nationalists is not a good one since the very insertion of troops can antagonize local populations and undermine the ultimate battle for "hearts and minds." But George W. Bush later ignores how counterproductive counterinsurgent war is when he replaces the word *Vietnam* with *Iraq*.

The Women's Movement

It was Abigail Adams who reminded her husband and his fellow delegates at the Continental Congress in 1783 to "remember the ladies," with thinly veiled threats that otherwise "we will not hold ourselves bound by any Laws in which we have no voice, or Representation." Nearly 70 years passed before Seneca Falls created a public demand for the right to vote and another 70 years before the Nineteenth Amendment established it. And then, fulfilling New Jersey justice Arthur Vanderbilt's axiom that "reform is not for the short-winded," the next 60 years accelerate the movement toward gender equality, led by three feminists especially—first Margaret Sanger and then Betty Friedan and Gloria Steinem.

Sanger was indicted in 1914 (for violating obscenity laws by distributing literature on birth control), jailed in 1916 (for opening America's first birth control clinic), and derided as a "menace to society" by a judge at her sentencing. Decades later she partners with an heiress friend, Katherine McCormick, to sponsor trials for a drug that McCormick had first conceived of—a simple pill whose use is entirely controlled by women. As soon as the FDA approves Enovid-10 in 1960, excessive expectations are attached to the pill's promise—a cure for divorce, an end to poverty. But what it does do is allow women and men to plan their families and permit women to join the workforce if they choose—and millions do.

Despite the Nineteenth Amendment, the American public in the following decades overwhelmingly opposes married women entering the workforce. George Gallup says the opposition is unlike anything he's ever seen in polling. This is the America in which Bettye Gold-stein grows up, in Peoria, Illinois, "marching to tunes that others had not yet heard," according to her brother. She changes her name to Betty Friedan and becomes a suburban wife and ad agency copy-writer. Then in 1963 she names "the problem with no name" in her seminal work, *The Feminine Mystique.*

Her hugely popular book documents stories of women who make their own path but then, standing on the precipice of new lives, turn back. One student interested in exploring cancer research switches to home economics deciding she'd rather work in a department store after college. Friedan explains to *Life* magazine, "Some people think I'm saying, 'Women of the world unite—you have nothing to lose but your men.' It's not true. You have nothing to lose but your vacuum cleaners."

Friedan's writings and followers attract national attention and, consequently, the White House, which convenes a largely symbolic National Conference of Commissions on the Status of Women in June 1966. Stymied by the inability to pass resolutions—"it was a weekend of lip service," Friedan observes—women pass napkins around the lunch tables at the Washington Hilton outlining their demands. That lays the foundation for what becomes the National Organization for Women "to take the actions needed to bring women into the main-stream of American society, now . . . in fully equal partnership with men." Friedan achieves her goal to create, in her words, an "NAACP for women."

Gloria Steinem eyes tap dancing as her ticket out of Toledo, out of a dreary childhood in a family burdened by heavy debts. She lives in a house-trailer during winters, crisscrossing the country while her father sells antiques, and doesn't regularly attend public school until she's 12, sparing her the socialization of school that would likely have constricted her expanding worldview. Steinem enters Smith College in an era of limited options—and fewer role models. "In my growing up years there was Eleanor Roosevelt, but to be her you had to marry a president," she says wryly to the author in a 2014 interview.

She comes to New York to be a writer but is confined to "wom-en's interests," such as writing about a candidate's wife, not the can-didate. But her reporting on a 1969 meeting in the basement of a Greenwich Village church on the state's abortion laws changes her life. "It was the first time," Steinem recounts, "that I had ever heard women standing up and telling the truth about something that can only happen to women. I had an abortion myself and never talked about it. Suddenly it just dawned on me—it's crazy that one in three women has had an abortion . . . Why is it so dangerous, why is there all kinds of sexual harassment in order to get one, not to mention physical danger?"

Inspired and radicalized, she starts moving into circles with other leaders, like Bella Abzug, whom she adores, and Betty Friedan, whom she doesn't. Then her brainy critiques, media-friendly looks, signature aviator glasses, and aplomb bring her celebrity, which she shrewdly invests to further her cause. Starting in the early Seventies, she leads the fight for an Equal Rights Amendment, a greater challenge than the women's movement anticipated. "We assumed that it was such simple justice that it wouldn't be difficult to win," she recalls with regret in her voice. But the right-wing forces of Phyllis Schlafly, along with reactionary state legislatures, slow, stall, and then stop the amendment three states short of ratification. Yes to *Roe v. Wade* in 1973 but no to the ERA.

What lesson does Steinem learn? "We were probably much too nice, much too well mannered, not enough demonstrations and courting the press to counter the distortions about bra-burning." ("Nobody ever burned a bra, that's made up," she says.) But as the movement's public face, she maintains her public composure, which she attributes to her roots. "It's Midwestern," she laughs.

The Environmental Movement

It started with fire ants.

They came aboard cargo ships in Alabama's Gulf coast around the 1930s and each decade came farther inland, reaching North Carolina and Arkansas, devastating many plants and animals, eating even electrical equipment. An increasingly alarmed U.S. Department of Agriculture brought pesticides into the fight, spraying 1 million acres with dieldrin and heptachlor by 1958. Missing its intended target, the pesticides began killing off quails, wild turkeys, armadillos, and meadowlarks.

Rachel Carson—a 55-year-old biologist from Pennsylvania battling cancer and donning a wig following her chemotherapy treatment—is horrified by the indiscriminate spraying of pesticides and begins exposing its dangers. The pushback is intense. Monsanto prints 5,000 copies of a parody brochure entitled "The Desolate Year" of a world without pesticides, a world dominated by insects, vermin, and famines. President Kennedy, however, orders his science committee to investigate her findings and then in September 1962 Carson's *Silent Spring*—referring to songbirds that had stopped singing—is published to instant success. Though she dies less than two years after its release, her account of the dangers of DDT leads to its prohibition in America and, within a decade, a global treaty banning 12 pesticides ("the dirty dozen").

Questions about pesticides lead to questions about other pollutants. Thanksgiving 1966 sees the weather conspire to unleash a temperature inversion—in which warm air traps polluted air—over Manhattan. Bombarding the atmosphere of New York are more man-made contaminants than any other big city in the country—almost two pounds of soot and noxious gases for every man, woman, and child. The city shuts off all of its 11 incinerators, but hospitals report a surge in deaths from pulmonary emphysema and chronic bronchitis. The smog hanging over the city exacerbates heart and lung conditions and leaves 168 people dead.

Such events prod Congress to enact the 1967 Air Quality Act, which passes the Senate *unanimously*. Three years later, the Clean Air Act of 1970 passes Congress, again with no nay votes, this being an era when environmental harm is seen as afflicting people irrespective of whether they have Republican or Democratic lungs. Then the Cuyahoga River in Ohio catches fire. Since rivers are supposed to flow, not ignite, this event draws public attention to why it's legal to dump toxic chemicals in our streams and rivers.

Drawing from the era's anti-war protests, Senator Gaylord Nelson (D-WI) comes up with the idea for a massive grassroots "teach-in" about environmental issues. He chooses April 22 as the first-ever Earth Day. If only 40 or so campuses hold teach-ins, he thinks, he'd consider it a success. By day's end, 2,000 colleges, 10,000 high schools, and 2,000 communities join in—in all, 20 million participate in what is, still, the largest mass mobilization in American history.

"The reason Earth Day worked," Nelson says later, "is that it organized itself. The idea was out there and everybody grabbed it. I wanted a demonstration by so many people that politicians would say, 'Holy cow, people care about this.'"

Wary of aligning with the same activists who denounce him as a war criminal in demonstrations, President Richard Nixon tells a top advisor, "Just keep me out of trouble on environmental issues." On December 2, 1970, Nixon signs the executive order that creates the Environmental Protection Agency because he's also an astute politician aware of the bipartisan popularity of an issue that so intimately affects the health of all American families.

Conservationist John McCormick concludes that no other mass movement over the past century "wrought so universal or so fundamental a change in human values." Carson and Nelson spawn a new environmental revolution that looks to government regulation to reduce dangerous pollution, and sees a surge in growth of existing groups like the Sierra Club and the birth of new ones like the Natural Resources Defense Council and Greenpeace. Of course there is corporate backlash arguing that job growth and environmental health are incompatible.

The fight is joined.

The Health-Care Movement

After Otto Von Bismarck sewed together his safety net in Germany, ex-president Teddy Roosevelt ran a third-party candidacy based on the chancellor's national health insurance model. TR's Bull Moose candidacy died but not his cause. His fifth cousin and namesake tried to make it a key element in his New Deal edifice. But when the American Medical Association opposition to his "cradle to grave" health insurance plan threatened to sink Social Security legislation, FDR—a pragmatist far more than an ideologue—dropped the insurance provision.

Then it's President Harry Truman's turn to try and fail when the AMA replays its "socialized medicine" card during the height of the Cold War. After a determined President Kennedy re-raises the issue at a huge Madison Square Garden speech, the AMA slaps him down in a prime-time infomercial that warns that decisions about a patient's care may be made by "some intangible, callous government committee" (presaging "death panels" a half century later).

Finally, fulfilling Voltaire's famous axiom about "an idea whose time has come," this cycle of failure is broken. When Lyndon Johnson crushes Barry Goldwater by 16 million votes and with 61 percent of the vote—and 37 of the AMA's best friends in Congress are defeated in that same November election—the AMA realizes its vulnerability and LBJ seizes his opportunity.

For years Wilbur Mills, always called the "powerful chairman of the House Ways and Means committee," had opposed comprehensive health insurance in part fearing that the AMA might threaten his safe seat. But given the election and Johnson's agenda, Mills proposes a new idea: combine some proposed AMA voluntary programs into LBJ's expansive proposal with parts that cover hospital insurance through the Social Security tax; pay for the cost of doctors by a monthly premium matched by government funds; and create Medicaid, a program for those unable to afford health care yet ineligible for Social Security.

This one omnibus bill supported by Johnson and Mills breaks the 60-year logjam that held up national health care. Medicare and Medicaid reimagine government's role and assure America's elderly and indigent of their right to health care. It passes each chamber by better than 2–1 and is signed by President Johnson on July 30, 1965, at a ceremony in Independence, Missouri, home of Harry Truman, who had been so maligned in his pursuit of national health insurance.

The decade witnesses a second health revolution destined to save millions of lives over decades—the pro-health war on tobacco.

When the Sixties begins, half of American men smoke, with another 21 percent being former smokers. Ashtrays are a ubiquitous part of everyday life—on planes, in offices, in restaurants. Cartoon staples like Fred Flintstone endorse cigarettes. Lucky Strike and Viceroy even advertise the healthful effect of their products. Among the celebrity salesmen, actor Ronald Reagan.

The link between smoking and cancer has been developing for decades. A heavily circulated *Reader's Digest* article, "Cancer by the Carton," in 1952 leads to the biggest drop in smoking in 20 years. The tobacco industry quickly conducts their own studies, which amazingly enough refute medical studies, and, with the release of filtered and low-tar cigarettes, win back many of these customers.

Seeking to settle the debate, President Kennedy appoints a panel led by Surgeon General Luther Terry to weigh the evidence. Terry assures an anxious tobacco industry that his panel will be impartial and even allows industry officials to vet committee members; indeed, half of the committee's ten members—like the surgeon general himself—are not only smokers but even smoke during their meetings.

Though bearing the anodyne title "Smoking and Health," the report is perhaps the most influential ever published in the U.S. on a health issue. Released January 11, 1964—a Saturday so as not to spook the markets, and so that it would blanket the Sunday papers—it provides inconvertible proof that smoking causes lung cancer: "Cigarette smoking is a health hazard of sufficient importance [to require] appropriate remedial action."

From 1963 to 1964, smoking dips 3.5 percent. Most press accounts conclude that while smoking may temporarily decline, over time it will again increase. The coming half century will prove them wrong.

The Terry report joins *Silent Spring, The Feminine Mystique, Unsafe at Any Speed,* and *The Other America* as publications that shift the axis of policy in America. Thirty-five years later Joe Camel ads came down and a half century later use of tobacco has fallen by more than half. The *Journal of American Medicine* estimates that since the report's release, 8 *million* American lives have been saved.

The Drug Reform Movement

When *Time* magazine chooses those "25 and under" as its Person of the Year in 1966, it writes, "He has clearly signaled his determination to live according to his own lights and rights." In few areas is this transformation as clear as the rise of drug use.

Drug use stays largely underground with the Beats and jazz musicians in the 1950s, as Louis Armstrong explains that "it relaxes you, makes you forget all the bad things that happen to a Negro." Then marijuana enters the bloodstream of the mainstream in the Sixties.

It begins mid-decade in San Francisco, initially inspired by Timothy Leary, a Harvard doctor thrown out with a colleague for his experimentations with drugs. Scott McKenzie's "San Francisco (Be Sure to Wear Flowers in Your Hair)" hits the radio in the spring of 1967, and thousands start flooding the city looking for weed.

By the end of summer, Haight-Ashbury is lost to darker drugs like LSD and speed (methamphetamine). The drug of choice on college campuses remains marijuana, with nearly half of all students having tried it by the end of the decade. It becomes a symbolic badge against the war but is also easily confused with the more dangerous LSD in the public mind. From 1965 to 1970, marijuana arrests jump tenfold. Decades-old laws, like those in Virginia that mandate 20 years in prison for possession of any amount of marijuana, remained on the books.

Alarmed by growing numbers of servicemen returning from Vietnam addicted to heroin, President Nixon worries that this epidemic threatens his title as the "law and order" president. This fear, however, turns out to be unfounded: 95 percent of addicts in Vietnam do not stay addicted upon their return to the United States. But Nixon simply transfers his contempt to marijuana users. Aide John Ehrlichman admits, "We understood that drugs were not the health problem we were making them out to be, but it was such a perfect issue for the Nixon White House that we couldn't resist it." Operatives on the RNC payroll disrupt the Democratic National Convention in 1972 by flying banners reading "Pot Peace Prosperity—vote McGovern." Arrests related to marijuana use soon exceed the number of all the nation's violent crimes.

The president's other top aide, H. R. Haldeman, writes in his diary how Nixon "emphasized that you have to face the fact that the whole problem is really the blacks. The key is to devise a system that recognizes this while not appearing to." These are the mind-set and actions behind Nixon's rhetorically vibrant "War on Drugs"—which begins a perversion of criminal justice that haunts American life still in 2016.

Partly in reaction to the disgraced president after Watergate, penalties for marijuana are reduced in 28 states for possession as the magazine *High Times* starts appearing on newsstands in 1974. But Ronald Reagan's election in 1980 and federal sentencing guidelines— as well Governor Nelson Rockefeller's notorious drug laws in New York—explode the prison population, as largely young men of color overwhelm jails. In New York drug offenders total one in three inmates. According to Governor David Paterson in 2009, "I can't think of a criminal justice strategy that has been more unsuccessful than the Rockefeller Drug Laws."

A century ago, the war on liquor created Prohibition, which had to be undone by constitutional amendment. In 2016, the war on drugs is inspiring a bipartisan countermovement to be more smart than merely "tough" on drugs.

The Gay Rights Movement

For most of the twentieth century, gays in America were seen as emotionally disturbed, an opinion fully sanctioned by the American Psychological Association. For decades, California's Atascadero State Prison subjected gays to torture and lobotomies, earning the notoriously cruel prison the nickname "Dachau for queers." When petitioning for their rights, activists strained to point out that they weren't seeking to win the right to marry or adopt children, only that their love no longer be considered criminal. "You weren't just in the closet," poet Quincy Troupe wrote in the late 1940s, "you were in the basement. Under the basement floor."

Things began to change when an inspired Harry Hay, a Marxist activist, raced home from an LA party late one night in 1948 and, while his wife and children slept, scrambled to write down a gay manifesto. It contained a demand that was a profoundly radical notion for a puritanical America 80 years after enactment of the Fourteenth Amendment: gays and lesbians deserve the same rights as everyone else. The Mattachine Society is born.

The Sixties opens with the first-ever reversal of an "Other Than Honorable" discharge for a gay woman in the U.S. Air Force. Illinois governor Otto Kerner in 1962 makes consensual same-gender sex legal—the first state to do so. Pickets start popping up across the country. Starting in 1965, at Philadelphia's Independence Hall on the Fourth of July, comes the Annual Reminder—a march of gays telling the country that "15 million homosexual Americans [are] being denied their rights under the law." The marches receive little attention in the press, save for mockery: one magazine headlines a story "Homos on the March." A bookstore opens in Greenwich Village featuring gay and lesbian authors, the first of its kind.

Then in the spring of 1967, just before the so-called Summer of Love begins, *CBS Reports* airs "The Homosexuals." Despite having a star of the stature of Mike Wallace, the program comes across almost like a *Reefer Madness* for gays, dripping with fear-mongering, stereotypes, and hyperbole. "The average homosexual, if there be such, is promiscuous," Wallace intones. "He is not interested or capable of a lasting relationship like that of a heterosexual marriage. Even on the streets of the city—the pick-up, the one night stand, these are characteristics of the homosexual relationship." Police raids of gay bars are then commonplace, like the one at the Stonewall Inn on a hazy evening in 1969.

Operating without a liquor license and backed by Mafia investors, Stonewall is a den of watered-down liquor and poor service protected by police officers being regularly paid off. Still, it's a refuge, one of the few places where men can embrace in a slow dance. But 20 minutes after 1 a.m. on June 28, eight police officers enter the bar, announcing, "Police! . . . The place is under arrest. When you exit, have some identification and it'll be over in a short time."

But it's not. Instead, a cross-dressing Stormé DeLarverie angrily pushes back, lighting a fuse that would explode old values and assumptions. "The cop hit me, and I hit him back. The cops got what they gave," she says. Years later, one man who was there excitedly recounts in a documentary: "In the Civil Rights Movement, we ran from the police; in the peace movement, we ran from the police. That night, the police ran from us, the lowliest of the low. And it was fantastic." In a seminal *Village Voice* piece, Lucian Truscott IV puts the city and the country on notice: "Watch out. The liberation is under way."

Today it's called either the Stonewall Riot or the Stonewall Rebellion, depending on your politics. Whatever the label, a cultural revolution is born that night which, speaking of "fantastic," over time leads to marriage equality nationally by 2015.

The Consumer Movement

The aphorism *caveat emptor*—literally "let the buyer beware" but figuratively "good luck, fella" in a seller-dominated marketplace—begins to change meaning in 1966. That's when two women likely paid by General Motors separately approach Ralph Nader in Washington, D.C., supermarkets to try to compromise him and, consequently, his advocacy. That ham-handed effort leads to a sensational Senate hearing, an auto safety law and agency in 1966–70, and a new way of holding corporations accountable for the hidden dangers they impose on consumers and workers, as will be detailed in the next chapter.

WHEN ASKED his opinion of the French Revolution, Chinese president Chou En-Lai memorably replied, "It's too soon to tell." When

Tom Brokaw wrote *Boom!* in 2007, he similarly concluded that it was too soon to issue a verdict on the impact of the multi-faceted Sixties. From my vantage point, however, as an outside consumer advocate and inside progressive politician who lived through them and then applied their values to public policy, it's past time for an accounting. Then, a generation wouldn't stay quiet about the cavernous gulf between American ideals and American practices. Now, tensions over racial justice, access to health care, women's and gay equality, diplomacy and war, and economic and political inequality are reemerging as new chapters in the continuing story of America.

TWO

NADER

Present at the Creation of the Consumer Movement

Law Student: "How do you live up to your image?"
Ralph Nader: "I don't. My image lives up to me."

—Ralph Nader, Harvard Law School, 1977

Patriotism is not a short and frenzied burst of emotion but the long and
studied dedication of a lifetime.

—Governor Adlai Stevenson

THE BOY FROM WINSTED

It's 1937, and Rose Nader of Winsted, Connecticut, is taking her four young children to visit their homeland of Lebanon. While the three oldest have struggled to learn the Lebanese national anthem in Arabic to impress relatives, it's the youngest, four-year-old Ralph, who unexpectedly steps forward and sings it flawlessly to his astonished extended family. He shyly admits that he had been listening in a nearby room during his siblings' lessons.

That same trip, the Nader family is in line to meet an archbishop of the Greek Orthodox Church in the city of Zahle. But when it's Ralph's turn to kiss the ring, he refuses. "I don't have to. I'm an American!" he announces. An unruffled archbishop looks down, pats Ralph's short black hair, and says, "A lot of ideas are going to come from this boy's head."

NINETEEN-YEAR-OLD Nathra Nader arrives in America in 1912 with a sixth-grade education and $20. The thin, diligent tradesman works in various jobs and places—the Maxwell Auto Works in Detroit, a machine shop in Newark—before returning to Zahle to wed Rose Bouziane in an arranged marriage. They eventually settle in the mid-1920s in Winsted, Connecticut—a Capra-esque New England town of under 10,000 nestled 26 miles above Hartford in the Berkshires near the Massachusetts border. It's a place of lush, sloping lawns, small shops, and local mills, where everyone seems to know everyone. Eventually, Nathra saves enough to buy a two-story, ten-room white clapboard house as well as a building in town that becomes the Highland Arms, the Nader family restaurant where all four of his children work at one time or another.

The father serves food with a side of civics, as the restaurant becomes a sort of town square where his views are as strong as the coffee. "When I went by the Statue of Liberty," he tells one Nader biographer, "I took it seriously." Rose too has firm views, in particular about parenting. When a child complains about something they think unfair, she says, "I believe it's *you*. Go do something about it." According to sister Laura Nader in a 2015 interview, "Ralph is a combination of our father's idealism and vision and our mother's practicality."

Early on Rose spots unusual things about young Ralph. Without instruction, he starts telling time at age three. When he comes home late from school around age eight, she asks where he's been: "In court. I like to listen to the arguments." At age 14, he carries home armfuls of the small-type *Congressional Record,* which he reads from start to finish. "You have a very good storage space," she tells him, touching his forehead. "You should fill it up and take it out when you need it."

Ralph is a newspaper boy for the Winsted *Register Citizen,* plays sandlot ball for hours on end with, among others, classmate David Halberstam, develops an ardor for "Iron Man" Lou Gehrig because of his durability and dependability, displays an encyclopedic knowledge of baseball stats, reads Hardy Boys books and biographies about turn-of-the-century muckrakers, and especially enjoys working the cash register at the Highland Arms. He compulsively engages customers to satisfy his developing curiosity. (Similarly, after Winsted, he would hitchhike to and from college and law school because "it was [one of the] greatest educations in the world. You meet all kinds of people: executives, tree surgeons, bricklayers, doctors, truck drivers. Not only did I learn a lot but you had to adapt to all kinds of personalities.")

Tall, thin, with an angular face and deep-set eyes, the shy student leaves Winsted for Princeton in 1951. Ralph is attracted by its declared mission—"Princeton in the Nation's Service"—and its excellence in foreign affairs and Oriental Studies, then his passions. And he falls for, in his words, "its beautiful open stack library" where he reads an average of a book a day *outside* of his required course work. Classmates walking by him en route to a big football game teasingly call him "a dirty grind." What Princeton's famous eating clubs are to generations of its tweedy students, the Harvey S. Firestone Library becomes to Nader.

He also learns some Russian, Chinese, and Spanish, in addition to the Arabic he occasionally speaks at home. Six years before Rachel Carson's *Silent Spring*, he wonders whether all the dead birds on campus result from the spraying of DDT. When he carries one to the *Daily Princetonian* to urge that they investigate, he's blown off. "We have some of the smartest chemists in the world here," an upper-classman editor assures him. "If there was a problem, they'd let us know."

While at college, he's exposed to great thinkers, especially Alpheus Mason, the leading biographer of Louis Brandeis, and Norman Thomas (Princeton '05). "What was your greatest achievement?" asks Ralph of the famous socialist and six-time socialist presidential candidate after a speech. Thomas replies, "Having the Democrats steal my agenda."

His scholarship and fertile mind deeply impress one professor, who tries unsuccessfully to convince him to get a PhD rather than going to law school. "For me," recalls Nader, "it was always the law." In a recommendation, this faculty member describes him as "a natural leader . . . Ralph is a man of possible 'greatness.' I think he is going to be one of the most distinguished men in our country in years to come."

Then Harvard Law School. "From day one I laughed at the game— to prepare corporate lawyers. If anyone fell off the bandwagon and became a lawyer for the poor, it was viewed as a random event. [For example], I took Landlord-Tenant Law, only we never got to the tenant. They made minds sharp by making them narrow."

Bored by his courses, Nader is periodically and mysteriously gone for days on end, hitchhiking around the country and researching Indian rights, migrant workers, the status of Puerto Rico. He also starts reading about auto safety after seeing car crashes in his travels, including one where a young girl is nearly beheaded in a low-speed crash when the glove compartment pops open. He writes and publishes articles on all these topics as a writer for and the top editor of the *Harvard Law Record,* and his third-year paper is on the issue of auto company liability for defects that result in death and injury. His idiosyncratic approach to HLS is seen when he's called into the dean's office and asked about a course in which he had gotten an A on the final exam. Ralph nods his head. "But there is one problem," says the dean. "You are not signed up for this course. Did you attend the classes?" Ralph admits that he had not. He had just thought he was enrolled in the course, so he took the exam.

In the five years after law school, Nader continues his intellectual progress, traveling to the Soviet Union, Scandinavia, and Latin/South America, writing dispatches on his portable Smith Corona (for the *Christian Science Monitor, New Republic,* and the *Atlantic*), scoring interviews with Fidel Castro in Cuba in 1959 and Salvadore Allende in Chile in 1963. He churns out two or three pieces a week. "I could go into a country and very quickly have a real grasp of the situation," he says, reflecting his phenomenal self-confidence combined with a deep appreciation of other cultures gleaned from his anthropologist sister Laura.

More routinely, he teaches at the University of Hartford, learns everything he can about the aerodynamics of cars, and opens a local law practice (where his big problem is having to charge clients), fulfills his military commitment in reserve training doing kitchen work at Fort Dix in New Jersey in 1959 (buying a dozen pairs of army combat boots for $6 a pair that he wears into the 1980s), and lobbies his state legislature to consider a local ombudsman office like the one he studied when visiting Helsinki. He even begins research on a muckraking book on women's rights, pre-Friedan, that he never finishes because "no one collected the kind of data I needed and my auto work took over. Amazingly, eleven states didn't allow women on juries!"

So by the time he sets off for the nation's capital in 1963 hoping to make an impact, Ralph Nader has already met his future—from running for president about as often as Norman Thomas to storing increasing reams of information in his own cranial search engine, much as his mother suggested.

MR. NADER GOES TO WASHINGTON

While so many young activists and professionals are drawn to Washington and to civil rights during the Kennedy years, the 29-year-old Nader hitches from Hartford to D.C. with a knapsack and a reservation at the YMCA, intent on working on what he calls "body rights."

He gets a job consulting to an assistant secretary of labor in the Kennedy administration who also has an unusual talent for policy and language as well as a specific interest in highway safety, which he had worked on as a young assistant to New York governor Averell Harriman. Indeed, Daniel Patrick Moynihan had written one of the first magazine articles on the subject in 1959, coincidentally two weeks after Nader's own groundbreaking piece in *The Nation* magazine on April 11, 1959, entitled "The Safe Car You Can't Buy." Moynihan considers Nader a furtive, brilliant figure who is rarely in his office yet does produce a 235-page report—*Context, Condition, and Recommended Direction of Federal Activity in Highway Safety*—that garners as much public attention as expected from a report with that title.

About the same time, a tiny New York publisher, Richard Grossman, is searching for someone to write a book on cars and hears about Nader from journalist James Ridgeway. They agree to a $3,000 contract for an "untitled book on auto safety." Continuing the original research that he began as a law student, Nader has a near-finished manuscript in mid-1964 when he leaves the only copy in a cab in Washington, D.C.! He then rewrites it from scratch.

I ask Ralph decades later, "So, how'd you feel when you first realized you had left it behind?"

Sighing at the memory, he replies, "Empty."

"Did you consider not rewriting it?"

"Never, I wouldn't give GM the satisfaction."

Unsafe at Any Speed: The Designed-In Dangers of the American Automobile comes out in November 1965. Its thesis is that the reason for most car crashes is "not the nut behind the wheel but the nut in the wheel" and "the second collision" of riders with interiors—that is, cars designed for style, not safety. With a showman's flair, Grossman sends an invitation to all auto company executives and Detroit media to hear Ralph speak about the book and take questions from all comers. He arrives at the Sheraton Cadillac on January 6, 1966, where he performs, entertains, and disarms critics (though no top executives attend). Grossman is thrilled and surprised: "That day, I suddenly realized his genius for handling the media. He was unflappable . . . and a couple of questions ahead of the reporters the whole time."

During these months in early 1966, while also working as an unpaid advisor to Senator Abe Ribicoff (D-CT) on projected auto safety hearings, Nader suspects that he's being followed. Friends and allies scoff at what they consider his amusing paranoia. Then he's approached twice by attractive women while shopping at stores near his boarding house, whose come-ons he rebuffs. When the *Washington Post* also gets a tip from a congressional security guard that people acting like detectives were looking for someone named Ralph Nader, articles about the snoops appear in the *Post* and the *New Republic* by two reporters who connect the dots—Morton Mintz and James Ridgeway, respectively. An outraged Ribicoff calls for a special hearing both because it's a federal crime to harass a congressional witness and because senators don't appreciate outsiders messing with their prerogatives.

The rest unspools like a screenplay for a Hollywood thriller. Though scheduled as the opening witness on March 20, 1966, before the Senate Select Subcommittee on Executive Reorganization, Nader—in what would become his signature uniform of dark suit, thin tie, and combat boots—arrives 40 minutes late. He then slumps quietly in the back of the packed Caucus Room of the Old Senate Office Building (the Senate's largest chamber, where JFK announced his candidacy in 1960). It seems that he couldn't find a timely cab on this biggest day of his professional life.

So Ribicoff first calls and puts under oath James Roche, the CEO of GM, a company then larger in gross sales at $18 billion than the GNPs of all countries other than the U.S. and U.S.S.R. With renowned lawyer Ted Sorensen counseling and sitting beside him, the executive immediately apologizes. Yes, someone in his company (who turned out to have been its general counsel) had indeed hired a detective agency to ostensibly investigate whether the subject was soliciting Corvair owners to sue GM. In fact, here is what the lead private dick had told his agents assigned to Nader: "Our job is to check out his life and current activities to determine what makes him tick

. . . his politics, his marital status, his friends, his women, his boys, and so forth, his drinking, dope, jobs—in fact all facets of his life."

Among the most offended senators is Robert Kennedy of New York, who deflates the culpable detective, a barrel-chested, blunt-talking, Clouseau-ish character named Vince Gillen. While testifying that he needed to check out rumors "in fairness to Ralph," Kennedy interrupts in his high-pitched voice. "What the hell is 'fairness to Ralph'? You have to keep proving he's not queer and he's not anti-Semitic? 'In fairness to Ralph'? Ralph is doing all right."

Then it's Nader's turn and he again proves to be a "natural"—calm, fluent, occasionally humorous, "a machine gun with facts" in one journalist's phrase. "I am responsible for my actions, but who is responsible for those of General Motors?" he solemnly wonders, gaining everyone's complete attention. "An individual's capital and soul is basically his integrity. He can lose only once. A corporation can lose many times and not be affected." Some senators then trot out the industry line that auto regulation is not the federal government's business. Ralph vaporizes their contention. Fifty thousand people a year die in America from car crashes, he observes, and you think this should only be a matter for *private* businesses, not *public* government interested in our health and safety?

When Carl Curtis, a bumptious Republican senator from Nebraska, implies that the witness's main goal is "to sell books," Senator Kennedy again interrupts. "Why are you doing all of this?" he asks Ralph, trying to coax a rebuttal. If he were trying to prevent cruelty to animals, comes the response, no one would doubt him. "But because I happen to have a scale of priorities which leads me to engage in the prevention of cruelty to humans, my motives are constantly inquired into." His shoulders hunched, his voice rising, his dark eyebrows arched in emphasis, he concludes, "Is it wrong to talk about defective cars, diseased meats, corporate cheating? Is it really distasteful that a person cares enough about issues like these to dedicate his life to changing them?"

The immediate upshot: that morning, Nader is a Cassandra warning about dangerous cars; by the next morning—after saturation of TV, radio, and print coverage—he's a certified truth-teller, perhaps the leading real-life example of a David slaying Goliath. *Unsafe* becomes a best-seller and is listed by the Library of Congress as one of the 100 Books That Shaped America.

The longer-term upshot, however, is even more profound.

First, within only five months, Congress unanimously passes—by 331–0 in the House and 76–0 in the Senate—and President Johnson signs into law, at a ceremony that Ralph attends, the creation of the National Highway Traffic Safety Administration (NHTSA). According to Dr. Robert Brenner, a pioneer in the field of auto safety, "All the twenty years of research which preceded Nader's book did not have its impact. It was one of the turning points of our civilization." Over the next 50 years, its design standards and recalls would reduce the rate of death per mile driven by nearly 80 percent, saving over 3.5 million lives and avoiding several million serious injuries.

Second, as if planning for this one-in-a-million moment his whole life, Nader expands horizontally into other consumer and democracy issues. He begins to raise and spend money to hire what comes to be called "Nader's Raiders." This moniker, coined by journalist William Greider, is initially considered trivializing and mocking but is then embraced by Ralph as memorable branding—not unlike the term "muckrakers" from Teddy Roosevelt 60 years before.

"You might call it my obsession," he tells me in 2015 about his thinking back then, as we sit in the huge, marbled conference room of the Carnegie Building on 15th Street in D.C. that is his current work home. "Others may be trapped by their earliest success to keep doing what they're doing," Nader says in his usual matter-of-fact tone. "I'm not interested in the Lone Ranger effect . . . The more groups I can help create, the more deeply rooted this whole process of consumer and citizen sovereignty becomes." He repeats a favorite comment of Jean Monnet, considered the father of the European Union: "Without people, nothing is possible. Without institutions, nothing is lasting."

So the modern consumer movement is born—not with the combined big bang of *Unsafe*/the Roche apology/auto safety law, but with one individual's strategic judgment to hire, over time, thousands of Raiders to work on cars . . . and nuclear power, pipeline safety, food and drug safety, airline safety, water and air pollution, anti-trust enforcement, corporate governance and shareholder democracy, clean energy, tax reform, income and wealth inequality, advertising, campaign finance reform, pension rights, old age homes, coal mine safety, occupational hazards, health care, hospital technology, smoking, freedom of information laws, civil service, multinationals, the Educational Testing Service, sports, veterans affairs, land management, corporate welfare, the oceanic environment, biogenetics, whistle-blowing, trade policy, insurance, procurement . . .

MANY NADERS

With requests for paying speeches pouring in and collecting a $425,000 settlement from his invasion of privacy civil suit against GM—courtesy, in one sense, of Brandeis, whose famous 1890 *Harvard Law Review* article created this "right"—Nader launches a five-decade drive to empower citizens to challenge corporate abuse.

He has a very specific model to build on—the original muck-rakers at the turn of the century that he learned about as a boy. The Nader-figure at that time was Frank McClure, the dynamic founder of *McClure's Magazine,* something of a cross between the Government Accountability Office, a Swedish ombudsman, and an investigative journalist. In editorial board meetings surrounded by the leading writers of that era, the idea-a-minute McClure would lead discussions of various social ills and then make assignments, working closely with his writers for the months or even years it would take to complete the article or book. His philosophy: "the vitality of democracy . . . depends on popular knowledge of complex questions." Their work product is still the gold standard, especially Ida Tarbell's *Standard Oil,* Lincoln Steffens's *The Shame of the Cities,* and Upton Sinclair's *The Jungle.*

Nader, however, wants something more. The early muckrakers, he observes, "only did 20 percent of the job. They stopped at exposure. They didn't follow through by mobilizing a concerned constituency." So while journalists are hired—including such later stars as James Fallows, Michael Moore, David Ignatius, Jonathan Alter, and Michael Kinsley—he leans toward young multi-talented lawyers who can analyze, write, speak, and anchor institutions that endure.

He starts in 1968 by hiring five lawyers and researchers working out of a couple of rented rooms in the National Press Building on 14th Street NW in Washington, D.C. Then in 1969 and 1970, there's a second wave of several dozen more—I'm among them—in the Public Interest Research Group (PIRG) and Center for Study of Responsive Law. Our stories are similar. Most wrote letters to "Ralph Nader, Washington D.C.," since there was no office to call or mail, and out of the thousands sent, somehow ours magically came to his attention. He'd usually interview students en route to a speech or airport . . . and then make a snap hiring decision. "He has this knack of picking bright people without ego problems," says Joan Claybrook, an early and continuing ally who would go on to become the head of the NHTSA under President Jimmy Carter.

Harrison Wellford, for example, has a prestigious position lined up with Henry Kissinger at Harvard, but Nader turns him, saying, "I promise you two things—you'll never be bored and will go home every night with a transcendent sense of accomplishment." With a reelected Nixon in the White House and the Vietnam War raging, many other young professionals and students flock to this guru for wonky idealists.

The PIRG lawyers formally start on a hot day, July 1, 1970, on the sixth floor at 1025 15th Street, when a dozen sit in a semicircle of chairs in a room without other furniture. Up front and holding onto his yellow pad is the 36-year-old Nader. "What will you tell your grandchildren that you did this year?" he rhetorically asks, and then plunges in by asking the lawyers to raise their hand when they hear a subject that interests them. "It's always better if someone agrees to an area they want than simply be ordered to take one," he explains years later in what he refers to as "*The* Assignment Meeting." Recalls one in the room: "There were areas like taxes, food and drugs, transportation, health, and safety [civil service, banking, pensions, whistleblowing]. When it was all over we each had a field and that was that." Each gets a desk, a phone, a pad of paper. For most, their task lasts a lifetime.

Ralph's template on auto safety is the model, which means the preliminary task is to find or create a sympathetic network to advance her/his issue. Scour the professional and popular literature. Speak to friendly, former administrators in target agencies. Make contacts with Hill staff and congressional members who respond to "Ralph Nader urged me to call . . ." Meet journalists who understand the advantage of a two-way exchange with information junkies. That means speaking their language. According to biographer Robert Buckhorn, "Nader has perfected the art of turning his legalistic arguments into readable copy designed to hold the attention of news editors." His tongue-in-cheeky phrasemaking—"crime in the suites," "fatfurters," "withering heights" for Congress—is playful and quotable. Not confused for Dylan's eloquent lyrics but successful in their realm.

As for workplaces, there is an unspoken presumption against ri-
valries, excessive egotism, factual sloppiness, and long weekends. Or
weekends at all, actually. When Reuben Robertson describes how he
and his wife relax on vacation, Ralph responds, "And what do you do
on the *next* day?" There is the collegiality of an all-for-one/one-for-
all movement akin to the original muckrakers and suffragettes, labor
organizers in the Thirties, ban-the-bomb protestors in the Fifties,
civil rights organizers in the Sixties.

The most prominent of the early exposés is the *Nader Report on
the Federal Trade Commission* in 1969. Six lawyers in their mid-20s
interview and research how this original consumer agency, the brain-
child of President Wilson, has declined into desuetude, patronage,
and trivia. Among the Raiders are William Howard Taft IV, great-
grandson of a president; Ed Cox, then going through a Weatherman-
like phase before becoming President Nixon's son-in-law; Judy Areen,
a future dean at Georgetown Law School; Peter Bradford, later the
chairman of both the New York and Vermont power commissions;
and Robert Fellmeth, a former Goldwater supporter from Hawaii
whose kinetic personality and prodigious work habits—he will also
author a 3,000-page Nader study of California land use—spawn the
in-house adjective "Fellmyth-ian."

The FTC chairman, Paul Rand Dixon, is not happy with their
effort, forcibly throwing one of the researchers out of his office and
concluding that the final report is "an hysterical, anti-business dia-
tribe." But the study's reporting and subsequent publicity provoke
the American Bar Association to appoint a panel to do its own analysis, which validates the Nader report. President Nixon then appoints
a new reform-minded chairman—Caspar Weinberger (*that* Caspar
Weinberger)—who hires Taft as his legal advisor, cleans house, and
revives the agency.

Fellmeth is delighted and amazed at their outsized impact. "It
made headlines all over the country. Are these people crazy? We're
just a bunch of students!"

It's heady stuff—an adoring public, admiring Congress, a president either supportive or at least not hostile. With an 80 percent favorable rating in polls and receiving some 90,000 letters a year, Nader
is widely regarded as in effect playing 50 simultaneous games of chess
while speeding at 70 ideas per hour. The result is stunning: beyond
the Auto Safety standards, in the decade between 1965 and 1975 he

either initiated or played an essential role in creating the Occupational Safety and Health Administration, Consumer Product Safety Commission, Environmental Protection Agency, Amendments to the Freedom of Information Act, Amendments to the Clean Water and Clean Air Acts, and Gas Pipeline Safety law.

But a looming cloud appears in 1971 in the form of the "Powell Memo" by Lewis Powell, a Virginia corporate lawyer who represents Philip Morris and the U.S. Chamber of Commerce and is named later that year to the Supreme Court by President Nixon. He lays out for clients and business lobbies how to strategically deploy donations, foundations, and the media to do what GM didn't—discredit extremists "like Ralph Nader."

RALPH AND ME

In early 1969, as noted, Nader convinces me to switch styles and venues, from city politics to national advocacy. We first meet in person in late spring 1969, when he squeezes his tall frame into my cramped basement office of the *Harvard Civil Rights–Civil Liberties Law Review*. We discuss where his project ideas may overlap with my interests. When he sees my enthusiasm for macroeconomics, the legal profession, and popular writing, he suggests two areas of concentration: the institutional power of Washington lawyers and anti-trust and regulatory law enforcement. Done. My dance card for the following decade is now largely full. We then move to a larger conference room where he woos several of my classmates to also work with him, before he walks into a large lecture hall where he further exhorts 600 in the audience.

It's not entirely clear why Ralph and I—from different generations and places—click so well or why we come to trust each other so completely.

I'm properly awed by him, gushing to a biographer at that time, "Nader is incredibly modest. You hardly ever hear a word of self-aggrandizement from him and this is contagious. Where else could a guy my age have the impact I have . . . ?" And he in turn tells an inquiring reporter, "One of the first things that struck me was how efficient he was, how consistent in his work habits. He has very high standards of scholarship yet is very well-rounded."

I find his brainy analyses and ironic humor hard to resist, and then there's the personal warmth that few outsiders see. When Deni is pregnant with Jenya, Ralph will invariably begin phone conversations by announcing "Baby Watch!" and then dispense some recent information he's come across about pre- or post-natal care. Our daily midnight calls for ten years provide the greatest public education of my professional life. In these talks, it's as if we're just two peers shooting the breeze. Which we're not. But it's part of his common touch—he seems to treat everyone, from waitresses to presidents, the same . . . like we're all customers at the Highland Arms.

In turn, he seems to appreciate my New York brand of kibitzing about everything and our mutual teasing. He calls me "the Mark of Excellence" using GM's slogan in a way that was never intended; I call him "the Nader of the Lost Mark" when I'm away. My addiction to hot dogs provokes him to conclude that "you're probably 90 percent rat feces and rodent hair by now"; I shoot back with something about his limited sartorial choices, lack of cultural awareness ("quick, who's Linda Ronstadt?"), and a sweet tooth tracing back to his youthful diet of cookies. (Alas, there aren't many other vices to taunt since he stopped smoking in '61.)

We laugh about our absurd encounters with the famous. During a meeting with Rev. Jesse Jackson in about 1975, for example, an aide suddenly jumps up and silently begins combing his Afro with a big pic, as Jackson doesn't miss a beat. Ralph shoots me an almost imperceptible glance that unmistakably says, "You'll never have to do that to *me*." We attend the wedding reception of Ed Cox and Tricia Nixon at the White House when, separately on a receiving line with the father of the bride, President Nixon actually utters the same malapropism to each of us: "So, you're a Raider's Nader!" Comparing notes later, we each realize that we each said to ourselves, "Thank you, Nixon Richard!"

Beyond chemistry is synergy—he has big ideas and I try to implement them. *Let's do the first citizen critique ever of federal anti-trust law enforcement.* Okey dokey—500 interviews and 1,200 pages later, I become the go-to expert on a subject that until then was monopolized by the anti-trust bar and corporate executives.

"So, what's he *like?*" I'm commonly asked, the assumption being that at night he rips off his mask of virtue to reveal some reptilian alien beneath. But I got nothin' because he's the embodiment of the cliché "what you is see is what you get." He's uniformly regarded by a dozen former Raiders whom I talk to for this book as persistent, consistent, indefatigable, austere, stubborn, sleepless, focused, unflappable, insatiable, honest, blunt, never defensive, never vain, funny, considerate, relentless—and with a photographic memory. Ralph's so comfortable in his own skin that he wears it all the time—and sounds exactly the same in late-night phone conversations as in public speeches. "He has a unity of personality seldom found," writes biographer Charles McCarry, "except in children or historical figures."

I also come to see two additional aspects away from public view—he despises violence and shuns coercion. He invariably edits warlike metaphors out of my writing and 70 years later recounts with unusual disgust how he hated bullies in middle school: "sometimes I would intervene, to my disadvantage." Nor can I really recall any instances when he spends the coin of coercion that's the currency of political insiders from Lyndon Johnson to Andrew Cuomo—"if you don't do X, I'll do Z to you." Instead of leverage, he's all logic and data, like a real-life Mr. Spock marshaling the best arguments to prevail. When some local officials in Winsted complain that he's bigfooting them on a project in the town, he replies, "Nobody's telling anyone what to do. If you don't have millions of dollars and employ hundreds of people, the only way you can tell people what to do is democratically."

In other words, he's a terrible opponent but, except for the pay and hours, a great boss and teacher.

THERE'S NO "Theory of Everything" that controls our work in the Seventies.

But like dots in a pointillist painting that become a discernible shape, a philosophy of government and business emerges out of the hundreds of books, columns, reports, testimonies, and speeches—it's called "consumerism" by others. It combines private sector investment and efficiency with public government insistence on disclosure, fairness, and competition. Lengthy articles by Ralph in 1968 in the *New York Review of Books* and by me in the *Yale Law Review* lay out our thinking.

The conceptually clean dichotomy between private and public sectors—privately owned businesses in one sphere, democratically elected government in another—has broken down now that huge corporations and billionaires are trying to buy public government in hostile takeover bids. According to scholar Andrew Hacker in 1973, "As matters now stand, government . . . is a subsidiary branch of the corporate community."

There's no marketplace in nature. Free-market fundamentalists may pretend that the business form is divine but conveniently ignore how "laissez isn't always fair" due to consumer ignorance, business fraud, monopolies. That's when lawmakers reflecting a democratic consensus can change the rules: first, by government prohibition (like child labor and racial discrimination in hiring); second, by government regulation establishing floors of behavior (this much pollution but not more); or third, by government-mandated disclosure (nutritional labels, tar and nicotine content on cigarette packages).

All regulation, we argue in our writings and testimony, can be divided into two parts. There can be bad "cartel regulation" and good "health/safety regulation." As the deregulation movement of the 1970s showed, if market competition can work, it should be allowed to work—hence the abolition of rate-setting that decade by the Interstate Commerce Commission (ICC) and Civil Aeronautics Board (CAB). But when markets are afflicted by hidden hazards that individual consumers can't discern or avoid—think of industrial pollution, dangerous cars, cribs that kill—then health-safety standards are essential. Voluntary virtue can't cut it in a profit-driven economy. And it's far smarter to locate guardrails at the top of a cliff than ambulances below.

I'm pretty confident that even the most rabid anti-regulation Republicans who talk endlessly about "freedom" do not want their children flying through shattered glass no matter how much they adore the regulatory philosophy of Milton Friedman. Nor is it obvious how seniors or the poor were more "free" when they couldn't afford health insurance before Medicare and Medicaid. Sometimes the "freedom to choose" is a libertarian euphemism for the "freedom to lose" life and limb.

The job of the consumer movement then is this: to make corporations more accountable, either based on H. L. Mencken's view that "conscience is the sense that someone may be looking" or based on democratically enacted rules that establish minimally accepted market behavior. Private contracts are of course essential to a modern economy. But so is the social contract to protect people from the "externalities" of production like pollution and injury. Frederick Hayek calls that serfdom, but we instead embrace this practical blend of Capitalism with Democracy since each needs the other to survive.

FROM WHEN I LEAVE Harvard Law School in 1970 to when I leave Ralph in 1980, I juggle some offbeat assignments but concentrate in the four areas that follow: regulating business, monitoring Congress, reforming the legal profession, and enacting a federal Consumer Protection Agency. Two out-of-portfolio assignments this decade, however, provide exhilarating diversions: Ralph hosting *Saturday Night Live* and flirting with a presidential campaign.

SNL & POTUS. I call Lorne Michaels in 1977 to suggest the counter-programming of having Ralph as a host. "He's really funny when he's not testifying," I say, defensively explaining how a scold can do comedy. Lorne, the show's founder and still its guiding force 40 years later, responds, "He has to be to devote his life to getting rid of dangerous hood ornaments on cars."

I spend a week in mid-January 1977 working out of 30 Rock, meeting talent and sitting in the writers' meetings to help steer Ralph through something outside his ken. It's exciting though sobering for a person who regards himself as culturally literate, if not funny, to be respectfully but consistently turned down when I suggest ideas that are standard laugh lines for Ralph and me in speeches. (One that gets through the process teases energy companies trying to own the sun; it bombs.) But I get to meet folks who later support my own candidacies—Chevy Chase, Gilda Radner, Al Franken, and, in what is his first *SNL* show ever, a new comedian named Bill Murray.

Late in the week Ralph arrives, learns his lines and paces, and is friendly to all though treated like some deity by the performers (though of course that's how we regard *them*). Two sketches stand out.

In the opening, a manic Ralph comes off the elevator, according to the director's notes, "wearing a flashy, fringed, rhinestone-encrusted cowboy outfit and a white ten gallon hat on his head, [saying] 'call me Ralphie!'" An excited Laraine Newman says, "I'm a big admirer of yours, I really am. I just can't help myself, I've gotta hug you." An air bag hidden in his shirt is then supposed to inflate to keep her at bay . . . which works perfectly during rehearsal earlier in the evening but merely emits a loud hiss during the live show. Ralph pauses a fraction of a second, knowing full well that 10 million viewers are scratching their heads, says "Whoops!" and then, displaying a show-must-go-on panache, shouts the familiar opening into the camera—"LIVE FROM NEW YORK, IT'S SATURDAY NIGHT!"

In a later sketch, Ralph is living with two inflatable party dolls—who he affectionately calls Pam and Rita—in order to test their durability for a consumer exposé, "Party Dolls: Turn-on or Rip-off?" "You have no idea how exhausting these tests are. I have to dress and undress them every day, brush their little teeth, paint their little nails," he tells Garrett Morris, adding that "Rita is beginning to leak." Morris responds, "You mean you have to pump her up, huh?" Ralph: "Not today. I have a yeast infection." (Twelve years later at a twentieth-anniversary celebration of the Raiders, Ralph admits, "No, I did *not* then know what a yeast infection was.")

Walking on a street the next week in Washington, a young guy approaches, saying, "I know who you are . . . you're the comedian, right?" Ralph loves it.

Running for president, however, is not a joke to some admirers. Pleas that he run for Tom Dodd's Connecticut seat in 1970, after Dodd's censure by the Senate, are ignored, Ralph understanding that he's both essential to all his start-ups and more influential than any freshman senator. In 1972 columnists Mike Royko and Nicholas von Hoffman, author Gore Vidal, and something called the New Party repeatedly push for a presidential run—and get no response. But the public seems intrigued. When Royko includes a mail-in questionnaire in a column to his *Chicago Daily News* readers, the results are startling: 1,614 for Nader, 148 for Ed Muskie, 42 for Ted Kennedy, 41 for George McGovern, and 11 for Hubert Humphrey.

Then, after vice presidential nominee Tom Eagleton in 1972 quits the Democratic ticket because of his history of undisclosed electroshock treatments, nominee George McGovern calls Ralph to ask if he'd consider replacing Eagleton on the ticket. Ralph politely demurs right away, saying, "I'm an advocate for justice and that doesn't mix with the needs of politics."*

---

*At a 1989 event honoring Ralph, McGovern offers this jesting toast: "I wished we'd gone that route. What a ticket McGovern-Nader would have been! And after my presidency, Ralph would have served another eight. Well, what about 1992?" At least I assume he was jesting.

In 1976, the attorney general of Massachusetts, who has the statutory authority, decides to put Nadar's name on the Democratic primary ballot, adding that he'll only take it off if the candidate swears not to run. Ralph, however, thinks it a big-brother-ish, undemocratic imposition to require a citizen to affirmatively say he's *not* running when he's given no indication of doing so. For a few weeks there's a stalemate and nothing happens—and then the campaigns of Senator Fred Harris, Representative Morris Udall, and Governor Jimmy Carter start calling me to say, *Hey, he's not going to run, right?* When I dutifully convey all this to Ralph, he shrugs, largely amused by the situation, yet, in my view, curious how the public conversation plays out. Polls appear showing that he's competitive with the existing candidates. Finally, however, with principle but not law on his side, it's Ralph who has to blink.

When he gives me his notarized letter of declination to the state's AG to bring to the post office, a diabolical thought crosses my mind en route—what if I "sewer-service" the envelope (i.e., when official papers are thrown away though claimed to have been served)? Then he'd appear on the Massachusetts ballot and then there'd be a national draft movement and . . . my reverie ends and I mail it off. And that was that, presidentially. I thought.

September 11, 1973. *Ralph and I meet at 9 a.m. at the Eastern Shuttle counter at the third-worldish National Airport in D.C. to fly up to New York City for our testimony to the United Nations about multinational corporations. He buys our tickets with cash ($25 a person!) because he refuses to carry a credit card. I'm in a corduroy suit and coiffed with a frizzy "Hebrew-National" while Ralph's in the same dark suit and skinny tie that he apparently wore in utero. And he's clomping around in a pair of those army combat boots he took with him after leaving Fort Dix in 1959.*

On the flight, Ralph barely looks up from his accordion folder of newspapers, magazines, and transcripts that is his third arm, reflecting a mania for reading he developed in boyhood. We grab a cab and get to the UN only a half hour before our remarks to a panel of the General Assembly in the Great Hall.

After, we head right back out to LaGuardia. But heading north on the FDR Drive, we hear on the radio that Chilean president Salvadore Allende has been killed in a right-wing coup. Ralph bolts upright in his seat, upset, eyes narrowing, having interviewed the elected socialist five years before. He's largely quiet on the flight back but, as we begin our descent to National Airport, abruptly says, "You know, Mark, that's among the reasons I'll never run for office. Look what they just did to Allende."

It's a pledge he keeps for a couple of decades, despite devotees who implore him to invest his huge popularity into a symbolic or even serious candidacy for president. But then, dismayed by how big-money interests continued to have a de facto veto over progressive legislation from the Seventies to Nineties, he does an about-face and runs for president four times, including his eventful candidacy in the Bush-Gore contest of 2000. He of course survives intact, his reputation less so.

Business Regulation. While there are Nader's Raiders working on specific market impacts—pensions, pollution, food safety, dangerous workplaces—Ralph in 1970 is concerned that no one group is working on the very structure of corporate capitalism. What's the corporate governance *within* firms that produces bad decisions and allows managers to avoid accountability? What's the competitive relationship *between* firms in the marketplace? What's the role of government regulation *over* corporations when markets fail? His view: shareholder democracy, "free markets," and government regulation are either weak or fictitious restraints on big businesses. He tasks me with starting the Corporate Accountability Research Group to expose and strengthen this underperforming "closed enterprise system."

In effect, he wants to launch another anti-trust movement. The first, during the Robber Baron era of interlocking directorates and the railroad monopoly, stretched from 1890 through 1914 and produced the Sherman Antitrust Act, prosecutions of Standard Oil, and creation of the Federal Trade Commission. Crusading Tennessee senator Estes Kefauver, who had gained fame leading sensational congressional hearings against organized crime in the early 1950s, later attempts to do the same in hearings against "administered prices" by "private socialism." But the Mob being more exciting than Monopoly—and with growing acceptance of an economy dominated by big business and big labor (Galbraith's "countervailing powers")—his drive for new legislation dies with him in 1963.

As the populist heir of TR and Kefauver, Ralph has a three-part plan. First, an investigation of anti-trust law enforcement—don't we want more competition and fewer shared monopolies? Second, a proposal for a system of federal, not state, chartering of corporations—shouldn't national companies have national charters? Last, an approach to health/safety regulation that highlights the often-ignored benefit side of the cost-benefit equation.

I enjoy the challenge of long odds more than most, but the opposing lineup seems unusually forbidding. Undergirding the status quo are companies worth trillions spending billions on campaign gifts and fleets of lawyers, lobbyists, economists, and scientists—all held together by the consensus philosophy of laissez-faire capitalism. And while citizens can understand racial prejudice or a polluted river, it's hard to get many aroused over "market shares" and "oligopolies." In describing why anti-monopoly activism is "the faded passion of American reform," Richard Hofstadter in 1963 concludes that it was a "complex, difficult and boring" subject. That helps explain why there's a priesthood of insider anti-trust lawyers and corporate executives on one side and unorganized, unsophisticated consumers on the other.

So where to start? If you're going to break into the Bellagio of capitalism, you need real talent. I recruit two of the smartest people I have ever known, both law school classmates—Bruce Wasserstein, whom we met in chapter 1, and Beverly C. Moore Jr., who will become the leading class action analyst in the country. I later add Joel Seligman, who in the 1990s would write the definitive 11-volume history of the SEC before becoming president of the University of Rochester. Filling out our starting five is an amazing find: 69-year-old Irene Till, who had been the chief economist under Kefauver and co-wrote his book on monopoly power, *In a Few Hands.*

I spend 16 hours a day burrowing into the Justice Department's Antitrust Division and the Federal Trade Commission Bureau of Competition, since these two agencies divide up enforcement of the Sherman Act and the Federal Trade Commission Act. Our team initially reads everything written about competition theory and anti-trust enforcement but then engages in the best way to decipher the process—interview current and former staff at these agencies as well as those who monitor it in Congress. As described by Ralph's Pulitzer Prize–winning childhood friend, David Halberstam: "If there were one thing I could teach a young journalist working on a major story, it's what I would call the sequence of interviews . . . how each interview sets up the next interview. You don't go on the very first day to the central person because you won't be prepared and he *will* be prepared."

With Bruce, Beverly, and me digging in and Ralph reviewing and commenting on every page, the four of us release our 1,148-page document—*The Closed Enterprise System*—at a Washington press conference on Saturday, June 5, 1971. Ralph is in good form—understated in tone but cutting in content: "This is a report on crime in the suites and its human, political and economic costs to Americans. It is finally a study of corporate radicalism so deeply insinuated into the politico-economic fabric of the society to be considered any longer a mere deviation from the norm."

I then tick off a few case studies showing when these agencies shy away from challenging big mergers; why consent decrees that settle cases are kept secret; how "shared monopolies" dominate two-thirds of American manufacturing so they can jack up prices and worsen inequality; and how political influence undermines white-collar law enforcement—the leading examples being the Nixon White House and Johnson attorney general Nicholas Katzenbach.

Am I shocked and thrilled when the *New York Times* the next day publishes a long, front-page article with the headline and sub-head, "Nader Asserts Monopolies Mulct the Public of Billions . . . Report Charges Political Power Aids Giants in Blocking Antitrust Suits"? Yes. I. Am.

There is a big reaction. Senators Hart, Metzenbaum, and Magnuson embrace the report and schedule hearings. AG Katzenbach says, "No third year law student at Harvard is going to tell me how to run anti-trust enforcement." (Which begs the question whether he is distressed by our analysis or our law school.) Conservative scholars in reviews, however, are critical: Yale Law School professor Arthur Leff calls it "unconvincing" in the *New York Times Book Review;* Chicago Law professor and conservative luminary Richard Posner writes, "It is a highly tendentious work—scholarship it is not."

But our preliminary goal is achieved—we're taken seriously as the first public critique of anti-trust enforcement and earn a seat at a table that previously had only heard a monologue on monopolies. When two years later Jack Anderson runs scandalized columns about how ITT strong-armed the White House and Department of Justice (DoJ) to allow the ITT–Hartford Fire merger—which we had covered in our study—the public and congressional reaction renews interest in our work. Throughout the decade, Ralph and I produce a stream of articles, books, speeches, and bills in an effort to convince the public and public officials to embrace real market competition, not oligopolies.

The results are mixed.

On the one hand, we write a bill with Senator John Tunney (D-CA)—the first pro–anti-trust legislation to become law in 25 years. It requires that consent decrees must be made public and that criminal penalties be raised from misdemeanors to felonies punishable by up to $1 million (for firms). Later, we get the Senate to enact the Hart-Scott-Rodino bill requiring that companies give the FTC advance notice of large mergers to allow for a legal challenge pre-consummation. We convince Attorney General Edward Levi to create a specialized unit to investigate white-collar crime and to publicly release correspondence between companies and the DoJ. And Ralph and I begin the practice of briefing new assistant attorneys general in charge of anti-trust about our views—and they, knowing of our reach into their staff and the media, seem attentive.

But while there is a continuing public conversation about the value of large anti-oligopoly cases, they're never filed. The very well-regarded Senator Phil Hart (D-MI), chair of the Senate Antitrust Subcommittee, holds hearings, but there's little appetite among politicians to bite the hand that funds them. Washington names a Senate Office Building after Hart but not a law.

Dented but unbowed, we continue our work on the structure of the marketplace but also add the structure of the corporation itself.

Ever since states gave companies charters to conduct business as "creatures of the state," no one questions the requirement of public charters to do business with the public. But who issues them? In a largely agrarian economy, it made some sense that local firms were chartered by states where they only did business. But 1789 businesses resemble 1970s businesses only to those who think that a minnow is no different than a shark since they both swim. States don't print money or conscript armies since these are obviously national functions. So why do states by the twentieth century continue to charter national if not multi-national corporations?

When I'm in law school, I don't question why corporate law seems to be all about Delaware law. When Ralph is in law school the prior decade, however, he figures out the back-scratching system that leads over half the Fortune 500 to incorporate there—i.e., Delaware gets one-fourth of its state revenues from chartering fees while the companies get state law and courts that defer to management prerogatives. It's a law-for-sale, race-to-the-bottom that enables Delaware to become the Reno, Nevada, of corporate law. Or as Ralph would often joke, "General Motors could buy Delaware . . . if DuPont were willing to sell it."

In the mid-1970s, he assigns me and Joel Seligman, aided by Irene Till, to try to expose and change a system that works well for big business and Delaware, but not so much for other stakeholders of corporations—millions of employees, shareholders, communities, and consumers.

As with our anti-trust work, we read everything we can on the corporate form, which is largely formalistic, rarely empirical. We then interview legal experts and scholars about ways to make sure that these "private governments" are more accountable to those they employ and affect. We discover that the federal chartering of companies was discussed twice by Jefferson at the Constitutional Convention, though never voted on. Presidents Roosevelt, Taft, and Wilson also considered it during the Populist Era but opted instead for anti-trust as the preferred mechanism of accountability.

We release our 433-page report—*Constitutionalizing the Corporation: The Case for the Federal Chartering of Federal Corporations*—at a packed press conference on January 24, 1976, in D.C. We highlight workable alternatives to unaccountable corporate power: the top 700 corporations required to have a majority of board members "independent" of management domination; an Employee Bill of Rights with whistle-blower protections; Community Impact Statements before plants move; additional disclosure requirements (political gifts, minority hiring data, toxins in the workplace); more shareholder rights to close the gap between ownership and control. And we continue pressing our analysis from our anti-trust work about how oligopoly entrenches oligarchy and worsens income inequality when concentrated private sector power—to cite the much-used word 40 years later—"rigs" both the economy and politics.

Coverage is extensive, hearings are held. We publish *Taming the Giant Corporation* later that year, and my study *The Corporate Lobbies,* on the U.S. Chamber of Commerce and the Business Roundtable, the next. Under the auspices of Senator Howard Metzenbaum (D-OH), I meet monthly for six months with a small group of national leaders—including Irving Shapiro, head of both DuPont and the

Business Roundtable, and Bill Winpisinger, head of the Machinists Union—to see if there's any common ground we could all agree on. (Answer: no.) We organize a large labor-environmental-consumer coalition of 25 organizations—including the AFL-CIO—and prominent experts like John Kenneth Galbraith, Michael Harrington, and Barry Commoner that lobbies Congress and conducts a "Big Business Day" in 1980 in 110 cities modeled on Earth Day, though far smaller.

Again, some specific ideas are enacted, like a pre-notification for plant closings and pay-for-performance data per firm. But we do not cut the Gordian knot strangling our system of corporate governance. Business exploits the very phrase "federal chartering" to imply that we are seeking "a federal takeover of American business." (Of course, either way corporations stay privately owned.) But as with anti-oligopoly bills earlier and a Consumer Protection Agency later, the powerful corporate-legal-congressional complex prevails to keep the profitable status quo intact.

First-year law students still sit in corporate law classes based largely on Delaware judicial decisions . . . and, like me, no doubt wonder why.

Our efforts to protect federal health and safety regulation, however, go better for a simple reason—the burden for change here is on corporate interests, not on consumer advocates. Business's "war on regulation" is a one-trick pony that focuses on exaggerated cost data provided by the affected industries and on rhetorical attacks on "big government." And the more outlandish and abstract the attacks, the better. So there is talk about supposed $200 toilet seats required by OSHA but not the 1 in 11 workers in the private economy with a job-related injury or illness in 1976. Talk about jobs lost but not jobs produced in the environmental controls and non–fossil fuel energy sectors. And don't bother to debate high miscarriage rates and birth defects around the contaminated town of Love Canal or families incinerated by low-speed rear-end collisions because of ruptured gas tanks.

Although business lobbies just assert that any new rule will bankrupt them—like putting air bags in cars or taking fluorocarbons out of spray cans—once these reforms are implemented, they're either easily absorbed into the cost of production or provoke innovation that meets standards. This intellectual fraud finds its apotheosis in St. Louis economist Murray Weidenbaum, who is lavishly quoted and amply financed by big business groups when he merely lists dubious estimates of the costs of regulation. A nice round $200 billion is his favorite number in the Seventies.

Rebutting such ideological arithmetic proves easy. We and other advocates (a) highlight reduced cancer rates and a sharp decline in crib deaths, among many other savings, to expose the hollow rhetorical war against the federal bureaucracy and (b) aggregate the best available benefits studies in 1979 that far exceed Weidenbaum's cost estimates.

Armed with examples and data, we proselytize for smart regulation in numerous publications and professional forums. I edit a volume in 1972 called *The Monopoly Makers* that explains our critical distinction between cartel regulation where "regulatory capture" leads to excessive rates and health/safety regulation that reduces the "externalities" of production that markets don't. Then, using the existing Freedom of Information law, I sue Secretary of Commerce Philip Klutznick to disclose those American companies secretly complying with the Arab States' boycott of Israel. Prevailing in *Green v. Klutznick,* I release the names of 1,400 chagrined companies that put their profits over America's ally.

I spend considerable time with two talents on Senator Ted Kennedy's staff who would go on to illustrious careers—Stephen Breyer and David Boies—collaborating to end Civil Aeronautics Board and Interstate Commerce Commission rate regulation. Working with economist Gar Alperovitz, we create COIN—Consumer Inflation in the Necessities—a consumer/labor alliance arguing that inflation is the result not only of monetary policy but also of specific sectoral problems. We meet with President Carter, who agrees to push this framework.

And I periodically debate regulation in Bar forums and before corporate audiences. A couple of times I face a charming but largely fact-free Washington lawyer by the name of Antonin Scalia. Another time I go up against Irving Kristol—the so-called "godfather of neoconservatism"—at a J. C. Penney forum, with very good results according to the corporate host afterward. ("Jeez, you clobbered him.")

Lawyer Reform. Before there was Nader, there was Shaw, opining that "all professions are conspiracies against the laity."

Ralph's skepticism about the performance of the legal profession to advance the public interest begins in law school, which he regards as a factory "engineering law students into corporate thinking, legal minutiae and wooden logic . . . impervious to what Oliver Wendell Holmes once called the 'felt necessities of our times.'" Coaxed by him a dozen years later, I draft a survey that the law school agrees to send to all recruiting law firms before they're allowed to interview students, which I enter into a primitive spreadsheet so students know what firms to see and what to ask. It's still there two decades later.

About every year in the 1970s, the two of us would go together to Cambridge, and, usually to a full house, we'd be a tag team on "Law Firms and Law Schools: The Ethical Imperative." Here's one Nader biographer, Hays Gorey, writing about it:

> His wild mane of wavy brown hair swinging from side to side, Green took the podium first, shaking his head and describing in moving terms the challenge and satisfactions of public interest law . . . Why couldn't more of them follow him into public interest law? Working up to an angry climax, Green pinpointed the perfectly obvious reason: money. "But there are other currencies, you know . . ."
>
> Nader [is] freshly and somewhat ridiculously barbered, yet the different styles and modes of dress and hair did not conceal from anyone the essential oneness of their purposes and views. The same fire burned in both men . . . He asked the students why it should not concern them that "most Americans are shut out of the legal system—priced, delayed, politicized, mystified out of it." [At the end], the law students rose out of their chairs and Austin hall throbbed with prolonged cheers and applause.

But his earlier MO of pulling a few resumes out of a pile and then interviewing someone en route to somewhere has now run its course. I annually also visit laws schools to recruit talent for Ralph's growing network, numbingly interviewing 20 applicants a day in half-hour intervals for five straight days at five law schools—usually Harvard, Yale, NYU, Columbia, and George Washington or Georgetown.

I then weed the 100 down to 20, who are interviewed back in D.C. by Ralph, me, and a few others. Often, among more substantive inquiries, Ralph asks, "Do you smoke pot?" I watch top students writhe under the pressure of either lying to Ralph Nader or losing the job of their dreams. After he does this a few times, I pull him aside and say, "Ralph, you just can't ask this anymore. Almost everyone smokes at some point and it's not morally disqualifying." He looks at me in mock horror and says, smirking, "Oh no, not you too, Mark!" His modern imitation of Cotton Mather mercifully ceases.

Beyond recruiting, Ralph is eager to write a book on the influence of Washington lawyers and law firms. The idea starts when he's in one Senate anteroom and Lloyd Cutler, the auto industry's lawyer, is in another as drafts of the 1966 auto safety report ping-pong between them. Though the process produces a largely strong bill, Ralph is nettled when Cutler successfully defeats the imposition of criminal penalties for knowingly manufacturing dangerous cars in Senate and House floor votes. This experience contributes to Ralph's testimony three years later before Senator Ribicoff's subcommittee about how Washington lawyers operate: "The gentlemen who run these operations are eminent specialists in cutting down consumer programs in their incipiency or undermining them if they mature. They are masters of *ex parte* contact, the private deal and tradeoff, the softening of the bureaucrat's will . . . I think you can learn more about the consumer movement and its problems by asking them just how they go about doing it on the other side."

When Ribicoff does invite several to testify, all politely refuse, with Cutler chiding Nader for not believing in the adversarial system of justice. That does it. He asks me to spend my maiden summer of 1969 investigating Cutler as well as Covington & Burling, the largest corporate firm in the nation's capital. "Since they're powerful institutions in D.C.," he explains, "they shouldn't hide behind client confidentiality but should account for their impact on public policy."

I research Cutler and Covington intermittently along with my work on *The Closed Enterprise System* and federal chartering. But a couple of problems emerge: though I ship all my research in boxes to a hotel room where Ralph intends to write the book, he's now the Nader of 1973, not 1963, and the obligations of fame and numerous public interest groups don't permit him the time to do it. Finally, pressured by his own guilt and by me, he gives me a green light to start writing. Unfortunately, however, a book on the same subject by a skilled Washington journalist, Joseph C. Goulden, beats us to the market in 1972. *The Superlawyers* is a big best-seller.

I plow ahead and in 1975 publish *The Other Government: The Unseen Power of Washington Lawyers*. Based on 300 interviews and exhaustive research, it argues that these "power lawyers" lack "a sense of consequence" about their anti-social impact. The book shows how they usually get their way in closed meetings with no adversary counsel anywhere and based on politics plus lobbyists. These lawyers ignore the part of the *Code of Professional Responsibility* requiring counsel to be "officers of the court," and they fail to even understand, in Brandeis's ideal, how to be "lawyers for the situation."

While reviews are positive, especially John Kenneth Galbraith's in the *New York Times Book Review,* when the ranking partner at Covington, H. Thomas Austern, is asked about Nader and the book, his only comment is "Fuck him."

Ralph and I produce a compendium volume and conference, *Verdicts on Lawyers,* with essays that chronicle how lawyers have tilted the scales of justice and priced themselves out of the market for nearly all Americans. The volume complains about "legal featherbedding," price-fixing, the lack of inexpensive alternatives to justice, and inadequate pro bono hours at law firms. We explain that lawyers remind us of "meat manufacturers in 1906 and auto manufacturers in 1966 . . . who believe they are capable of self-regulation." I tell James Fallows, who at the time is President Carter's speechwriter, that "90 percent of lawyers represent just 10 percent of the people" and, in a new experience for me, hear a president use this line in a speech urging parallel reforms. (Alas, I probably got the numbers wrong—looking back, it should have been 90 percent and 1 percent.) Eventually we turn over our analysis and materials to a newly created Equal Justice Foundation, which has continued this work to this day.

I also work with Nader's top litigator, Alan Morrison, on how best to break up this professional guild. As head of Ralph's Public Citizen Litigation Group, Alan brings lawsuits against bar associations' "minimum fee schedules" and bans on advertising—which together stunt competition and raise prices—that result in two Supreme Court decisions in the mid-Seventies striking down both. (Amazingly, bar associations of lawyers lose before the country's top judicial panel of lawyers by votes of 8–0 and 8–1!) All of our Naderian efforts combined produce probably the biggest change in the profession in decades.

Another legal collaboration involves President Nixon's infamous firing of Special Prosecutor Archibald Cox in October 1973 in what came to be called the Saturday Night Massacre. That night Ralph calls several of us urgently saying, "We have to do something." We convene early the next morning at the Litigation Group to brainstorm how to best respond. Ralph cares deeply about this event, in part because in 1972, before Watergate became a synonym for scandal, he called the Nixon administration "the most corrupt in history" due to excessive surveillance, extralegal policies, tolerance of financial corruption, and its undemocratic "fascism of the mind." For which he was chided as exaggerating.

After several go-rounds, it's decided that Ralph and a few members of Congress (including Representative Bella Abzug) will sue the president for violating the special prosecutor law forbidding his removal except for "extraordinary improprieties on his part." Six months later, Morrison persuades federal district court judge Gerhard Gessell to declare Cox's firing illegal. But by then the case is moot, since Cox is back at Harvard and a new special prosecutor, Leon Jaworski, is continuing the probe. Yet *Nader v. Bork* has the effect of letting Nixon know that Jaworski must now be considered truly independent of the White House. There are no more legal massacres, if you don't count Nixon's massacre of himself.

What I remember most from this period is how, leaving the Corporate Accountability Research Group (CARG) every night about 1:30 a.m., I'd motorcycle by the Mayflower Hotel on Connecticut Avenue to scoop up that morning's *Washington Post* to read Woodward and Bernstein on "Nixon's Richard." In my then-Manichean world of black-and-white hats and in the context of Nixon's villainy, it's probably the most emotionally satisfying few months in a life of fighting the Right.

The Congress Project. "Nader's Biggest Raid," in the estimation of *Time* magazine, emerges in 1971 out of several intersecting thoughts in Ralph's mind. Though very successful on Capitol Hill in the late Sixties, he worries about the tightening grip that big donations have on elections and laws. Lamenting the lack of civic education, he wonders out loud whether a student army studying Congress could do for citizenship "what the Arthur Murray Dance Studio does for aspiring dancers."

On November 2, 1971, at the National Press Club, Ralph announces "probably the most comprehensive and detailed study of Congress since its establishment." It's an audacious effort to enlist 1,000 volunteers and 50 full-time Raiders to research and write profiles of 484 congressional members either running for reelection in 1972 or holding Senate seats, plus book-length reports on six major committees. While the product will be nonpartisan and informational, it will also no doubt be controversial, so Ralph pledges to finance it with only his lecture fees and not foundation funds. He accelerates his lecturing, hitting a high of eight one day in Oregon, with only one rule: he refuses to be driven in Volkswagens because "they're portable funeral parlors."

On June 19, 1972, Ralph holds an orientation session at a George Washington University college dorm to excite his "army." According to author Justin Martin, "The atmosphere was electric . . . Nader began by comparing the project to the Wright Brothers' first flight. 'Many of you are too smart for the courses you're going through but let me assure you, you'll be really sweating, literally and figuratively.' Nader warns against pot smoking. It's illegal and if anyone gets busted it would reflect poorly on the Project . . . [And there was] an extremely tight deadline. 'If it's not met, there's no tomorrow.'"

Running it are two of his most trusted aides, Joan Claybrook and Bob Fellmeth. True to form, Bob drafts a 633-question survey that takes an average of ten hours for a congressperson to answer. An effort of this magnitude generates a significant pushback: from members who resent the time imposition, from liberal members who assume Nader would merely be on their side with no questions asked, and from the profilers themselves who think that nine profiles averaging 30 pages each to be a bit much. After they balk at the volume and deadline, Ralph slightly relents and reduces the workload to only eight profiles with an additional week tacked on.

Then Oscar Dystel, the head of Bantam Books and the acknowledged godfather of paperback books in America, gives Ralph a big idea—publish a soft-cover book based on all the research that could "make Congress *readable*." In June he conscripts me, Fallows, and environmentalist David Zwick to write it in under two months. *Who Runs Congress?* proves to be about the most intense professional experience of my life. We three drop everything else and spend day and night at CARG's underground office at 18th and M Street splitting up the research and writing.

I watch how Fallows, who in my opinion goes on to be the premier journalist of his generation at the *Atlantic,* knocks out first drafts that are publishable as is, rendering editors largely extraneous.

My research excavates two quotes that become benchmarks for future discussions of Congress: first, Will Rogers saying, "We have the best Congress money can buy"; second, Boies Penrose, a turn-of-the-last-century, 300-pound Pennsylvania Republican senator with refreshing candor, telling his donors, "I believe in a division of labor. You send us to Congress; we pass laws under which you make money . . . and out of your profits you further contribute to our campaign funds to send us back again to pass more laws to enable you to make more money."

Everything miraculously comes out in October. The profiles are extensively used in campaigns by incumbents, challengers, or both. Hays Gorey writes, "It may still be one of Nader's most significant and enduring contributions to revitalizing the United States system [of governance.]" *Who Runs Congress?* proves to be controversial, popular, and influential. Congressman Gerald Ford is upset that "it calls some Members criminals." Senate Majority Leader Mike Mansfield lauds it as "having a good deal of meat and validity." David Bollier, a historian of the consumer movement, concludes:

> Much of The Congress Project's impact stemmed from the success of "Who Runs Congress?" The book was a brisk, tough-minded, witty overview of Congress, drawing upon Congress Project research and other materials, both original and derivative. [It] took off like a rocket . . . and was #1 on the *New York Times* best-seller list for the month of November, 1972. Eventually going through four different editions and print runs of more than one million copies, it remains the best-selling book ever written on the Congress.
>
> While it is difficult to measure the impact of any single book, there is no question that "Who Runs Congress?" helped change the climate of public opinion toward Congress and Congress's own perception of itself. The book was widely read among the incoming batch of legislators in 1974, the famous class of "Watergate Babies" that included 47 freshmen Democrats.

Given Ralph's penchant for creating enduring organizations, perhaps the greatest impact of the project and book is that they led to the establishment of Public Citizen's Congress Watch to permanently monitor Capitol Hill. Claybrook is its first executive director from 1973 to 1977, and I'm the second from 1977 to 1980. Those years running the most influential consumer lobby in Washington shape me for years to come and ignite my own ambition to try to answer the book title's question with "Why not me?"

Present at the Stillbirth of the Consumer Protection Agency. While Congress Watch's eight staff hardly even the odds against several thousand business lobbyists, the disparity in federal agencies is geometrically worse.

James Madison's theories in *Federalist # 10* about competing factions balancing each other out read like naïve fiction two centuries later. According to all 14 members of the Senate Governmental Affairs Committee in 1977: "[At] agency after agency, participation by the regulated industry predominates—often overwhelmingly . . . For more than half of the proceedings, there is no consumer participation whatsoever. In those proceedings where participation by public groups does take place, typically it is a small fraction of the participation by the regulated industry." This is insider democracy, as citizens inquiring about process or policy are often rebuffed by the query "Who ya with?"

To fix this flaw, Senators Hubert Humphrey and Estes Kefauver in 1959 introduce a bill to create a Department of Consumer Affairs that would unite all consumer functions under one roof and provide counsel to speak up for voiceless consumers. It goes nowhere. By the late 1960s, Nader and Rep. Benjamin Rosenthal (D-NY) team up to develop a proposal for a Consumer Protection Agency (CPA) that wouldn't combine all functions in one place—where Ralph fears it could be more easily stymied by concentrated business power— but would provide countervailing advocates before existing health, safety, and environmental agencies. He calls the bill "the most important piece of consumer legislation ever to come before Congress." Five times between 1970 and 1976 it passes either the Senate or House but never both because of the fortuities of scheduling, bickering over individual provisions, and Republican opposition.

Then, at the start of the 95th Congress in 1977, it's strongly supported by the newly sworn-in President Carter; Speaker Tip O'Neill; 150 labor, senior, and citizen groups; and a 2-to-1 majority in public polls. Ralph assigns me to run the campaign to secure final enactment. Given the lineup and merits, we're optimistic.

Beneath this broad public support, however, there's a troubling undercurrent—we keep hearing generalized complaints about "big government" and "not more government" and "not another OSHA." We explain that the CPA can't regulate anything, but as an office with an annual budget of $15 million will only provide consumer advocates to argue positions before existing regulatory agencies. Reasoned arguments, however, are not the fuel of lobbying—money and grassroots pressure are. So we develop two counter-strategies.

First, we create Congress Watch Locals in 83 swing congressional districts because local pressure beats pleading off the House floor any day. But we now confront the first all-out organized business opposition since the Powell Memo laid out its how-to manual in 1971. The Business Roundtable in 1977 hires Leon Jaworski to lead the lobbying against the bill. The *Wall Street Journal* runs a front-page piece with the headline "Business Lobby Gains More Power as It Rides Antigovernment Tide." Speaker O'Neill says that he has "never seen such extensive lobbying" in his quarter century in Congress.

Second, to counter the cliché of "more big government," I organize the Nickel Campaign to get at least 500 local residents in each of these 83 districts to send in actual nickels to wavering members to symbolically and puckishly explain that this "big new government bureaucracy" will cost citizens only about five cents each. Many members are annoyed since they don't know what to do with this shower of 40,000+ nickels. One actually complains, "It's a form of bribery," which forces me to explain that "if they can be bought for a nickel, they're aiming too low." Allies worry that such a move risks turning off moderates who resent such public mockery. To which Admiral Hyman Rickover replies, "They never complain when business tries to buy them, only when someone stands up for the people." (Eventually, the 83 members split 42 to 41 on the final vote.)

I work daily for months with the Speaker's office and the White House, especially Esther Peterson, the beloved 71-year-old consumer advisor to President Kennedy and now Carter. She's constantly rattled by Ralph's public comments and attacks—once telling him that "I shouldn't spend my energy picking up the pieces with the people you've offended"—though we consider that as one of the only ways to lean on wavering members. In any event, according to biographer Charles McCarry, "Ralph doesn't think politics is the art of the possible but a system of imperatives."

O'Neill, Nader, and our team are increasingly worried about Democrats overanxious about corporate money in Washington and small businesses in the district. One backs off, saying that he just "can't explain 500 times back home why this isn't just more big government." Another tells Ralph outright, "I'm worried that the Chamber [of Commerce] will run a candidate against me in the primary."

Shortly before the culminating vote in February, there's a triple whammy: Representative Tom Foley jumps ship after watching a fellow Democrat lose in a nearby district to a far-right Republican, which in turn enables Democrats such as Patricia Schroder, Leon Panetta,* and others to follow suit. Then, in a move that astonishes both the pro- and anti-CPA sides, the *Washington Post,* which had editorially supported a consumer agency for years, switches to oppose it the day before the final vote; it writes gibberish about how it's no longer needed since Carter had appointed many consumer advocates to his agencies. (Brandeis is on the bench so no need for defense counsel?) Then President Carter, who for months had been promising to hit the phones, calls the first 6 out of a list of 24 members that we provide, gets none saying yes, and stops calling.

The bill fails 227 to 189 on February 8. When I reach Ralph, who is traveling in Nevada, with the news, the line goes silent for a few seconds. "This is the world's greatest country," he says more in regret than anger, "but it's being run by a bunch of pinheads."

This is a big, historic loss.† Looking back, February 1978 starts a long comparative shift in consumer power and corporate power in Washington, D.C. The forces that pull down the CPA are seen in the passage of the Prop 13 property tax referendum in California that year, in the defeat of the Labor Law Reform bill also that year, and,

---

* I'm furious with my *Harvard Civil Rights–Civil Liberties* book reviewer Panetta. I call my friend folk singer Harry Chapin, who had promised to do a fund-raising concert for Panetta, and convince him to withdraw. Hanging up the phone, I say to my assistant Dan Becker, "Not usual for a public interest lobbyist to have economic leverage over a member and use it. Better enjoy this because it may not happen again." Don't think that it did.

† In 1976, Congress Watch came within one vote of breaking the business lobby–supported CPA filibuster, which required 67 Senate votes. One unanticipated, huge side benefit of the five failed cloture votes was the decision of a frustrated Majority leader Robert Byrd to amend the filibuster rules and require only 60 votes to stop a filibuster. The bill's death therefore gave life to this key Senate reform, which is still the standard.

of course, in Reagan's 1980 victory. Conservative arguments against big government—except when it comes to corporate welfare, defense spending, gay rights, reproductive choice, imposition of the death penalty—still reverberate in 2016.

WITHIN A MONTH of CPA's demise, I get an unexpected call from Peterson saying that she'd like to retire and intends to urge President Carter to choose me as her successor. "Are you interested?" While I usually like to prepare and think ahead, in this case I'm mute with indecision. "Um, um, well, thanks . . . and, um." "Mark, can you think about it and at least come in for an interview with Eizenstat?" President Carter's top advisor gatekeeper, Stuart Eizenstat, is a smart, smooth, fair-minded guy. He emphasizes Carter's consumer bona fides, which I'm pretty familiar with after the CPA battle.

Now, I'm not immune to the prestige of a White House appointment that at the least provides a clinching answer to my parents' question: "So, when are you going to get a *real* job?" But the job might only be for a year, that year being when Carter is running for reelection and trying to not appear anti-business in order to raise campaign funds from elite donors. Given the likely clash between Carter's needs and my Naderian inclinations, it's pretty clear which would prevail. I inform a disappointed Peterson and explain to the *Washington Star* that I declined because my current work "was important and rewarding and because they deserve someone more loyal than I can be to their important energy program."

The Carter offer, however, does stir something in me. The mix of writing, lecturing, lawyering, and lobbying is nearly the exact job description I would have designed for myself in law school, but might there be something of even more satisfaction and sway? Then, like anyone who works on and around Congress, the idea starts growing—why not *in* Congress? Can I meld advocacy skills and political office to expand my impact? Can someone do both?

A year later I leave the security of what I know for a high-risk bid for a U.S. House seat in a New York City already bursting with talent. Ralph is surprised, not shocked, yet supportive. While he's never before endorsed a candidate, he agrees to make an exception under our new rule: *if someone works for Ralph ten years or more, thereby forfeiting significant income and a Rolodex of rich business friends, he may try to even the playing field.*

There's subsequently one moment when he inquires if I'd return. At 11 p.m. the night I lose my 1980 general election, he calls to offer political condolences and then raises the prospect of me returning as the head of Public Citizen during what's likely to be the coming crisis of the Reagan presidency. But I choose to remain and keep my family in New York and see where it leads. Like the Carter decision, I've come to a fork in the road and taken it, which of course changes my life. So in 1969 I ditch Lindsay in New York for Nader in Washington . . . and in 1980 stay in New York, nearly ending up in Lindsay's job two decades later.

1981–2016: NADER ON THE ROAD AND ON THE PHONE

The nightly phone calls end when I leave, replaced by monthly ones that feel like two college roommates catching up years later. Ralph's always curious to know what I'm learning and how I'm faring in Gotham politics while I cherish the opportunities to pick his brain. Deni says she can always tell when he's on the line because my voice shifts to a warmer, more substantive, and deferential register—once a young aide, apparently always one.

The Eighties, however, prove very challenging for Ralph. At a personal level, his adored older brother Shafeek dies around the time that Ralph contracts Bell's palsy in 1986, which makes his eye and face droop to the point that he wears sunglasses to hide the distortion. Yet he travels to 48 states that fall to stop the insurance industry from restricting tort liability and quips to audiences wondering about his appearance, "Well, you can't accuse me of speaking out of both sides of my mouth." Politically, the Powell Memo ripens into a corporate counteroffensive that finds its man in GE's Ronald Reagan. President Reagan's anti-consumer, anti-government progeny don't so much reverse consumer and environmental laws—they're too popular for that—but instead his administration largely stops enforcing them. Since "government is the problem," the fortieth head of the American government tells us in his first inaugural address, he appoints people like James Watt to Interior and Anne Gorsuch to the EPA, who obligingly fail at their jobs. The joke in right-wing circles is that the administration's credo is "Don't just do something, stand there!"

At the same time, Congress wearies of someone they see as an annoying Old Testament prophet. It was said that the people of Greece turned against Aristedes because he was always called "Aristedes the Just." In Henrik Ibsen's play *An Enemy of the People,* the "enemy" people got mad at was not so much the company that polluted its water supply but the town scold who kept insisting that something be done about it.

The media too, as almost always happens, has moved on—other stories, other players, other issues. News implies new . . . which Nader isn't. And he knows it. "My approach is not in fashion," he says dispassionately mid-decade, "but a non-adversarial approach means abdication." He adds that *"The Post* and *Times* don't pay attention, and therefore the networks don't pick us up. You've got to come at them with a national outcry."

So he switches gears.

Over the next three-plus decades, he seeks new spheres of influence that don't require permission slips from powerful interests. He organizes locally, pressures Washington from outside Washington, runs for president, travels to Cuba to confer with Castro, writes more of his own books, creates an American Museum of Tort Law in Winsted, and erupts with a steady lava of letters to power brokers.

Local grassroots organizing and politicking means even more out-of-town lectures and better-targeted issue campaigns. Nader organizer Don Ross, backed up by Ralph when necessary, travels the country for much of the decade starting local PIRGs based on student fees. If tuition automatically includes football equipment, why not lawyers the students hire to work for them? (Twenty-six PIRGs still exist.)

One campaign that works is Prop 103 in California in 1988. When the insurance industry proposes to jack up rates by double digits, a former Raider, Harvey Rosenfield, creates a new organization, *Voter Revolt!* He invites Ralph to campaign for a referendum that would instead roll back rates by 20 percent and create an elected state insurance commissioner to monitor the industry. Though outspent $70 million to $3 million, 103 prevails 51 percent to 49 percent almost entirely because of Ralph's saturation-proselytizing around the state. Over time, several billion dollars shift from companies to consumers.

"The competing proposals were very complicated," reports one glum insurance industry lobbyist afterward, "but people figure that if Nader was for 103, it couldn't be bad." Bill Schneider, a well-known CNN and *LA Times* commentator, provides a political interpretation: "There were a lot of stories that he was old hat in the 1980s. But he resurrected his image at a stroke by winning Proposition 103. The victory came as a big shock to people in Washington who didn't realize he continued to have that clout. But he managed, rather incredibly, to maintain this image of saintliness, that he is [*sic*] uncorruptible."

A similar sentiment is heard from Speaker Jim Wright a year later when Nader leads a nationwide effort that successfully defeats a 50 percent congressional pay raise: "Where did this guy come from? I thought he had his day." A victory that reduces congressional pay, however, does not endear him to an already resentful Congress. But afterward, one political wag—theatrically getting down on her knees on Connecticut Avenue—told Claybrook, "They may not like you, but they respect you."

Perhaps the biggest success in this post-1980 era results from his original advocacy, when the Supreme Court rules 9–0 against Reagan's attempt to block NHTSA's air-bag rule, allowing the agency to require them by 1989. If there's one perfect example of "big government" intervening in an imperfect marketplace to save lives, this is probably it.

Not all of his ideas, however, catch on. He advocates with little result the "Audience Network," where consumers would band together to buy and run low-frequency TV stations. He proposes "Citizen Utility Boards" (or CUBs), where ratepayers would agree to pay a few bucks a month to finance their own lawyers to challenge utilities in rate-making bodies and court; only Illinois and a handful of other states adopt it. Another tactic is charming but fanciful. "I wanted four-person strike forces to parachute in to company towns—including a lawyer, organizer, PR person, and a sage saying 'you can't do *that*'"—as in *actually* parachuting in to get attention. This Hindenburg, however, never gets off the ground. What happened? I inquire. "My problem is that I'm bolder than the people working under me. I'm not gonna be reined in but I can't do things like that without these people."

Speaking of not being reined in, there are of course his four presidential campaigns.

After years of suing Nixon, being disillusioned by Carter, disgusted by Reagan, shunned by Congress and the national media, disappointed later by Clinton and Gore—who refuse to ever meet with him, even on auto safety—Nader begins considering a symbolic presidential run to elevate ignored issues. His usual formulation was that he'd run for elective office only if "there was an invasion from Mars." So what changed? "There was an invasion from Wall Street . . . and the model of expose and reform wasn't working because of a kept Congress. Something had to change."

Enjoying his experience campaigning all over California for Prop 103, in 1992 he allows his name to stay in the New Hampshire primary ballot, campaigns for three weeks largely in favor of legally allowing "NOTA" in future races—establishing a "none of the above" line—and receives 6,311 votes. In 1996, the Green Party gets him on 21 state ballots. He pushes a long agenda of pro-democracy and pro-consumer reforms but seeks no contributions, runs no ads, and spends under $5,000 of his own money. And gets 684,871 votes.

Against the near-unanimous advice of his closest friends and allies, he chooses an all-out run in 2000, campaigning in 50 states and getting on the ballots of nearly all of them. Some former Nader's Raiders organize a petition to publicly denounce his candidacy, but I'd rather stab myself in the eye than him the back—and refuse to join. But as the ranking elected Democrat then in NYC, I endorse Vice President Al Gore, explaining to my mentor, "If you campaign for Greatest Advocate of the Century, you have my vote. But if the question is who can actually keep the Republicans from continuing to control the Executive Branch, then I'm with Gore."*

His race has some low points, like never being able to get into the debates. And when he says that Bush and Gore are equally bad (using a too-glib "Bore vs. Gush" formulation), he means that they and both parties are too indebted to big money, not that they are identical on social or foreign policy. But the nuance is lost and damage done among angry Democrats. There are some high notes as well:

---

* Privately, like many of his friends, I suggest that he adopt the "Ivins Plan," named for writer Molly Ivins, to urge people vote for Gore in swing states but Ralph in very Red and Blue states. He declines since he's trying to maximize his vote to reach the 5 percent threshold that generates another round of public funds. Later, critics will claim that he intentionally went into swing states, like Florida, to try to defeat Gore. But independent scholars who have studied his schedule of appearances confirm that he was out to get votes, not defeat Gore.

he raises an unexpected $8 million and pioneers what are called "super-rallies" where thousands *pay* up to $25 to hear him speak; they culminate in nearly 20,000 at Madison Square Garden (including my admiring son Jonah) who collectively roar when he opens with "Welcome to the politics of joy and justice!" (After one long speech, he pesters an aide, "Did I mention that Pentagon point and my idea on health care?" Aide: "What are you worrying about? They loved it!" Ralph: "You don't understand at all. You never know what thought or line will connect to someone and change their thinking or their life.")

Ralph starts at 6 percent in national polls, aims for at least 5 percent of the vote in order to qualify for matching funds in any future presidential campaign, but ends up with 2.7 percent. Worse, of course, Bush wins Florida after a recount by 537 votes while Ralph gets 96,915 there. He becomes even more of a pariah to ranking Democrats. Todd Gitlin says, "I think [his candidacy] borders on the wicked." James Carville adds, "No one in the history of the world is on a bigger ego trip than Ralph Nader . . . I am going to shun him and any good Democrat should." Notes Senator Joe Biden, "Ralph Nader is not going to be welcome anywhere near the corridors. He cost us the election. God save me the purists."

He is now faced with the worst of all possible worlds—most Republicans loathe him because he's regarded as an anti-business liberal; many Democrats loathe him for electing Bush.

Asked about his blame for Bush in December 2015, he replies: "Apparently I was unusually influential since I made Gore lose his home state of Tennessee, got Florida to design its butterfly ballot, convinced Gov. Jeb Bush to strike thousands of eligible minority names from voter rolls, stopped the recount short of the whole state, and persuaded the Supreme Court to make Bush president." He also contends that unless the Democratic Party fears progressives, it will always take them for granted and give them lip service. In 2007, Lawrence O'Donnell agrees: "If you want to pull the major party that is closest to the way you're thinking, you must—you *must*—show them that you're capable of not voting for them."

When asked directly if, knowing what he knows now, he regrets running in 2000, he answers, "If I could do it over, I'd have run all out in 1992 when the field didn't have a strong favorite. Look at how well even Paul Tsongas did." Well, did you ever visualize yourself as

president and what you'd do? "I did visualize what I'd do in terms
of a program, which is to devolve power to people, especially at the
state and local level. Unless you do that, you can't get anything done
in Washington."

For all the exceptional events of 1966 that catapulted him to national prominence, November 2000 sees the nightmare of Bush winning the closest presidential election ever due to an even less plausible
combination of events that made the numerical loser the winner. If
Gore had lawfully won, Ralph's candidacy presumably wouldn't have
been held against him ever since and might have even helped resur-
rect him as the national progressive leader holding President Gore's
feet to the fire.

But "if" and "might" are not arguments—they're unprovable
counterfactuals,* maybe someday an Amazon alternate-history series. Especially after 9/11 and the calamity of Iraq, most Democrats
automatically accept that Nader is responsible for Bush-Cheney. Period. Making matters worse, Nader again runs in 2004 and 2008. I
make my opinion known in a December 2, 2003, handwritten note:
"Ralph, I have only two words why I believe it would hurt our values
and our country if you run in '04—'President Bush.'" I help arrange
a meeting between him and nominee John Kerry, whose campaign
I'm co-running in New York State. Ralph urges him "to draw sharper
distinctions with Bush, like on the very popular minimum wage increase," but, in Ralph's later view, "he instead blurred himself. If he
had done it, he'd have likely carried Ohio and the White House."
Nader ends up making no discernible difference, garnering less than
1 percent.

My frustration over his choices and my personal quandary of being part-politician/part-Raider, however, leads me to say something
foolish and out of character. During the 2004 Republican Convention at Madison Square Garden in July, I happen to see him crossing
the street at 34th and 8th. We shout hello, embrace, and I hear myself
say out loud, "Ralph, why are you doing this again? You're risking my
children's lives by possibly helping Bush win reelection." He looks

---

* Another interesting hypothetical—based on Bernie Sanders's later successes as a
Democrat—is what would have happened if he hadn't promised his father that he'd
never join either of the two major parties and had run as a Democrat in either 2000
or 1992. That's now, however, merely an intriguing chimera.

startled and dismayed, having heard such comments from many adversaries but not often from a protégé. I don't think I've ever regretted saying anything more.

But those saying he ran because of some personal "ego trip" are completely misreading him and looking at an unconventional person through a conventional lens. Taking the long view beyond 2000, his goal was always, like Norman Thomas, to advance a progressive agenda in the hope of its eventual enactment, which is different than getting his picture in the *New York Times*. I've known a lot of prominent people who get the shakes if they're not getting frequent media validation but none who are as personally modest (if publicly grandiose) as him. Or as he says privately, "I don't like to toot my own horn."

After these presidential detours, he returns to more familiar ground—traveling, conferencing, lecturing, writing.

In 2002 he goes to Cuba for 15 hours of conversations with Fidel Castro.

According to his "Sleepless in Havana" strategy, Castro invites Nader and his seven-person group to his offices for three dinners from 10 p.m. to 4 a.m. with plenty of fruit, berries, nuts, and wine in between. Oregon lawyer Gregory Kafoury recalls their wide-ranging conversations about history, economics, politics, culture, and whether Cuba can steer a path between capitalism and communism. "It was as if each had spent a lifetime looking to meet someone as grand and brilliant—and found him." Nader also pitches his specific plan for the United States and Cuba to exchange what each has in abundance—U.S. technology and Cuban doctors, respectively. Castro agrees but the Bush administration nixes it.

Also on the trip, the American advocate meets with a group of some 40 Cuban intellectuals for a wide-ranging conversation about the two countries, with the Cuban group led by Ricardo Alarcon, something of the Revolution's Hamilton and Franklin, having fought with Fidel and then performed for decades as a resident intellectual, author, economic czar, legislator, diplomat. Nader opens with a question: "Can any society withstand the pressure of corporate, commercial capitalism?" After three hours of conversation, Alarcon says for his group that he believes they can because "we are a society of resistance." Then on the final day of the trip, *El Presidente* attends a lecture that Ralph gives at the University of Havana. Nader aide

John Richard asks Castro what he thinks of the talk. Castro replies, "And they say that I give long speeches!" For another example, I ask Ralph in 2000 about the length of his acceptance speech that day at the Green Party nominating convention. "Only an hour and a half," he says, self-mockingly.

He continues to visit cabinet secretaries on a variety of issues, call public interest groups with his ideas of what they should be doing, and bang out a column a week, *In the Public Interest,* for what is by now a total of over 2,000. He also spends more time in his Winsted family home writing books very different from each other and from those he supervised a decade before.

He publishes five in five years between 2011 and 2015. One is a lyrical, almost poetical paean about the family values of the Naders from Connecticut—*The Seventeen Traditions.* Then there's a mammoth work of what he calls "political fiction" and "utopian realism" called *Only the Super-Rich Can Save Us.* It's an extended parable with real named billionaires who decide to pool their wealth to change America. He no doubt hopes that the book is predictive but realistically thinks that "these people don't believe in anything they haven't thought of themselves."

Ralph's especially pleased at his deep dive into original sources to research the history of conservative thought in his 2013 book, *Unstoppable: The Emerging Left-Right Alliance to Dismantle the Corporate State.* But he's displeased three weeks later when he tells me that the *Times* won't even be reviewing it.

He now appears so infrequently on national TV, including the cable shows, that when he's on MSNBC's *Hardball* in October 2014, the irrepressibly exuberant host, Chris Matthews (himself a former Nader's Raider), can't stop remarking, "Wow, Ralph Nader, It's really you. You're really here!" channeling Twain's famous observation about reports of one's premature death. Given hosts' and bookers' reluctance to reach out to him, he instead tries to reach out directly to citizens via social media, writing a separate column for the *Huffington Post,* tweeting daily, hosting a weekly radio podcast.

Our freewheeling monthly talks in recent years provide an updated answer to that long-asked question, "What makes him *tick?*" For I hear someone now in his early 80s who sounds almost exactly like he did in his 30s.

- Infuriating Ralph are "defeatist Democrats," as he calls them. In a phone conversation in March of 2010, he's angry and prescient: "Look at how Democrats and the media got rolled in 2002 by Republicans always pushing for more war—like Hearst's papers and TR before the Spanish-American War . . . We now have the best House chairs in a long time—Waxman, Miller, Markey, Conyers—yet things are worse than ever because they don't take on the Republicans for the vicious politicians they are. Why not at least list the 100 proposals they're against that the majority of people are for? Self-defeatism is unseemly when 30 million people can't afford to put food on the table . . . Their problem is so deep that only psychiatric language can describe it. We have to save the Democratic Party from the Democratic Party."

- When I tell him that I saw Al Franken burst out crying at his own U.S. Senate fund-raiser as he talked about the plight of Native Americans on reservations in Minnesota, Ralph is impressed. "That's very good. It shows a level of empathy few have in his position."

- After the *Citizens United* decision in January 2010, we speculate about its potential impact. "It won't last," he says confidently. "The public will never put up with such an obvious system of political corruption. It'll eventually be reversed."

- During the 2012 presidential campaign, he's itching for Obama to "stand for something beyond being against Bain Capital. He needs a more compelling message to help Democrats in Congress, more of a clash of philosophies. Otherwise, iceberg ahead for Democrats."

- In recent years, he's disappointed by how progressive allies "don't even read each other's books—we don't work together or help each other out like the right wing does." Accordingly, he has a hobby of secretly buying their remaindered books at auction to distribute to libraries and audiences and tweets about their good works to get the word around. He functions as a conveyor belt of progressive intel. About once a month, I still get an envelope with a clip or book from him with a handwritten note or hand-typed letter on his Underwood (replacing his Smith Corona) explaining why I should pay attention to the enclosure. I'm not the only one on his version of e-mail. (He's not online and doesn't have a smart phone.) In 2014 he lauds my earlier book, *Losing Our Democracy*, which he has just re-read. How many people do you know *re*-read books?

- He's dismayed and impressed by the modern GOP. "They aim high. Gingrich toppled Wright and Foley but there's an intensity gap between the Right and Left." He sees the Republican Party "as about the most radical party in American history. They don't want a modern economy but want to go back to Andrew Mellon. They want to return to prehistory, like the Taliban. OK, they don't want to cut off hands but look at what Bork and Bolton want to go back to."

- We repeatedly disagree about Hillary Clinton, whom he thinks is a "militarist" and "corporatist" while I see her as more a Wellesley boomer than a Wall Street pawn who's also a brilliant center-left politician who will do no more opportunistic things than FDR and JFK to win. Wouldn't he vote for her against any Republican? "Well, you don't have to be morally complicit though."

- Once I ask him to be introspective about his phenomenal drive. Incredibly, he challenges my premise and then follows with an uncharacteristic, wandering, revealing self-analysis:

> I don't see myself as driven. You're more driven than I am [*sic*]. I've accomplished less than 1 percent of what I should have. If I were driven, I would have spent the time to get more billionaires to fund our expansion earlier. But really rich people were so demanding for a quid pro quo or their own little hobbyhorse that it turned me off. I said, "Do I really want to get into this quagmire?" As you know, Mark, something happens between pleader and giver. After a while, it affects you. If I went through that trap door and became too subservient, I'd lose my credibility with the public. That's why I was so fanatical about not living high on the hog—you have to set an example.

"I'm struck by your combination of personal humility along with outsized public ambitions," I tell him in a final interview for this book. "Isn't that unusual?"

"Not at all, they go together. If I got all wound up in my own ego then I'd burn out. In order to get big things done, you've got to put ego aside and focus on working with whoever you have to. What I really try to do is elevate people. I just visited with Transportation Secretary Anthony Foxx and explained that he should imagine that drivers are hanging by a thread from his window and only he can save them—and there's no better time than now when his boss isn't running for reelection and there's all this attention to the scandals of GM and VW. He and his people liked that. Basically, my approach traces back to something that constitutional law professor Paul Freund once said in class. It seemed to go over the head of the students but I've never forgotten it: 'What makes us brothers and sisters is the infinite power of the universe.'"

An hour later, I realize when I've heard a version of this lesson about ego and result before. It was in the fall of 2001 when Senator Hillary Clinton reached me in my car between campaign events to offer advice for my general election for mayor. To paraphrase from memory since I took no notes: "Mark, you'll now obviously be attracting a lot of attention and criticism. You really have to put all that aside, not let it get to you, bother you. Instead, just concentrate on what you need to do that day or week to become mayor."

Ralph and Hillary are different in many obvious ways. Yet they also both possess a very large bandwidth, wonky earnestness, progressive values at least domestically, implacable public self-confidence, the resolve of a fighter, appear undauntable and unsinkable, are both loved and loathed, and focus on mission over ego. If only they could have an easy meal together about policy. But given their current roles as Mr. Outside and Ms. Inside and Ralph's instinctive skepticism of powerful politicians, that doesn't seem likely anytime soon.

- Finally, he lists various new organizations he wants to launch after the fiftieth anniversary of *Unsafe* in November 2015, including one called The Secretariat composed of a couple hundred former military leaders to speak up on defense cuts and war/peace. "With $200 million, they could have stopped the Iraqi invasion. There are now hundreds of them out of uniform with strong views but no vehicle to express them," he asserts. "OK," I respond, "but do you really think you can pull such a group together?" Ralph pauses: "You never know unless you try."

In other words, there's no quit in this guy, no acknowledgment, privately or publicly, of any lion-in-winter phase, or any sign that ostracism has dampened his optimism. His pace and imagination appear undiminished. This national icon seems to get as excited about lower-order efforts—a letter to the editor, a debate on C-SPAN—as he did when writing law after law in the late 1960s, enjoying a river of lecture invitations, or packing the Garden. "When I see something wrong," he says, like a progressive Peter Pan refusing to grow up, "I feel like I'm 19 again." Speeches in the Sixties and 2016 contain the same signature line: "The only aging is the erosion of ideals."

AN AMERICAN ORIGINAL:
THE LEDGER OF A LIFE

Although Nader says his legacy or critics don't concern him—"What will they do, pull seat belts and airbags out of cars?"—two questions interest me as a friend and author: how could one person do so much, and what's his place in history?

As for his impact, there are three essential truths.

First, events have largely vindicated his principles. Big corporations have been abusing consumers and citizens—because of purchased politicians and sympathetic corporate judges—throwing off the desired balance between Democracy and Capitalism. His overarching goal of a system of regulated capitalism is one that is vital and widely popular.

Second, he has an unusual combination of skills that have enabled him for decades to recruit adherents, win public support, and be unaffected by odds or obstacles. Of course, he's a joyful workaholic with unusual stamina. He notes with uncharacteristic pride that he has an entry in the *Guinness Book of World Records* of having had the most political campaign stops (in different communities) in one day when he engaged in 21 from 6 a.m. to 1 a.m. in Massachusetts in 2000, ending in the revolutionary war town of Sheffield. When Harrison Wellford asks him in March 2015 after a reunion dinner of Raiders what he's doing later that night, Ralph says, "Going home to edit. I love staying up all night reading a report." His stamina and resilience owe to a rare mental architecture that shakes off a defeat like a great pitcher who's just thrown a home run ball. "I don't get all clutched or nervous if things go wrong," he tells one journalist. "I have an inner consistency that carries me through."

When a group of original Nader's Raiders reminisce about his traits, I ask them if he ever raised his voice or yelled at any of them. None could remember an instance except one time, when Congress Watch failed by one vote in the House to enact an auto safety provision. He was crestfallen, fell silent for a moment, then said to Claybrook, "Well, don't ever do that again!" When I later ask Ralph if he recalls ever yelling at staff for some costly blunder, he says, "Never. Since any such conversation would not be between two people with an equal relationship that would make me a bully, which would make me sick." Despite his prominence, he doesn't so much dictate top-down to subordinates like a standard senator, governor, or CEO but rather embodies the ethic of Albert Schweitzer: "Leadership is example."

Third, for all his decades of tedious consistency, Ralph is also a bundle of seeming contradictions. He combines personal humility with public hubris and is both of Winsted and the world, grounded in small-town virtues along with obvious intellectual and political sophistication. He's alternately an accountant and philosopher, fretting small details while advancing big visions. (Alan Morrison once told Ralph he could never be president "because you won't be able to sign 3 million checks a day.")

He's an American radical—as in challenging orthodoxy and getting to the root of problems—who works within the system to change it.

IT IS RARE that one person can make a decisive historical difference, although arguments can be made, most obviously, for Lenin, Hitler, Churchill, Gandhi. Usually, movements make leaders far more often than leaders make movements. It seems likely that the civil rights, women's, environmental, and gay rights movements in the Sixties would have grown and prevailed eventually because of real grievances even without the inspiration of a King, Steinem, Carson, and Milk, all of whom amplified and organized the voices of dissent. But no Nader, probably no consumer/corporate accountability movement, or at least nothing remotely resembling the groups and laws that sprung from his initiatives.

His failures have been large: the 2000 presidential race, no Consumer Protection Agency, and corporations more politically powerful than ever because of influential adversaries from Lewis Powell to John Roberts to the Koch brothers. It's hard, however, to think of many private citizens in American history with more public influence on more issues over a longer time than Nader.*

Of course there are individuals with monumental impact in a particular area—no one can match Dr. King for the greatest influence on our greatest social movement. But in terms of range, who? And in terms of his longevity, who? Nader's breakout moment came exactly 50 years ago. Yet he hasn't gone away and isn't likely to anytime soon—his parents lived to be 100.

While there's still resentment among liberals over 2000 and some of his rhetorical excesses—against Obama and the Clintons, for example—there's also a consensus about his historic role. Former vice president Walter Mondale said he thinks Nader is "a man without parallel in American history." Liberal essayist Michael Kinsley, who once worked for him, argues, "No living American is responsible for more concrete improvement in society. Ralph is living proof that there isn't much difference between a fanatic and a saint. I'll bet you Mother Teresa is impossible to deal with too." His four biographers—Gorey, Buckhorn, McCarry, and Martin—regard him, in Ribicoff's phrase, as "an American original."

---

*It would require a full-length, current biography to chronicle the breadth of his impact: he helped enact a score of major laws, such as the Auto Safety Acts, Occupational Safety and Health Administration, Environmental Protection Agency, Consumer Product Safety Commission, Freedom of Information Amendments, Clean Water Act, Consumer Credit Disclosure law, Consumer Co-Op Bank, Foreign Corrupt Practices Act, Mine Health and Safety Act, Whistleblower Protection Act, Wholesome Meat Act.

He created some 100 separate organizations on particular issues (Pension Rights Center) or in the states (PIRGs); sponsored 125 books and wrote a dozen. Thousands of young advocates have worked either directly for him or in satellite organizations over 50 years, including numerous leaders in public service, journalism, academe, business, and politics, such as: Joan Claybrook, Sidney Wolfe, Alan Morrison, Harrison Wellford, Clarence Ditlow, Gene Karpinski, Peter Bradford, Michael Waldman, Miles Rapoport; Michael Moore, James Fallows, E. J. Dionne, Michael Kinsley, David Ignatius, Chuck Todd, Chris Matthews, Amy Goodman; Robert Fellmeth, Judy Areen, Joel Seligman; Bruce Wasserstein; Ed Cox, Donna Edwards, and Barack Obama (NYPIRG).

People had high-jumped for millennia, but when Dick Fosbury in the 1960s started jumping head-first rather than the traditional feet-first scissor-kick, "the Fosbury Flop" took the event to, well, new heights. Other originals, paradigm-shapers in their different fields: Hearst, Brandeis, Ford, Lloyd Wright, Houdini, Robinson, Elvis, Brando, Kerouac, Dylan, Salinger, King, Friedan, Baldwin, Ali. We know it when we see it in the arts, sciences, sports, business—that combination, as James Lipton said of Brando, "of talent and technique" that creates something very *different*.

Nader is very different. There were public advocates before him, of course. But like Fosbury, he dives head-first into high bars. I'm reminded of what tennis great Ille Nastase said of his rival Bjorn Borg in the late 1970s: "We're playing tennis, he's playing something else."

In 2015 I mischievously ask a well-known author on a book tour for his opinion of who, not counting public officials, has had a comparable or greater impact on public affairs over time on such a broad range of problems as Citizen Nader. After no hesitation or self-consciousness, Ralph responds, "Benjamin Franklin. Look what he did, from creating the postal service and volunteer fire departments to starting public libraries and of course his *Almanac*. Then there are his scientific inventions—did you know that he was a member of the Royal Academy of Science in England?"

NADER'S TORT MUSEUM

A Tort Museum? In Winsted, Connecticut (population now 7,563)?

Even allies became cynics when Nader first mentions the idea in 1998 after he visits plaintiff's lawyer William Trine in Boulder, Colorado, to look at files in a major litigation Trine had won. "What do trial lawyers do with key exhibits in such cases when they're over?" Ralph asks. "Well, they either store them in boxes somewhere or throw them out." Light bulb! He then begins raising money toward his dream of a Tort Museum to advance understanding of what is, in the phrase of historian Eric Foner, "a weapon of the weak."

"Tort" is French for "wrong." From the Common Law through the Seventh Amendment's right to trial by jury, tort law is a system to ensure that victims of wrongful acts or products get compensation. But Nader watches with growing alarm over 30 years as this mechanism of corporate and personal accountability is undermined by a successful corporate campaign to re-translate tort law into "frivolous lawsuits" and the work of "greedy trial lawyers."

That's why on a perfect fall day in September 2015, Deni and I drive two hours north to Winsted, down Main Street by Jessie's Barber Shop and ABC Pizza, to the former Winsted Bank Building that Nader bought in 2012 for $525,000 to house the American Museum of Tort Law. It's actually the first museum in the world on *any* aspect of law. At its opening, we join some 500 guests to listen to an illustrious panel of lawyers and public figures and to Patti Smith perform "People Have the Power." Nader welcomes everyone, including a group of Chinese students in Chinese. (The Princeton Sinologist urges them to "go back to your country and start a system of civil justice there.") Then, in his usual subdued tone, he explains his mission for the museum:

> Tort law protects our freedom and safety. It's a system of civil justice and direct democracy with checks and balances—a jury of your peers and the right to appeal. Can't get better than that . . . Tort law broke open how the tobacco industry takes 400,000 lives a year, how asbestos has killed so many in this corporate cover-up—and product defects in automobiles, pharmaceuticals, hospitals. All of these cases generated a message to the owners, the people who control these companies, that it's cheaper to be safe than unsafe and inflict terrible injuries on innocent people whether they're customers, workers or just people living in a community. That's what this museum is all about.
>
> A slavery museum recently opened in Louisiana on a plantation, organized by a trial lawyer whose distant relative had owned the place. In a sense, slavery was the ultimate tort.

Entering the 6,000-square-foot museum, visitors walk past a large quote from Judge Learned Hand: "Thou shalt not ration justice." Then they see an eye-catching, mint-condition red Corvair, with its (in)famous rear-end engine that made it the centerpiece of *Unsafe at Any Speed*, as well as the lathe that established strict liability for manufacturers making dangerous products. A short film on the history of product liability, narrated by Phil Donahue, is complemented by colorful illustrations of major moments in tort law, from the thirteenth century through Nader's successful lawsuit against

GM for invasion of privacy. Plans are now under way to build a model courtroom, conduct mock trials on the Internet, take exhibits on the road, and make the museum not merely a destination location but an "educational enterprise" so the law of wrongful injury can stay strong and adapt to new situations (what happens when driverless cars get involved in accidents?).

As for why Winsted, he says, "Why not Winsted? Why should all these things go into the big cities? It was here that workers in manufacturing mills over decades were injured or killed." As for whether it will help beat back the anti–civil justice assault of big business, sitting in the audience I am brought back to another David-Goliath battle 50 years earlier when people were understandably skeptical about his long-odds crusade for an auto safety law and his attack on General Motors. Now its Corvair is a museum piece—in Nader's museum.

THREE

THE ADVOCATE

Consumer Cop and Democracy Czar

For the first half of the 19th century, a Bostonian named John Chapman planted apple seeds in wilderness areas. Tens of thousands of trees made up his environmental legacy . . . He became widely known as Johnny Appleseed.

—Ralph Nader, column, *In the Public Interest*, 1987

As through this world I've wandered, I've met lots of funny men / Some will rob you with a six-gun. And some with a fountain pen.

—Woody Guthrie, "Pretty Boy Floyd"

Mark's an elected Public Advocate. I don't know if there's another city in America that has an elected public advocate. But think about what that means. Someone who is standing up for people at large, right? . . . I'm sort of the country's public advocate.

—President Bill Clinton, April 15, 1997

I HANG UP WITH RALPH LATE ON THE NIGHT I LOSE MY 1980 congressional race, conflicted but knowing that I'll be staying in my native New York. Could I now become one of Ralph's apple seeds replanted here?

Until I can realize my dream of combining outside advocacy with inside public office, I decide to set up my own shop called "The Democracy Project." Based on a decade with Ralph, I push my theme of "tugboat liberals"—how small groups can steer big policies through the smart application of pressure—especially now that Reagan runs the White House and Republicans the Senate.

Recalling Bernard Baruch's axiom that he got rich "by buying when everyone was selling and selling when everyone was buying," it seems like a good time to try to update liberalism from my new venue. It was only a few years earlier that the Heritage Foundation brought together different disciplines under one conservative umbrella to affect policy, but there was next to nothing like that on our side. I conscript Harry Chapin, the dynamic folk singer and story-teller ("Taxi," "Cat's in the Cradle"), a pal from Long Island and Democratic politics and founder of WHY (World Hunger Year). At the level of a Pete Seeger and Peter, Paul and Mary, he's a "citizen-artist" who tells me, "I can provide you something rare—intellectual risk capital. My theory of life is that I do one concert for me, then one for the other guy."

He commits to perform once a month to kick-start this smaller version of Heritage while I put together other funding, a mission statement, and a strong board of directors (which will include Ramsey Clark, Sidney Harman, Norman Lear, and Stanley Sheinbaum).

Then tragedy. On July 20, 1981, Harry is killed in a freak car accident at exit 40 of the Long Island Expressway en route to a concert. His loss staggers his family, his fans, and our nascent effort. I find a plaintiff's lawyer for his widow, Sandy, who eventually recovers several million dollars for the family due to a car defect. Our Democracy Project plunges ahead, though it stays undercapitalized for years to come.

Our time is spent trying to formulate a progressive agenda on the economy, regulation, and crime via, again, public events, books, and television.

Democracy Project forums engage clashing Left and Right luminaries, from John Kenneth Galbraith, Bill Moyers, and I. F. Stone to Bill Buckley, Pat Buchanan, and Kevin Phillips. They also put presidential candidates in front of large audiences of NYC political and money "machers." In 1984, they include Walter Mondale, Gary Hart, and John Glenn; in 1988, Michael Dukakis, Jesse Jackson, and Al Gore; in 2004, John Kerry, Howard Dean, and John Edwards.

Senator Glenn makes news in February 1984 when I ask him before an audience of 500, "Do you think a person's sexual orientation is a matter of biology or choice?" This American hero immediately and sincerely answers, "It's a matter of personal choice," presumably reflecting his small-town views of gay Americans. The audience starts murmuring and, standing on the platform next to him, I can see he has no idea why. *Did I just screw over John Glenn? Should I step in and somehow bail him out? No,* I decide. *I'm the referee, not a coach.* Until then he's a top-tier candidate, but his New York support soon evaporates.

After Dukakis's workman-like appearance four years later at our forum at the Ethical Culture Society, he pulls me aside to ask my opinion how Mayor Ed Koch's typically loud endorsement of Senator Al Gore will affect his chances in New York. When I tell him that "Gore may survive it," he can't stop laughing and we begin a mutual admiration society.

But no one on our side is in a laughing mood after George Herbert Walker Bush's victory. Early the next year, I host a "Retreat to Advance" at a hotel near DuPont Circle in D.C. where 100 leading Democrats convene to discuss how to reorganize and rethink. As keynote speaker focusing on education, we invite the young southern governor, Bill Clinton of Arkansas. He's policy heavy and impressive as hell.

Also in early 1989, I contact my friend, actor Ron Silver, with an idea—since NYC has so many talented progressive actors/celebrities each going off in their own directions on public affairs, why not harness them into one focused group pushing for various causes and candidates? Ron and I then co-host a three-hour organizational meeting at my apartment a block from Gracie Mansion on 90th Street to discuss whether and how to do it. Among the 30 in attendance are Wendy Wasserstein, Blythe Danner, Mandy Patinkin, Susan Sarandon, Tim Robbins, Peter Yarrow, and Olympia Dukakis. Out of that emerges a 501c3 "Creative Coalition" that is still going strong in 2016 and that hosts forums and lobbying campaigns around specific issues. *(I withdrew shortly after formation since it had to be for and run by performers and not merely the subsidiary of a think tank, and Ron had the skills to do it. Later, after 9/11, he became a Bush conservative though he voted for Obama before sadly dying at only age 62 of cancer.)*

Over these same years, Democracy Project books attempt to reframe issues to keep Reagan from inaugurating a conservative era based on personal charm wedded to stories he read in the reactionary

Human Events magazine. In 1982 Bantam Books publishes my *Winning Back America,* a liberal manifesto laying out alternative ideas in 31 policy areas. While nominated for a National Book Award, it's no *Silent Spring* in terms of changing America. *Reagan's Reign of Error* in 1985 documents several hundred examples when Dutch says something that's either false, misleading, ignorant, or all three—like saying that some nuclear missiles are recallable. As I promote the book on *Good Morning America,* Reagan's chief of staff James Baker is watching in the Green Room and says out loud in the presence of my aide, "No, no, he doesn't *know* what he's saying is wrong."

In 1986, we publish two volumes that, in my view, add value to the debate over regulation. On assignment, Joan Claybrook and journalist/historian David Bollier write the best book I've ever read on the benefits of federal regulations: *Freedom from Harm: The Civilizing Influence of Health, Safety and Environmental Regulation.* Then we go further to scrutinize not the federal but the *corporate* bureaucracy, which I call "corpocracy" in *The Challenge of Hidden Profits.* Coauthor John Berry and I conclude that "corporate bloat erodes efficiency, reduces profits and weakens our ability to compete internationally." Adding up the documented waste due to uncompetitive, polluting, worker-injuring, consumer-abusing corporations, we calculate that it comes to roughly $862 billion a year. That's the result of real-world corporations that ignore market theory and prefer to fatten their own bureaucracies and pockets. *Fortune* lauds "a new kind of Naderism" that concerns itself with making business both more efficient and accountable. And the term "corpocracy" enters popular parlance after Reagan's deputy treasury secretary, Richard Darman, appropriates and spreads, literally, the word. No longer is "bureaucracy" exclusively an epithet hurled at Washington.

Then in 1988 and 1992, we gather some of the best liberal scholars and advocates to produce citizen transition books in the tradition of the 1980 Heritage Foundation's *Mandate for Leadership* for Reagan. The 1988 version is slender and, obviously, not much used by presidential winner Bush. The 1992 version, however, comes out of a conversation with Governor Bill Clinton in October 1991 as he and I linger late one night after a DNC event at the Tavern on the Green. When I explain my idea for the project, this policy-prone candidate brightens, pulls me toward him, and says, "Do it. Sure hope I'm the one who benefits."

Weighing in at 781 pages, *Changing America* comes out in November 1992. This anthology by 50 progressive leaders—Jamie Galbraith, Bob Kuttner, Aryeh Neier, Marian Wright Edelman, Henry Louis Gates, among others—explains agency by agency how to shift gears from Reagan-Bush to Clinton-Gore (turns out that Al does survive Koch's endorsement). My stopped-clock-right-twice-a-day strategy for transition policy books finally succeeds when the candidate who inspires the volume then enthusiastically uses it as president-elect, according to him.

I also appear increasingly on TV, including scores of times on *Firing Line* or sitting "on the left" on *Crossfire*. Yes, it's fun tangling with Buckley, Buchanan, Bob Novak, Newt Gingrich, Edward Teller, Alexander Haig . . . but ultimately unfulfilling. Family and friends watch and applaud as my ego is tickled. But the events, books, and debates are essentially academic, reflecting policy rather than making it.

The decade's end arrives awash in frustration: Reagan dominates public discourse, Hart self-immolates, and Dukakis flounders, while I win a U.S. Senate nomination in 1986 (see next chapter) but not a Senate seat.

Then something happens to shift my course.

An underestimated David Dinkins, the Manhattan borough president, handily defeats a battle- and scandal-scarred Mayor Koch in 1989 to be elected the first African American mayor of the city. As an early and vigorous supporter, I'm on a short list being considered by Dinkins's transition team to lead his Department of Consumer Affairs (DCA), a post made famous 20 years before when former Miss America Bess Myerson held it. Some on the panel are enthusiastic because of my history as a consumer advocate, others worried at my headstrong public reputation.

But Dave's vote is the only one that counts. When he makes the offer, I initially hesitate, wondering whether I want to be "just" a local commissioner. Then I recall an experience from 1977 when I accompany my friend Linda Blitz to buy shoes at a store on upper Connecticut Ave. When she asks if there's a cash discount since the store saves money by avoiding a fee to the credit card company, she's told no by a baffled clerk. "Why not?" I ask a manager. "Because the credit card companies won't let us in their contracts with us." *Bingo!* Yale law professor Paul Gewirtz sues the store and AmEx in a case that successfully ends such anticompetitive clauses. The idea that I could make law like this regularly as a public official becomes tantalizing.

Then too, Ralph encourages me: "You can be a prototype on how to enforce consumer protection laws." Soon I shake off my national hubris, realizing that there are truly worse things than having a staff of 300 licensing 50,000 companies in 82 lines of commerce and the legal authority to prosecute fraud and enact reforms. Believing it's put-up or shut-up time, I say yes and am sworn in on February 20, 1990.

"I, MARK GREEN, do solemnly swear . . ." I hear myself saying in City Hall, full of excess adrenaline and surrounded by my beaming family. Dinkins—a politician whose external mildness sheaths a tough, sometimes prickly persona—talks up my consumer cred as a "Nader Raider." My son Jonah, then six, can't resist grabbing the mic to say a few words. Then he allows me my turn to declare that I want to "especially protect seniors, children, women, the disabled, and minorities who most need government help."

"Go get 'em, Dad," my 11-year-old daughter Jenya stage-whispers when I conclude.

So I do, in the spirit of Alexander Hamilton, who shrewdly understood that "in politics as in war, the first blow is half the battle." An hour later and three blocks north at the frayed offices of the DCA, I hold a press conference denouncing R. J. Reynolds for "commercial child abuse" because of the way it uses the cartoon figure Joe Camel to addict 13-year-olds—the average age of a first-time smoker—to a lifelong if not life-ending habit.

Tumult! The mayor's office understandably feels blindsided since, in my enthusiasm, I hadn't checked in with them beforehand. During an angry phone call, City Hall press secretary Albert Scardino expresses amazement that I would do that in my first hour on my first day in office. In the future, he insists, "you have to clear such press conferences and statements with my office." "Sorry, can't do that," I reply, worried that waiting for permission could compromise my law enforcement judgments and inevitably bog down my file full of ready-to-go initiatives in his press bureaucracy. I assume, or rather hope, that it would be untenable to fire me so early for this impertinence.

Scardino grudgingly backs off while Dinkins is too busy juggling bigger crises than this small contretemps. From a mayoral perspective, of course, Dinkins-Scardino were probably managerially right. CEOs like to know about and coordinate what their subordinates are doing. But I win this round simply because I *cared* far more than they on a matter so essential to my plans, which I'm confident will bring credit to City Hall. As a result, I have lots of leeway to investigate bad actors and reform bad laws on behalf of powerless, screwed consumers.

Four years later, I get elected—and in 1997 reelected—the city's first public advocate. It's an office that traces back to 1831, is one-fifth the size of DCA, lacks law enforcement authority, and has been a perennial underachiever.* But since it's elected citywide and constitutionally next in line to the mayor, I see the potential to elevate it from lapdog to watchdog . . . as long as I stay alert to likely efforts to eliminate it by hostile tabloids and mayors unenthusiastic about such an institutional critic.

Except for occasional attacks on the office's very existence, from 1990 to 2001, the political planets are in alignment for someone who believes in aggressive government and progressive values. Or to quote President Clinton, as we ride in his limousine across 45th Street after a March 1994 speech to the United Nations, "Do you feel like you died and went to heaven?"

ELEVEN YEARS IN ADVOCATE HEAVEN

I make several private vows at the start of my public service: to structure my office as a Nader-like public interest law firm; put into practice the liberal ideas I've been advocating for 20 years; work every day with NBA-playoff intensity since I can't know how long I'll be able

---

* Originally called the "president of the Board of Aldermen," the 162-year-old office has been held by such luminaries as Al Smith (1917) and Fiorello La Guardia (1920), as well as four others who rose to the mayoralty. It became "City Council President" in 1937 and acquired ombudsman authority in the 1970s—a reform supported by both William Buckley Jr. and socialist Michael Harrington—to handle citizen complaints and monitor city agencies. Finally, the city council changed the name once more in 1993 to "Public Advocate" because the Speaker of the council, who really ran it, resented being confused with the presiding officer, the president of the City Council, who didn't.

to merge advocacy and office; and go big not small—"if St. George had slain a dragonfly rather than a dragon," it's said in the screenplay *Inherit the Wind*, "who would remember him?"

That approach and the leverage of the world's premiere city enable me from 1990 to 2001 to churn out some 320 reports, lawsuits, and laws—first under the Democratic Dinkins as an appointed official, then under the Republican Rudy Giuliani as an elected one.

Here are six areas that describe how progressive values from the Sixties are adapted and enacted by Nineties activist government.*

1. Kicking Joe Camel's Butt

I'm thinking hard about an opening initiative in January 1990, recalling the wisdom of Ronald Reagan, who said to an aide in 1966, "Politics is just like show business. You have a hell of an opening . . . [and] a hell of a close." Over the course of one day I see the Joe Camel "smooth character" at a newsstand, in an ad on my crosstown 86th Street bus, in my subway car, and finally in the February 8 issue of *Rolling Stone*. Then it hits me—who the hell relates to a cartoon figure extolling the coolness of smoking in a hip cultural magazine except teens and preteens? How is this possible more than 25 years since the groundbreaking exposé of the lethality of smoking in the surgeon general's report?

Now, I have never smoked and I obsessively lectured my two children that they can never, never light up. But what about everyone else's children? I resolve to use my government perch both to warn about tobacco ads targeting kids and to use the law to do something about it.

But I can't persuade City Corporation counsel, the talented Victor Kovner, to pursue legal action to take down Joe Camel ads on public transit, on billboards in sports stadiums, and in the minority communities where they especially proliferate since fewer kids of color smoke. We respectfully disagree: after numerous legal memoranda go back and forth, Kovner sees it more as a speech than a

---

* For reasons of space and theme, the following section omits nearly all actions involving general consumer law enforcement and Public Advocate ombudsman work.

health issue, and a federal one rather than a local one; I consider it misleading under existing "false and misleading advertising" laws to imply that smoking is more likely to enhance than end your life.

As commissioner, however, I pursue several alternate steps to publicize rather than romanticize such products.

First, Mayor Dinkins, who's both personally proud that he quit smoking in 1961 and adores all children, enthusiastically agrees to push for a ban on the distribution of free samples and on cigarette vending machines in all public venues like movies, bars, and restaurants. "It would be considered crazy to have vending machines for liquor," I testify to the city council. "Why do we have vending machines for a product considered more dangerous? Two hundred city children on average per day start a habit, usually at a vending machine, that a third of them will die from." It passes easily, making our ban the first of its kind in a major American city.

Second, the mayor and I lean on the Yankees and Mets, and, with stars like Billie Jean King, on the Virginia Slims tennis tournament to stop their tobacco sponsorships since children go to games or see the billboards prominently displayed on TV screens. When a representative from Philip Morris threatens to pull their offices out of the city if we keep pushing our campaign, Dinkins tells me, "Send them a token." A few years later, the billboards and ads come down. Teams that lease their stadiums from the city rationally don't want to aggravate their landlords.

Third, I file a petition with the Federal Trade Commission in 1990 to bar cartoons in tobacco ads as "inherently misleading" under the FTC act. Despite enormous legal opposition from tobacco interests, seven years later the FTC staff agrees and urges the full five-member commission to move forward with such a rule. Two months later, on July 10, 1997, and before the agency can formally act, R.J. Reynolds "voluntarily" ends its ad campaign and thereby kills off the second-most-famous advertising brand in the country (the Marlboro Man being number one).

Last, I develop an idea for Kick Butts Day, modeled on the 1970 Earth Day and our 1980 Big Business Day. What better way for targeted children to learn about the lethality of tobacco than to enlist their participation in their own school in a fun day of poster contests, skits, rap performances, local essays, undercover surveys of stores that sell to minors, and letters to legislators? Appreciating the branding brilliance of Joe Camel, I persuade *Doonesbury*'s Garry Trudeau to design our own memorable logo for the day and then woo President Clinton—with White House lawyer Elena Kagan as our enthusiastic contact—to sign on.

Our first Kick Butts Day takes place in May 1996 when the president speaks from Woodbridge High in New Jersey to our event at P.S. 10 in Queens and then is hooked up to student audiences in ten other venues. Ciara Pack, a 13-year-old eighth-grader at I.S. 10, tells her awed classmates and an impressed president that "tobacco firms say they are not trying to target kids—but we're not stupid. They are trying to get us to smoke now so we add to their profits later."

The next year, President Clinton travels to the Andries Hudde Junior High School in Brooklyn, in crutches because of a bad spill at a golf club, to personally address a throng of children, parents, school and public officials, plus now 100 linked cities. Local congressman Chuck Schumer warmly welcomes the president since it's the first time in memory that a U.S. president has visited a Brooklyn public school (not to mention that Schumer's daughter is a student there). Clinton is typically overgenerous, saying that "Mark's Kick Butts Day involves about 2 million students [via closed circuit TV]. And he was the first official to ask to ban cartoon figures in tobacco ads" . . . then musing in this chapter's opening quote about how *he's* the real "Public Advocate."

In April 2001, first lady and Senate candidate Hillary Clinton—she also being a famously doting mother interested in health issues—joins me for that year's Kick Butts Day at the Salk School of Science on Manhattan's East Side. While she always has a genuine big smile at public appearances, the senator appears to really get into a program where children take responsibility for protecting themselves while displaying their artistic and dramatic skills. "Standing up with students," she tells an overflowing crowd, "we today send a clear message to the tobacco industry—stop targeting our children with your deadly products." Then as we watch students rapping their anti-smoking lyrics, she whispers, "This is *such* a great idea—you've got to continue it."

But since this idea has now gone national—we reach 4,000 schools by 2001—it's not something for one local official to oversee. I formally turn it over to the Campaign for Tobacco-Free Kids headquartered in Washington, D.C., which has capably run the Kick Butts

Day every April from then to 2016, engaging many millions of participating students.

This tobacco work begins a three-administration crusade—Dinkins, Giuliani, and Michael Bloomberg each making major strides—so that by 2015 the rate of smoking in NYC has fallen two-thirds among youth and nearly as much among adults.

2. What Do Women Want? Equality

Sanger, Steinem, and Friedan help deliver women into the twentieth century medically, politically, and legally. Now, in its last decade, is there anything a local official can do to build on their genius and enhance the quality of life for women? Relying especially on our female professional staff, we make specific progress in the courts, marketplace, workplace, and health care.

When a group of divorced women from Westchester ask to see me in 1990, at first I decline since they're not in my geographic jurisdiction. But they're insistent that their problems affect thousands of "unmonied spouses" in the city. At my meeting with a dozen of them, led by Monica Getz, a graceful and forceful advocate who had once been married to jazz legend Stan Getz, they describe a stacked system of "justice" under which well-off husbands hire top legal talent to coerce wives who lack the resources to navigate a complicated system.

Can the DCA help?

We spend a year interviewing 150 divorce lawyers and litigants, documenting this de facto gender discrimination in *Women in Divorce: Lawyers, Ethics, Fees & Fairness,* a report written by research assistant Karen Winner. (She goes on to devote much of her professional life to this cause.) It documents numerous cases where middle-aged women tragically lose almost everything—homes, children—because of a one-sided process that, like the old Soviet constitution, works fine on paper but not so well in practice.

This turns out to be a real fight with two well-matched sides. Divorce lawyers are plentiful and powerful, vigorously arguing that the status quo is fine (i.e., profitable) and that I'm biased against them. But we have on our side Monica's group—the Coalition for Family Justice—as well as Gloria Steinem and Judith Kaye.

Gloria, as high-minded and engaged as ever, helps host meetings to expand our array of women's groups and to appear when her star luster is needed. Judith Kaye is the chief judge in New York State, the successor to Chief Judge Sol Wachtler. He had gained fame first by ruling that marriage is not justification for marital rape and then by resigning in 1993 after admitting that he had physically threatened a former lover and her daughter. Oh, and Judge Kaye is then the decider over the rules of matrimonial law since they're drafted by the court system.

Women in Divorce and its subsequent publicity prod the Court of Appeals to convene its own blue ribbon panel of judges to independently investigate our criticisms and proposals. Seventeen months later, Judge Kaye and the panel, according to the *New York Law Journal,* "announce sweeping changes in the matrimonial law system, banning non-refundable retainers, requiring binding arbitration of fee disputes and—in the strictest regulation of lawyer conduct in the nation—prohibiting sexual relations between attorney and client during the course of representation." Also, a "Client's Bill of Rights" must now be handed to all potential clients that specifically lays out their rights, including "You are under no legal obligation . . . to agree to a lien or mortgage on your home to cover legal fees." According to Judge Leo Milonas, who heads the group of jurists, our DCA report "was the catalyst for the changes that we adopted."

Monica and Gloria are ecstatic at our success, which spans both my consumer affairs and public advocate roles. Our PA general counsel, Laurel Eisner, who has worked with me on this issue, then walks into my office not just to celebrate but with another long-ignored gender-based pathology—women being fired at work because of abusive partners. We gather the grim data: a third of American women report being physically or sexually abused by a husband or boyfriend in their lifetimes; 70 percent of employed battered women say that their abusers harassed them at work; and a quarter of such women report losing a job at least in part due to domestic violence.

Among others, I sit down with Rosa Schirripa from Staten Island, who shares with me her grief at trying to keep her family together and stay employed despite an abusive husband, only to lose her job when he harasses her at work and her employer doesn't want to put up with any hassle. This is both heartbreaking and little discussed in an era before domestic violence became a big issue.

Laurel and I organize the public-private Safe@Work coalition with a dozen women's, labor, and corporate organizations—including NOW, the Communications Workers of America, and Verizon, Liz Claiborne, and Philip Morris. Over the course of a couple of years, we hold hearings, organize the city's first march against domestic violence with 3,000 participating, and exchange strategies about how to protect women like Rosa when traditional corporate law allows employers to fire employees at will (unless unionized).

Because of business opposition within our broad group, we can't unite behind a proposal to affirmatively provide special protection in workplaces. We do, however, craft a bill that forbids firms from firing women because they merely *asked* for accommodations—like some time off for court appearances, desks away from doors—or because of "their actual or perceived status as domestic violence victims." This anti-discrimination protection, we believe, can encourage women in the shadows to come forward, knowing they at least won't suffer retaliatory firing.

With half the city council as cosponsors, I introduce the first-of-its-kind bill in 1998—it's soon after adopted by California, Maine, and then, finally, by NYC in January 2001. Mayor Giuliani signs it at a smiley-face bill ceremony, one of the very few that we two share in our eight-year relationship. New York State, under Governor David Paterson, enacts it as well in 2009.

Separately, Nancy Youman, my executive assistant, shares her annoyance about the double indignity of women underpaid at work yet then overcharged in the marketplace. "Every place I've had my hair cut charged women more than men," she says. "I asked the guy who cuts my hair why and he said things like 'Women are more temperamental. They want to talk to you. They just take longer.'"

In 1992, we publish *Gypped by Gender: A Study of Price Bias Against Women in the Marketplace,* which documents how women pay 25 to 30 percent more than men for the same dry cleaning and haircuts; they are even charged more by car dealers two-fifths of the time. While many men dismiss our findings, most women get it and are grateful.

As with *Women in Divorce,* our empirical report garners national attention, local headlines, and council support. Again, as public advocate with council cosponsors, I introduce a bill that bans both the posting of differential prices and the charging of them. It passes and becomes law.

Last are two health initiatives, involving reproductive rights.

When it comes to reproductive rights, New York State is a leader, legalizing abortion in 1970 three years before *Roe v. Wade*. But continuing right-to-life political pressure in the early Nineties scares off Roussel Uclaf, the French manufacturer of RU-486, a nonsurgical "abortifacient," from testing or selling it in the United States. The company doesn't want its American subsidiary to be picketed and boycotted. Yet hundreds of thousands of women in Great Britain, France, and China are safely using this chemical procedure that stops fertilized eggs from lodging in uterine walls.

As consumer commissioner, I get Mayor Dinkins's approval to organize a 30-mayor national coalition to let the firm know that officials representing millions of women want the company to allow it to be tested and then sold in the United States. Based on this effort, I encourage Bill Clinton to talk up RU-486 in his presidential campaign; he does and then, in his first month as president, issues an executive order to the Health and Human Services Department to figure out how to get the drug imported for testing. His administration persuades Roussel Uclaf to transfer its patent for mifepristone, the chemical name, to the Population Council to begin testing. In 1996, the FDA clears it as safe and finally, in 2000, it becomes available for sale under the trade name of Mifeprex. This puts reproductive choice where it ideally belongs, in the privacy of a physician's office rather than in what can be the public gauntlet of an abortion clinic.

As public advocate, I read a squib in the *Daily News* in October 1994 about the ordeal of a Brooklyn art teacher who is raped and then sits for hours at Woodhull Hospital in a flimsy examination smock in a general waiting room near handcuffed prisoners. It's astounding to allow the re-victimization of someone who has suffered such physical and psychological trauma.

We launch an investigation into how the 11 municipal hospitals treat women in these fraught circumstances. With 20 rapes a day in the city and only 5 percent of rapists ever prosecuted, the very least hospitals can do is ensure the emotional and physical well-being of rape survivors. Based on site visits and 100 interviews with hospital officials, workers, advocates, and counselors, a year later we release a report that documents how women in this situation lack separate rooms, special showers, and psychological and social welfare aides. Naming the top and worst hospitals, we create a kind of competition among facilities to see which can respond best. Two years later, we re-investigate and find that every municipal hospital now has special rape treatment and counseling protocols.

3. Poor Pay More? The "Sunlight" of Disclosure

To stressed seniors and families, nickels and dimes add up. In my first few months as consumer commissioner, one senior on a fixed income writes a long, anguished, handwritten letter about paying a nickel more for a drug he needed—*a nickel!* Another woman on a phone call starts sobbing about a fly-by-night contractor who had taken several hundred dollars for kitchen repair but then departed, leaving her stranded with a nonfunctioning kitchen, normally the center of her family life.

These and thousands of other examples reflect both an earlier consumer classic as well as my own research. In his seminal 1963 *The Poor Pay More: Consumer Practices of Low-Income Families,* Columbia professor David Caplovitz analyzed how, without any businessman waking up wanting to screw the poor, cultural and market failures produced that perverse result. *The Closed Enterprise System* in 1971 documented how anti-competitive practices worsen inequality by transferring billions of dollars from average consumers to the wealthier shareholders and managers of large companies.

A moralist could make an argument for progressive pricing as we have progressive taxation, but no one can reasonably justify *regressive* pricing where poverty compounds itself. How and why does this happen? I decide to update Caplovitz.

Our counterintuitive findings come out in a series of four major studies called *The Poor Pay More . . . For Less:* in food, banking, auto insurance, and home improvement contracting. The food problem is that big supermarket chains often shun low-income, minority communities, citing pilferage and culture. "It would be difficult for an Anglo-Saxon store like Sloan's to do business [in a Hispanic community]," says the CEO of Sloan's. "They would view our presence as impersonal."

These areas are served largely by small bodegas and convenience stories that lack healthy, fresh foods and can't compete with lower prices and bulk buying. There are an average of 17,232 people per supermarket in Harlem versus 6,580 residents per supermarket in

Manhattan's middle-income and wealthier neighborhoods. On average, economically distressed ZIP codes pay 8.8 percent more—or $350 a year—for the same 21 items as shoppers in more affluent ones, as tallied by a human calculator who, fortunately for me, is our Director of Research Glenn von Nostitz. At the release of our findings in 1993 on 161st Street in the Bronx, Congressman José Serrano complains with cheeky humor, "I don't think that I [should] have to pay and dust at the same time."

DCA uses our study to urge city development agencies to provide various tax credits to lure supermarkets back in. The Dinkins administration proposes to encourage the construction of a first supermarket in East Harlem. But by the time formal approval is required, the Giuliani administration is balking, largely because it doesn't want to do anything associated with Dinkins and also because local bodegas are complaining. Finally, a Pathmark supermarket is narrowly approved in 1995 under the leadership of Democratic city councilman Guillermo Linares and Manhattan borough president Ruth Messenger.

This pathology of poverty is also true for low-income, underbanked communities. Because of fewer branches and ATM machines and the red-lining of entire neighborhoods, the financial industry—commercial and savings banks—is forcing working and poor families into check-cashing outlets that charge $500 a year for what would otherwise cost $60 at a typical bank.* We use this data to pressure Citibank into opening more branches since there *are* depositors in East New York and the South Bronx with money to save and fees to pay. Indeed, when Citi wants to merge with Travelers in 1998, I protest with Gloria Steinem at the Travelers Building downtown to urge the Office of the Comptroller of the Currency to reject the proposed merger until Citi performs better under Community Reinvestment Act criteria.†

---

* It's the same deal with auto insurers: black and Latino drivers with the same safety records as white drivers can pay three times more if they live in minority areas.

† I propose one other idea: given that low-income communities pay more for access to their money, suffer more crime, and often endure tense relationships with the police, let's locate ATM machines within or next to police precinct buildings. Police Commissioner Bill Bratton loves it but Giuliani doesn't—and it goes nowhere . . .

Following up this financial services report, we produce an annual survey called *Ranking Banking* with state senator Franz Leichter. It gathers information about bounced check fees, minimum balance requirements, and interest paid on various accounts of some 50 banks and then ranks their consumer-friendliness. As expected, top-ranked banks—usually smaller ones lacking big-name market power—brag about it in their ads while lower-rated ones bark at us, but we get thousands of requests from interested customers to mail them our price surveys (this being pre-Internet).

Beyond these specific sectoral studies, we come up with a way to vividly convey how growing inequality is taxing us. Our study, *The New Poverty*, shows that in 1972, it took 2.8 years of work, on average, to purchase a house, and 6.9 years in 1990; college tuition, 14.2 weeks in 1972, 23.9 weeks in 1990; a Chevy sedan, 18.4 weeks in 1972, 24.5 weeks in 1990; a doctor's visit, 1.7 hours in 1972, 4.7 hours in 1992. That is, because real wages are falling for most New Yorkers, average families have to run faster even to stay in place.

Of course, with some exceptions like natural monopolies and utility rates, government doesn't set prices in a capitalist economy. But it can publicize prices and ingredients. In the spirit of Louis Brandeis's famous axiom that "sunlight is the best disinfectant"—and looking to tar and nicotine labeling on cigarettes as an example—we pursue a disclosure model that facilitates comparison shopping so that economically stressed families can get more for their money.

Too much fat and calories in fast food? Neither the FDA nor I can dictate exactly what to put in a hamburger (though no *E. coli* bacteria or salmonella!). But as the consumer commissioner, I introduce a bill in August 1991 to require fast food chains, which feed one in five Americans daily, to list their fat and caloric content for each meal. (We're years away from a national campaign against obesity.) Joining me in front of a brightly colored poster with this information is CEO Barry J. Gibbons of Burger King, the country's second-largest fast food chain, in one of his 80 NYC restaurants. That's gutsy in one sense since his most popular offering—a Whopper with cheese, fries, and a Coke—has 80 percent of a day's fat allowance as well as 1,342

---

until Bratton proposes it again 20 years later in his second tour as PC under Mayor de Blasio. He tells me in late 2015 that this time it'll happen.

calories. But he announces that he wants his brand to take the lead "in the passage of this historic law." A few years later, the city and then many cities mandate such postings for the billions of fast food meals served annually.

We also conduct periodic surveys of drug stores and gas stations to compare prices of the same drugs and grades, attracting enormous media coverage because of reader and viewer interest. An average person does *not* want to pay $400 more for a basket of drugs at the most expensive drug stores as compared to the least expensive, with spreads of 30 percent on the most popular drugs. Nor does anyone, neither Bentley nor Buick owners, want to pay 30 percent more for the same-octane gas.

My favorite price disclosure project is the Passover Pledge. There is a religious tradition, passed along for generations, that I first encounter as a boy in Elmont: kosher-for-Passover foodstuffs rise in price before the Seders. Though almost no one seems to know or even wonder why this happens, to me it smacks of price-gouging based on religious necessity, akin to electric generators spiking in price during a blackout.

In 1990, we inaugurate our annual Passover price survey: first, we print and distribute thousands of handheld cards listing the high, low, and average prices for various Seder-related foods by borough (matzo, gefilte fish, cheeses, chicken, canned fruits, etc.); second, stores that jack up prices the most are publicized in our "Hall of Shonda" (shame) press release; and third, we organize 82 Jewish groups into a "Kosher Coalition" to petition hundreds of stores to take the Passover Pledge not to increase prices during the holiday. Ninety-seven stores agree. My son calls me "Knish-ener Green."

While all this sounds like good, clean fun, in fact, for the first time in memory prices do not jump for the Seders. And Jewish families, especially large Orthodox ones on modest incomes, do not overspend by hundreds of dollars in order to observe their religion.

RUDY AND ME

Rudy's father, Harold Giuliani, teaches him how to box at just two years old to toughen him up for the world outside their insular Flatbush environs. In high school, Rudy—encouraged by his doting mother—spends hours in his room listening to operas and imagining a world of a never-ending battle between good and evil.

After attending NYU law school, in 1970 he joins the office of the U.S. Attorney in the Southern District where he meets Harold Tyler, the deputy U.S. attorney general, who's struck by Giuliani's sharp intelligence and prodigious work ethic. It's there as a 30-year-old prosecutor that he wins a fearsome reputation with a withering cross-examination of Democratic congressman Bertram Podell, charged with bribery and who, in Rudy's retelling, breaks down on the stand, then confesses. Very Perry Mason, very operatic. Except those present say that the congressman already planned to make his guilty plea and kept his composure. Nonetheless, this story enhances Giuliani's legend and reflects a lifelong habit of blending hyperbole and ferocity.

Becoming a mentor for life, Tyler plucks Giuliani from his Manhattan office and brings him to Washington. After serving as Reagan's number three at the Justice Department (and after getting an annulment claiming he didn't know that his wife was his second cousin), his new fiancée's promotion to a New York television station proves fortuitous. Senator Alfonse D'Amato has been seeking to nominate just such a candidate who could tackle New York's mushrooming drug-fueled crime wave.

It takes just three days into Giuliani's work as U.S. attorney for him to announce his initial indictment, the first in a series of high-profile cases against Mafia dons and tax evaders while slapping handcuffs on trembling brokers on the trading floor. His crusades earn him a national profile. But his style also rankles—an insatiable appetite for publicly leaking charges to reporters, pioneering use of the "perp walk," timing announcements of his office's work for the six o'clock news. When Rudy Giuliani announces in early 1989 that he's quitting his post—after an unusual standoff with Senator D'Amato, who Giuliani implies might appoint a successor who'd kill his big cases—the *New York Times* editorializes that "New Yorkers have seen enough to hope that one day he'll return to public office."

They don't have to wait long. That spring, Giuliani launches his race for mayor, losing to David Dinkins by a three-point margin. It is a bruising campaign that, like the rematch that followed four years later, is inflected by the ethnic tensions that roiled New York in the 1980s and 1990s . . . and hints at Rudy's racial edge that would bluntly emerge in 2015.

Before our elections on the same day in November 1993, Giuliani and I have only a glancing relationship. We debate once in 1992 on

CNN on the topic of white-collar crime, when he doesn't seem to appreciate my on-air criticism that he wasn't tough enough in seeking penalties on business crooks. Also, bizarrely, we reside several dozen feet from each for a few years in the late Eighties when he and his wife live on the 35th floor of 420 East 86th Street while Deni and I live on the 34th floor of the same building, though our interactions are limited to nods as we hurry by each other in the lobby.

At one level, we have certain traits in common: two publicly spirited lawyers originating from Long Island who enjoy giving as much as getting, and we respect each other's combat skills. But coming from very different places politically, we end up fighting monthly for the eight years that we're the ranking Republican and Democratic elected officials in NYC.

He proves to be a formidable adversary, displaying the smarts and drive that so impressed Tyler. Deputy Mayor Joe Lhota recalls admiringly how he would hand Mayor Giuliani pages of budget documents to read and how he'd then return rather than file them, yet would recall them with enough specificity months later to question Lhota if something seemed awry. During the 1997 State of the City address, which all leading city officials dutifully attend, he does something unusual—instead of reading from a text or a prompter, he delivers 40 minutes of remarks from memory. Our top counsel Laurel Eisner, no fan, seems stunned. "My god," she blurts out, "he could be president!"

As for Rudy and me, we get off on the wrong foot on the day of our swearings-in and, frankly, never recover. He speaks for 22 minutes about his hopes for the city to the 2,000 people packed in to City Hall Park. But nearly all the attention is grabbed by his seven-year-old son Andrew, who stands next to him the whole time mouthing the words that he learned during Rudy's rehearsals, and that is famously mocked by Chris Farley on *SNL* that week. I'm allotted and speak ten minutes by City Hall, which I fill with my aspirations as the first public advocate.

Two hours later, I take a phone call from Peter Powers, the first deputy mayor, informing me, "The mayor didn't like your remarks." Huh? Why not?

"He thought they were too mayoral."

"Well, Peter, always happy to talk to you about the mayor's editorial views but I don't work for him and thought I gave a speech about

Public Advocate, it never occurring to me it was in any way mayoral." But they truly believe that it was. In an interview for this book years later, Randy Mastro, Giuliani's top City Hall lawyer, tells me, "When we heard it, we were taken aback."*

Two months later, I release my second investigation of a municipal service, suggesting that auto maintenance and repair at the NYPD should be contracted out to car repair shops to free up an estimated $11 million for street policing. Commissioner Bratton confides that he thinks it's a good idea. The report and press release nowhere mentions the mayor's name.

About four o'clock the day of its release, I start getting calls from journalists reporting that they just got off the phone not with the mayor's press secretary, not with a NYPD person, but with *the mayor,* who attacks my "stupid idea—what happens if a terrorist is able to plant a bomb under the police vehicle while it's in their shop?" I'm amazed at his punching down on a simple, nonpartisan, reinventing government idea. We quickly find out that the FBI outsources auto repair, as does the NYC Housing Authority. QED.

These two unpleasant interactions, however, presage what's to come. As Bette Davis famously said in *All About Eve,* "Fasten your seat belts, it's gonna be a bumpy night."

A month later on March 1, my car gets off the FDR Drive onto the ramp to City Hall at about 10:20. But 15 minutes later, there's a shooting at that exact spot, which turns out to be an actual terrorist attack. A crazed Arab gunman, later admitting that "I only shot them because they were Jewish," fired rounds into a van of Hasidic students, striking 16-year-old Yeshiva student Ari Halberstam. He's rushed to nearby St. Vincent's Hospital in critical condition. I decide to go over to the hospital but en route get a call from mayoral aide Mastro telling me the mayor doesn't want me to go.

"Why not?"

"It would cause a media circus."

---

* Here are a few key sentences: "I accept your strong mandate to be a watchdog for the working families of all five boroughs who feel shut out, left out, let down and ripped off by the government they pay for. This new Public Advocate office will be a quality-of-life cop patrolling the bureaucracy beat—without fear or favor or flinching, and no matter whose toes we may have to step on." To me, that was me being me. To them, it was a threat.

"What am I, Mick Jagger? I'm going and won't disrupt anything."

I'm escorted by police to a waiting room where I try to console Devorah Halberstam, Ari's distraught mother. An hour later, we get the news that he'd been shot in the head and is in critical condition; he dies four days later. (Through this ordeal, Devorah and I subsequently become friends—and I'm able to deliver to her at the Shiva a handwritten condolence letter that I get President Clinton to write.)

In our opening months, the mayor and Speaker Peter Vallone shake hands on the city's $31.6 billion budget, but Giuliani then almost immediately calls him back. Here's what happens next, according to Vallone in his memoir, *Learning to Govern:*

> "I forgot something," [Rudy] began. "We have to de-fund the Public Advocate's office."
>
> "What are you talking about? Every agency has already taken a cut."
>
> "Well, cut Mark Green more—don't you realize he's going to run against you? This is a good time to get rid of him."

Hearing about his effort, I speak to all living former mayors—Lindsay, Beame, Dinkins, even Koch, a Rudy supporter and no fan of mine—who send him a joint letter protesting that "none of us ever used the budget to retaliate against our next-in-line city council presidents when we may have had disagreements with them." I also line up friend and super-lawyer David Boies to represent me if the mayor actually gets to the brink of illegally eliminating a charter-mandated office via the backdoor of the budget without a required public vote.

Speaker Vallone honorably rejects the proposed axing but does go along with an additional 13 percent reduction on top of a 27 percent one the prior year.

My friend John LoCicero calls out of concern. Few know City Hall politics like John since he was a close Koch advisor for his 12 years as mayor. "Are you crazy taking on Rudy like this? He's the mayor. He can *kill* you!" He calls my brother to urge him to get me to pull my throttle back, to which Steve says, affectionately, "You know Mark." I appreciate John's wise and sincere counsel but think I really have no choice when I'm in a cage match with a world-class kickboxer.

Giuliani's not done with me and my office.

*My brother Steve, my father
Irving, my mother Anne,
and me in the Catskills,
1953.*

*Varsity Tennis, Great Neck
South High School, 1963.*

*With Tama in dance contest,
Great Neck South High School,
1963. Credit: Bob Gruen.*

At the United Nations, 1973. Credit: UN/Chen

Poster *for* Who Runs Congress?, *1972.*

"Ralph Nader's Biggest Raid" *Time*

Who Runs Congress?

The President, Big Business, or You?

First time in print.
An eye-opening and urgent report!

A Bantam Book

On Sale Here

New Yorker *cartoon, 1972. Credit: Joseph Mirachi*

"If you can't trust one of Nader's Raiders, who can you trust?"

White House meeting on consumer agenda: I'm next to Esther Peterson and Ralph two seats to President Carter's left, 1978.

Caricature of me as a congressional candidate, 1980. Credit: David Levine

Campaigning for Congress with Jenya and Senator Ted Kennedy, 1980.

During Ramsey Clark for Senate campaign, 1974.

At Nuclear Freeze Rally organized by wife Deni with one million people at Central Park, June 12, 1982.

Marching for reproductive choice in Washington, D.C., 1989.

Picketing Eastern Airlines with Jenya, 1989.

At fund-raising party for Senator Hart with Warren Beatty and Terry McAuliffe, 1984. Credit: J. Ross Baughman

With Fidel Castro in Havana, 1987.

Hosting Democracy Project presidential forum with Senator Al Gore, 1988.

*With Deni,
children,
and parents
winning
Democratic
nomination for
U.S. Senate,
1986.*

*Campaigning for U.S.
Senate with Gov. Mario
Cuomo.*

*"Singing"
with
Mandy
Patinkin
and Carly
Simon at
gala fund-
raiser.*

On CNN Crossfire *set with Pat Buchanan at 1988 Republican Convention.*

With Buckley pre-air and then on set of Firing Line *with Buckley and Koch, 1988.*

In early 1999, I hear rumors that he may create a special Charter Commission to alter the rules of succession. He wants to be sure that if he defeated Hillary Clinton for the U.S. Senate seat of the retiring Daniel Patrick Moynihan in 2000, I'd serve only 60 days, not the remainder of his term, which had been the charter precedent for over a century. At a cocktail party with city officials, I spot Deputy Mayor Joe Lhota, one of Rudy's best appointees (and later the GOP mayoral nominee in 2013). "Joe, don't do it. It'll look like a vendetta, and he'll lose. Can't any of you reason with him? Personally I'd rather not have to waste the time." When Lhota murmurs something inaudible, which is the language used when Yes-Rudys are put on the spot, I reasonably suspect something's up.

A couple months later, he announces a commission of 12 hand-picked appointees, chaired by the pugnacious Mastro. While Randy knows to only talk about their good government intentions—and indeed there is a plausible general argument about who should succeed a chief executive in case of a vacancy and for how long—Rudy to his credit is unsubtle. He's quoted in the *New York Times Magazine* saying "This is politics. That's what I do . . . I can't imagine there is anyone in the city that doesn't know my opinion of Mark Green."

I start organizing a large citywide coalition of civic, labor, and elected leaders to denounce, in my words, his "power grab to change the rules in the middle of the game because of political vengeance." Again, all the former mayors criticize him. Editorial opinion is nearly unanimously hostile. I particularly enjoy the *Jewish Press,* an orthodox, right-wing paper that's always supported Rudy: "While we may share his disdain for Mr. Green's politics," concludes the paper's editorial, "we Jews have an important stake in a government of laws rather than personalities. We are simply horrified that the law of the land might be altered . . . to accommodate one powerful individual's disdain for another."

Since the integrity of my office is at risk and his personalization of the contest is on the record, I do not hold back in my 1999 testimony before his commission at a packed cheering and jeering crowd of 300 in a Queens Borough Hall basement:

> I'd like to thank Mayor Giuliani and Chair Mastro for launching an unprincipled and unprecedented attack on [this office] because it's given me an opportunity to explain (a) why no prior Charter

Commission this century saw a problem with the current system of mayoral succession and (b) why the Mayor is using you as a Show Trial to satisfy a political vendetta . . . Either withdraw your proposal [or] suffer an historic defeat. If you don't like these choices, don't blame me. Blame a mayor who governs by enemies-list and who's using you as political pawns.

I don't stop there, going on to school a politician who prefers only to dish it out:

The Mayor should heed the words of Fiorello LaGuardia, one of my predecessors as President of the Board of Aldermen: "If they disagree with me, I understand it. If they agree with me, I appreciate it. If they abuse me, I take it. And I still believe in a democracy."

They alter their proposal under public pressure so that any approved succession changes would only be for after the next election, not for 2000. But like trying to rub mustard out of your clothing, it's too late. Since my narrative that this is more about Rudy's ruthlessness than the order of succession, we win the November vote 76 percent to 24 percent. "The controversy Rudy's fixation engendered," writes Peter Vallone in his memoirs, "was a political bonanza for Mark Green in his campaign for mayor."

This prosecutor-mayor, however, cannot easily abandon a menacing MO that's gotten him to the mayoralty and who knows where else. True, Giuliani says after his reelection that he wants to establish "a tone of civility throughout the city" and will later write in his bestselling book *Leadership* that he lived by his father's credo: "Never pick on someone smaller than yourself, never be a bully." Of course, to me, his guiding ethic is more of reverse Lincoln: "with malice for all and charity to none." His terrorizing persona—"better to be feared than loved," wrote Machiavelli in *The Prince*—helps keep both enemies and friends off-balance and in line. Or as one holdover Dinkins appointee, Marilyn Gelber, later reports, "There were constant loyalty tests [like] will you shoot your brother . . . People were marked for destruction for disloyal jokes."

The number of incidents over his eight years in office when Giuliani is a bully in his pulpit could fill a separate book. Here are just three:

In order to tamp down a damaging story about his Youth Services commissioner near the start of his term, Giuliani leaks shocking allegations that *Dinkins's* Youth Services head, Richard Murphy, had signed off on millions in contracts to Dinkins's political supporters and that someone had destroyed hard drives to cover it up. It works—the media run after this newer shiny object instead of Rudy's. Although Giuliani's own Department of Investigations later exonerates Murphy, the damage is done. In an interview shortly before his death in 2013, Murphy says, "I was soiled merchandise—the taint just lingers."

A 49-year-old chauffeur and amateur photographer, James Schillaci, videotapes police setting a speed trap on Fordham Road in front of the Bronx Zoo by triggering a quick light change in order to ticket otherwise innocent drivers. When his complaints to the NYPD go nowhere, my office shows the videotape to the *Daily News*, which plasters it on its August 26, 1997, front page with the headline "GOT-CHA!" Then, that same day, Schillaci is arrested and handcuffed at his home for a 13-year-old outstanding traffic warrant (which is dismissed as dated); the NYPD releases his rap sheet of arrests going back 14 years, saying he had been convicted of sodomy, which is false; and the mayor dismisses criticism of his department's handling of this matter as "police bashing," adding, "Mr. Schillaci was posing as an altruistic whistle-blower [but] maybe he's dishonest enough to lie about police officers."

According to a *New York Times* account, "Mr. Schillaci suffered an emotional breakdown, was briefly hospitalized and later received a $290,000 legal settlement from the City." Remember, he is not some political opponent of Giuliani's but merely a private citizen reporting abuse. "This isn't police brutality," writes columnist Jim Dwyer of the *Daily News*, "it is mayoral brutality."

Then there's Mark Berkowitz, the seven-year-old son of an observant Jew in my office, who wonders why there isn't kosher food at Shea and Yankee stadiums when he goes to ball games. He asks his mom, Adena, to get me to look into it. Can't say no to that.

I organize a group of Rabbis and Jewish groups in 1997 and we eventually persuade both teams to open small Glatt Kosher stands there for the 1998 season. We plan an announcement at Shea Stadium at noon on May 19 before a Mets-Cincinnati double-header. On radio at 10 a.m., I proudly note that this will be happening later that day . . .

but at 11 a.m., I'm called by the office of Mets owner Fred Wilpon to say that the event is being called off—seems that the mayor's office is not happy about it. I leave this message for Wilpon, who is a good guy and no doubt unhappy at his predicament: "Fred, you may want to cancel but I'm still showing up at noon with the excited children, their parents, their Rabbis, and the media to laud the Mets and cut a ribbon or be escorted out in front of the media. Up to you. Be there in 40 minutes."

It works perfectly. We walk in without incident as I applaud the Mets' community spirit—and the Yankees' two weeks later—because now "Jewish children can nosh and cheer at the same time." Rudy's choice of political payback over children goes unmentioned since I strive to maintain the "tone of civility" that the mayor is urging for others.

But Giuliani apparently does not forget setbacks. And at a vulnerable time in my 2001 mayoral campaign, he seeks timely revenge, as we shall see.

4. Police and Race

Predating the Ferguson and Baltimore riots of 2015, police relations with minority communities have often been tense, sometime explosive. Harlem, 1935. Detroit, 1943. Watts, 1965. Newark and Detroit, 1967. This tension is especially palpable during Giuliani's tenure.

Accelerating a reduction in crime that began under predecessor David Dinkins, Mayor Giuliani and Commissioner Bratton preside over record declines in their first two years in office. While no one seems to know exactly why crime falls so precipitously around the country, their policies of "broken windows" and CompStat in NYC—i.e., aggressively policing quality-of-life violations and targeting crime increases by computer mapping—are widely given credit.

But at the same time, my Public Advocate office hears numerous complaints about police mistreatment of minority youth, who appear to be stopped, frisked, and insulted in large numbers. Is that the inevitable price we pay to reduce crime?

Since I have never personally been pulled over for "driving while Jewish," I sit down in 1995 with several minority Public Advocate staff to hear their experiences. Michael Gaspard, Philip Cooke, and Cleon Jones, reflecting the common experience of their friends, tell me how routine and infuriating these interactions are. I then also visit the local precinct commander whenever I hold a monthly community town hall to better familiarize myself with cop-community issues.

Beginning an investigation of the police disciplinary process in January 1997, we request internal records (with officer names blacked out) to determine whether documented Civilian Complaint Review Board (CCRB) cases of police abuse lead to NYPD sanctions, from lost vacation days to severance. But Commissioner Howard Safir refuses to cooperate, despite what I think is our obvious authority under the City Charter. I file suit in the New York State Supreme Court, where I'm represented by civil rights lawyer Richard Emery, who had brought the historic lawsuit that led the U.S. Supreme Court to abolish the Board of Estimate in 1988 and would himself become head of the CCRB under Mayor Bill de Blasio 20 years later.

During this year, the 70th Precinct torture of Abner Louima attracts more public attention to the issue of police abuse. I also formally petition Attorney General Janet Reno in August to investigate whether the NYPD engages in a "pattern and practice" of misconduct under federal civil rights law to justify the appointment of an independent monitor over the department; shortly thereafter, U.S. Attorney for the Eastern District Loretta Lynch launches an investigation.*

In October, we win a convincing victory in *Green* v. *Safir*. According to State Supreme Court judge Edward Lehner, the intent of the Charter Commission was to make the Public Advocate a "watchdog" over city government and a counterweight to the powers of the mayor. The vision of the office was an independent public official to monitor the operations of city agencies with the view to publicizing any inadequacies, inefficiencies, mismanagement, and misfeasance, with the end goal of pointing the way to right the wrongs of government.

Lehner's opinion, upheld 4–0 on appeal, is the most important judicial decision in the history of the Public Advocate office, clearly articulating our authority and responsibility as well as allowing our probe to go forward. Given this context and Giuliani's hostility, we

---

* At the end of successor Michael Bloomberg's tenure, such a federal monitor is imposed on the NYPD by Attorney General Eric Holder, which his successor, the same Loretta Lynch, is now monitoring.

understand that we have to do our investigation in the most thorough way possible; I raise $300,000 in supplemental funds from foundations and assign a dream team of talent to oversee the effort, led by experts David Eichenthal and Richard Aborn.

Analyzing 760 substantiated cases of misconduct involving 1,084 officers between 1998 and 2000, our massive Public Advocate report—*Disciplining Police: Solving the Problem of Police Misconduct*—finds that only 5 percent of all CCRB complaints result in a "substantiated complaint" being sent to the NYPD for further action; that only 30 percent of this 5 percent lead to charges filed against the officers. That is, less than 2 percent of all civilian complaints lead to any disciplinary action. Here's one typical example from our report:

> The Victim was told by the police officer to stop holding the back of a truck as he was riding his bike. The Victim complied but says the officer later intentionally opened his car door in the bike's path. When the victim requested the officer's badge number, the officer allegedly slammed him into the window of a restaurant, handcuffed him, punched him and made racial and other remarks such as "nigger" and "your mother is a 50 cent bitch." Officer pled guilty, accepted five lost vacation days, and charges were then dismissed and did not become part of his record.

Our conclusion:

> This is a systemic failure that neither punishes nor deters substantiated cases of police [abuse] . . . Widespread resentment in minority communities against police misconduct imposes huge costs on our City. Consider the anger felt and multiplied when a public official behind a badge racially slurs, punches or hospitalizes a victim and is then "punished" by a reprimand in a file or two lost vacation days, before the next promotion . . . [But] since effective policing needs residents to report crimes and provide evidence, the NYPD must now adopt reforms to rebuild the trust between cops and communities of color as a crime-fighting measure.

We propose 24 changes to repair this broken system, especially increasing the severity and likelihood of individual sanctions after a complaint is substantiated.

Guiliani has two responses. First he calls me "pro-crime," which is an odd accusation against someone who's raising his two children in this city; second, he otherwise appears to blithely ignore our effort, the first entirely independent, outside investigation of the police disciplinary process in the context of racial grievances. But the *New York Times* editorially backs us up: "Mark Green's interim report gives disturbing evidence of how lax New York City's Police Department has been in past years on following through on citizen complaints."

While we cannot determine what, if anything, the mayor and commissioner specifically do in response, our final report in my last month in office documents some good news: the percentage of substantiated CCRB cases investigated by the NYPD rises from 5 percent to over 20 percent, and the percentage of those cases that lead to some punishment jumps from 30 percent to 70 percent. Now not 2 percent but 15+ percent of civilian complaints lead to some kind of punishment. It appears that City Hall has without acknowledgment reacted positively, fulfilling Judge Lehner's description of the Public Advocate as being a "watchdog over City Hall . . . right[ing] the wrongs of government."

During this lengthy process, there are other horrible racial incidents that roil the city and dominate the news. After an unarmed Amadou Diallo, a 22-year-old immigrant from Guinea, is shot 19 times on his Bronx doorstep by four police officers in a special Street Crimes Unit in March 1999, there are mass protests and criminal indictments but no convictions.

This time I don't wait years for data. I suggest on a Friday in late March that Safir resign because "tripling a street crime unit with officers of less experience pursuing fewer criminals, yet with the same unspoken quotas, foolishly created a powder keg waiting for a spark . . . There's nothing more pro-police than weeding out bad cops who tarnish the reputation of the vast majority of the police force." He should accept responsibility for failed police-community relations, in my view, and allow the mayor to rebuild a more accountable NYPD.

While Rudy is angry at my public slap, Safir doesn't help his cause when he tries to bow out of important city council testimony on this topic that coming Monday because of his schedule . . . and then is spotted on the red carpet on Sunday at the Oscars in California! (He takes a red-eye to get to the testimony.) I suspect that my call for him to be fired gave him immediate job security but did change his travel plans.

When Safir finally leaves two years later and is replaced by Giuliani's former driver and bodyguard (and future felon) Bernard Kerik, I ask for departmental memos on why there has been no internal discipline even though the officers who shot Diallo were all forced to surrender their firearms. Our surmise is that Giuliani had simply tanked the case because of Giuliani's early, prejudicial comments that the officers involved had done nothing wrong. When Kerik refuses, I remind him of the *Green* v. *Safir* precedent and that we'll again go to court unless he turns over the requested material by five o'clock on May 8, 2000. He does, with a few hours to spare, and confirms our suspicion that, in the view of Arnie Kriss, a former NYPD ranking official and advisor on our CCRB study, "it was a dump job. The cops should have been disciplined with the standard of proof not the criminal one of 'beyond a reasonable doubt' but rather the 'preponderance of evidence.'"

Then as final evidence of why Giuliani is so widely disliked by the African American community, exactly a year later an innocent, unarmed black vendor, 26-year-old Patrick Dorismond, is shot and killed on West 28th Street by police who mistake him for a drug dealer. The next day, the mayor releases Dorismond's juvenile records and contends that "he wasn't an altar boy." Other than the fact that he literally *was* an altar boy (at Giuliani's own Catholic boys' school), this breach of confidentiality rules strikes me as disgraceful—and unlawful. But since the files are now public and no apology can be expected, I sue the mayor—supported by most of the black political leadership of the city, led by the "dean" of the congressional delegation, Charles Rangel—under a never-before-used provision of the City Charter established in 1873, Section 1109. It allows a citywide official to seek a "summary judicial inquiry" to investigate whether a mayor has violated or neglected his duty. Or according to my affidavit to the court: "No Mayor can put himself above the law by unilaterally releasing confidential information to vilify a victim."

Judge Louise Gruner Gans rules in our favor in *Green* v. *Giuliani* on November 21, 2000, ordering that an inquiry go forward within no later than 21 days to answer my questions of how the mayor obtained the sealed records and whether his release was illegal. Giuliani appeals her ruling, but our terms expire before the inquiry can be conducted. Her decision, however, still stands as precedent against mayoral abuse. It is also yet another in a series of judicial rebukes—involving protests on the steps of City Hall, legality of the Independent Budget Office, retaliation against the Brooklyn Museum of Art, the attempted privatization of the city's public access channel for Rupert Murdoch—all driven by the antipathies of this lawyer-mayor rather than by the law.

The fires next time between cops and communities of color are not played out in reports and courts but, in an era of cell phones and body cameras 15 years later, seen around the world.

5. The Mob Tax

In June 1990 Forrest Smith visits me in my commissioner's office at 80 Lafayette Street. He's in his mid-40s, silver-haired, intense, with a stocky, athletic physique—indeed, he once held the world speed record for power watercraft. And a big pair of brass balls, it turns out.

"Commissioner, I'm a small businessman who runs several Mc-Donald's franchises in the city. I've long thought that carters were overcharging me, so I measured my refuse before they picked it up and now know that they overestimate my waste by a third. But when I told them that I would complain unless they lowered their charges, one said, 'If you do, we'll kill you.' Can you help?"

The DCA licenses and sets the rates of commercial garbage haulers because of the industry's long history of being dominated by organized crime. During my sit-downs with predecessors, the venerable Commissioner-of-Everything Elinor Guggenheimer tells me at a Regency Hotel breakfast, "Of course, the one industry you really can't do much about is carting"—which of course piques my interest.

Now comes Forrest Smith. As he's speaking, I'm thinking two things: it's very, very unlikely that the mob would kill a public grunt like me and, in any event, I've taken an oath of office to enforce the law without fear or favor. "Sure," I say to his request for help, beginning a beautiful relationship with this hardscrabble guy—who grew up in Ithaca and never went to college—that'd last 12 years until his death in 2003, when I'd deliver the eulogy.

That meeting spurs an agency task force, led by Deputy Commissioner Rich Schrader, to figure out how to reduce what I call the "$500 million mob tax." Paid by our 250,000 New York City small businesses and private organizations, that number is based on the 40 to 100 percent price differentials between what carters charge in the city as compared to other metropolitan areas: a maximum $14.70 per cubic yard here versus $9 in LA, $5.30 in Boston, $5 in Chicago. Why is New York City so high? Because once a carter has a route, no one tries to underbid it for fear of retaliation by organized crime. It's all run by a 72-year-old James Failla, a former boss in the Gambino crime family, nicknamed Jimmy Brown for his brown suits. He hobbles on two canes into weekly meetings at the downtown offices of the Association of Trade Waste Removers, where he carves up and enforces routes for scores of carters . . . for 30 years! DCA has been, in effect, a "useful idiot" providing legal cover by going along with the exorbitant rates.

We then spend months lowering the rates, imposing significant fines and withdrawing licenses from carters that fail to provide us with adequate information on routes and fees or are convicted of various crimes. The Dinkins administration introduces my bill in the city council to establish "Competition Zones" within which the city would competitively bid out routes and impose an innovative law enforcement technique called IPSIGs—"independent private sector inspector generals"—to police and report back everything a carter does. Most significantly, I meet several times with William Ruckelshaus, the chairman of Browning-Ferris Industries—and the former EPA commissioner and Nixon attorney general of "Saturday Night Massacre" fame—to convince him to enter the NYC market and provide some competition. Working with law enforcement, we promise protection, which essentially works, except for that time that a German shepherd's head is found on the Westchester lawn of a BFI executive with this note in the dog's mouth: "Welcome to New York." Also, there is another time when someone calls my apartment and tells my daughter Jenya that they are going to kill me. (They don't.)

Initially, the results of our anti-mob campaign are mixed. Ruckelshaus and BFI do help bring down rates where the firm operates by 40 percent. Later, overlapping with our efforts and bolstering them, Manhattan DA Robert Morgenthau indicts 44 individuals, companies, and trade groups on racketeering charges. But our lowered maximum rate is thrown out in court on technical grounds. Interrupting everything is the election of Giuliani as mayor and me as public advocate. When Rudy and I have a courtesy meeting in early December 1993 before our terms begin, we swap campaign stories, but I also emphasize how we can work together on at least one issue: as the ranking Republican and Democrat in the city, a famous mob-busting U.S. attorney and the citywide official with experience regulating carting firms, we should collaborate on breaking up this mob cartel. He agrees, proudly talking up his big cases and the cost of such economic terrorism.

For several months in 1995, City Hall chief of staff Mastro, Brooklyn city councilman Ken Fisher, and I negotiate a joint bill that would restructure the industry. On behalf of the mayor, Mastro prefers a new agency tightly auditing and overseeing every aspect of the entire industry rather than our Competition Zones/IPSIG approach. We hammer out one bill that combines both ideas, leaning toward a new agency because, well, he's the mayor and his could be the better approach.

We plan a big announcement on November 30 at City Hall. But that morning I'm surprised to read a front-page *New York Times* article by its organized crime reporter, Selwyn Raab, laying out how Mayor "Eliot Ness" would be tackling mob carters. So much for team play. I make a few mental notes: that it's "good to be king," that Mastro is one shrewd operator, and that this mayor is indeed especially credible on this issue. But mostly, I feel the satisfaction of getting something big done governmentally. The tableau that day—eight of us speaking and arrayed around the mayor, including DA Morgenthau and the FBI Organized Crime Task Force—impressively conveys our united front.

The city council then passes the "Giuliani-Green" bill and the mayor signs it, creating a new Trade Waste Commission that takes jurisdiction away from DCA and more strictly oversees the industry. Rates soon fall 50 percent as city businesses save a half-billion dollars annually. Forrest Smith invites my family to join his family power-boating around Cayuga's waters—not at world-record speeds—and pronounces himself "proud as hell." Me too, actually.

6. A Democracy Czar

"All of the ills of democracy can be cured," said Governor Al Smith, "by more democracy." I always liked his tautology until discovering that, by the mid-Nineties, the state with the forty-seventh worst voter turnout was Smith's own New York.

Now, "democracy" is in my bones, both as a big D and small d Democrat; as author of a book on how the legislature of the world's greatest democracy isn't very democratic; and as an admirer of Martin Luther King Jr.'s seminal speech at the Washington Monument in 1957 beseeching Congress, "Give us the ballot! Give us the ballot!" Which it did in the historic 1965 Voting Rights Act.*

In my Public Advocate campaign, I said that I wanted to be a "Democracy Czar" "plugging people into the socket of government." How to do that?

One opportunity is to fix NYC's pioneering 1989 campaign finance law to make it *"more* perfect." While it usefully provides matching public funds of 1:1 for the first $1,000 contributed from a city resident, that does little to effectively counter the still-huge contributions from individual donors and special interests to candidates who choose not to opt in. In my 1997 reelection-night victory speech, I announce that the top goal of my second term will be to change the law to reduce by half the maximum contribution ($8,500 to $4,500), prohibit matching funds to candidates who accept corporate contributions (banned federally since 1907), and raise the match to 4:1 for gifts under $250 to motivate more people to donate because of their increased leverage.

The bill proves to be an easy lift. I repeatedly cite my earlier Democracy Project study showing that public financing is *cheaper* than the existing corporate financing of elections due to fewer expensive loopholes, subsidies, bailouts, and preferences. No doubt members also realize that the proposed changes will facilitate their fund-raising toward the spending cap. Most significantly, I convince Speaker Peter Vallone, who controls the city council, to put his name first on our bill. Giuliani, however, vetoes it in September on spending grounds.

---

* Approaching the fortieth anniversary of President Johnson signing that landmark law, Rev. Jesse Jackson asks me to join him, Rep. John Lewis, a score of other leaders, and thousands of activists on August 6, 2005, to again march over the Edmund Pettus Bridge to pressure Bush 43 into renewing the law. My assignment is to contact and bring any Cheney, Goodman, and Schwerner family members and then speak on their behalf at the march. Which I do on a sweltering, moving day in Selma. Bush later signs the extension.

With me as a very pleased presiding officer wielding the council gavel a month later, we easily override him 44–4.

By the next decade, the percentage of funds coming from small donors rises from 20 to 40 percent in NYC, while it stays the same at only 15 percent statewide. With spending caps, bigger matches, and term limits, far more minorities and working people begin running and winning office in the city. The *New York Times* now frequently refers to it as "the best municipal campaign finance law in the country."

Voter registration, however, is still proving to be an extra hurdle for many people. Sociologists Richard Cloward and Francis Fox Piven develop a model of "agency-based registration." Instead of hoping that busy people will each individually figure out how to register at their Board of Elections, the husband-wife team of Cloward and Piven believe it far better to register people already interacting with government when, for example, they're obtaining driver's licenses, food stamps, or welfare checks. It's included in the National Voter Registration Act for federal agencies that President Clinton signs in 1993, gaining the catchy moniker, "Motor Voter." Two years later, New York State follows suit.

But the Republican mayor doesn't appear to be making it a priority to enfranchise such (likely Democratic) citizens when they visit municipal agencies dispensing federal and state benefits. So in 1995, we conduct an undercover investigation showing that agencies are complying only about 50 percent of the time with the requirement that voter registration forms and assistance be affirmatively offered. Properly embarrassed, the fingered agencies promise to retrain their workers and do better.

This failure and a city turnout rate in 1996 that's seven points lower than the national average (42 percent to 49 percent) leads me to launch the "Shop & Vote" campaign in 1997 because "registering to vote should be as easy as shopping for bread or a book." Our public-private coalition—including the Board of Elections, Food Industry Alliance, UFCW, 21 supermarkets, and Barnes & Noble—place forms in attractive kiosks in 600 supermarkets and bookstores. Also, I collaborate with Councilman Gifford Miller to enact a Voter Assistance Commission that is supposed to propose structural reforms to boost registration and voting. To help somewhat even the playing field against wealthier opponents, it requires the mailing of a brochure to every voter where each candidate summarizes her/his story and the videotaping of a voter appeal available on the city's cable TV channel (and later e-mail lists).

Unfortunately, all these worthy, labor-intensive efforts do little to boost registration and voting. By the time that I run for a third term as public advocate in 2009 (after sitting out eight years), a pathetic 12 percent of Democratic voters turn out to choose nominees who are effectively the winners in a 5–1 Democratic city.

To restore our democracy—so that, per a century-plus ago, an 80 percent turnout chooses public officials, not 12 percent—means junking the current system that elevates money over voters. Chapter 8 summarizes such a Democracy Agenda, the twin cornerstones being universal voter enrollment and overturning the pernicious 2010 Supreme Court decision in *Citizens United*.

Finally, a more responsive bureaucracy is another way to restore faith in our democratic public sector. In 2001, I see that the city of Baltimore has a 311 system allowing residents to call one dedicated number to be connected to complaint handlers and ombudsmen to cut red tape and provide essential information or services. I propose and run on it in my 2001 mayoral campaign. A few months later, Mayor Bloomberg, a bottom-line businessman and efficiency maven, does implement it with much fanfare. At a Citizen's Budget Commission dinner the next June at the majestic Cipriani downtown, he spots me in the large audience and thoughtfully says, "I want to thank Mark for giving me the idea for 311." I happen to be sitting at the same table as Peter Powers, Mayor Giuliani's former deputy mayor and the person who chided my "too mayoral" swearing-in remarks. "Peter, can you imagine Rudy crediting someone else for one of his successes?" We smile together at the improbability.

From 2003 to 2015, 200 million calls—about 15 million a year—are made to the 311 "socket of government."

FOUR

WHAT IT'S LIKE—
NEW YORK POLITICS

There's definitely a very slim chance we'll survive.

—Bill Murray facing the Stay Puft
Marshmallow Man in *Ghostbusters*

The politics in New York are no different than the politics in Massachusetts except that in New York they lie more.

—Robert F. Kennedy, 1964

POLITICALLY I'M IN WASHINGTON, D.C., FOR MOST OF the Seventies, but culturally I'm a New "Yawker." I'd long assumed that someday the sirens of the city would woo me back for the reasons best understood by filmmaker Ric Burns, who said in his epic eight-part documentary *New York* that this place is "a continuing experiment to see if all the peoples of the world can live together in one small space."

For me politics starts pre-birth in 1940 when my father runs for the state senate as a Republican on the Lower East Side, a factoid lodged in some synapse of mine waiting to be awakened. Three-plus decades later, I fall hard for Congress after the Intern Letter, Nader Congress Project, *Who Runs Congress?*, and working the Hill on consumer justice issues. Over time I begin thinking, *Why can't I be an advocate* inside *the system?*

In 1974 I get a call from close friend Victor Navasky—author, former *New York Times* magazine editor, and later editor and publisher of *The Nation* magazine for 20 years. It sets in motion a half-year stint in New York City working for Ramsey Clark, running for the U.S. Senate, and eventually a permanent move from D.C. to NYC—four hours but really four planets away in terms of the political zeitgeist. Some allies think it's foolish, almost unsavory, to exit the public interest for self-interested realpolitik. But just as it's said that war is politics by other means, for me it's just one side of the same progressive coin.

That begins my participation in three campaigns that, together, end up shaping state politics for decades.

A. 1976–2000: WELCOME TO NEW YORK

Ramsey Clark: The West Village Texan

William Ramsey Clark grows up the son of a well-connected Texas politician who himself rises to become United States attorney general and a Supreme Court justice. Ramsey is quiet, studious, hoping to become a historian and teacher. But he also possesses a powerful impulse against injustice, especially racial injustice. After serving in private practice for a decade, he joins the Kennedy Justice Department in 1961 and plays an instrumental role in the 1965 March on Selma and the Voting Rights Act, then rises to deputy attorney general.

Only 39, Clark becomes attorney general when a cunning LBJ figures out that this choice would likely compel his father, Tom Clark, to resign his Supreme Court seat to avoid the appearance of a conflict of interest whenever the Department of Justice defends the United States in the Supreme Court. By this one maneuver, President Johnson successfully sends the first African American ever to the high court—civil rights icon Thurgood Marshall—and the youngest attorney general ever to the third floor of the DoJ building on Pennsylvania Avenue.

Clark soon also becomes one of most famous AGs when Richard Nixon, at his 1968 Republican Convention and throughout that fall, regularly denounces the liberal AG. "If we are going to restore order and respect for law in this country, there is one place we are going to begin," declares the former vice president to inevitable GOP cheers. "We are going to have a new Attorney General of the United States of America!"

Nixon wins . . . and Clark in 1969 moves to NYC to practice law. There being few famous, liberal, former AGs in the city at the time, a little-known but rising local star is impressed by a kindred political intellectual whom he barely knows. Queens lawyer Mario Cuomo visits Clark at his West Village apartment in 1970 with an out-of-the-box idea: run in 1974 against three-term Republican incumbent Jacob Javits. Clark is intrigued but wonders whether his Texas twang and leftish politics can work in this ethnic melting pot. He decides to try.

This implausible candidate then improbably asks Navasky—a person of enormous intellect, integrity, and mirth who's the opposite of a political pro—to be his campaign manager. Having met while he was researching his best-selling book, *Kennedy Justice,* he in turn recruits me to join the campaign as the Policy Guy. Here's my chance to meld outsider idealism with insider authority—Ralph Nader and Philip Hart. The answer is *yes.* (I too admire Ramsey's Lincolnian bearing, am ready for a break from the one-crop political capital, and think two things: this is one way to learn about New York politics, and maybe I'll meet a great New York woman. Three years later, Ramsey campaign worker Deni Frand's answer is also *Yes!*)

The opponent is Lee Alexander, a handsome, ho-hum mayor of Syracuse (who will go to jail in 1988 for tax evasion and racketeering). But a more worrisome potential rival is former one-term congressman and Eleanor Roosevelt protégé Al Lowenstein. Every spring the frantic, brilliant Lowenstein looks around for a seat to run for and, in 1974, he too thinks that Javits, especially after Watergate, might be vulnerable. I'm confident that he won't run and thereby split the downstate liberal base, which would allow the more conservative Alexander to win with a plurality.

Lowenstein goes to the State Democratic Convention and is put on the ballot, but only an hour before the deadline to withdraw, he flinches and chooses instead to run for a Long Island house seat (which he ends up losing).

While Ramsey is now a well-known front-runner for the nomination, as an actual candidate, he turns out to be somewhere between exotic and ingenious.

First, he befriends whistle-blower Frank Serpico, who stays over at Ramsey's the night before he famously testifies against corrupt cops at the Knapp Commission hearings. Serpico slips into and then out of the back door of the residential building on West 12th Street and keeps several guns with him since, having been shot in an earlier police raid and hated as a turncoat by other cops, he fears for his life. The candidate decides to ask him and ex-con Herbert X. Blyden (a prison-educated civil rights advocate and chief spokesman for Attica inmates during the 1971 riots) to put his name in nomination at the Democratic State Convention to make a symbolic point about political inclusion.

All that's unusual. What's ingenious is Ramsey's idea of limiting contributions to a maximum of only $100, not the $1,000 limit permitted in federal law. He's warned that this tactic will deny him the several million dollars needed for a serious candidacy. But he argues that it reflects his sincere embrace of campaign finance reform against the big-money incumbent and, ideally, will also inspire more small gifts to make up any shortfall. In our version of Lincoln's Cabinet (the nays are 11, the yeas are 1, the yeas have it), the $100 limit becomes the thematic spine of Clark-for-Senate.

Though this is well before Internet fund-raising that can raise millions when sticky messages go viral, indeed the $100 limit does convince 35,000 people to contribute a total of $800,000, impressive numbers at that time given the self-imposed ceiling. It clarifies that the fall contest, in our theory of the case, will be a breath of fresh air in the year of Watergate against "the Senator from Big Business."

After Ramsey beats Alexander by 20 points, I see that Javits has accepted $15,000 from Governor Nelson Rockefeller, which taken alone is not strange, given Rocky's wealth and party. But it's not hard to persuade Ramsey to demand that Javits return the money since the senator will shortly vote on Rockefeller's nomination to be President Ford's VP following Nixon's resignation. Just as a judge cannot accept money from a plaintiff, we argue, a senator judging such a nomination shouldn't accept money from an interested nominee either. The demand annoys Javits, buoys Clark, and scores points when Javits refuses to admit error and potentially insult Rockefeller.

This race deepens my nonexistent campaign experience. During the general election, I meet Ramsey with a traveling aide at LaGuardia arriving from upstate. In the van to the city, we review the draft of his policy paper on a Palestinian state. After I note that he essentially supports one, he says, "Well, no, Mark, I do not explicitly call for that."

"But, Ramsey, you do in the draft," I reply.

Then after a minute of the candidate and his policy director bickering over what he believes, Ramsey glares at me and introduces his "traveling companion." "Oh, Mark, have you met Steve Weisman of the *New York Times,* who's covering me today?" *Arrrgh.* Did you know that the first three letters of the word "assume" is "ass"?

In a three-way general election—with a Conservative Party candidate also on the ballot—the incumbent wins 45 to 37 percent. Respectable. I return to Washington and Nader.

IN 1976, incumbent senator James Buckley, brother of Bill, is up for reelection in New York. He snuck into the seat on the conservative line with only 39 percent in a three-way race against two liberals in 1970. Could Clark build on his political success in 1974 and run again? Or was Alice Roosevelt Longworth right that "a soufflé can't rise twice"?

The process begins mid-August 1975 when, on the shuttle from D.C. to NYC, Ramsey pops the question: "I'll be running next year—would you be my campaign manager?"

I'm surprised. "But don't you want to win?" I sputter. "Don't you want an ideologically acceptable Clifton White [a Republican pro associated with Goldwater and Reagan]?"

Ramsey gets that earnest look when he's saying something that permits no dissent. "No, that's just what I don't want. I want you."

All right. All right. All right.

At that time, Ramsey is leading in polls after his 1974 prominence. But possible heavyweight Democratic opponents include UN Ambassador Daniel Patrick Moynihan, Representative Bella Abzug, and former city council president Paul O'Dwyer.

On October 19, Moynihan takes himself out of contention on *Face the Nation,* saying that it would be "dishonorable" to leave his position as UN ambassador to run for any office and that if he did "people should vote against me." Well, I think, that takes care of that.

Bella and Paul, however, keep coming. Abzug of course is a bona fide force of nature, a three-term anti-war congresswoman who was born with a megaphone for a larynx and now offers a vibrant rationale to a core constituency, viz., "Isn't it time for more women in the Senate?" Paul is sort of an Irish Ramsey, most famous for running guns to the IRA in the 1940s. Nor does it hurt that, from the head up, he's a reincarnation of labor titan John L. Lewis.

It's March 15, announcement day. Ramsey agrees to do it in Manhattan and two upstate cities but not three "because I won't miss the Brooklyn Law School course I teach at four that afternoon just to hit a third upstate city. The only reason you say it four times in four places is to get on TV and after a while people don't think you're for real."

His comment implies a problem with his candidacy throughout: he's so consistently high-minded as to be easy to love but hard for political professionals to take seriously. Along with Ken Lerer—our young but preternaturally astute number two*—we spend endless hours in Ramsey's spacious, book-laden apartment on West 12th Street trying to get him to do candidate stuff. Like making money calls to big shots who could help bundle small checks (again we have a $100 limit). Like making political calls to seek support from admirers including Ethel Kennedy, Mayor Bob Wagner, the Beach Boys. But it turns out that Ramsey is burdened by modesty and doesn't like pressuring or even asking people for help. Instead, he continues to spend much time on his pro bono causes, for example, asking Ethel to be on the board of his anti-handgun group Disarm rather than to endorse him.

Then Moynihan and Abzug jump in the race.

Moynihan's convincing declination of October creates barely a flicker of embarrassment once the ambassador starts to run. But he has trouble morphing from sociologist, professor, and appointee to candidate. On June 7, Frank Lynn of the *Times* writes a story headlined "Moynihan Backing Off on Senate Bid." On June 11, Mickey Carroll of the *Times* runs a story headlined "Moynihan Enters U.S. Senate Race." On June 17, Moynihan campaign manager Sandy

---

* Lerer will go on to become one of my closest friends and among the leading digital investors in the modern era, co-founding the *Huffington Post* with Arianna Huffington and *BuzzFeed* with Jonah Peretti.

Frucher privately moans to Lerer, "My job is to keep Pat from saying stupid things," such as when he lectures several TV reporters and their crews at his announcement to stop blocking the views of newspaper correspondents "because there are some journalists here." Then he misses the must-attend Godfrey Sperling/*Christian Science Monitor* breakfast with reporters, explaining that he had been "dazed" for a couple of days. In July, Frucher et al. slow down Moynihan's pace and schedule him to deliver a few well-received policy addresses—his wheelhouse—which successfully stabilize his candidacy.

Abzug has a different quandary. Should she give up a secure House seat that's her base or try to make history in the U.S. Senate? She has a moment of doubt when her finance committee tells her that money is only trickling in, and, if Clark stays in, they'll split the liberal vote, possibly allowing the then center-right Moynihan to grab the nomination. On a warm spring day in June, she has to sweat out whether to go up or out, the same dilemma that Lowenstein faced in the prior cycle. At 10:30 p.m. on June 8, with a declination letter sitting on her desk, she announces that she's in the Senate race for good. I'm disappointed, though admiring.

The campaigns settle in to the familiar political pattern of vilifying anyone who stands between their guy/gal and immortality: Bella's people see Ramsey as a soft-headed, sanctimonious carpetbagger who's not only not a woman but also prosecuted Benjamin Spock and William Sloan Coffin (conscientious objectors who later donate to their prosecutor); Ramsey's people see Bella as a screaming bully who chews up staff and can't play well with others in a legislative body; and both camps regard Moynihan as an iffy Democrat who threw in with the Nixon White House and wrote the infamous "benign neglect" memo that seemed to suggest a retreat from concern for minorities. Of course, the truth is that each of these three has special skills to be a standout New York and national senator.

Then like a plane with two bad engines, Ramsey's candidacy sputters, stalls, and begins a permanent descent.

With party leaders favoring the "electable" Moynihan—an egghead combining Hell's Kitchen and Harvard—the State Convention decides to put all the major candidates on the ballot for a September primary. This sounds very-small-d democratic except that it's cleverly designed to ensure that three liberals split the 60 percent liberal vote to allow Moynihan to win with a plurality.

Then comes my worst day in political life until 2001. I take Ramsey's call in our headquarters. "Mark, I think we have a problem," says the candidate evenly. "[Party chief] Joe Crangle has just called to ask why our campaign has not filed a required form formally accepting the State Convention ballot line for the primary." My stomach knots. "Well, I think this has to be a priority," Ramsey adds, with considerable understatement since his political career appears to be hanging by a thread. I'm grateful for his patience and wracked by anxiety and self-loathing.

We spend the next week trying to get around the fact that while we filed Y form, we hadn't also filed Z form. Not able to escape that detail, we get on the ballot as in 1974 by the sweat equity of obtaining at least the 20,000 Democratic signatures on nominating petitions over the summer. It's embarrassing though not fatal.

Once on the ballot, Ramsey takes me along to his editorial board meeting in August with *New York Times* publisher Arthur (Punch) Sulzberger. It goes badly.

Early small talk raises a recent *Times* series on Sidney Korshak, a prominent labor and Hollywood lawyer with alleged mob ties, which leads Ramsey to spend a third of his time with the publisher chiding that coverage since "Korshak has never been convicted of anything." True. But this (a) has zero to do with his Senate campaign and (b) doesn't impress Sulzberger, who not surprisingly sticks up for his paper's coverage. (Later the editorial board wants Abzug but the publisher, as is his prerogative, overrules them. Moynihan gets the crucial endorsement.)

Ramsey's endearing high-mindedness and insouciance ultimately prove fatal. I nearly give up on getting him to make essential calls since he apparently hasn't reconciled himself to the 75-year-old technology called the telephone. But Bella believes in the telephone. And when she's not cowing waverers on the horn, she's prowling the aisles for media hits and political support at the mid-July Democratic National Convention at Madison Square Garden. Rather than admirably teaching a law school class or doing pro bono work, she's doing pro se political work. My feverish spinning about Ramsey's progress and substance works on newbie journalists but few others. Assuming that "energy is genius," as Justice Holmes remarked, Bella's a genius. "If there was a period when Bella took off," her close associate Dorothy Samuels recalls, "it was convention week and all that exposure."

We see the upshot in late July when the press starts implying that it's a two-way race between Pat and Bella. Then the phone stops ringing in mid-August. Just stops. It's so abrupt that we actually check with the New York Telephone Company if lines are down somewhere. No, it's the silent sounds of bad word of mouth, like an eagerly anticipated big-budget movie that earns just $6 million opening weekend.

An otherwise-rising Abzug then commits an amazing unforced error—she mentions that if Moynihan were the nominee, she might not support him. This undisciplined, offhand blunder plays into her stereotype as a my-way-or-the-highway egotist and encourages the *Times* to run one negative story after the other.

An alarmed Abzug campaign asks me to lunch a week before the primary. At the elegant Warwick Hotel on West 54th Street, Ronnie Eldridge, a friend of the Kennedys and later Jimmy Breslin's wife, and Dick Aurelio, the former Javits aide who goes on to found NY1, urge me to urge Ramsey to drop out to keep Moynihan from winning. I explain that his supporters believe him to be the best potential senator and it's not my job to pick between Moynihan and Abzug.

But I understand their argument and why Frucher is telling me privately that Moynihan's tracking polls "only have Clark moving up." That is, either he's telling me the truth or conning me to keep Ramsey on the ballot. Either way, I'm obliged to lay all this out to my candidate. I hear back what I expect: "It would be wrong to play games with the process at this point and not let the voters decide. And I could never do that to all the people who have gotten us here."

I tell Ronnie and Dick. They're not surprised.

Two weeks later—and two days before the September 14 primary—I'm Abzuged. Walking out of a WPIX debate, Bella spots me in a hallway and publicly surrenders to late-campaign, private bitterness. In a husky voice, she yells, "You are a disgrace to everything that Ralph Nader and you have ever stood for!"

Then her assistant, presumably believing it wrong per se to run against a credible female candidate, chimes in, "Women are niggers, is that it?"

Bella now turns to her husband. "Let's go home, Martin. This is just a staff dispute."

Moynihan beats Abzug 36 to 35 percent and goes on to serve four much-lauded terms and elevate the Senate's collective IQ by several points on his own. Bella later runs unsuccessfully for both mayor in

1977 and the East Side congressional seat vacated by Mayor Koch in 1978. Ramsey and O'Dwyer get only 10 and 9 percent respectively, as the former goes on to a renowned and controversial career of representing hated clients—Charles Taylor, Slobodan Milošević, Saddam Hussein, Lyndon LaRouche—in devotion to the principle of equal justice under law. When I ask Ramsey in 2014 what he thinks went wrong in 1976, he says, "I was sort of an outsider with no real base while Bella had a very strong group of activist women who pushed hard for her . . . Even if I had won, I probably would have been a loner in the Senate given my views, and not likely have sought reelection in 1982."

Oh, and Deni and I get married on August 13, 1977. At the wedding, I tell Ramsey, "Sorry that you lost but I won."

Green[2]

When Abzug first hears that I've moved back to NYC in 1980 to run for Bill Green's East Side congressional seat, which she herself sought in the prior election, she's dismissive. "Ha," Bella tells a friend, "he's just a staff guy."

But given my youthful crush on Congress—and after my pal Chuck Blitz tells me that his mantra for life is "If you don't swing, you don't hit"—I want to take some cuts myself, in the spirit of Patti Smith who in 1968 thought to herself as she watched Jim Morrison perform, "I could do that." Not to mention that it's good for Deni, me, and Jenya to be back in our natural habitat and near family.

I first call some political acquaintances in the city to test the waters and hear back from Henry Stern, a prominent city councilman-at-large and later parks commissioner, about my prospects. When he says that he can detect no interest in me coming back as a candidate, I decide that the time is right.

Bill Green is an heir to the Grand Union supermarket family and a Javits-like "moderate Republican." He upset both Bella Abzug and then the wealthy Carter Burden in 1977 and 1978, respectively, to win the district, a long skinny sliver from the high-income, high-brow Upper East Side down through the Lower East Side of sheitels and delis.

There's one big obstacle, however—Lowenstein, again.

He's even more of a liberal icon than in 1974 and, no matter my willfulness, impossible to compete with if he decides to enter. So I set up a 5 p.m. meeting with him on March 14, 1980, to ask him directly. I'm with Nader that afternoon at the Essex Hotel on Central Park South where he's preparing to go on *SNL* at NBC's studio at 30 Rock. At 4:25, as I'm leaving to walk to Al's office, coincidentally at 50 Rockefeller Plaza, Deni reaches me by phone. "Joe Rauh just called! He heard that Lowenstein was shot and killed at his office!"

I'm stunned, nauseous, and speak to Rauh to confirm what happened. I go through the motions at Ralph's *SNL* run-through in the very complex where Lowenstein was shot hours before by a deranged former associate. On Tuesday I attend his funeral at the soaring sanctuary of what will become my temple, Central Synagogue. Ted Kennedy and Bill Buckley speak; Peter, Paul and Mary and Harry Chapin sing; and there in the audience are Governor Carey, Senator Moynihan, Mayor Koch, and two women familiar with gun violence, Jackie Onassis and Coretta Scott King.

But what I recall most given my link to Al that week is Rep. Andy Jacobs (D-IN). His eulogy includes the story of a little-known member of Congress asking Jacobs about Lowenstein the year before. "I say, 'Al, do you know who he is?' Al doesn't. I respond, 'Well, he knows who you are so why do you think that you always have to run for Congress to be well-known and have an influence?'"*

I then begin an all-out campaign against two little-known primary opponents. Recalls Mark Weinstein, our volunteer coordinator, "You were the young guy who wrote all those books and so attracted a stream of idealistic volunteers day and night. Four hundred plus by that summer. They really ran the campaign because of the lack of money." Winning the nomination easily, I run in the general election as the "Democratic Shade of Green" hoping that, with President Carter at the top of the ticket, his coattails can make the difference against a Republican incumbent in a marginally Democratic district. But Bill turns out to be a living embodiment of one

---

*I never do find out if Lowenstein would have run had he not been killed. Media guru Bob Shrum had scheduled Al to edit "Ted Kennedy for President" spots at David Sawyer's office that evening and doubts he could have extricated himself from the Kennedy campaign for his own candidacy. The *Washington Post*, however, reports the next month that their sources believe that he did intend to run. Lowenstein friend David Bender, who had dinner with him the night before the shooting, says the subject did not come up and today guesses it was 50–50.

of my themes in *Who Runs Congress?*—an incumbent who works the district hard. He schleps to subway stop after supermarket, even in the rain (especially in the rain), and becomes nearly universally regarded as "not a bad guy," an organic and accurate phrase I hear several thousand times.

I'm a rookie candidate making rookie mistakes, such as handing out my "lit" *during* an outdoor concert to annoyed listeners in Central Park. Worse, I arrive 45 minutes late to our first debate when there's complete gridlock in Midtown as I sit sweating in my cab before running the final ten blocks. I develop a decent stump speech full of issues and attempted humor, including the line "I'm running against one of the few *un*indicted members of Congress," this being the year of ABSCAM (see the film *American Hustle*). I'm amazed and dismayed when Herbert Brownell, Eisenhower's former attorney general, attacks me for implying that Bill's a crook! I think (a) no, no, the joke is that he's *not* a crook, and (b) really, this is what former attorneys general do? I learn a lesson—humor is high risk when people have a political motive to misconstrue you.

Then I nearly self-immolate with a gaffe—which is when you tell not a lie but the truth, according to the Kinsley Rule—one that will reverberate throughout my New York political career. At a small cocktail party of presumed supporters, someone asks me what I think of Mayor Koch. I answer as if I'm a talk show commentator, not a candidate on a mission. "Well, he's dynamic and getting lots done but I worry about how he contributes to the racial divide in the city"—such as his hot rhetoric about shutting Sydenham Hospital in Harlem and his cutting remarks about black civic and political leaders. It turns out that the questioner is an aide to Koch who reports to him the next morning what the Democratic nominee in his old district has said. It turns out that he's not happy, not happy at all, and enthusiastically belittles me whenever asked and even when not asked.

In the end, I'm endorsed by *The Nation* magazine. That's helpful. But it's way more helpful to Bill when he's endorsed by the *New York Times*: "We would like to see Mark Green in Congress . . . but losing Bill Green—a man of outstanding character and intelligence—would be too high a price."

I lose 57 to 43 percent. But my consolation prize is that I do get my feet very wet, cutting radio ads with irascible radio guru Tony Schwartz (he of the famous "Daisy" spot), learning about fund-raising from a cloyingly gregarious Syracuse businessman by the name of Terry McAuliffe, being gob-smacked by the mayor of New York at every turn, learning about edgy humor in politics.

My friend Derek Shearer of California calls to cheer me up. "Don't worry. You're now in the big leagues and can credibly run for anything."

Failing Upward: The United States Senate

I decide to take Derek's admonition seriously.

After a half decade of building up my Democracy Project and a few months immersing myself in Senator Gary Hart's campaign for president, I decide to run for the U.S. Senate seat of Al D'Amato. After all, I had lost a House race, been on *Oprah* and *Larry King*, an early poll showed me with a statewide recognition of 2 percent, and I'd written a book on Congress that perhaps .001 percent of the state had read.

Whether I take too literally Woody Allen's line that "success is being turned down by a better class of date," looking back now, it was nervy, probably crazy. But not far crazier than Alfonse D'Amato himself when, as a local Long Island pol, he successfully challenged popular four-term Senator Jacob Javits in the Republican primary. D'Amato won the very conservative primary and then the office when Javits stayed on the Liberal Party line, allowing Al to eke out a 1 percent plurality over the Democratic nominee, Rep. Elizabeth Holtzman.

Since U.S. Senate seats in New York are not handed out like Halloween candy, another big obstacle looms—former VP nominee Geraldine Ferraro is making noises about running.

Though a risk taker, I'm not completely insane. So in a "be prepared" Boy Scout mode, I move around a lot in late 1985 paying courtesy calls in case she doesn't run.

The morning of December 11, I'm in my two-room Democracy Project office at 19th and Park when a journalist calls to ask my reaction to Ferraro's statement that she won't be a candidate due to a pending Justice Department investigation. As if ejected from a catapult, I immediately start calling down my prepared list and barely look up from the phone for several hours. Turns out that Governor Mario Cuomo, no slouch at thinking ahead, has been trying to call me that entire time to cool my jets since he has already recruited a candidate to run. That would be the very wealthy John Dyson, an upstate businessman and the former head of three state agencies— the Power Authority and the Agriculture and Commerce Departments—and a six-figure donor to Cuomo's campaigns. But Mario doesn't get through to me that day.

Like me, Dyson lost a House race against a moderate Republican (Ham Fish III, 1968), attended Cornell, and is, at 43, just two years older than me. But that's where the similarities end. He's also a self-financing scion, shunning street campaigning and enjoying long Midtown lunches where he orders his food in Italian. I'm pretty much the opposite. In one typical article, the *Albany Times Union* contrasts my exposed-pipes office in the dowdy West 30s with his Fifth Avenue splendor—that is, according to the article, my "chopped liver" fundraising with his "pâté" style.

He's far ahead in his polls, I'm told (unable to afford any of my own). I hit subway stops every morning and evening in the vote-rich NYC and trudge to every Democratic club and union that will hear me explain my rationale: "I'm a "progressive subway Democrat" while he's a "wealthy closet Conservative" who contributed to Republican and Conservative Party candidates in the past. For his part, after initially trying to ignore me, John hits back repeatedly that I'm a nobody "with no record and no money."

Before the crucial Democratic State Convention in June, I manage to anger Governor Mario Cuomo, twice. He laughs when I privately tease him, "You gonna throw your halo into the ring for president?" . . . but he's furious when he sees the jest in cold print in *Newsweek*. Nevertheless, the governor arranges for Dyson and me to get the 25 percent of delegates necessary to appear on the September primary ballot. (We file the necessary paperwork!) But when, for the twentieth time, I'm asked why the governor secretly supports Dyson, instead of repeating per usual that "he says he's neutral," I get creative. "Why do you listen to leaks from the governor's aides? You should listen to the organ grinder, not the monkeys. And he says that he's neutral."

Well, this Jewish kid from Long Island is completely unfamiliar with the fact that "organ grinder" is a famous anti-Italian slur from the 1930s, in the same category as "money-lenders" is to Jews. And he's famously conscious of ethnic and class distinctions, once confiding to me that he'd never appeared on *Firing Line* because of Buckley's instinctual distinction "between 'Castle Irish' and 'Field Irish.'" I take an unpleasant call from Andrew Cuomo asking me what the hell I'm doing. I grovel, apologize, plead ignorance, and explain, "You know, probably the very last thing I'd intentionally do is insult my Italian-American governor at his Democratic Convention where he's putting me on the ballot."

I'm rattled but survive. John and I each then address the 1,000 convention delegates. He recites his significant appointive experience. After walking in to the podium to the cheeky chords of "If I Were a Rich Man" from *Fiddler on the Roof,* I try to light a fire under delegates who don't know much at all about me: "I may not have been the head of the Power Authority but I'm an authority on power," I semi-shout to a galvanized crowd. "And the best way to defeat D'Amato is to sharply contrast with him and not be a pale Democratic version of him."

Before and after that convention, however, I encounter three potentially fatal problems: the governor publicly chastises any criticism of the other lest we play into D'Amato's hands; the immensely famous/popular Harry Belafonte says that he's thinking of running; and I find out that Dyson intends to spend a good chunk of his $25 million inherited fortune (from his father, Charles, inventor of the leveraged buyout). What political leverage do I have to go around or through any of these brick walls? Frankly, it's my outsider status and any Naderian skills that I bring to this war zone.

First, I respond publicly to the governor: "I promise not to criticize Dyson any more than you criticized Koch in your 1982 gubernatorial primary when you were the underdog." I'm told Mario doesn't like my impertinence, but he then ceases to dwell on this objection. With Dyson trying to sound more Democratic despite his previously conservative leanings, like supporting the Shoreham Nuclear Plant on Long Island that the governor opposed (and shut), it's essential that I underscore how he may memorize the lyrics but can't get the beat.

Second, as Belafonte is publicly mulling a candidacy, we end up attending the same Peter, Paul and Mary anti-apartheid concert in February at the Kennedy Center in D.C. Gloria Steinem acknowledges him from the stage as "the next senator from New York," which 3,000 people cheer as I shrivel in my seat. Yet when I see him milling around after the event, I walk over (we knew each other from when

Deni worked for him in the music business in the Seventies) and say with feigned confidence, "Harry, good luck in your decision." But then staring directly into his impossibly handsome face and sparkling eyes, I say with complete faux confidence, "But please know that I'm running no matter what because I believe I have the background to be a strong candidate and senator."

Why so blunt and brash? If he thinks that he has a clear path to a nomination and can fame his way into the U.S. Senate, he'll be more likely to run. But if he thinks that a feisty, informed progressive lawyer will be biting his ankle the whole primary, maybe he'll think twice. Whatever his reasons, he opts out shortly afterward. (Not surprisingly, he harbors a resentment of me until we make up in 2008 through the intervention of Deni and Navasky.)

Third, my Sisyphean financial challenge becomes clearer at a June Democratic primary event in Roslyn, New York. After both of us speak, Dyson's media guru, Hank Morris, comes up to me and snarls with little subtlety, "There are millions of reasons you're gonna lose, Green!" *(Twelve years later, he guides Schumer to a win over me in the 1998 Democratic Senate primary and then State Comptroller Alan Hevesi to a loss in our 2001 mayoral primary. Sadly, however, this talented operative goes to jail in 2005, for corrupting the controller's office.)*

In mid-August, "body guy" Barry Grodenchik is driving me around upstate when we hear on the radio that Dyson has filed his financial disclosure statements. He reports spending $7 million in his primary campaign, adding that "Mark Green can't raise a dime . . . and you need resources to beat D'Amato."

I think to myself, well, I might not have run if I had known my opponent would set a national record for a self-financed primary. Barry, however, is buoyed: "Wonderful," he earnestly says, "he must think he's losing!" After calming down later that day, I rationalize my peril: since it's too late to quit, maybe the odds have now shifted for the *New York Times* endorsement since they hate money buying elections and perhaps I can jujitsu his arrogance into an asset. I announce the "Mark of Dimes" campaign against my "heir-head" opponent, try to raise small donations to defeat his big check, and end up with a treasury of $700,000, enough for one TV ad aired four times. But I repeatedly ask him, "Where in the U.S. Constitution is there a wealth test for high office?"

I also have an ace up my sleeve—a staff of young talent eager to counterpunch. They include Michael Waldman, later to be President Clinton's chief speechwriter and head of the Brennan Center for Legal Justice at NYU, and David Corn, who will go on to win a George Polk Award for reporting on the Romney "47 percent" tape for *Mother Jones* in 2012. I tell them that since Dyson has the advantage of money, let's turn that lemonade into a lemon—surely he has some investments that won't sound kosher to Democratic voters.

Wait. That's it!

Since my 1978 lawsuit against the Department of Commerce forced the public release of companies complying with the Arab States' boycott of Israel, I task David and Michael with trying to tie Dyson to the boycott. And while they're at it, could they check any investments going to firms doing business in South Africa since he opposed disinvestment while a trustee at Cornell? If he gets a big political benefit from his personal wealth, can he pay a political penalty as well?

It works. They come up with 27 firms in Dyson's financial portfolio investing in South Africa and others cooperating with the Arab boycott, which we know about because of my lawsuit. I gather a group of black supporters—including Arthur Ashe, Rev. Calvin Butts, and David Paterson—to issue a statement in July demanding that he divest: "We expect our elected representatives to lead the fight against apartheid, not profit from it." A week later, Dyson does sell off $3 million from firms doing business there, attributing his change of heart supposedly to Governor Cuomo's request that any possible fall ticket have a unified approach on such investments.

Saving the Arab boycott financials for our first debate in Oneonta in August, I enjoy a near Bentsen-Quayle moment in front of 200 curious rural Democrats and statewide media in what the *Times* calls "one of the most vituperative political debates in New York in recent years." During a discussion of Israel, I unload: "John, if you're such a big supporter as you say, then why did you invest funds in companies cooperating with the Arab boycott of Israel? And why did you invest millions more in South Africa?" He looks stunned, presumably trying to recall and explain these Israel-related investments and understand how such revelations will affect the Jewish and black vote, which together total about half of the primary. All in about a second. He can't. Nobody could.

Then I develop a closing line in all my talks that, more than any other in my political career, I repeat because it emotionally connects me to audiences and also empowers them. "Please help this candidacy and this cause. Then, on election night, when you see Deni and me holding up our arms after an upset victory, you won't simply say, '*He* did it.' But rather, '*We* did it.'"

September 9, primary night. I'm with family and supporters in a small suite in the Halloran House on Lexington Avenue. Jan Pierce, the head of the local Communications Workers of America and an ardent supporter, is on the phone getting early tallies from his people in Nassau County. "Mark, based on how you're overperforming in these state senate districts, I think we're going to win." My brother, who's the very, very bottom-line sibling, is stunned. "Whaaat! You're going to actually win?"

I do, by 54 to 46 percent, and take a gracious concession call from Dyson; then I walk to a quickly swelling ballroom of ecstatic supporters and triumphantly shout, "*We* really did it! Message beat money!" The next day's *New York Times* has a big front-page picture of Deni, Jenya, Jonah, me, and my beaming parents.

We enjoy a day of exhilaration before crashing back to earth when the following day's front-page *Times* headline says that Democratic mayor Ed Koch has crossed party lines to endorse the Republican senator. Our tit-for-tat relationship apparently continues, though it is far from over. Privately, I invoke the old Irish joke that if, God forbid, Ed got Alzheimer's, he'd forget everything except his vendettas.

Senator Al D'Amato: "What Hump?"

If Bill Green was a hardworking incumbent, Al D'Amato is a political genius. How else to explain his ability to be a "fugitive from the law of averages," in Bill Mauldin's term, a conservative Republican senator who stays popular in a state with 1 million more Democratic voters?

By the dint of relentless fund-raising, relentless "bringing home the bacon," and relentless stand-ups on the six o'clock news, D'Amato has earned his way to a 60 percent favorable rating by the start of the election year (with a 50-point lead over me in the earliest poll, 66 to 16 percent). And with $6 million in the bank—or 6 million more

than I have on September 10—I appear to be not so much an underdog as a non-dog.

I cheerfully announce that "this is the clearest choice in a generation" and that, since it's widely considered a David-Goliath contest,
"I'm a stone's throw from the U.S. Senate."

But it will take more than one-liners to dethrone this political
king. Unable to finance much paid media, we throw ourselves into
free media by holding some 30 press conferences blending attacks
on his ethics and votes with my "50 New Solutions for New York,"
or about one a day in the general election. When press conferences
occasionally draw no media, which ignore content for something
about the "horse-race," our news releases puckishly begin, "In his eagerly awaited 37th 'New Solution,' Democratic Senate nominee Mark
Green today urged . . ." We document how D'Amato again and again
cuts ribbons for federal contracts in the state while voting to cut to
ribbons these same programs at the behest of his big donors in Washington, D.C.

But for all of D'Amato's political strengths, he's also regarded as
a charming rogue or just a rogue. He says in 1980, "I'll do anything
short of killing Javits to win this nomination," and later runs ads
questioning whether the 76-year-old incumbent will even survive
another term. In 1984 he declares that he'd be a character witness
for subway killer Bernard Goetz. He and then U.S. Attorney Giuliani
dress up in sunglasses, army jackets, and Hell's Angels attire to buy
$20 worth of a cocaine derivative in Washington Heights to attract
media coverage; he also enforces an illegal scheme, according to a
court decision, that coerces Nassau County Republican appointees to
kick back 1 percent of their salaries to the party. And there are reams
of articles in major media about his method of delivering for donors.
"If you don't contribute," says one stockbroker about the chair of
the Senate Securities Subcommittee to the *Wall Street Journal*, "they
don't return your phone calls."

Because I view the senator as a "walking quid pro quo," I announce that I'll be the only major party candidate in the country that
cycle to refuse all PAC gifts, an idea inspired by Ramsey's $100 limit.
Since virtue should not be its own reward, I'm hoping this step also
contrasts sharply with D'Amato and attracts additional donations
to fill the gap. With bad polls and few business donors, I use celebrity friends to host concerts—Crosby, Stills & Nash; Peter, Paul and

Mary; Pete Seeger; Judy Collins; Mandy Patinkin and Carly Simon—
as well as organize numerous fund-raising parties once I realize that,
for some reason, a party with me alone doesn't do quite as well as one
with Warren Beatty and me.

Warren, who became a friend during and after the '84 Hart campaign (see chapter 5), is now providing a private plane to ferry the two
of us and staff around upstate. Local media and average citizens in
Buffalo, Rochester, Syracuse, and Albany barely know me but go nuts
for such a bona fide Hollywood star. In Buffalo, after I do a WKBW
news segment, I convince this usually publicly shy leading man to do
the weather report, which he ends by saying, "It'll be sunny tomorrow . . . if Mark Green becomes your senator."

The result: 20,000 donors and $1.5 million. Which sounds like
a lot to me . . . except as compared to Al's eventual then-record $13
million war chest to buy TV and radio spots to sway voters.

D'Amato's response to all my attacks and exertions is to stonewall, i.e., simply ignore the "pay-to-play" articles that I recite. It's as
if he studied the Marty Feldman character in *Young Frankenstein*
who responds to a sympathetic comment about a grotesque two-foot
hump on his back by saying, "What hump?" After chasing cameras
for six years, he follows the front-runners' playbook nearly perfectly:
he refuses to comment on anything I do or say and schedules two debates within 12 hours of each other (the first opposite the Mets World
Series) so we need to speed from upstate to downstate to get back in
time. At each he just stares straight ahead when I pummel him on
policies and ethics.

There are two post-debate exceptions to his refusal to engage.
When I say that his "pothole" reputation shows how little he matters in Washington since senators can always hire staff to handle
local problems, his campaign spanks me because it sounds snobby
. . . because it is. Then his staff combs through my books and argues
that I'm a radical for proposing to decriminalize (not eliminate) laws
against marijuana. "If you think it's desirable to imprison Reagan's
children," I respond, "say so." The issue disappears.

Throughout, Governor Cuomo looms. As the party leader and
hugely popular top of the ticket, the question becomes—will he
help?

Grodenchik and I drive up to the executive mansion in Albany
a week after our upset victory in the primary. A burly guard eyes

our '68 Oldsmobile, barks out, "Halt, who are you?," and peers in. "Oh, the giant-killer," he says in a lower octave and waves us in. Over lunch, I thank the governor for staying publicly neutral in the primary and for helping convince Dyson to withdraw from the Liberal Party line allowing for a two-way general election. He's very flattering about my performance in the primary, likening it to his underdog win over Koch because both victories turned on debate performances and a more progressive base coming out for their guy. "If you can get him on TV with you where you shine, you win."

That's nice. But since I can't "get him on TV," as we both know, I plunge ahead to make the expected request. "Obviously you have your own race, but it'd be great if you could campaign with me and help in any way with fund-raising." He assents generally.

But when nothing happens for several weeks, there's a lot of press criticism and bad word of mouth that the popular governor isn't helping his long-odds undercard. Senator Moynihan says publicly, "Of course there was a nonaggression pact between Governor Cuomo and Senator D'Amato. That's not a theory; that's a fact." Stung, Cuomo calls with two weeks to go to tell me that he's moving $50,000 from his party-controlled account to my Senate account and would campaign twice with me. And does.

Desperate for cash, I traipse to D.C. to meet with the Democratic Senate Campaign Committee to ask for funds. The good news is that I have a great conversation with Senators Bradley, Durbin, Metzenbaum, Reid, and others, as Bradley says after I make my case, "Hey, you're like a white Jesse Jackson." (I *think* he intends that as a compliment.) But these pros know too much about politics, polls, and odds to do anything more than spring for a modest five-figure amount.

November 10, Election Day. D'Amato wins 57 to 41 percent, about as expected. I put in the standard congratulatory call. It's not taken or returned. In my concession speech, I thank the governor "for doing everything he could to help our campaign." The crowd loudly boos.

I return to Democracy Project work. But two weeks later, the Iran-Contra story explodes, reducing President Reagan's approval rating nearly 20 points in a month and, with it, party ratings across the board. Also, I read a steady flow of articles over the next two years documenting a continuing pattern of unseemly if not unethical favors that D'Amato performs for his donors. Then I completely violate the tradition that losers are supposed to suffer in quiet dignity.

Believing that vindication is no excuse for silence, I file a 32-page complaint with the Senate Ethics Committee in July 1989 arguing that exposés since the '86 election—in the *New York Times, Wall Street Journal, Newsday, Daily News*—justify some official sanction against the senator. D'Amato calls me "an obviously distraught former candidate." My complaint anticipates his belittlement: "Since I've spent most of my 20-year public career working on issues of public ethics and campaign finance, I'm filing these papers not because of my campaign but despite it."

Since the real problem of legal graft is shaking down donors so long as you don't say "OK, in exchange I'll now vote for your bill," I don't expect much of a result. After all, if the committee punishes D'Amato, they'd establish a standard where they could be next. But I believe it's important at least to further expose a corrupt process.

The complaint gains surprising attention and traction. The committee decides there's enough evidence to open a formal investigation that lasts 21 months and calls 53 witnesses, including D'Amato himself, over four days that covers 900 transcript pages. (Thirty others refuse to appear, citing their right against self-incrimination.) On August 3, 1991, the Senate Ethics Committee releases its ten-page report, unanimously finding no criminal misconduct but officially reprimanding him for "being negligent in failing to establish appropriate standards for the operation of his office" because his brother Armand D'Amato "misused [his office] for personal gain." As for the senator's denial that he knew anything about how his brother exploited his Senate office to help a client, Wedtech, get Pentagon business, Senator Rudman writes in the report, "Based on how all of us run Senate offices, it strains credulity that a member would be unaware how his own brother was lobbying his staff on behalf of a major interest group."

Nonetheless, D'Amato immediately and shrewdly frames the story line that he's been "completely exonerated." He refuses to publicly release his testimony and goes on to head the Senate Banking Committee's Whitewater investigation demanding that the Clintons make "a full disclosure" of all their records. He wins reelection in 1992 by one percentage point when his Democratic opponent, state attorney general Robert Abrams, boots it away by remarkably calling the Italian senator a "fascist" at a late campaign rally in Binghamton. In his book *Power, Pasta and Politics,* D'Amato uses 12 pages to denounce me (and implicitly all those newspapers that ran articles about his fund-raising practices) as an anti-Italian smear artist.

Finally, in 1998, starting with the highest negative numbers of any incumbent running that year, he loses to Congressman Chuck Schumer by a large margin and cites his decline in popularity as stemming from my ethics petition.

Five years later, the former senator attends the opening in 2003 of the Alfonse M. D'Amato United States Courthouse in Central Islip. In a reversal worthy of a novel, then-senator Hillary Clinton artfully jokes that "if a few years ago someone had in the same sentence said Al D'Amato, Hillary Clinton and courthouse, I don't think this is what we would have had in mind. But life is full of surprises." The audience, including D'Amato, erupts in laughter.

Finally, as regular panelists, Al and I appear some 200 times together from 2002 to 2015 on NY1's *Wiseguys* program. In his world of eye-for-an-eye politics, that's actually laudable. We get along fine on the show. Well, except for that one time when during a break he threatens to punch me out, wrongly fretting I was going to talk about his ethics on air.

Dinkins, Green, Schumer: Three Winning Campaigns

It's January 1989. An ardent Black/Latino/Liberal-Jewish coalition is trying to draft a reluctant David Dinkins to challenge three-term mayor Ed Koch to become the city's first black mayor. Dinkins enjoys serving as Manhattan borough president, a job that took him three campaigns to win. But when polls show him ahead by 10 points over Koch—whose third term is marred by the scandals of his appointees—the lure of City Hall proves too powerful.

I'm among the many co-chairs of the Dinkins campaign. Dave is a friend who is impossible not to like personally and who is the opposite of the formidable loudmouth who, in my view, has racially divided a diverse city. That's what I indiscreetly said as a candidate about Koch in 1980 that began our feud. When I visit him in 1985 to inform him about my intended U.S. Senate bid, Koch merely kvetches, "Have you ever said anything nice about me?" Can't say that I have.

Ed can be infuriating and admirable. A nebbishy Jewish kid from the Bronx, he ends up in World War II's European theater dangerously foraging at night for food for his unit. On one mission, a partner walking next to him steps on a land mine that blows off his leg. Koch loyalists John LoCicero and George Arzt believe that his particular wiring and wartime experiences produce a person who leaned into conflict and "would never back down," says LoCicero. "It's probably why he ran for a fourth term in '89 when we told him he couldn't win."*

I surrogate for Dinkins around the city, usually at white political clubs and Jewish organizations because he needs at least a quarter of the former and third of the latter (there's obviously some overlap) to win. Then two related episodes break the election open.

The killing of black youth Yusef Hawkins by a white mob reminds voters that it's time for a more healing mayor. And the very popular Governor Cuomo, who chooses words carefully, echoes that conclusion at the Labor Day Parade by saying that the winner will be the person who can "best bring this city together." Hint. But Koch, predictably, responds that he's the one who can unite the city when he comes out in favor of the death penalty for *any* racially related deaths, black or white.

Early returns election night show a rout. Given my fractious relationship with Koch, I'm in the satisfying position of being the MC at the microphone of the Sheraton Center ballroom as 2,000 screaming Democrats celebrate Dinkins's expected historic win. My job is to alternate speakers so the platform collectively reflects the "Gorgeous Mosaic of New York," Dave's favorite metaphor for a city of 178 distinct nationalities.

I dive deep into my talk show persona and joyfully rotate every race, gender, and creed to convey how Dinkins will bring everyone together. Then I spot Rev. Jesse Jackson moving toward the stage. I introduce him as "one of the cornerstones of our campaign" since it's when he carries the five boroughs in the '88 Democratic presidential primary that Dave realizes that he can really win. No Jackson,

---

* In one area, I can confirm this almost chemical impulse to fight. Koch too is on NY1's *Wiseguys* for the decade that I'm a regular. He would invariably be pleasant before and after any show. But on air, if he thought I was about to criticize his point of view, he'd compulsively lean forward, fix his eyes on me, and start getting bumptious and ad hominem—"Green, that's just like you . . ."—anything to win the argument. I get used to it and rarely take the bait of counter-denouncing an 80-something three-term former mayor.

no Dinkins. After Jesse delivers a resoundingly Jacksonian address, provoking cheers and tears, he and several of his entourage position themselves behind me in the camera shot.

When the stage gets too overcrowded, in a sweet aside I suggest that Jesse exit right as all other speakers have done to make room for new ones to shine—coming back to share the stage with the candidate later. He laughs easily, pulls me toward his large frame, and says, "No. Arrest me." Uh oh. When I yell into the mic ten minutes later that "the networks have just officially announced that David Dinkins has won the Democratic nomina—," I'm drowned out by the joyous crowd, with Jackson and his growing group largely occupying the platform with me.

By the time Dave and Joyce Dinkins come out for his victory speech a half hour later, the stage has been completely taken over by the reverend and a sea of African American male faces, a visual far more monochromatic than mosaic.

The rest of the momentous Dinkins-Giuliani rivalry is well known. Dave wins by nearly three points in 1989, as Rudy at his concession speech screams somewhat hysterically at his crowd to stop booing his mentions of Dinkins. Then after an industrious four-year tutorial in the politics and communities of NYC, Rudy comes back to win by nearly three in 1993. He's significantly helped when Governor Cuomo inexplicably allows Republican Staten Island to vote on a secession referendum, boosting that pro-Rudy vote and angering Dave, as his memoirs make clear. Mario giveth and Mario taketh away.

The '93 result differs from '89 largely because Dave's been in office four years. He's offended a small but crucial number of swing white voters due to a barrage of criticism after two wrenching events: an illegal black boycott of Korean grocers that he's slow to respond to and a Crown Heights riot that leaves one Jewish student dead. Giuliani predictably and hyperbolically calls it "a pogrom."

Election night '93 is sad and awkward. I win election as public advocate and Alan Hevesi as comptroller. But I'm subdued since a friend who helped launch my electoral career loses. I stand next to Dinkins at his eloquent concession speech ("Mayors come and go. But the life of the City must endure") though some of his supporters are livid. Percy Sutton, the Apollo owner and ex–Manhattan borough president, loudly wonders, "Why did the two white citywide candidates win but not the black one?" According to Dinkins's memoirs,

Al Sharpton threatens not to shake my hand as we all commiserate in Dave's suite. The mayor, knowing of my all-out efforts for him, restrains the Rev from causing a scene. Turns out this is a Sharpton prequel.

IN EARLY 1993 I'm immensely enjoying my work as the Consumer Affairs commissioner. My friend Ezra Friedlander, a very politically shrewd Orthodox Jew, calls. "I have an idea for you—why don't you run for city council president since [Andy] Stein is leaving to run for mayor and you'd win?" I hadn't seriously thought about that but, at first blush, his logic is sound. But would I want to hold an office that has been a ceremonial dead end? Then the powerful city council speaker, Peter Vallone, who doesn't enjoy being confused with the less powerful city council president, enacts a law changing its name in 1992 to "Public Advocate." Fritz Schwarz, the influential head of the recent NYC Charter Commission and former City Corporation counsel, publicly says the change indicates that someone "like Mark Green" should hold the position. Others agree privately to me.

Like my initial reluctance to be a commissioner, I conclude that this is an office I can win, shape, and revive. After announcing my candidacy, the two-term incumbent Andrew Stein drops out of the mayor's race saying that he will now run for reelection. To me he's a big name who's lost his fastball . . . but also now the third rich guy in a row I may run against in a line of work where wealth can matter. At a hastily arranged presser, I'm pelted with variations of the question whether I'd now drop out. "No." "Would anything make you drop out?" "Death!" I respond, which pretty much sums up my determination and shuts down further speculation.

Stein's pollster is now privately telling him that he can't beat me no matter how much he spends. Also, my campaign lawyer, John Siegal, has won a court ruling that the money Stein spent running for mayor counts against his public advocate cap, hobbling him financially. Two weeks later, I'm campaigning early one evening at the 23rd Street and Eighth Avenue subway stop when I get a call from veteran *Times* reporter Sam Roberts. "Mark, Stein just told me that he's dropping out to spend more time with his two children. Your thoughts?" I can't say a word for a sustained ten seconds. "Come on, I've never known you to be so tongue-tied," says Sam with a wink

I could almost see through the phone. Fact is, I'm paralyzed by the combination of giddiness and confusion as I struggle to say something gracious about Stein after weeks of thinking him as, well, not stellar. I finally mumble something sort of nice about his career and get back to leafleting.

One of my rivals is state senator David Paterson, enormously smart and funny, like stand-up comic funny. Although he and I have been friends since we cross-endorsed in our 1986 races, he wants to ascend politically and friendship almost never beats ambition. So when his own father and the black mayor suggest that Paterson not run since two African Americans at the top of the Democratic ticket is not ideal and I'd bring "diversity" in this instance, David ignores his elders and runs anyway. That's impressive.

During the race we have a very chummy dinner at my home, something that doesn't happen often in a campaign, perhaps never. (When 16 years later as lieutenant governor he succeeds Eliot Spitzer following a prostitution scandal, David teases me, "You know, perhaps if you had let me win Public Advocate, today *you'd* be governor!")

Throughout the summer and fall, I rotate volunteer drivers in a rented campaign car since I no longer can use a city vehicle. One is an enthusiastic, very sharp 25-year-old Columbia Law School student originally from India by the name of Preet Bharara . . . who of course goes on to well-earned fame as an anti-corruption U.S. Attorney in the Southern District, Giuliani's old office.

The campaign is not very eventful or competitive. The *New York Times* endorsement is ideally on to something when it concludes that "the voluble Mr. Green is so enthusiastic about public service that he might actually find a rationale for a city post that now has little meaning." The day after my primary win, four of the losing Democrats agree, per custom, to join me at a victory rally at City Hall. But one candidate who comes in third at 12 percent won't come unless we have a private meeting and separate public event, which doesn't happen. That would be Assemblyman Robert Ramirez of the Bronx, whom I'd be bumping heads with, for higher stakes, eight years later.

I'm sworn in at our home on the evening of December 31 by Dinkins in one of his final acts as mayor. A moment later, my precocious nine-year-old son Jonah grabs the handheld mic and raises a glass of soda to make a toast to his dad. "Ask not what you can do for your city," he says with authority, "but what your city can do for you!" Close enough.

I've now reversed Daniel Patrick Moynihan's career. He first loses for city council president (aka public advocate) before winning for U.S. Senate in 1976. I lose for U.S. Senate before winning for public advocate, "proving you're the better politician," I would periodically remind him to his Irish delight.

IN 1982, I bump into a young staffer with Congressman Schumer on Capitol Hill. Recalling how Chuck keeps stockpiling his money from cycle to cycle, hitting up big donors two, three times each because federal law, unlike city law, allows transferring funds to future races, I playfully ask, "Who's the schmuck that Schumer will end up spending all his money against?"

That would be me 16 years later. (The staffer is John Siegal, whom we met two pages ago and who later becomes one of my closest advisors and counsel to my public advocate and mayoral races.)

In 1996, Michael Tomasky writes in *New York* magazine that many folks are waiting to see if, given my poll numbers, I'll next run for mayor against Giuliani or Senate against D'Amato—at the time I'm tied with Rudy and far ahead of Al. Indeed I am toggling for a month between a next race against one or the other. But I choose the office I fell in love with as a congressional intern, previously held by my hero, Senator Robert Kennedy, and previously sought by me. Not to mention against the target of my ethics complaint.

When I announce for reelection in January, the mayor uncharacteristically tells the *New York Post* that "he's relieved" and invites me into City Hall for one of only two private meetings over eight years. Now that I'll never be a direct rival, he's relaxed and chatty. "I'm amazed that you can announce for one office, Public Advocate, yet also say that you'll likely run for another the following year. How can you do that?"

It's unusual, I agree, "but if I level with voters, instead of the usual BS of saying I intend to finish the term when I don't, they'll respect my candor. At least I hope they will."

Other major Democrats, however, are also not unaware of D'Amato's vulnerability because voters are tired of his shtick and scandals. They include Congressman Schumer and Geraldine Ferraro, bitter that she had to pass up her chance in '86 and that she lost to Abrams in the '92 primary after what she regarded as anti-Italian assaults on her family.

One constant rumor involves John F. Kennedy Jr., who is famous, gorgeous, and modest, an irresistible combination. At a benefit at the Whitney Museum in mid-1997, I make a beeline to him. No Belafonte antics this time. "John, I'm working my tail off preparing for a Senate race while you just wake up in the morning, brush your teeth, and boom, you're ahead by 20 points. How can that be?" We both laugh knowing the core truth of who I am and who *he* is. "Hey, I'm loving putting out *George* magazine and don't think about it," he replies.

In a state stockpiled with talent and bold-faced names, I feel like a child on a Disneyland water ride as different monsters emerge from the darkness to threaten my boat. As the field is forming in 1997, I see Liz Moynihan, the senator's wife and chief strategist, at the Al Smith Dinner in October. For some reason she and I have bonded since that time in 1976 that I ran a campaign against her husband. This evening she confides that I should think about waiting because the 1998 field looks to be very strong and "you never know about the other Senate seat." Years later she tells me that she was signaling but couldn't explicitly say that Pat wasn't going to run again and she hoped that I would.

Not that it matters. According to mutual friends, in late 1998 Kennedy does start to think seriously about running in 2000, anticipating Moynihan's declination at age 71; but he is tragically killed in a plane crash in mid-1999. By then, Hillary Clinton is on her "listening tour." The rest is herstory.

I keep pursuing the Senate seat through 1997 on my entrepreneurial theory from 1980 and 1986 that you have to risk a humiliating loss to a late entrant to have a chance to win such a coveted prize. My close friend Bruce Wasserstein tells me that Schumer confirmed to him that he's undecided between running for governor or Senate, before concluding, "but could you contribute as I make the decision?" In August 1997, Deni and I combine a vacation in Paris with Bruce's wedding. En route to the airport, a journalist calls to let me know that Chuck is now telling his inner circle that he's going for the Senate. I spend half my time in Paris calling political and financial leaders to try to get to them before Schumer does, which would have been hard enough if I were in Manhattan but impossible against this political tornado.*

Whatever the exact standards for a "force of nature," Chuck is a Category 5. Anthony Weiner, an early Schumer protégé, tells me, "There probably aren't ten people on the planet with as keen a sense of how something will politically play than Chuck." His template for success is imprinted on all his assembly and congressional campaigns and terms over the 24 years leading up to our Senate contest.

First, he's the Stephen King of fund-raising, meaning no matter how many books or dollars each produces, they're compelled to want more. He enjoys cold-calling big donors and, like a spastic colon, impulsively and shamelessly asking a target for money again and again. New York lawyer Bernard Nussbaum tells me how "Schumer would keep calling me until I finally picked up the phone and agreed to give him $1,000 but only on the condition that he stop calling. But sure enough, two weeks later he asks for another thousand . . . and keeps calling until I give again just to get rid of him."

He can't be outworked—witness his near-impossible feat later of visiting all 62 New York State counties as a senator . . . every year; Moynihan maybe did that over his 24 years in the Senate. Schumer also has a huge legislative record of proposals and laws involving banks, guns, consumer issues. Not to mention that he apparently lives on the Washington shuttle, attending nearly every significant NYC event where he insists on speaking when he arrives—always taking a bit longer than the program allows—and then rushing off to the next event.

Finally, he works the media aggressively and successfully, to the point that Senator Bob Dole annoys Chuck by saying in a much-repeated phrase that "the most dangerous place in Washington is between Chuck Schumer and a camera." Years later I hear Schumer address a Metropolitan Council on Jewish Poverty breakfast where

---

* Seventeen years later, I ask Chuck how close he came to running for governor instead. His explanation is interesting and revealing: "Not very close, although I thought I had about the same chance of beating Pataki as D'Amato. Look, if you're the governor and you go somewhere, you have the cars, the plane, and 50 people line up to tell you how great the shirt you're wearing looks because they want a road in Elmira. But it's all transactional. A senator? Maybe five people come over. But you're working on bigger issues affecting more people. I'm a legislator."

he refers to this reputation and makes a thoughtful admission: "You know, if that's the worst thing they can say about me, I'll take it."

Ferraro too runs, with the initial poll putting the race at Ferraro 50 percent, Green 25 percent, Schumer 16 percent. Our few debates in the campaign entail Ferraro and me occasionally sparring while Chuck, confident that his war chest and record will be decisive, largely hangs back.

At one in Saratoga Springs, I chide Ferraro for accepting a $10,000 speaking fee from a tobacco firm. She retorts, "You've accepted tobacco money too!"

"When?"

Geraldine pauses. "Well, Shirley in the audience [her research assistant] has the information and . . ."

I interrupt her. "But Shirley isn't running for the U.S. Senate, you are. I've never accepted lecture fees or PAC money from tobacco interests."

It turns out that she's talking about a $100 contribution from an individual employee at Philip Morris. To a reporter afterward, I conclude, "She's running on the fumes of fame," which is harsh but not untrue. Chuck's only too happy to watch the two of us collide.

Then a coup. I persuade President Clinton (see chapter 3) to come to a city school on Kick Butts Day in April 1997. My staff chooses the Hudde Junior High School in Brooklyn for the event, which is a perfect venue . . . except for the political weirdness that Jessica Schumer is a seventh-grade student there. The congressman and I end up sharing the stage and spotlight. A decade later at a party, Chuck relishes that moment. "Once I saw that you and the president would be there, I knew I would be all over the school and you'd have to share the credit."

The race in August settles into a dangerous rhythm. Gerry stumbling, Chuck unleashing a tidal wave of ads, while I travel upstate to rural counties where I'm unrecognized. I write and mail out a charming 12-page "Travel-Blog" about Deni and me touring upstate, complete with shots of us petting a camel . . . that maybe a few dozen people read. Deni finds the trip demoralizing and foreboding. It's as if I'm trying to catch fish with my hands in a pond while my competitor is netting off the Great Banks.

By primary day, Chuck raises a total of $9 million (counting that stockpiled money), Gerry and I $3 million each. He impressively wins 51 percent to 25 percent and 19 percent for, respectively, Gerry and me. I beat Ferraro in NYC, which is a small silver lining for the future. Schumer goes on to easily defeat a weakened D'Amato 55 to 44 percent as I stand behind him on the crowded stage election night, yelling "The era of D'Amato is over!" Schumer serves three terms (so far) and recognition as the most influential U.S. senator from New York in the modern era—and overwhelming favorite to be the Democratic leader of the Senate starting in 2017.

He won because he was the better politician and candidate.

On the Street and on the Phone

There are two political imperatives behind the headlines, debates, and polls—street campaigning and fund-raising.

Given that NYC is a compact place where 6 million people a day take public transit, meeting voters means campaigning at subway stops primarily and then churches, supermarkets, street fairs, and "walking tours." All serve the dual purpose of showing up locally to show you care and learning from people about what matters to them. Running in NYC is like campaigning to be head of the UN. On a weekend day, it's an Orthodox breakfast event in Borough Park, then shaking hands in Korean Sunset Park, street fairs in Astoria and Washington Heights munching baklava and fried plantains, a march in Harlem up Adam Clayton Powell Blvd., early evening to an Italian political club in Bay Ridge, then back to Manhattan for two elegant charitable events. It's not clear if all this gains votes or pounds, but it's certainly the cost of political ambition.

I hit a subway nearly every morning and evening over the course of every campaign so that a couple hundred thousand New Yorkers per election either shake my hand and say later to family and friends "Yeah, I've met Mark Green" or millions of others can at least see me in person and take my measure. The repetition is so mind-numbingly unbelievable—"Hi, I'm Mark Green for Senate . . . Hi, I'm Mark Green for Senate . . . Hi, I'm . . ."—that once, before I complete my spiel, the woman entering the subway station at 86th and Lex says back, "I know, honey, we're married." In 1980, someone asks my almost-two-year-old her name, and Jenya says, "Mark Green for Congress."

When you do something this often, you learn about whole categories of people. With apologies, here are un-PC opinions: older black churchgoing women almost always shake my offered hand in apparent gratitude for either my gesture and/or my record on issues they care about; younger professional white women rarely do, usually eyeing me like someone about to deliver a pickup line at a bar; white businessmen, never; older Jewish women look on me as a favored son.

But while there are patterns, there are also interactions that educate you, inspire you, stay with you, and are why I come to really enjoy street campaigning. One favorite was Kenza Martin, a nine-year-old African American girl I met near the Jamaica train station while campaigning for Public Advocate reelection in 1997. "Kenza, if you study hard, you could become a Public Advocate someday." She flashed a huge, toothy smile and announced, "Oh no, Mr. Green. I intend to be the first black female president of the United States!" (Not yet so far, but it's early.)

Daily News columnist Michael Kramer in 2001 writes that I'm a "New York Bill Clinton" for my street chops. Still, after thousands of stops over a decade, I wonder why no scholar has ever done a serious cost-benefit analysis of such person-to-person fleeting interactions. Am I investing enormous effort at the political equivalent of dial-up?

Then there are the six hours a day set aside for fund-raising calls.

When I begin my maiden campaign in 1980, a D.C. friend with experience in fund-raising, Alvin Rosenbaum, advises me to first list all the people I know who could possibly contribute since I have the liability of knowing more public interest advocates and intellectuals than well-off business executives. When I then proudly show him the 80 names I had gathered, he cackles and tells me to come back with at least 500 names after better scouring all the people I know from childhood, the tennis circuit, high school, college, law school, Nader days, the parents of old girl friends. When I hit that benchmark, he's satisfied . . . and I'm off and running.

Fund-raising-wise, it's a long way from 1980 to 2000.

In my race for mayor, I put out 30,000 calls over two years—that is not a typo—in what eventually becomes an assembly-line process. Two callers (three in the general election) with key information on one-sheets sit in front of my desk as I read a newspaper and ink letters while they put out an average of 80 calls a day, usually querying an assistant, "Is Mr. Smith available to take a call from Mark Green?" About 15 to 20 a day either take the call or call back. I then have perhaps two seconds to glance down at my binder of names with their history of donations listed, pick up the phone, and figure out how to start (how's the family? the Knicks? your work? the latest news stories?) and what the "ask" should be. You don't want to raise $500 from a potential $4,500 donor, which means that, in the parlance of fund-raising, you "leave $4,000 on the table."

"Dialing for Dollars" may be like running in sand for hours a day, but it's unlikely there will ever be an app for that, given the personal touch donors want and expect. I don't particularly mind it as the price of a ticket to The Show, in baseball parlance. But I'm told by someone who was there that Attorney General Bob Abrams, a mild-mannered man pushed beyond his limits in his 1992 race against D'Amato, actually picked up his phone and smashed it against the wall. He then pulled himself together and continued calling.

Nor can you take anything personally, given the large majority who refuse to take the call or denounce you for requesting a lot of money, something that in fact would be strange in normal life. *Hey, neighbor, got a grand for me?* During this process, you raise money but also hear about terrible business or personal reverses, listen to carping about some policy or yourself, find out that the person you're calling is deceased, or experience true eccentrics like Ace Greenberg, a Wall Street Master of the Universe. If he takes the call while sitting in his office directing billions of dollars, he'll give you maybe five to ten seconds to make your case or else he simply hangs up—as in *click . . . dial tone*—not because he's angry but because you're now wasting too much time, given his opportunity cost. Eventually I get it down to "Can you help me become mayor by giving $4,500?" That one finally works.

If, however, you're not the favorite of the money elites, there's also the avenue of hundreds of house parties raising $2,500 to $10,000 at a time or even celebrity-laden big gala dinners. With opponents having the war chests or wealth of a Bill Green, John Dyson, Al D'Amato, Andrew Cuomo, Chuck Schumer, and Mike Bloomberg, I become a combination of party planner and theatrical agent.

I'm often asked how I'm able to get musical groups like those previously mentioned—and folks like Paul Newman, Alec Baldwin, Sarah Jessica Parker, Martin Sheen, Itzhak Perlman, Christopher Reeve, Bill Murray, Al Franken, Bon Jovi, Buster Poindexter, John McEnroe, Richard Dreyfuss, Bob Balaban—to pitch in. With few exceptions, you have to meet them in an authentic situation and bond personally.

I gave a living room speech in California in 1986 and 21-year-old Sarah Jessica was in the audience—she remembers me later. When I fly to Las Vegas to protest nuclear testing, I march with Martin Sheen, and we stay in touch. I push for accessible buses and "curb cuts" for people bound to wheelchairs, as Perlman is. Reeve and I initially collaborate with others on my "Tuesday Night Out" initiative for Broadway when we coax theater owners to lower ticket prices on Tuesdays during a recession.* Franken and I get simpatico when Nader does *SNL* and it appears that he has political sophistication and interests (duh). Navasky gets me together with *Nation* magazine investor Paul Newman, and my tennis background doesn't hurt when his successor, Katrina vanden Heuvel, introduces me to her pal John McEnroe. We play tennis together. I let him win. He hosts a gala.†

Who doesn't enjoy rubbing elbows with people of renown and talent? But while fun, celebrity fund-raisers can be fraught.

In my 1980 congressional race, Paul Simon agrees to be the name host of an ice cream party at the top of the Empire State Building. Only I barely see him there for the first hour; I find him on the floor above making out with Carrie Fisher (they subsequently marry, then unmarry). Late in that campaign, he agrees to perform a concert, but his schedule will only permit it after the election. "OK, I'll take out a loan on the understanding that your concert will enable me to pay it back." After the election, however, he explains that his schedule has changed and he can't do the promised event.

That same year, Carl Sagan, whom I got to know from Cornell ties, agrees to come into the city to host a fund-raiser—with one

---

* Reeve turns out to be a joy and a prince, as people came to know. After his riding accident and paralysis, in mid-1998 I drive to his Westchester home on a large, landscaped few acres in northern Westchester. We have an easy lunch chatting away about politics and national affairs and then he shoots a commercial from his wheelchair in one take: "I know Mark. He's been there for you on [here he rattles off a few issues], so please be there for him on Primary Day next week."

† Such support can have the added political benefit of demoralizing opponents, I discover. When Johnny Mac invites me to his TV booth to commentate for part of a U.S. Open match in the 2001 mayoral race, rival Peter Vallone goes into a frenzy because he's such an fanatical fan—and strong-arms his way into the booth during a later match as well. Another opponent, Alan Hevesi, like me a huge *West Wing* devotee, shares how crestfallen he was when he turned on his car radio in August 2001 to hear Sheen as the distinctive voice of my mayoral ad.

condition. He needs security. Now, we can hardly afford to fly him in, much less provide formal bodyguards . . . so we get a couple of beefy volunteers to put on their best dark suits and dark sunglasses; they then rent earpieces and shuffle Carl around all day. He is happy and so are we.

Bill Murray is as eccentric and charming as his reputation. He requires everyone—agents, producers, *everyone*—to contact him by calling an 800 number and leaving a message on his voicemail or by sending a request to a P.O. Box, neither of which he regularly checks. I do so a couple of times, asking for a contribution and his attendance at a fund-raiser at a comedy club. For months I hear nothing, then I receive an envelope with what looked like some origami figure, which when unfolded proves to be a $1,000 check from Bill—and he just shows up at our party and does a hysterical stand-up for some 20 minutes.

Before his serious turn as an unusually thoughtful U.S. senator, comedian Al Franken hosts a big fund-raiser for my 1986 Senate race, during which he says of Cardinal John O'Connor, "Boy . . . isn't he a dickhead!" (New York has more than a few Catholics.)

Most thrilling is Lewis Black, who agrees to host a night of comedy at Caroline's—"Politics, What's So Funny?"—in the summer of 2001. Three hundred paying guests wait but he never shows and doesn't call. I assume he's either dead or has two personalities. I'm more relieved than angry when he tells me the next afternoon that he and friends had rented a bus to moon tourists at Times Square, for which he's thrown in jail for the night. And he calls his lawyer, not his candidate. Being a charmer and a mensch, however, he pledges to do two more events at some future time—and does.

Ultimately, the key to fund-raising is having real friends in different sectors who hit up their friends with a version of "this one matters to me." Whether it's when I raise $103,000 in my 1980 congressional race or $12.5 million for mayor, that would be my brother Steve in real estate, Bruce Wasserstein on Wall Street, David Boies and Jeh Johnson with lawyers, Ken Lerer in media and tech, Andrew Rasiej in digital/social media, my nephew Gary Green among young entrepreneurs. Calling, hosting, bundling—it takes years of development for a liberal Democrat like me, who lacks the power or inclination to play the give-to-get money chase, to raise $20 million over a decade and half, but we do.

Yet it's not enough because of the Mario-Andrew Cuomo network, Alfonse's special-interest piggy bank, and the Bloomberg desktop terminal combined with the 1976 Supreme Court decision *Buckley* v. *Valeo*, which overturns the post-Watergate campaign finance law that limits self-funding candidates to $25,000. Now rich people can spend as much of their fortune as they want. Justice William Brennan, in the majority in *Buckley*, comes to regret his vote. Me too.

B. THE 9/11 ELECTION:
A GATHERING "PERFECT STORM"

"Clinton should resign! What he did is disgraceful!"

I'm at a January 1999 cocktail party at the Century Country Club in Westchester County as the guest of Elinor Guggenheimer, a prominent leader of society and government, listening to the first words I ever hear Michael Bloomberg say. Of course, I know who he is due to his business notoriety but also because of his status as the thrower of the best parties at national political conventions, which I happily attend. One more thing—there's also a teeny-tiny rumor that he may want to run for NYC mayor in 2001. But no self-funding businessman has ever seriously run for mayor in the city, much less won.

I'm enjoying his corporate Cosell-ish way of speaking, something I don't hear often if ever on the political circuit. Politely disagreeing with his Clinton judgment, I comment that "he should resign only if you think that private peccadillos count for more than public performance, not to mention two national elections." But when the conversation turns to Bloomberg's famous convention parties—with mountains of steaks, burgers, and lobsters between life-sized ice statues and human acrobats—I get frisky. "Mike, can we make a deal—should we ever run against each other for mayor, if you win I'll help you with your inaugural speech; if I win, you cater my inaugural party?"

He enjoys the ribbing. Seems like a good guy, I think, with a locker room/boardroom kind of humor. But I can't imagine how he'd go over in person in Canarsie or the South Bronx or anywhere for that matter outside of the monied Uptown and Wall Street ZIP codes.

Then there's Fernando Ferrer, a rising Latino star, whom I sit down with in 1997 for lunch at his favorite Washington Heights restaurant as I'm starting up my '98 race for the U.S. Senate. Freddy is pleasant, deliberate, fluent in government, and appointed to the major office he's holding—Bronx borough president—when a vacancy came up between elections.

We exchange backstories before getting to the main course—would he consider supporting me for Senate next year? I lay out my record generally as commissioner and advocate, particularly my accomplishments in communities of color. "I would consider that but only if you support me for mayor in 2001," he says candidly. That strikes me as reasonable but something of a stretch since it's almost four years away. Then, of course, there's the unmentionable reality that, should my Senate bid fail, it's possible I could run for mayor since Giuliani is term-limited. I politely decline and we part amicably.

After my Senate loss, I do think more seriously about mayor. While my early history and interests have been largely national, I've served since 1994 as the number-two citywide official and tangled regularly with Giuliani. The opportunity to convert ideas into policy in office—my original impetus back in 1980—and the ego gratification to run the greatest city of the world's greatest democracy is inviting, and then becomes irresistible. Service and ego—always two strands in the same rope of ambition.

Deni and I have our sit-down in mid-1999 to discuss a mayoral candidacy. This is when I explain out loud that I have a good chance of winning "if there's no external event" that can unexpectedly shift the electorate. While everything's probabilities and I believe this one, I also privately worry about Olympic short-track speed skating as a metaphor for an Olympic-scale election. On ice, superbly trained competitors basically glide around the rink for seven turns bunched together with a nominal leader, and then there's a frantic dash at the end when some fall, others get shoved, and one skater lunges at the tape to win by inches. After four years of work, a chance event and a fraction of a second can separate one hero from several losers.

Gliding through the Preliminaries

Other than Freddy and me, the field includes City Comptroller Alan Hevesi and city council Speaker Peter Vallone.* The early line is

---

* The tabloids can't help but speculate whether President Clinton, who will be moving to New York where his wife is the senator, might run for mayor. There's actually a poll that pits me against him among prime Democrats: he's ahead 45 to 18 percent,

mixed to favorable, according to a *Village Voice* cheat sheet of pluses and minuses:

Green: wide reputation as fighter on populist issues, maintains singularly high numbers with black voters, smart and telegenic, engaged Giuliani in more headlined combat than any other candidate . . . but too glib and arrogant for many voters, alarms elites even while appearing elitist himself.

Ferrer: starts with vast Latino base, has nascent alliance with Rev. Al Sharpton and Bronx black leadership that could lead to Dinkins-like coalition . . . but his sudden pullout in 1997 race feeds doubts about character, creature of Bronx machine, gets Sharpton baggage as well as his blessing.

Hevesi: wide reputation as competent and careful manager, probably candidate of the *New York Times*, the United Federation of Teachers, the Liberal Party . . . but perceived as "Rudy Lite" due to years of accommodation, may be too centrist and establishment for primary voters, could get hammered in news stories about the appearance of contributions from city contractors.

Vallone: his 14-year track record as council leader adds up to an unparalleled municipal experience, lays claim to white Catholic base . . . but appears too close to Giuliani, too tied to Real Estate Board and array of special interest lobbyists.

Two outside forces that could significantly influence the race are Rudy and the Rev.

---

as I wonder who those 18 percent are since I'm not among them. Jonah and I attend the last White House dinner of the Clinton administration in mid-December 2000. As we approach the president and first lady, I say in a loud voice, "Jonah, this is exciting—meet the next mayor of New York City!" POTUS, FLOTUS, and the Greens all belly-laugh. But being no dummy, the president knows to say "Mark, that's not gonna happen." Of course, Moynihan said he wouldn't run for the U.S. Senate from the UN, but this guy at this time I believe.

By 2001, Rudy and I are exchanging insults. When asked how I'd be different as mayor, I answer, "I wouldn't arrest the homeless at Thanksgiving. I wouldn't govern by enemies list. I'd try to manage this city more in a collegial Joe Torre kind of way than an angry Billy Martin kind of way." But I can't see how he can undermine me in a Democratic primary where he's particularly unpopular. Except for a few potshots here and there, he plays next to no role in the primary scheduled for September 11.

Indeed, it appears likely that Rudy will be running against Hillary Clinton for the vacated U.S. Senate seat of Pat Moynihan. This creates the anomalous situation that if my nemesis beats my friend and leaves City Hall for Washington, I become mayor by law since I'm next in line of succession. When I speak to Hillary early in 1999 about my governing experience with Giuliani, I ask her if she's seen the Kevin Spacey movie *The Usual Suspects*.

"Sure. Why?"

"Because basically he's Keyser Söze, who will kill his own kids so they can't be taken hostage as negotiating chips by kidnappers."

"Oh my God!" she exclaims with feigned fear, as we go on to seriously analyze what he'd be like as an opponent. Since these two political goliaths are then tied in early match-up polls, I'm thinking to myself a not-unobvious thought—whoever wins this titanic contest for a seat in the Senate could someday be president.

For months people wink and ask me who I'm *really* supporting for Senate, given my unavoidable self-interest. I insist to everyone that, because I couldn't otherwise look in a mirror again, I'll do *anything* to help a Democrat I adore win. Concludes the *New Yorker*, "To his credit, it is not at all difficult to imagine him doing that." But while occupying center stage for months, this play closes before Broadway when it turns out that Giuliani dislikes going upstate, dislikes the idea of being in a collaborative body, and "in a divine intervention," as one top Rudy aide says to me, he withdraws from that race when he is diagnosed with early prostate cancer.

Then there's the mercurial, multi-talented Sharpton, with a high IQ, higher EQ, and even higher skill to work the media like a trainer feeding fish to seals. I first encounter him in 1986 when the then-rotund radical preacher oddly endorses Republican D'Amato and—what a coincidence—subsequently benefits from a $500,000 HUD grant arranged by Senator D'Amato. But he's become a double-edged sword by 2001, probably the most divisive figure in the history of New York City as measured by the stunning 50-point-plus gap, according to my early polling, between his black and white favorable ratings.

We've been largely friendly over the years: I'm the ranking Jewish Democrat to support Dinkins over Koch in 1989 and the leading white public official attacking Giuliani on police misconduct. At his office in 1998, he tells me, "You know how you're different from Schumer? You come out of a movement and act like it in office"; and he tells the *New Yorker* that he's impressed that, in the September 1999 African American Day Parade, "[Green] got a better reception than some of the Harlem politicians."

How to treat him? He's very likely to endorse Ferrer, given Sharpton's political base and Freddy's Brown-Black coalition strategy. That's understandable also because, as *New York Times* columnist Bob Herbert writes, "How does a New York politician court Jewish voters while he's chasing Al Sharpton for his endorsement?" Given my base and campaign slogan of "A Mayor for *All*," an endorsement from the Rev is neither essential nor desirable.

I inform my political staff that I've decided to shower him with respect as a civil rights leader but not seek his formal support. That way he and everyone would understand that in any Green administration, he'd no longer be treated as a pariah like under Giuliani. Also, no endorsement means that I won't appear to be under any obligation to him because of how shrewdly he's able to appear to own events and candidates. Governor Mario Cuomo sums up his influence and motives when he reminds all the mayoral candidates to pay attention to this power broker while knowing that "in the end, what he does will benefit Sharpton."

He comes over to my apartment for breakfast in early 2001 to discuss city, political, and racial issues. Deni and I invite him, his then-wife Kathy, and mutual friend Allen Roskoff to see opening night of *Judgment at Nuremberg* on Broadway and then go out for dinner. In late August, after he endorses Ferrer, I go to the renewals of his wedding vows at an elegant event at the Puck Building; in his list of acknowledgments from the dais, he graciously tells his 200 assembled friends, "Mark Green is here and I thank him for that given what I'm doing politically in the mayor's race. This says something good about him."

With the field set and not much happening on the Rudy and Rev front, we're off and . . . strolling. Frankly, not much happens for months. Newspaper headlines reflect press exasperation—"The Big Snore Four" *(Daily News),* and "4 Democrats Spar Cordially" *(New York Times).* Journalists, especially at the *New York Post* and *Daily News,* privately egg me on to attack Sharpton, but, consistent with my strategy and relationship, I won't and don't. It gets to the point that, testing the mics for sound before one debate at CUNY, I lose my self-discipline and playfully repeat, "I'll try for a contentious debate, I'll try for a contentious debate . . ."

I announce my candidacy before 300 supporters and press at Brooklyn's Prospect Park on April 24, where I'm introduced by Russell Simmons and Bill Bratton and joined by four New Yorkers whom I've personally helped as public advocate. "I've fought City Hall. I've worked with City Hall," I say in a 16-page speech written the month before while visiting Jenya at Cornell. "Now I'm ready to run City Hall." It's well received though perhaps too much of a good thing. Adam Nagourney, in the next day's *Times,* notes the delivery from memory without text or prompter but also admonishes me for my "uncommonly long" 39-minute speech. Despite my annoyance, he's right. Caught up in the moment of a captive, immediate, and city-wide audience, I'm too comprehensive. Ten minutes would have been far better. Lesson learned.

I may have been excited but the primary isn't, in part because of the New York City runoff structure. No one wants to attack any of the other three candidates too explicitly, not knowing whose support you'll need in a one-on-one runoff. The gentlemanly Vallone, however, in a debate tries to change the dynamic by attacking Ferrer for "dividing the city racially" by his "other New York theme"—i.e., ignored communities of color. None of us responds.

That's about the only time race comes up in the entire primary, except when Sharpton says in May that he'll support Ferrer but only on the condition that Freddy promises to support two other possible black candidates in future campaigns. Vallone, Hevesi, and I immediately chastise this racial litmus test and, eventually, an embarrassed Ferrer does as well. Sharpton then disingenuously tells the *New York Times* that Freddy "is the one who has given conditions to us by saying this is a Black-Latino coalition. I didn't bring race in, he did." The episode reminds me why I intend to work with him but not make deals with him.

Like any athlete exercising, I establish arbitrary goals to get through the months of repeat motions. I aim to and visit 50 schools to meet with principals and students to better understand public education; do 200 subway stops; and visit 150 churches over four years to the point that staff think I've converted based on the number of "Praise Gods" I utter every Sunday morning.

I enlist RFK Jr., Gloria Steinem, the 32 BJ doormen and janitor's union, and, most importantly, David Dinkins and Bill Bratton.* When the latter two frequently campaign together with me, it's considered a bold stroke that simultaneously disrupts Ferrer's Black-Brown coalition and implicitly rebuts critics who claim that I'm weak on crime because of my much-publicized scrutiny of the NYPD.

Freddy wins over state comptroller Carl McCall, Senator Moynihan, former Rep. and VP nominee Geraldine Ferraro, and the 1199 Hospital Workers, the most powerful local union with 210,000 members and a $3 million budget to organize voters. That comes after a long, wine-splashed dinner with union president Dennis Rivera when he asks but I decline to allow him to select one of my deputy mayors should I become mayor. Not to advise me on a choice but actually, in his word, to "select" the person. That's when he grouses that I'm "too . . . too . . . independent." Later, Rivera endorses Ferrer and pledges to produce over 5,000 "volunteers" on Election Day for him, or five times what any other union can.

Throughout, I focus on four core issues: reducing class size; economically developing downtown Brooklyn and tech as the next growth sector; bridging the racial divides in the city; and improving police-community relations. I'm chided by the mainstream media for an election-year moderation makeover. "While he's been the official noodge of the city for the last seven years," says political consultant Norman Adler, in a widely held view, "now he has to come across as someone who is going to be a leader."

---

* Bratton tells me at a Regency breakfast in February, "I was thinking about running for mayor myself but came to realize that's not my thing. I love being a police professional." That's when I convince him that I have a good chance to win and will be tough and smart dealing with crime and police. We never explicitly discuss whether he'd return as commissioner. It's unspoken though presumably assumed . . . and, of course, Bill's skills and reputation do earn him a return as police commissioner under a progressive Democratic mayor, albeit 12 years later.

Basically, we're gliding in our lanes, avoiding spills, awaiting the final frantic few days.

As we approach September, I win two key endorsements— the *New York Times* and the *Village Voice*. (Vallone gets the *Daily News*.) My son Jonah—who's shooting a video for a school project— captures me on film taking a call from Nagourney in late August alerting me about the *Times,* which most thought would go to Hevesi. While I'm grinning with pleasure and chatting about this development, my daughter Jenya—who's delayed law school for a year to be my volunteer coordinator—is seen passing me this hand-written note: "Say something more MODEST." After which I remember to mutter, "I'm very gratified to have earned such an important endorsement."

Which brings us to Monday night, September 10. Leaving my campaign office early that evening, supporters Bill Bratton and Jerry Hauer suggest that I meet later that night for drinks with them and John O'Neill, the head of security at the World Trade Center and former leader of the FBI Counterterrorism Task Force investigating Osama bin Laden. I beg off because I want to spend the remainder of that last primary day quietly with Deni.

I tell her at dinner, with relief and joy, that "there's been no ex-ternal event" to alter the campaign's expected trajectory and it looks like there will be a runoff between me and Ferrer, one I believe that I'll win. As of then, I've felt calm and confident throughout, can't remember a bad day, and impressed my wife, which is pretty hard to do. While downing Deni's roasted chicken, I'm playing with my likely statement the next night about being excited to be in a runoff. At that moment in Portland, Maine, however, Mohammed Atta is having dinner at Pizza Hut and anticipating his morning flights, first a commuter run to Boston and then on American Airlines Flight 11 bound for Los Angeles.

9/11: The Day

The next morning, I vote at the Richard R. Green High School at 88th Street and York Avenue and am driven downtown to my last scheduled stop of the day at PS 41 on 11th Street and Sixth Avenue. After urging parents to vote *today,* I have the final handshake of the primary at exactly 8:46, as mentioned as the end of the Introduction, when I hear people around me gasp. I look up to see smoke and flames billowing out of the North Tower of the World Trade Center. This is so outside my experience that I cannot emotionally process what's happening. For a moment, I solipsistically think, *This can't be happening, it's primary day!* Then, I hear a parent shout, "A plane's accidentally hit the World Trade Center." On this perfectly clear, blue day, I snap back to reality. *That's no accident,* I think.

My bias for action is to go downtown as a citywide official to see what's happening and try to help. With me, however, is deputy campaign manager Jeremy Ben-Ami, who quickly figures out that this is something for the mayor and relevant uniformed services, not someone who's regarded on this particular day as more political than governmental. "Let's go back to the apartment," he suggests.

So we drive north, not south. Within that hour, John O'Neill, the WTC security chief and former FBI official hunting bin Laden, has been killed by his nemesis. Giuliani reportedly nearly dies when he's trapped underground in a building near the collapsed World Trade Tower.

Fifteen family, staff, and security members hang in my apartment for hours, like everyone else in the city and country mesmerized by the sickening images on TV of trapped victims jumping from the high floors while also processing how all this will affect families, our city, and, in my case, also the election. I have no idea.

At 11 a.m., I get a call from Governor George Pataki's office to say that he's postponed the primary to some date to be determined. Later, it's reported that exit polls as of that morning show me hovering around the magic 40 percent threshold needed to avert a run-off, although it's usually evening when the "pull operations" of big unions begin their work.

That night, my Harvard Law School roommate Sandy Berger, who was President Clinton's national security advisor, stays over after a speech since he can't get out of town with the airports closed. Picking at take-out Ecuadorian chicken while watching experts on *Charlie Rose* review the day's monumental events, I ask, "You guys ever anticipate a terrorist attack by plane?"

"Nope," he says, adding, "I told Condi [Rice] in our last briefing nine months ago that terrorism would be Bush's number one foreign-policy problem. I held a meeting every morning on al-Qaeda for the four months before the millennium because we worried about an attack that day. But the Cold War–oriented Bush people didn't believe us about the threat of terrorism, at least not until this morning."

Primary Redux

"Can't wait till September 11"—the phrase Deni and I had been privately exchanging for two years—now has an entirely different meaning.

I visit Ground Zero on Thursday to thank emergency personnel and look at the wreckage firsthand. Seeing the mountains of twisted steel, looking at scattered files on the ground from exploded offices, it feels like, in Senator Clinton's description after her visit, "what you would imagine hell to be like." When flights resume, around the city children look up, frightened; many residents carry water bottles to clear throats raspy from the metallic atmosphere. Hospitals wait to treat the injured who never come because, with few exceptions, people either died or escaped.

Throughout these days, the world sees a Giuliani who rises to the occasion, displaying courage, empathy, wisdom. He rallies the city emotionally, oversees the recovery effort, guides groups of foreign dignitaries and congressional leaders through downtown, and attends funerals of lost firefighters, a department that in an hour loses half as many men, 343, than in the prior century.

My friend Jonathan Alter, writing for *Newsweek,* covers and watches Giuliani closely for much of that week. "He conveyed a sense of calm with, like the smart lawyer he is, a masterful grasp of detail. When acting from instinct, he made all the right decisions." I agree with that assessment based on one personal interaction. As a courtesy to me as public advocate and as a potential next mayor, Giuliani invites me to one briefing of his cabinet on the West Side piers where a shuttered City Hall has in effect been moved. As his staff reports on an enormously complicated logistical recovery effort, he absorbs the information with a steady competence both in the meeting and then at his daily press briefing, when I stand with him.

By being so dangerously at Ground Zero, as repeatedly replayed video shows, Alter thinks that "Giuliani's stature and renown grew since, unlike Bush and Pataki, he had been touched by fire." He opens

SNL that weekend to soothe not just the city but the nation. "Rudy the Rock" is what French president Jacques Chirac calls him, and it sticks.

My friend Forrest Smith, who helped start our anti-mob carting effort, now owns an Outback franchise. We decide to organize a tent under the FDR Drive near the South Street Seaport to cook and serve steaks to hundreds of exhausted (and, we later learned, contaminated) emergency personnel. They are surprised to see a politician with an apron handing out the food, with no cameras or media allowed. It feels satisfying . . . until I remember why we're there at all. Later that day I visit one of the few injured survivors at New York Hospital. Part of one of the Towers fell on this Port Authority cop and mangled his legs. "Don't worry, Mr. Green," he says in a hushed but clear voice. "When the tower fell on me, it didn't crush me and can't crush our city either."

I attend several funerals of fallen uniformed personnel. The first is the saddest—my friend Father Mychal Judge, a Franciscan priest and the Fire Department chaplain. A beloved figure, Father Mike is the very first recorded fatality on September 11. He was giving last rites to a firefighter when a large piece of debris killed him. Former President Clinton, Senator Clinton, Cardinal Egan, Mayor Giuliani, and I deliver eulogies four days later to 3,000 mourners downtown at the St. Francis of Assisi Roman Catholic Church. Looking at the throng of family and friends, including gay men from the Alcoholics Anonymous sessions he attended for 23 years, I decide to indirectly acknowledge that Father Mike was gay, lauding his work "with every group and orientation in society." I'm glancing at Cardinal Egan, who doesn't flinch. Family members take me aside afterward to express their appreciation at the tribute and reference; "he would have wanted that," says one.

Politically, the campaign is frozen this week by common consent. And completely upended. For one thing, the mayor has gone from Nixon to Churchill in a day—now anything he says or does carries enormous weight. My jokes at his expense—"either you love him . . . or he hates you"—are never to return. No campaigning, no mailings, no appearances. But since third parties are not bound by this informal agreement, 1199—which Ferrer candidly refers to as his "marines"—are lining up their Election Day artillery behind the scenes.

Over this week, I spend time in our Public Advocate office, checking in with other public officials, checking up on staff, and trying to help constituents wherever possible as the city's ombudsman. But along with David Eichenthal, my chief of staff and an economic development expert, I'm also churning with thoughts on how to reemerge into this altered new world. Campaigning resumes the following Monday for the now-rescheduled September 25 primary. Opinion leaders are looking closely at which candidates respond thoughtfully, mayorally, to this unprecedented calamity. I deliver a series of three addresses on "the New York Comeback" starting with the recovery of the Lower Manhattan economy on September 20 and explain how the city must "unite to rebuild."

Borough President Ferrer's initial response to 9/11 is that he understands what the city needs because he's seen "rubble bounce" in the Bronx and experienced the 1990 Happy Land arson fire that killed 87; he adds that rebuilding funds should be "dispersed around the city" rather than merely go to rebuild the financial center downtown; and he sticks to his vow to give teachers a 30 percent raise despite what is likely to be a big hit to the city budget. Editorial opinion is very favorable to my remarks but critical of his, which sound more like patronage than recovery. The attack also has the effect of undermining Ferrer's slogan of "two New Yorks" and corroborating mine of "a Mayor for *All*" in what now seems like one New York pulling together.

At the same time, our team rightly worries about the 1199 machine organizing its minority membership around the exciting prospect of electing the first Latino mayor. I get that because when I was campaigning for Dinkins in 1989, I'd go to racially mixed Democratic audiences and declare, "Let's make history!" The unspoken subtle rule is that it's OK to be excited *for* a racial underdog while not being *against* someone purely on racial grounds. Late in the primary, for example, I'm campaigning in Midtown when a 20-something comes up to me and says, "Green, I think you're great but, hey, I'm a *Latino!*" We both laugh, do a guy-hug, and go our separate ways.

With a surge in Latino voting in the September 25 Democratic primary, Ferrer wins 35 percent of the vote, I get 31 percent. It's the runoff we thought, though about four points worse than anticipated.

But the first polls show me with a lead of 50 to 40 percent as far more Vallone and Hevesi supporters initially come over to our campaign.

Then there's a big surprise two days later.

Runoff: Rudy and Mario

It's 3:15, September 27, on Yom Kippur, two days into the runoff. The mayor's office is calling to ask that I meet with him at 5 p.m. at the West Side piers. The subject is not mentioned.

I'm ushered into a small, windowless room where I'm alone with Giuliani. Characteristically, he gets right to the point: "Look, Mark, the city is in an emergency and I have my cabinet working together every hour to get through this—and who knows if something else might happen? I'm asking each of the three remaining candidates [Bloomberg, Ferrer, me] to support a proposed legal change to give me and my experienced team 90 more days after the scheduled January 1 swearing-in to finish what we started."

Well, that's pretty creative and nervy, I think. "Mr. Mayor, I understand your desire to complete what you're doing. But even Lincoln during the Civil War, a worse emergency, went ahead with a scheduled election in 1864. Postponing the swearing in would set a bad precedent." The meeting lasts five minutes and ends with Giuliani asking me to "think about it more since Mike has already agreed."

En route home, top mayoral advisor Denny Young calls my cell to imply that the mayor will publicly condemn me if I don't agree to support a 90-day extension. This entire episode is occurring at the same time that Giuliani aides are openly speculating that "America's Mayor" might seek to change the term limits law and run on the Conservative Party line and Governor Pataki is suggesting that people write in his name on ballots—in effect, to cash in his newfound 90 percent popularity to run as the Indispensable Man.

I go home to a pre-Atonement dinner with my family. "You're not gonna believe what the mayor asked me to do," I say, going on to explain the details and debate what might come next as we down Deni's matzo ball soup and brisket. There's a split among family and top staff whether to acquiesce to an extension because, while unprecedented, (a) it's arguably in the city's interest to have continuity and institutional memory throughout the crisis, and (b) it's in my interest to avoid him running and winning a third term on the Conservative Party line. I can't get a read from assembly speaker Shelly Silver, an Orthodox Jew observing Yom Kippur, on what his chamber might do if the mayor made a request to change relevant state law.

After mulling this over during and after dinner, I change my mind and call Young to say that I'll go along if three months can be added to the next mayor's term. The upshot: Ferrer refuses Giuliani's entreaty and looks like a hero standing up to a bully. Silver shoots it down later, saying of me, "Quite honestly, I think it is a political calculation." My lead over Ferrer plunges ten points into a tie.

My eight years of standing up to Giuliani on everything from racial profiling to an incinerator in Brooklyn seems to be torched in a day. But I deserve it. I've allowed Rudy to corner me into violating my history and reputation as a straight-shooter because I'm worried about a potentially worse option. I'm not quick enough to realize that, if he is being authentic rather than political, I could have pledged instead to voluntarily retain his people in my first three months. But in the chaos of that evening, I didn't think of that. Nor did he suggest it. The reaction to my concession is mixed to negative, with liberals expressing surprise and disappointment while moderate voters seem to like an apparent nonpartisan approach to the tragedy. I vow, however, not to go against my gut again for largely political reasons . . . if there is an again.

A week later, on October 1, I'm in a bathrobe drinking coffee at 7:10 a.m. when I take a scheduled phone interview with Mark Riley of WLIB radio. After a few minutes of easy conversation, he asks, "If you had been mayor during 9/11, how would you have done?"

"I actually believe that if, God forbid, I had been mayor during such a calamity," I answer, "I would have done as well [as] or even better than Giuliani."

Stupid answer. The smart response when asked such lose-lose questions is to quickly say, "I don't answer hypotheticals. And, by the way, he did a great job on 9/11." But my actual answer, not the mulligan in my mind later, is regarded as a big gaffe by the standard Kinsley-ian definition of "telling not a lie but the truth" as you see it. For in my thinking, I'm not seeking office to do less well than the incumbent, and I'm indeed dismayed by how, as *Times* magazine profiler James Traub subsequently puts it, "Giuliani risked sacrificing some of his moral prestige when he tried to inveigle his way into a third term, or at least into a 90-day extension of his current term." Alter too thinks that when Giuliani started making "not instinctive but political decisions," he strayed from Rudy the Rock.

But part of being a successful politician is knowing how things will sound when you're not available to explain your thought process personally to each voter. So I go on *Imus* the next day to eat crow. Bloomberg, who prefers to run against Ferrer, predictably airs a ton of effective ads using my own voice saying "better than Giuliani" and ending with only the word on the screen—"Really?"

Approaching the final weekend before the Thursday vote (because of a Jewish holiday), I change tactics. Ferrer is beating me up good over the 90-days *contretemps* so I make three decisions to regain the offensive by reminding liberals who I am and who he is.

First, after weeks of negotiating with Andrew Cuomo over the endorsement of his father, we agree to their major condition—which is to endorse Andrew for governor the following year if I'm mayor, which is not illogical since he'll be running against Ferrer supporter Carl McCall. And Super Mario is the biggest-name liberal whose endorsement can actually move votes. Consequently on Monday, the father and I—along with Representatives Jerry Nadler and Carolyn Maloney, State Senator Eric Schneiderman, other brand-name liberals—gather at the CUNY studio space on 34th and Lexington Avenue to hear the governor say that I'm the "superior choice [to manage the] economic and fiscal crisis" after 9/11; and, as a long-time opponent of capital punishment, he chides Ferrer because "if you change your mind about the death penalty, then maybe you'll change your mind about taxes or this and that." Ferrer unwisely takes the bait, saying, "I would have thought that would be beneath him."

Second, it's not "beneath" either Cuomo *or* me. I take advantage of Ferrer's policy flip-flops—from supporting the death penalty and opposing many abortions ("Every time a mother hiccups," he said, "that's no reason to abort a child") when he ran as a moderate Democrat for mayor in 1997 to his newfound populism in 2001. Campaign staff come up with the funny and effective idea of a rally outside our office where supporters throw actual flips-flops back and forth with the words "Death Penalty" and "Choice" on the soles. On this same day, Donald Trump endorses Ferrer, which one supporter of mine thinks is perhaps what Freddy means by "the other New York."

Last, my media team shows our top staff, my brother, and me a tough, negative ad that they've crafted without my input. It cites the *Times* editorial that called Ferrer's 9/11 response "borderline irresponsible" and ends with "Can we afford to take a chance?" We have a vigorous back-and-forth whether to use it: no because it contradicts our strategy of a high-road, positive campaign; yes because it finally counters their drumbeat of criticism of me, gets us off the defensive, and is built on editorial opinion from the *New York Times* and also the *Daily News.* No one says that it may appear to be racial since, as Steve McMahon, who made the ad, later notes, "that's the standard language you use to argue that the less well-known person is a risk, like ads that ran against Gary Hart and Howard Dean. Remember the ringing red phone late at night?"

I pull the trigger and approve the ad.

Ferrer and his people are furious. Hazel Dukes, a local NAACP leader, says at a Ferrer women's breakfast, "I woke up and thought I was in Mississippi. They lynch you with new ads." A black journalist writes, "Mark Green, a Rudy Giuliani in the making, may have replaced the ironfisted Republican mayor as the most hated white man in the African American community. [Green should] stay out of Harlem." Ferrer himself calls the ad "ugly . . . it turned my stomach."

But almost no one outside their orbit agrees that an accurate if negative ad becomes racial per se merely because it involves a minority. Ed Koch publicly says, "That ad is defensible." Since Ferrer himself compares the spot to racially inflammatory ads that had run earlier that year against Antonio Villaraigosa, also a Latino and who was seeking the mayoralty in LA, I call him to ask if he thinks ours crosses a line. "Hey, my white opponent ran spots implying that I was a drug dealer," Villaraigosa tells me after listening to it. "Yours is within bounds."

The combination of Mario's endorsement, actual and rubber flip-flops, and the "borderline irresponsible" ad over the final three days combine to slow and stop Ferrer's advance. Our tracking polls show white liberals moving back to me. Late afternoon of the October 11 runoff, Jonah's camera captures me and family literally crying with joy when exit polls show us ahead by eight points. That night I'm declared the winner by four, 52 to 48 percent. Ferrer concedes in a phone call and then to his supporters. I "bound" onto the stage, to use the description of the *New York Times,* and immediately—knowing personally how an election-night defeat stings—laud him as "an extraordinary leader of idealism and vision. I need you and can't wait to speak to you and your supporters to unite with us and win in November."

Turns out that I did have to wait because a day later, it appears that there's been some inadvertent double counting by the Board of Elections in some polling places. During the few days it takes the Board to sort out the numbers, my lead shrinks from 32,000 to 16,000, an administrative snafu that incites Ferrer's campaign chairman, Robert Ramirez, to refer to the ol' faithful of southern officials stealing elections from blacks and, with zero evidence, to conclude that Green for Mayor had engaged in a "blatant effort to suppress the voting rights of many New York Democrats." Which at least is a step up from "lynching" them, in the vivid word of Dukes.

On the morning after the runoff, I'm again on the phone with WLIB host Marc Riley, this time fully dressed and wary. He asks about anti-Sharpton/Ferrer flyers and robocalls in white, conservative areas of Brooklyn. "I really have no idea what you're talking about," I reply, vowing to inquire after the interview. Staff send me a flyer with a *New York Post* cartoon depicting Ferrer kissing Sharpton's butt for an endorsement.

The *Post,* of course, is a place notoriously brutal to minority and liberal candidates. And everyone understands, especially Al and Freddy, that the borough president *was* "craving" the Rev's support (again, Bob Herbert's word) because he's long been the planned cornerstone of the Black-Brown strategy. Nadler later tells me that there's no reason to apologize for a cartoon that, however gross, reflects reality and that we didn't distribute in any event. However, because I never would have allowed such flyers or robocalls generally and certainly not into only white areas, I publicly denounce them as "reprehensible" and vow that any "asshole(s)" who did that would never work in any Green administration.

But the Ferrer camp, already miserable over their close loss, is again up in arms as it emotionally conflates my TV spot + a Board of Elections glitch + lit we didn't create. I find myself in a potentially dangerous place between Ferrer Democrats on my left crying foul, who in effect supply scripts for Bloomberg's avalanche of ads on my right.

General Election: Unfriendly Fire

I begin the truncated three-and-a-half-week general election in reasonably good shape—16 points ahead of Bloomberg, with a 67 to 18 percent favorable rating (and, in very hypothetical mayoral matchup, I'm ahead of Giuliani 50 to 42 percent). Rudy and David Garth, the legendary media advisor and now Bloomberg consultant,* are privately doubting that Mike can win.

Then, to quote Forrest Gump, shit happens.

"It's Mark Mellman on line three."

"So how are we doin'?" I ask my pollster, who's now conducting daily tracking polls.

"Well, I have good news and bad," he says, which of course means net bad. "I've never worked for a candidate who lost an election so far ahead so close to the election as you are but never worked either against a candidate spending a million-plus a day—not a month or a week but a *day*—and gaining a point a day. We may not see the full Bloomberg onslaught until too late." There are 20 days left and I do the math.

What now? Once I realize that it's impossible and illegal for me to set fire to his fortune, I have no option other than to raise what I can at our upcoming "Unity Dinner," continue to coalesce the Democratic base, and chide Bloomberg as a governmental novice as much as possible in the free media. That part is fun. "Mike wanting to be mayor is like me going this afternoon to knock on the door of Bloomberg LP and saying, 'Hi, I'm Mark Green. I've never run a company for a day in my life but I'd like to take over [yours]. Where do I apply?'" And I spend money and time talking up my proposals for change, including a novel disc we mail to hundreds of thousands of voters called "Mark Green's 100 New Ideas for New York." One, again, is a 311 for NYC.

But I'm also calling Ferrer all week after the runoff with no return call or endorsement, normally an automatic after a primary.

* In late 2000, I meet with Garth, who guided Lindsay, Koch, and Giuliani to their mayoral wins, to see if we could be a team. We're both polite but I realize that his well-known domineering MO—periodically threatening to quit if he didn't get his way—would be incompatible with my temperament and operation. Which makes him available to be hired later by Bloomberg. Which happens.

As I'm preparing for the annual Al Smith dinner at the Waldorf a week later, Ferrer's office calls: the borough president will see you tonight at his campaign office. Okay, good. At 9:30 p.m. I leave a dais of 100 religious and political celebrities and, incongruously attired in white tie and tails, go to 611 Broadway on the East Side, sweeping by several reporters who were tipped off about the meeting. I enter a small conference room with Ferrer doppelgänger Roberto Ramirez— my 1993 public advocate opponent wanting his own concession event—advisor and former Dinkins aide Bill Lynch, and Sharpton. I'm there with my campaign manager, Rich Schrader, and Assemblymen Denny Farrell and Clarence Norman Jr., two county chairmen and African American supporters. The grim faces of the Ferrer 3 convey the feeling of a police third degree, albeit without the lamp shining in my face.

But I'm relieved we're there, assuming that we'll finally come to some agreement since no serious Democrat, especially minority constituencies, would want our party further locked out of City Hall after Giuliani's two terms. Yet right off, Ramirez and Sharpton demand that Farrell and Norman leave since they're not a party at interest making campaign decisions. In that instant, I figure out that while the Hollywood version would have me say "they go, I go," in real life, the issue is not who's at a particular meeting but would the Ferrer camp do the right thing. Since I'm the nominee, I might as well concede some small ground to protect the priority. Instead of potentially blowing up the opportunity for a united party or making the obvious point that Sharpton too is neither a candidate nor campaign staff, I consent, containing my pique at their small-minded ploy to embarrass Denny and Clarence. They calmly exit.

The Ferrer folks then proceed to harangue me and Schrader about perceived offenses. Ramirez passionately decries what he regards as our "patronizing, condescending, insensitive, disrespectful" comments. Rich is getting annoyed at Roberto's hectoring style, which in turn sends the latter into even more shrill charges. Amazingly, a now-overwrought Schrader, who suffered a massive heart attack the year before that almost killed him, says, "That's it, I'm done," and marches out, leaving his surprised candidate alone to face the interrogators.

I continue solo to repeatedly explain that I knew nothing about the Brooklyn flyers, they appear to have been done by breakaway

Dems in the county, and I've again and again publicly denounced them. "What else can or should I do? But really, guys, does this justify turning the mayoralty to Republican control for four or eight more years?" (Twelve years did not then occur to me.) After 90 minutes of this, we all agree to reconvene the next morning.

About 9 a.m. I return, brush by a larger clutch of reporters, and meet with Freddy one on one. We're perfectly cordial for 45 minutes as he airs his familiar concerns and I re-pledge to get to the bottom of what happened and to focus on winning back City Hall with his team as part of mine, as I announced in my victory speech the previous week. We then go into a large main room where we're joined by some 50 of his most prominent supporters as well as a handful of mine. There's Dinkins, Spitzer, Rangel, McCall, Paterson, Norman, and Queens congressman Greg Meeks in what becomes a useful mutual therapy session. I repeat how much I need their help, how I'm competing with a billionaire Republican, how I've spent most of the past eight years fighting Giuliani on behalf of communities of color on issues like policing and price-gouging. "You know me and I know you."

Then in the fourth hour of meetings over 12 hours, I'm searching for new ways to gain their trust and unite the party. Despite the ambience of Mark in the Lion's Den, I still feel self-assured given my record and relationships, especially as compared to a Republican nominee nobody there knows and who quit four all-white clubs to run. I'm also aware that minority leaders are rightly sensitive to being taken for granted after an election and recall my published comment earlier summer that "the broadest, interracial coalition [is] not only the best way to win—it's the best way to govern." So in closing I comment that as much as I hope to win their support in the election, I especially want their participation in governing the city.

Freddy then announces to the group that he will endorse me at a press conference early that afternoon. Two hours later at the Sheraton New York, I stand with several dozen of the Democratic elite—DNC chair Terry McAuliffe, Senators Clinton and Schumer, Sharpton, Ramirez, McCall, Dinkins, Silver, Farrell. McAuliffe opens with his typical pep-rally fervor lauding all for coming together and warning against a divided party. The borough president is understandably downcast, staring at his shoes and speaking softly. But we all agree to work together based on a joint statement from both campaigns that condemns any racial incitement and includes Ferrer's stated support. "It was probably," reports *Newsday,* "the strongest showing of Democratic unity for a mayoral campaign in years."

Except I'm now sabotaged by a slander that has grown into an urban legend that cannot be unlearned by those who wish to embrace it. *Can you believe that Green said he didn't need us to win the election!* Whether I said in my extemporaneous remarks that morning that "I don't only need you to win the election but especially to help me govern" or left out the words "only" and "especially," I cannot recall 15 years later. Nor should such an inconsequential difference justify Freddy's supporters suggesting that Latino voters sit out the election to teach me a lesson. Spitzer understood the obvious context that I wanted us to be a team for the term. "You were complimenting them by emphasizing not politics but the more important matter of governing the city," recalls Spitzer about that moment. "But what you assumed was praise, some of them took as degradation."

Or in the axiom of a law professor of mine, "To the jaundiced eye all looks yellow."

In a game of racial gotcha, they convince themselves that I'm probably the first nominee in a Western democracy to beg for support from a natural constituency yet really mean the opposite. I naïvely can't even contemplate how, given my known record on race in a campaign co-chaired by David Dinkins, anyone could treat me like some race-baiter. But, politics usually being driven more by emotion than logic, that's exactly what they imply in those pivotal weeks and in the years since—"Green was 'disrespectful'" is their preferred euphemism.

For this book, I ask two people who were close to this episode for their dispassionate view—Arnie Segarra, a Latino political professional and ranking Ferrer insider, and Dominick Carter, probably the leading African American journalist in the city during the election. Their memories mesh:

Arnie Segarra:

> Freddy and crew thought you were arrogant. Actually, you were a smart son of a bitch who spoke from the heart and weren't dismissive or condescending. You could appeal to both tribes. Unlike Hevesi, you were the opponent where they could not say—where

had you been?—because you'd been there for us against Rudy even when it wasn't popular.

When you said "need you more to govern than to win," they were resentful mostly because it was their time to make history and you beat them. It was sour grapes.

Dominick Carter:

It went south after the word went out that you supposedly said you didn't need them. In fact, they wanted to bring you down whatever it took so that Freddy could run in '05.

You were basically the black candidate at the start of the campaign. No one in city government that decade, black or white, did more than you to help low-income and minority communities. It's what you dedicated your life to, yet that's thrown out of the window overnight when racial arsonists wanted you to kiss their butt and make Sharpton in effect a deputy mayor, like de Blasio has done. But they knew you were too independent to do that.

WITH ONLY TWO WEEKS to go, I turn to my actual opponent, a first-time candidate and the twenty-third-richest man in the world at that time.

Mike Bloomberg is easy to admire.

He's obviously immensely ambitious yet authentic in his blunt CEO way. (Remember "Clinton must resign!") His biographer, Joyce Purnick, reports that he told pals in college that he wanted three jobs: secretary general, head of the World Bank, or president of the United States. When I think about him I'm reminded of Andrew Undershaft in *Major Barbara:* when asked his religion, he answers, "Why, I'm a millionaire!"

But in October 2001 he's still learning the ropes as a candidate and it's not always pretty. He's used to asking questions, not answering them. At press events, after responding to any question, he invariably barks out "next!" to stay away from the quicksand of follow-ups. When asked why he's not disclosing his income and net worth statements like me and other candidates, he snaps, "That's fine. They don't make anything." When questioned about his public experience, he says, "Based on all the countries I deal with, I probably have more government experience than anyone in the world." (Looks like he's caught my superlative virus.) For nearly all of the contest, he seems to be a wallet in search of a rationale, until 9/11 allows this builder of businesses to argue why he can rebuild New York City.

He's struggling to pretend that he's a Mikey-from-the-Block despite marveling at how "real people" are, as if he's Margaret Mead in Samoa. Still, he has the guts to leave the comfort zone of his worlds of business and high society to seek office where a public humiliation is the likely result.

Bloomberg rarely engages the media—or me for that matter—because he doesn't have to. He needn't comply with the usual protocols of making endless fund-raising calls, campaigning daily at subway stops, showing up at every political club or group evening because his biggest asset, again, is his assets. He does, though, have to debate, which we do twice. Since I'm an experienced debater and he's not, the expectation is that I'll easily best him. But I recall thinking to myself late in our second debate on WABC-TV, *Wait, this guy is hanging in there with me! How's he doing that?*

Then, two hovering figures from offstage splashily re-enter the mayoral scene.

First, there's Giuliani with his Bunyan-esque approval ratings. He's now as needed by Bloomberg to attract outer borough white voters as Sharpton has been for Ferrer with African Americans. Yet he's playing hard to get for the Republican mayoral nominee. Some staff are urging him to stay above the fray and focus on helping the city recover rather than appearing political. Indeed, the first two times that Bloomberg's campaign books a large hotel suite with producers, equipment, and technicians to shoot an endorsement, Rudy cancels on the day of the taping.

But showing the tenacity that elevated him to the top of the business world, Bloomberg is a salesman who keeps coming back to close the deal. And does. On October 26, it takes only a few minutes for the mayor to walk down the steps of City Hall to give him a hug and say that "Mike understands how to create jobs because he's done it," which is enough to air what is just about the most influential TV spot at that time in New York history. Later, pollster Mickey Carroll remarks that Rudy and Mike are seen more frequently on TV during the final games of the Yankees' World Series that month than Derek Jeter. After the election, Garth says that the Giuliani ad alone shifts 16 net percentage points to Bloomberg.

Second, Sharpton now does what he does best, becoming a one-man show, the Kanye of politics barging onto a stage demanding attention. He's not subtle about his racial impetus, earlier not only insisting that poor Freddy pass a black litmus test in some other campaigns but also declaring that if Carl McCall didn't become the Democratic gubernatorial nominee the next year, it "would be the victim of the greatest form of political racial profiling in the history of the state." He's also been generating headlines over the previous months announcing that he might run himself, announcing that he won't run, leaking that that he might support Ferrer, then leaking that he didn't leak the original Ferrer leak, then endorsing Ferrer.

This zigzagging provokes an exasperated Jack Newfield to write a *Daily News* column with the headline "Rev. Al Trickster, the 'Source' of Lies."

> In 35 years in the newspaper business, I have never disclosed a source. But today—and never again—I have to break that rule. Al Sharpton was my source for my column that disclosed he had promised to endorse Fernando Ferrer for mayor. I am reporting this only because I've been listening to Sharpton say all week that Ferrer was my source.

Then he does a Full Sharpton in the general election, tossing racial anthrax my way. *New York* magazine writes in October that when "the tabloids were begging Green to pounce on Sharpton and, to his credit—we might have had a racial free-for-all if he had on our hands—he didn't do it." No matter. Despite his attendance at the "Unity Press Conference," headlines start appearing like "Sharpton Calls Green's Tactics 'Bigoted'" *(Newsday)*, "Bitter Rev Al Says Green Played the 'Race Card' to Beat Ferrer" *(New York Post)*, "Rev Al Warns Green: Black Nod's in Doubt" *(Daily News)*. He insists that I asked for his endorsement when I didn't. On and on, day after day—like his proven slander of white cop Steven Pagones in the infamous Tawana Brawley episode, Sharpton is convincingly lying. About me. But of course, unlike Pagones, I can't and won't sue.

9/11 + Sharpton/Ferrer/Ramirez are helping Bloomberg catch up. But none of that would have been enough to boost him into orbit without the fuel of his money. In April 2001, when asked if he might spend as much as $30 million, he responds that the number is both too high and "obscene." In any event, he adds that the public should be happy he's spending his own money. "As for the other candidates, I can't help it if your problem is that you can't afford to do it yourself."

But one thing you can say about Mike Bloomberg—he knows how much to spend to make a successful tender offer for a company or a city. In the final week, with Rudy's endorsement providing the grist for positive mailings and ads and Ferrer's team proving material for negative ones, Bloomberg pours it on, as Mellman had warned. He spends $17 million on daily direct mail—with no media attention, millions of pieces urge voters "not to go back to the Dinkins era," assert that I've accomplished nothing as public advocate, attack me as anti-police and anti-business—an amount that alone exceeds more than I spend for everything. "We killed Green in the mail and no one wrote about it," his direct mail guy, Duane Baughman, later says.

The *Daily News* writes, "Mike Bloomberg is trying to transform every channel into The Bloomberg Channel." Whenever I turn on the TV, look up at Madison Square Garden during a Knicks game, look down at the ground at subway stops, there he is, in English, Spanish, Chinese. I feel as if I'm playing in a World Series game where I get to bat in one inning versus his nine.

But all this probably still wouldn't have been enough to elect Bloomberg except for the turmoil of the final three days when the campaign veers into *Bonfire of the Vanities* territory.

A *Daily News* article the morning of October 30 carries the byline of a Larry Cohler-Esses and the provocative lead, "Contrary to repeated denials, Mark Green's mayoral campaign distributed the controversial flyers linking the Rev. Al Sharpton to the candidacy of Fernando Ferrer, sources told the *Daily News*."

The article reports that a dozen south Brooklyn pols had convened at Nick's Lobster House in Mill Basin just before the runoff, including Green staffers Jon Kest and Ralph Perfetto, to discuss how to use Sharpton's support of Ferrer to carry their largely white election districts. Ferrer is again livid, calling me on my car phone as I'm leaving a breakfast with Dinkins at Sylvia's Restaurant in Harlem. "What can I tell my people?" he says with anguish. "I need heads! Even a secretary's!"

I tell him that I'll speak to the staff mentioned in the article about what happened since this is the first I've heard about it. I ask Kest—our political director, a renowned liberal labor leader and the co-head of the grassroots organization ACORN—who looks me in the eye later that day and says that the Thomas Jefferson Club in Brooklyn had called and ran the meeting and that he adamantly told State Senator Carl Kruger and former Vallone advisor Bruce Bender, "That's precisely what Mark has resisted the entire campaign. We won't do that." Perfetto corroborates Kest's version to me.

Despite their denials, Ferrer insists that I fire Kest and Perfetto or some unspecified bad things would happen.

An hour later, our top staff meet at my apartment to figure out how to solve this political Rubik's Cube. Some suggest that I fire Kest and Perfetto, given the risks and their presence at Nick's Lobster House. Others think it weak to ruin loyal people who had opposed the suggestion of the hardliners at Nick's. At this pivotal moment, my outside public interest impulse wins out over my killer political one. I simply can't sacrifice two staff—not to mention that Kest, though white, helps lead a major black organization and Perfetto had recently recovered from leukemia—at the altar of Ferrer's anger. This is way beyond agreeing that Farrell and Norman leave a private meeting.

That night is our "Unity Dinner." In the spring, I had asked movie royalty Harvey Weinstein to start organizing a massive event for whoever would end up being the nominee (assuming that would be me). Harvey readily agreed. Speaking of forces of nature, Harvey is big in size and appetite, always more films, Oscars, causes. While many dislike his volcanic temperament, I admire his bigheartedness, including the way he periodically revisits his college pals back in Buffalo where he got his start selling videos door to door.

At the dinner that Friday evening, 1,200 leading donors, Democrats, and celebrities cram the Sheraton ballroom in Midtown Manhattan to hear emcees Jon Stewart and Jimmy Fallon joke and host the Clintons, the Cuomos, Dinkins, Spitzer, Hevesi, Vallone, and other Democratic luminaries. Bill is filmed affectionately nuzzling and hugging Hillary backstage in Jonah's film. I'm captured telling the audience how much change I'll bring to City Hall after Rudy because "I'm not running just to win an election . . . though that would certainly excite my mother-in-law." At which point said mother-in-law, Lucille Frand, with an Auntie Mame persona, jumps up in the audience and shouts, "YES, IT WOULD!"

We have fun, raise a million bucks, boost morale. But Ferrer refuses to show. The next day's *New York Times* carries the headline

"Unity Dinner Is Anything But, with Ferrer Absent." This fiasco dominates the news in the final three days of the general election.

Then, *mirabile dictu*, it gets worse.

It's Monday, November 5, and our "Greenmobile" is beginning my customary all-nighter before Election Day, hitting all five boroughs. I'm giddy with excitement and relief as I banter with United Federation of Teachers president Randi Weingarten and other supporters who rotate on and off. At 5:45 p.m., I get a call from Schrader: "I just spoke to your pal [mega-publicist] Ken Sunshine, who says that he's been holed up in the Four Seasons Hotel for the past several hours eating and drinking in a private suite with Harvey Weinstein, Sharpton, and Ferrer. They want President Clinton to come over right away to broker a peace between you and Freddy and then hold a late-night press conference with everyone."

Fifteen minutes later, Clinton calls to ask what I want to do, since "it's your campaign." We briefly review the pros and cons. "Bill, I want to end on today's great Bryant Park event with you and Ted [Kennedy]. That's what voters should see in their morning papers, not eleventh-hour theatrics with Sharpton," who's both unpredictable and unpopular with most voters . . . and likely to hijack any event for his own purposes. Who would rationally risk that? I'm sure Harvey and Ken mean well and intend a dramatic rescue. But this isn't a movie. Unless it's *Tin Men*, when home improvement contractors punch holes in a roof and then ring the doorbell asking if they can repair the damage. Another "unity press conference" without him—just Clinton, Ferrer, and me—might do some good; Ferrer, however, is insisting that the Rev be part of it. That's a deal breaker.

Clinton, a good friend of Weinstein's, goes to the hotel to let the group know my thinking. But when a scrum of press tipped off by Sharpton swarm his car as it pulls up, the president tells his driver to keep going because "I know when I've been set up." They escape down 58th Street with cameras capturing their taillights. Weinstein is beside himself, according to journalist Michael Wolfe, his "self-assigned centrality" having failed. "All I want to fucking do is unite this fucking city, and you won't let me," he shouts into a phone to someone—not me—according to a press report.

The next morning—Election Day itself—Weinstein switches sides and actually endorses Bloomberg! (In a *New Yorker* profile on him by Ken Auletta a year later, I choose not to be interviewed, except for one on-the-record comment: Since I go to the movies a lot, I ask Weinstein through Auletta, "Would he let me have final cut of *Shakespeare in Love?*") This same Election Day morning, Mayor Giuliani authoritatively tells his pal Howard Koeppel, "Green will win by four."

A few hours later, I'm told that public exit polls have me leading by two. Bloomberg's staff, expensively conducting their own exit polls, are startled that I'm overperforming by four points as compared to their pre-election tracking polls. They flood their poorly performing areas with $150,000 in phone calls, volunteers, and door-knockers that reach 1.5 million homes to get out their vote.

Election night. At my campaign suite are several dozen anxious family, friends, politicians, staff, and VIPs including President Clinton. "Be strong tonight and tomorrow for your father," he knowingly suggests to Jenya.

At 7 p.m., we're all guardedly optimistic because of those afternoon exit polls. At 9:50, Denny Farrell hands me tallies showing a lead of some 5,000 votes; about that moment across town, Bloomberg is telling former SEC chairman Arthur Levitt Jr. that he thinks he'll lose by two. At 10:33, it's even. I duck out to be alone in an adjacent bedroom to stare, emotionally frozen, for 15 minutes at draft victory and concession statements. *So this is sort of how it feels to be waiting for a jury verdict to find out if you'll go free or to jail.*

By 11:55, I've fallen behind by 8,000 in Farrell's count. In a suite eight blocks south at the Hilton Times Square, aide Kevin Sheekey pulls out of his pocket both victory and concession speeches, and hands Bloomberg the victory one. (No one later recalls his reaction, though Mike tells his biographer, "I didn't jump up and down cheering—that's not me.") When Detective Kim Jackson of my security detail tells me that there's a 15,000-vote deficit near midnight, I ask her, "Please get me Bloomberg on the phone."

"Well, Mike, congratulations. You're an Al Kaline, winning the batting crown in your rookie season," I say, lapsing into a jokey-jock persona that's my default position under stress.

To which the mayor-elect replies, "What time will you be conceding?"

At 12:20 a.m., my family and I take a freight elevator downstairs to a stage full of party leaders and a roomful of 800 stunned and deflated supporters. "We gave it our all but it wasn't enough," I say at the podium, having lost 50 to 48 percent in the closest mayoral election of the past century. "They sure got it right that 'it's NOT easy being Green.'"

Back home at 1:45 a.m., Deni makes chocolate chip cookies for me, Jenya, and Jonah, as recorded by our son's video. "What could be bad," announces my protective wife, "with a chocolate chip cookie?" A year later, Jonah sells his film, *Off the Record,* to the Sundance Channel, which rotates it with two other documentaries as its election year package—*The Perfect Candidate* about Ollie North's Virginia Senate race and *Unprecedented* about Bush-Gore. "I should thank you for such an exciting race," he says, tongue firmly in cheek. "It made for a better film."*

After-Report: What Happened

What happened is that he won and I lost because he got more votes.

Right after November 6, I refuse to be baited into blaming others for my loss . . . except for that one time I say privately to Schrader, "He bought it fair and square." Otherwise no one, *no* one, wants to hear from a self-serving loser why he lost, especially when some 2,852 New Yorkers and passengers lost not an election but their lives. That's why in an exit interview from the Public Advocate office a month later with the leading political reporters in the city, I turn aside their barrage of questions prodding me to comment on my campaign. They must have thought I had taken several Quaaludes when, despite a career of arguing, I decline to complain or explain. The result are uniform headlines, like "Green Takes a Gracious Tone" in the *Daily News* and "Green Admits Share of Mistakes" in *Newsday.*

Democrats happy about the loss of their party's nominee have no such compunction. Ed Koch, a *bête noire* since our 1980 exchange, says only two words could be blamed for my loss, "Mark and Green." Sharpton boasts that he's glad that he helped defeat me because people of color, having been brutalized historically "by the Bull Connors,"

---

* Readers interested in seeing Jonah's film about the campaign can see it at jonah green.com.

could not allow themselves to be so "disrespected." Al D'Amato says, "It's the greatest political upset in the history of New York." Ferrer warns *Newsweek* and *Newsday,* "No one better blame me. I supported Mark and felt bad when he lost." Greg David, the editor of *Crain's,* which endorsed me, writes that I lost because "voters didn't like or trust Mr. Green."

I also receive a ton of calls and mail from shocked and commiserating allies. The next morning, in order among others, Bob Reich, Al Franken, and Bill Clinton call with, in effect, the same story line: "I was so depressed when [respectively] I left the Labor Secretary's office/when my Stuart Smalley movie flopped/when I lost for governor in 1980 and basically curled up in bed for a month" . . . *so hang in there!* Governor Mario Cuomo writes three days later, "You ran hard all the way. You never sold out an important principle or tried to blame anyone for a campaign weakness or whine about unfairness. Believe me, you have a lot of good things left to do and enjoy. Thanks for giving me a chance to participate." Vartan Gregorian, then president of the Carnegie Foundation, takes me to lunch to suggest that I go on a sabbatical to London to put distance physically and emotionally from the defeat. (I don't.) Jonah offers up his version of Deni's chocolate chip cookies to me: "Nothing's changed except your expectations," adding Nick Carraway's comment to Gatsby, "You're worth the whole damn bunch put together."

Dismayed journalists weigh in. *New York's* Michael Tomasky: "Bloomberg's involvement in the life of the city was largely built around the act of opening his checkbook . . . When did $4 billion and no civic track record become better credentials—to Democrats!—than years of salaried public service spent aiming a sword at mobbed-up garbage carters and the tobacco lobby?" Joyce Purnick of the *Times,* who will go on to write a biography of Bloomberg, concludes that "the deconstruction of Mark Green suggests that a white candidate has to walk on eggshells when running against a black or Latino candidate. The campaign . . . left a legacy of political correctness masquerading as racial righteousness that could prove enduringly damaging." Her colleague Clyde Haberman, commenting on a campaign that had David Dinkins, Denny Farrell, and Russell Simmons in its leadership, adds that "from the way Mr. Sharpton talked about him before the November election, you'd have thought that Mr. Green paraded around town in white sheets and a hood."

We often hear from the beaming winners after bouts or elections, thanking their great supporters, sharing their wisdom. But not much from the losers, a far larger category. How does it *feel* to go from toast of the town to toast—to, in journalist Wayne Barrett's comment to me, "not being able the rest of your life to do what you were born to do?"

Heartbreaking, shocking, infuriating, humiliating, depressing, sickening, crushing. "The mornin' after a fight, ya' nothin' but like a large wound. I feel like calling a taxi to take me from bed to the bathroom," says Rocky to Adrian in that iconic first film.

After 25 years with a spouse who periodically has to calm down my overconfidence, Deni now lifts me up, starting with those chocolate chip cookies. You beat yourself up, fret that you let down so many talented young workers who cut their teeth with me and wanted/deserved to help govern the city. And all the while you keep these feelings bottled up, unwilling to sound self-pitying yourself in the aftermath of a national tragedy.

Remember driving by a wreck on the side of the road and you think selfishly, *Glad that's not me?* Except in this case it *is* you. Remember when you've lost the girl or the job and you're feeling blue? At least then, while walking down the street, no one knows it. But when you walk around New York City streets after you've lost the mayoralty, every person you pass looks at you with wide eyes or says a version of "Ohh, I'm sorry" or "I voted for you!" (Based on this scientific poll, I won with 97 percent.) Or occasionally remarks, "Ohh, I voted for you four times," which means primary day one, primary day two, the runoff, and the general election—which has never happened before and probably won't ever again. It gets to a point that I ask Deni to go out to get that half-gallon of milk rather than unnecessarily face this gauntlet again.

When friends start lauding my "courage and resilience," I laugh because once you make the relatively easy initial decision not to kill yourself, courage and resilience are sort of the only other choice. Then there are the five people who later thank me for saving their lives. How? "I was so excited to vote for you," explains one in words others use, "that I waited in line to vote in the morning and delayed getting to my office by 8:30 a.m. at the 102nd floor of the first World Trade Center . . ."

At the political level, of course I made "wrong mistakes," as Yogi Berra supposedly once put it, over the course of an unusual campaign.

I regret the 90 days decision, waiting until the last few days to robustly criticize Bloomberg, being one or two words off wooing Ferrer
supporters itching to be offended, not figuring out how to assuage
him when he flipped out at the overwrought *Daily News* article, failing to appreciate that the Bronx party would actually go on strike.
I thought that Ferrer Democrats would ultimately be rational, not
racial. That proved to be wrong. Nearly half of his runoff vote went to
Bloomberg. "I've seen a lot politically," says an angry state party chair
Judith Hope, "but was shocked to watch TV election night and see
Ramirez and Bronx party leaders partying at their headquarters with
unused phones piled in a corner."

To be fair, obviously my team and I made a lot of good decisions
that got us to the doorknob of City Hall. We convinced, for one, a
skeptical *New York Times* to endorse me: "We wondered if he had the
political finesse to reach a goal through negotiation rather than by
calling a press conference. But as a candidate for mayor he has been
extremely deft." Most political observers thought we had run a smart
and largely error-free campaign until 9/11 rewrote the script. Indeed,
until the final Bloomberg paid media assault and the Ferrer/Sharp-
ton political assault, we were very strong in polls—only to watch a 69
to 18 percent favorable rating in my private polls plummet to 46 to 42
percent over the course of the final three weeks.

According to Chris Smith in *New York* magazine, "Many old-
school Democrats believe that Bloomberg's 2001 victory over Mark
Green was a terrorist-provoked, money-soaked aberration." Ray
Kelly, who endorsed Bloomberg and later became his effective police commissioner, concluded in his memoir *Vigilance* that, after reviewing various factors for Bloomberg's victory, "one other thing was
more important than everything else combined—Bloomberg spent
$74 million, more than in any non-presidential campaign. Had it not
been for that and the terror attack, I'm sure New York would have
been preparing for the inauguration of Mayor Mark Green."

Until this book, I've never publicly discussed the reasons for my
loss. But I cannot disagree with Smith and Kelly. With Bloomberg,
Giuliani, Sharpton, Koch, Pataki, Garth, Ferrer/Ramirez/Rivera arrayed against us, I came to self-servingly wonder how I even got 48
percent in a perfect storm that a Tom Wolfe couldn't have made up.

My greatest regret, however, isn't the shock of election night or
even the racial innuendo and a near indictment (more on that later

in this chapter). Rather, after a lifetime of progressive activism, thick policy books, and reams of "new solutions," I just miss out on a once-in-ten-lifetimes opportunity to be an outside advocate who actually gets to convert ideas into policies in high public office.

After Walter Mondale lost the presidency in 1984, he famously asked George McGovern, who failed in 1972, when he got over it. McGovern reportedly replied, "I'll let you know when I do."

AFTERWARD

The Brooklyn Flyers. Fred Dicker of the *New York Post* writes in November that an unnamed "outer-borough Democratic state lawmaker was responsible for at least some of the racially charged runoff phone calls. 'We told the people who were called, "If you vote for Ferrer, you're going to have Sharpton at City Hall" and it scared the hell out of them.'" The lawmaker tells Dicker that "he arranged the calls without the knowledge of Democratic victor Mark Green."

Isaac Abraham, a Hasidic Jew and political operative in Brooklyn, proudly informs journalist Tom Robbins that he too was behind some of the unsigned flyers. "Abraham was asked if he had shown the letter . . . to the Green campaign. 'No, no. This we do on our own.'"

When weeks later I see Abraham at a Brooklyn event, I ask him heatedly, now knowing his outsized impact on the election, "Why the hell did you do that?" "Because we hated Sharpton," he answers.

Years later, assemblymen Frank Seddio and Bill Colton say they were shocked how the *Daily News* article sensationalized what happened at Nick's Lobster House that day. Seddio, now the widely respected Kings County Democratic leader, concluded in a 2015 interview that "the meeting ended with an agreement that no such literature would be distributed."

The "Kill It" Ad. Four days after the election, I call Bloomberg to apologize for a TV spot that we ran only on the very last day of the general election. It quotes from the sworn affidavit of a female Bloomberg LP employee claiming that, when she told Bloomberg she needed a pregnancy leave, he urged her to have an abortion, supposedly saying, "Kill It. Kill It." She settled for an undisclosed amount of money.

"I dismissed the ad for weeks out of hand and then overreacted to your deluge of negative ads," I tell the mayor-elect. "But I still shouldn't have gone there."

"Yeah, I don't know what she was talking about," he replies.

Bloomberg on Ferrer. A year after his victory, the mayor invites me to a friendly, fence-mending hour-and-a-quarter lunch at his favorite Midtown Italian restaurant, Paper Moon. We spend it mostly talking about our families and the impact of a political life. Toward the end, he says, "You know, I never would have won if Ferrer didn't have that fight with you." Or in the opinion of Koch's wise confidant, John LoCicero, "In New York City, race trumps everything."

My loss also turns out to be Ferrer's opportunity. He does run for mayor in 2005—as a Democrat, I support and campaign with him. He wins the nomination but loses to Mike by 19 points. He and supporters Charlie Rangel and Roberto Ramirez bitterly criticize disloyal Democrats who don't support him.

Koch and Green. Shortly after the election, I see Koch at a Jewish Museum event at the Sherry Netherland. "Ed, I'm probably not as good as I thought but not as bad as you thought."

"I don't think you're bad," he says.

"Ed, c'mon. I watch TV."

The exchange has no rancor. We agree to put past animosity behind us because, why not?

Fulani-Bloomberg. The Independence Party endorsed Bloomberg in the election. He got 50,000 votes on that line, or 14,000 more than his 36,000-vote margin of victory. Shortly after the election, *New York Sun* reporter Ben Smith reports that the mayor contributed $50,000 to Lenora Fulani's organization, the All Star Players; *Gothamist* later discloses that he gave a total of $1.7 million to her party or organization through 2008. When asked about Fulani's anti-Semitic remarks and his ties to her, Bloomberg snapped, "So what! *I'm* not anti-Semitic!"

Poster Boy. The verbal racial strife in the mayor's race directly influences the 2002 campaign for governor and 2005 contest for mayor. *Jewish Week* reports that its reporter hears Andrew Cuomo tell people at my election-night ballroom, "Carl [McCall] would be the second installment of that contract, that racial contract, and that can't happen." This comment adds to the racial tensions that ultimately force him out of the Democratic gubernatorial primary in September 2002. "The 44-year-old," wrote Wayne Barrett in the *Village Voice*, "did not want to go wind up a second-rate Green, racialized and ridiculed, a lifelong liberal . . . white man who gets in the way of ego-driven empowerment." Anthony Weiner in 2005 comes in a strong second to Ferrer in the Democratic mayoral primary but withdraws before the runoff, worrying both that he's unlikely to win and will also be racially slammed.

Post-Election—Bloomberg. Mike goes on to a largely successful mayoralty, despite his imperial override of term limits, and then to a uniquely influential post–City Hall life based on his Rolodex, media empire, and billions in philanthropy.

Post-Election—Giuliani. He goes on to earn millions off his reputation from 9/11, a tack that starts to appear tacky when Joe Biden memorably says in a 2008 presidential primary debate, "There's only three things he mentions in a sentence—a noun, a verb, and 9/11." He flames out running for president that year when folks get to see the snarls beneath the halo. He also loses much luster when he says in 2015 that Obama "doesn't love America" and that police shootings of unarmed black youth fail to take account of "black-on-black crime." For all his formidable fame and skills, he apparently cannot escape a parochial and professional background that's not very diverse.

Post-Election—Sharpton. The Rev goes on to even greater prominence. He's a riveting, entertaining "confidence man"—see *The Sting, Music Man*—who charms his way out of a list of particulars that would destroy anyone of lesser talent—mob ties and being an FBI informant against the mob, Tawana Brawley, IRS fines, multiple campaign finance violations, anti-Semitic comments, racial bullying. When Giuliani makes his repellent remarks in 2015 about Obama not loving America, Sharpton says, without a flicker of irony, that the former mayor "'will say anything or do anything to get attention." The Rev befriends and has open-door access to both President Obama and Mayor de Blasio and gets a coveted 6–7 p.m. show weeknights on MSNBC in 2013 until he's moved to one hour on Sundays in 2015.

Post-Election—Green. In early December 2001, NYU law dean John Sexton, a friend for years, invites me to his office to discuss my future around the time that the *New York Times* runs a piece headlined "What's Next for Green? Politics (and a Beard) May Be Out."

"Hey, you look like you've lost your aura," says Sexton, who then generously offers me a position for a year as a visiting scholar with a large office and student research assistants. Which I accept and which allows me to research two books that I later publish, *Selling Out* and *The Book on Bush*. The year at the law school leads to five years teaching a freshman honors seminar on "Personality on Policy: How LBJ, Bill Clinton, Ralph Nader, Rudy Giuliani and Mike Bloomberg Get It Done." I tell my students on the first day of class that "given my experience as a student of and participant in politics, if this isn't the best course in political science in your four years at NYU, you or I have done something wrong." That's arrogant and brash. But probably true.

Turns out that I love teaching.

C. 2006–2009: LESSONS LEARNED FROM "THE ARENA"

Andrew Cuomo: The Son Also Rises in 2006

As with Rudy, Andrew and I start off on the wrong foot—recall the awkwardness of our exchange over "Mario the organ grinder"—and then it gets worse. Three experiences deeply sour my view of this political thoroughbred.

The HUD undersecretary and NYC public advocate have a get-to-know-you lunch downtown in late 1996. It goes poorly from my perspective not because of language but body language. As we talk amiably about politics, I'm struck by how he never looks me in the eye but always speaks into the royal middle distance, as if I'm just lucky to be there with him. Frankly, I haven't had quite this experience before or since.

Then I announce in April 1997, as explained above, that I've decided to run for reelection and later perhaps for Senate, but not mayor that year. AP's Mark Humbert calls me later that afternoon asking for a response to Secretary Cuomo's comment that if I'm too chicken to run against Rudy, how could I against Al? *Whaaat?* I'm amazed at Mr. Buttinski's judgment in a race in which he has no apparent standing or interest. When told I'm pissed, first Cuomo says that he's been misquoted, which no one believes since Humbert is the leading journalist and straight-shooter in Albany. Then his staff lets me know that *I* can call *him* to discuss the matter. My mind immediately goes back to his princely airs at our first lunch—no, he took the gratuitous shot and if he's not going to call, then never mind.

Three years later, we're seated next to each other on the dais of the Al Smith dinner in 2000 with Bush and Gore seated in front of us with Cardinal O'Connor. At the time, everyone in politics understands that I'm running in the following year's mayoral race while he'll be challenging Carl McCall for the 2002 Democratic nomination for governor. We discuss both campaigns and I ask, "How can you oppose the state's ranking African American when you've effectively been out of the state for four years?"

He says, again with his gaze fixed on something other than me, "Mark, do you know the three pictures that every black family has on their walls?"

"Well, no."

He answers, "They have a picture of Jesus Christ, Martin Luther King, and either John or Robert Kennedy."

He stops and now I'm wondering what is he saying and then I realize—*because he's a Kennedy by marriage, he'll win black voters over McCall.* I'm speechless at what I regard as über-arrogant, tasteless, and politically naïve. He tells the exact same story to Eliot Spitzer. When asked about it by biographer Michael Shnayerson, he denies ever saying it to anyone.

He and I periodically speak on early-morning private calls during his aborted 2002 gubernatorial campaign since, if nothing else, his father helped me win the mayoral nomination and I pledged to endorse him in return, if I had won. When he's forced to withdraw a week before the primary by the combination of bad polls and former President Clinton, I call him the next weekend to privately commiserate, recalling how I felt after a crushing public loss. He's in understandable emotional pain, noting that his mother, Matilda Cuomo, said the night before to cheer the family up, "Well, no one died!"

Cut to mid-2005. Out of office for four years and back at the Democracy Project, I realize how much I enjoyed public service and that my history as a consumer advocate is a pretty strong rationale for state attorney general. About the same time, the Cuomo family decides that the ex-HUD secretary's comeback race will be for AG as well. But then both our plans are potentially altered when Robert Kennedy Jr., my friend and Andrew's former brother-in-law, says that he too may run. Shades of Lowenstein in '74 and '80, Belafonte in '86, JFK Jr. in 1998, Bill Clinton (sort of) in 2001! I'm back on a boat in a dark Disneyland tunnel.

The Kennedys—Ted, Bobby, Joe—often joke with me that, given my bushy hair and big teeth, I look like a "Jewish Kennedy." Bobby's statement of interest leads me to wonder, *Why the hell didn't I grow up in a small state, say Vermont or Rhode Island, without so many celebrity politicians clogging up the works? And while it's one thing to be considered a "Jewish Kennedy," it's quite another to run against a real one.* Andrew is also understandably sweating over running against an even bigger name than his own. When I'm asked about this by the *New York Post,* I fib, saying that I'm in the race for keeps since "though I love Bobby, I'd love to be Attorney General more." The loving parts are true but not the part about running no matter what. Bobby Kennedy is not Andrew Stein.

Bobby opts out, not because he couldn't have won but because he has six children, marital difficulties, and literally can't afford public office. Later, I have a friendly conversation with his mother, Ethel Kennedy, explaining the grinding ordeal of hours and hours elegantly begging people for their money, even for a famous candidate. When Bobby eventually decides not to run for anything else in subsequent years, Ethel tells friends that our conversation contributes to his conclusion that he's better suited to be a very influential environmental advocate than an ingratiating politician.

There are five people running on the Democratic side, including (future congressman) Sean Patrick Maloney and an affable African American Democrat, Charlie King. Despite an early private statewide poll that puts Andrew ahead of me 30 to 16 percent—I'm basically unknown upstate—an irrational confidence misleads me into believing that my record and history would eventually trump his record and name. That conclusion is influenced by an enormous number of insiders telling me how much they dislike the son for, in their view, his bullying temperament. One such person is Charlie King. At 2 percent in polls throughout the contest, he calls me every few weeks to share his opinion that "Andrew is a thug who cannot be allowed to get close to being attorney general."

Early on, I get a hint of Cuomo's political approach and strength. Although state contribution "limits" are a sky-high $50,000, his team tries to get labor allies to funnel more money into his effort. Turns out that his top advisor, Jennifer Cunningham, is also coordinating an "independent" office by the influential Service Employees International Union, which is illegal. When a journalist calls this "independent" phone line and she answers, it's an embarrassing moment. But then they simply rip out the line and ignore press inquiries about it.

It turns out that Andrew's lead is real and continuing, allowing him to ignore my criticisms of his HUD record and lean on wavering influential politicians and donors. His very connected parents are calling everyone they know for their son in his do-or-die campaign. A prominent city congressperson says that s/he can't support me. "Let me just say, mommy and daddy won't let me."

Looking back, there are four highlights in Andrew Cuomo's march to attorney general. First, given his 2002 performance and reputation, he tells everyone that there's a new Andrew and then personally charms hundreds of opinion leaders and donors one by one by displaying more honey than vinegar. I doubt there's been a personality change, but politically, he makes an enormous, admirable, and largely successful effort to convince skeptics.

Then at the Democratic State Convention in Albany, with many insiders under the sway of the popular former governor, I'm slightly short of the 25 percent needed to get on the ballot. But the also very popular AG Eliot Spitzer, the all-but-certain next governor, prefers me. We share populist values, and he had some miserable experiences with Andrew when both were vying to be the leader of gun-control initiatives in the late 1990s.

But Eliot's private assurance that he'd help me get the needed delegates wavers under behind-the-scenes brow-beating by the Cuomos. Eliot—who becomes a friend and whose family would contribute significantly to me—tells me that he has to stay neutral. I understand his predicament, eventually getting on the ballot the Ramsey Clark way, by petition. But Eliot is wary of a sharp-elbowed Andrew as a fellow statewide Democratic official. Indeed, "I got very close to cutting an ad attacking Cuomo as unworthy of the office," he informs me years later, but is talked out of it by staff smartly citing polls showing I'm losing. Much later, Spitzer tells a leading journalist, "Not endorsing Mark was one of my biggest mistakes in politics."

Eliot's not the only one they lean on, really lean on. When I'm straining to get to the 25 percent threshold, a Brooklyn delegate and supporter—Dilia Schack—signs an affidavit for me and then flees Albany to avoid more arm-twisting by Cuomo supporter Vito Lopez, the Kings County political boss. Except when Lopez finds out, he sends an aide to the airport who hurdles a barrier near the gate and forces a now-crying delegate to sign a new affidavit renouncing her prior one and supporting Cuomo.

In the final two weeks, the *New York Times* endorses me and then goes on to trash Andrew and worry that he'd allow the office to again become "a nesting place for political hacks" because his major concern at HUD "was burnishing a political resume." Andrew is personally staggered. The race now tightens into a tie, I'm told by his pollster (post-campaign). Then the money that Cuomo carries over after his 2002 gubernatorial withdrawal and his successful fund-raising in 2006 click in. He rolls out a barrage of TV spots with a blaring headline based on a negative quote from one *New York Times* article, which allows him to use the famous *Times* logo as if the paper is supporting him. I of course run ads heralding my actual *Times* endorsement, though far less frequently.

Cuomo starts pulling away again. A few days before the September primary, I hear rumors that Charlie King is pulling out to endorse the person he's repeatedly called "a thug." So when I'm told, "Mark, it's Charlie King on line one," I do something unprofessional: I don't, almost physically can't, take this call. An insulted King at his press conference that day not only endorses Cuomo but also denounces me (and my brother) for good measure.

Andrew wins by 51 to 31 percent. I call election night to congratulate and endorse him. Three days later, he tells the *New York Times* that "my father made maybe 10 phone calls for me." Nothing wrong with a parent going all out for a child seeking office—I would for mine. But what's revealing is that Andrew feels the need to misstate the number by several orders of magnitude based on research by his biographer, Michael Shnayerson, who calls dozens of country leaders and discovers that nearly all of them had heard from Mario. For example, Vince Monte of Rockland County supported Koch over Mario for governor in 1982 and had endorsed me early in 2005. He picks up the phone in June and hears a familiar voice shout the following: "Are you going to fuck Andrew like you fucked me?" Then he hears a click and a dial tone. And does what any rational politician would—he withdraws his endorsement of me, saying "I have no choice."

POSTSCRIPTS: I watch Cuomo first as AG and then as governor govern as he ran, the Wizard of Albany pulling all strings behind a curtain of surrogates and staff. Worse, he tells an official of the Working Families Party, a very influential amalgam of unions, "I'll spend whatever it takes, $5 million, $10 million, to destroy you if you don't endorse me" for reelection in 2014 over a minor progressive candidate. It then does, much to its later regret when, according to the official quoted above in an interview, he reneges on his pledges to go all out to win a Democratic state senate seat. Andrew reminds me of Senator Warren Magnuson's sage observation that "all anybody wants in life is an unfair advantage."

Although we don't speak for five years, in November 2011, I'm called by his chief of staff to ask if I'd be one of ten commissioners on a Moreland Commission investigating utilities and state performance after Superstorm Sandy, probably the most expensive natural disaster ever to hit the city and region. Since this is a public service involving neither pay nor politics, I immediately agree, assuming the commission would be largely independent, as was a Moreland Commission created by his father. That turns out to be a classic "triumph of hope over experience."

It's not at all independent but run as an extension of the "Second Floor" (as the governor's Albany office is referred to). I attend nearly every commissioners' meeting (Cuomo ally and my '86 opponent John Dyson is a fellow appointee), never speak to the media during its existence, and gain the confidence of Cuomo staff assigned to the project. But at a key moment, the governor falsely implies in our interim report's official release that all the commissioners support his preconceived plans to privatize the existing Long Island utility (called LIPA)—although three of us don't. I feel obliged to threaten to quit unless he and his office correct that misimpression and stop playing such games. They do and I stay, as we go on to produce a useful final report that fixes some Public Service Commission laws and replaces the despised, ineffectual LIPA.

But Moreland I is a harbinger of the far more troubled Moreland II (which I don't serve on) that looks into public corruption after a string of criminal cases involving capitol politicians. Although Cuomo initially announces that it is completely independent and can investigate anything concerning state government, six months later he announces that of course it can't investigate *him* since he appointed it. When he then prematurely pulls its plug during budget negotiations with Assembly Speaker Sheldon Silver, U.S. Attorney Preet Bharara publicly rebukes the governor, unleashing a river of negative publicity.

When Cuomo runs in 2014 against a compelling if unknown campaign finance champion, Fordham law professor Zephyr Teachout, I'm about the only name Democrat in the state to endorse her in the primary. Political friends think I'm nuts while the governor's Republican opponent, Westchester County executive Rob Astorino, privately calls to laud "my spine" in standing up to him. At a revealing but not surprising moment at the Labor Day Parade, there are pictures and video of Teachout being blocked from trying to shake the governor's hand while he looks directly at her, yet later denying that he ever saw her. She wins an unexpected third of the Democratic primary as Andrew goes on to win reelection in November with 53 percent of the vote. That's underwhelming given that he outspends Teachout by some 25–1—that includes "independent" expenditures and $53 million in state funding on saturation TV ads to publicize his Start-Up New York program (which generates just several dozen jobs and $1.7 million in new investment in its first two years).

Losing Is One Thing, Indictment Is Another

Brooklyn DA Joe Hynes is a politically ambitious prosecutor and a friend of Governor Mario Cuomo, who appointed him to the assignment that made him semi-famous—as special prosecutor to investigate the 1986 Howard Beach killing of Michael Griffith. A month after the mayoral race, a political opponent of mine urges him to investigate the racially provocative literature in Brooklyn because, assuming it was directed by my campaign, we didn't list on financial forms the few hundred dollars that it cost. Since no one seriously thinks I either approved or wanted them distributed and since this is not Watergate in any event, I'm not overly concerned.

But when Hynes impanels two grand juries between 2002 and 2005, which bring in many of my staff and supporters, each having to hire lawyers—and when his top prosecutor, Michael Vecchione, actually tells my lawyer, Richard Emery, "I'd love to indict Mark Green"— that gets my attention. Since this is the first time I've ever heard the words "indict" and "Mark Green" in proximity, I'm sick about the threat and the potential risk of becoming "a ham sandwich."

Four years of grand juries and leaks from his office later, it's the spring of 2006 and I'm running for attorney general. Dominick Carter, the anchor at NY1, asks me on June 21 what happened to the investigation. "I assume it's over," I reply, explaining that I haven't heard anything in over a year. Within the next couple of days, according to Ben Smith in the *Daily News,* "the head of the rackets bureau [tells] one potential witness, 'We're starting to look into this again. Could you come in and tell us what you know,' said a Brooklyn district leader. I was like, 'I've done this already, twice.'"

Since headlines like "DA Investigates AG Candidate" are not politically helpful, my patience is exhausted. These idiotic flyers contributed to one political loss and are now threatening another? Not if I can help it. So I instruct Emery to tell Hynes that I want to come in and testify under oath after which they should either charge or clear me. He advises against that as a matter of law but, while a lawyer and here a target, I'm also a public person whose candidacy and reputation are being potentially ruined. The DA agrees.

After reviewing our notes at a nearby bar, Emery and I then enter a back elevator from the trucking platform so as not to be seen. Seven of them led by Vecchione (though not Hynes) are seated around an oval conference table in a yellowish, windowless room. Emery begins by acknowledging that "sure, some rogue people were perhaps involved, which can happen in any large-scale campaign. But why is my client here? Do you have any evidence that Mark had any knowledge of this stuff?" After saying versions of hummina-hummina, in my view, it becomes clear that their unspoken premise is that I "couldn't have *not* known," which meets no known evidentiary standard.

When one specifically asks why I didn't know more about a particular expenditure, I (rhetorically) ask him if he's ever run for mayor or for anything. I then explain what a candidate for high office does, i.e., spends half his day raising money and half performing and strategizing, with zero time to be an auditor of particular bills or what some worker I've never met is doing in my name. Frankly, having a completely clear conscience, I'm not nervous but relieved to be facing my accusers.

The next morning, Hynes's office releases a letter exonerating me, saying, "Based on a four-year investigation of the distribution and financing of controversial literature in sections of Brooklyn on the eve of the mayoral runoff in 2001, my office has confirmed that Mark Green had no knowledge of these events." That's good. So is it when the tables are reversed. Documents start emerging in 2011 showing that Hynes's office has been systematically abusing its prosecutorial powers by intimidating witnesses and fabricating evidence in order to get convictions. Indeed, a formal Department of Investigation report alleges that he used public forfeiture money for political campaign purposes. Hynes loses his reelection in 2013 as courts and the new DA throw out many convictions.

As of this writing, he is under criminal investigation.

2009: De Blasio Rising

Though I don't approve of many of his policies or his means of ascent, I still like Mike, as I did when we first met. Bloomberg has an I-yam-what-I-yam persona that befits a multi-billionaire businessman and that certainly contrasts with standard political insincerity. Nor do I resent him for legally using his assets, and I almost admire his bottom-line focus—i.e., if you're still losing after spending $50 million, then increase your bid to $73.9 million if that is what it takes.

When he calls to ask me in 2005 to participate in a funny spoof for the annual Inner Circle charity dinner, I readily agree. After a sequence of people are taped sycophantically lauding his prior performances at the Inner Circle, I merely growl, "They stank! Big time!" I'm told it brings down the house at the dinner. (Perhaps you had to be there.)

But what he does at the 2008 Democratic Convention *does* stink. With nearly all major Democrats leaving for Denver, his office announces on a late Friday that Mike—after years of refusing—now supports a law to overturn term limits, which would allow him to run for a third term. Angered at this undemocratic, selfish about-face, I do as many stand-ups with local media at the convention as I can. I call and personally speak to the *Times* and *Daily News* publishers Arthur Sulzberger Jr. and Mort Zuckerman to urge them to editorially oppose a maneuver that directly contradicts two public referenda. But having previously been lined up by fellow billionaire Bloomberg, they politely listen and later editorially endorse his move.

Leading the fight against it back in the city is Brooklyn councilman Bill de Blasio, a personable and adept organizer tutored by such political pros as Harold Ickes and Bill Lynch, top strategists for the Clintons and Dinkins. He's planning to run for public advocate in 2009 once incumbent Betsy Gotbaum completes her two terms. I join his effort as he skillfully puts together a big coalition of liberals, labor, and good government groups. But it fails when, predictably, the city council self-servingly votes with Bloomberg since many of them too want to run for an extra term.

A month later my cell phone rings. "Mark, it's Patrick Gaspard. Got a minute?" Patrick was an ally back when he headed the SEIU's political operation in NYC (indeed, I asked him to run my AG campaign)—and is now the top political operative in President Obama's White House. Whereupon he explains that while he (him or the White House?) thinks that Rep. Anthony Weiner is "endlessly entertaining, there's concern whether he'd be a serious enough candidate in 2009 to oppose Bloomberg. Would you think about running again?"

Not a call I expected. However, not relishing again climbing what would be a $100 million mountain, I explain that I'm honored, though the answer is no.

But.

It apparently doesn't take much to unleash my juices about running and serving again. When Public Advocate Betsy Gotbaum says that she won't seek a third term, it dawns on me—if I ran and won again for PA in 2009,* then I (a) would have a good chance to win an office that I loved holding, and (b) would be in a strong position in 2013 to pursue the one that got away in 2001.

After mulling this big step and talking with family, I give an exclusive interview to Jonathan Hicks of the *New York Times,* who files a story that I'm going to run. Having announced his candidacy months earlier, de Blasio is shocked and upset since he has a long-term plan to win for city council, then PA, then mayor. He refuses to take my call for a week while he calms down and consults with advisors. They figure out that he could pull an inside straight because of a hand that includes a strong Brooklyn political base, the endorsements of nearly all of labor (including the influential Working Families Party that he helped found), and an appealing racially mixed family.

He stays in and we're off. I soon see Schumer as we exit Scott Stringer's State of the Borough Address. "Green, you're *incorrigible!*"

---

* Unlike the federal constitutional amendment, which disqualifies anyone from ever serving a third term for president, the City Charter allows someone to run for a third term if there's been at least a term in between.

he says in that now well-known nasal Brooklyn twang. Given the source, I take it as a compliment.

De Blasio and I have different assets. His three-year head start provides him a fund-raising edge and a lot of institutional support while my name and record recognition give me a huge early lead in polls. We then run the gauntlet of club meetings, donor calls, and several debates about our competing rationales. I argue that I know the job because I've done the job well and have ideas that I lay out on how to do it better. He runs on being a neighborhood family guy who represents a newer generation of talent. So far, so good. The other two candidates, councilman Eric Goia of Queens and civil rights lawyer Norman Siegel, have considerable skills but gain little political traction in this lineup.

Three events then prove influential.

De Blasio's first four citywide mailings are composed largely of pictures of him with his African American wife and mixed-race children. OK, we all have wives and children whom we love and campaign with, although I've never seen a candidate advertise his quite so much. (He originally plans to send them only to minority ZIP codes, but staff convince him that would look a bit obvious so they instead send it out broadly.) My polling shows de Blasio climbing among African Americans in general, black women in particular.

Then his second four mailings are not about his family but mine: they have a big picture of my brother with the headline, "Steve Green is one of the most corrupt landlords in New York City and his brother Mark is in his pocket." I ignore these mailings since denials will only elevate them into the media beyond mailboxes. Nor do I want to complain, which would convey anxiety and defensiveness. But I start to meet people on the street who say a version of "You the one with the landlord brother?" Then in late August, driving between events with campaign manager Anne Strahle, I take a call from Bill.

"Mark, we've debated two times, but I think we should debate more. What do you think?"

"That's interesting. Let me think about it. But now that you're on the phone and it's your dime, may I ask you a question?"

"Sure."

"What the hell are you doing falsely sliming my brother? I thought there's rule that candidates lay off family."

He smoothly begins responding, "Well, my research people tell me that—" I then interrupt and say, "You're so full of shit and we both know it. Good-bye." And I hang up on the 109th Mayor of New York City (not knowing that then), which I think is the only time I ever hang up on someone in my life.

"Politics ain't beanbag," it's said. In the heat of a campaign you say some things you regret, perhaps make a personal attack that exposes your opponent's character (or your own). But, for me, this de Blasio tactic is something of a deal breaker, in the sense of Churchill's observation that an opponent's action "was like the 13th chime that cast doubt on all that had preceded it."

Then the *New York Times,* a bit weary after supporting me twice for PA and four times for mayor (primary I, primary II, runoff, general), endorses Bill as a fresh face who'd do a good job while giving me a rhetorical gold watch. With the unusual combination of the *Times* and labor—plus a disciplined campaign making few mistakes—he catches up as we each get about a third of the vote in the primary. But he has overperformed and I have underperformed based on expectations, giving him momentum in a runoff. With his labor army pulling out a big share of the pathetically low 12 percent of the Democratic turnout, he easily wins round two.

Again, given my extensive experience with concession speeches, I bite my tongue . . . except once on primary night when I grouse to a reporter, "Based on turnout, today seemed more like a selection than an election."

Four years later, Bill runs another well-organized and strategically adept campaign, now for mayor. He benefits from a great political ad highlighting his son Dante's "fro" and from scandals that trip up both "the endlessly entertaining" front-runner, Anthony Weiner, and rival comptroller John Liu (due to staff misdeeds, not his own). During the campaign Bill visits my "corrupt" brother at his S. L. Green offices to ask for money, which Steve donates since he understands that he's with the likely next mayor. Bill's "tale of two cities" slogan didn't work when Ferrer attempted it, but, after 12 years of programs tilted to the Manhattan elite and months after Occupy Wall Street, the city largely admires Bloomberg but is ready for a change toward policies helping the "99 percent." Voters lurch from a short multi-billionaire capitalist to a very tall lefty labor organizer.

Lessons Learned

One thing I've learned from political campaigns is that a lot of folks either love you more than you deserve or hate you more than you deserve. There's probably too much at stake and too much adrenaline for it to be otherwise.

Still, it's pretty amazing in my mayoral campaign to have been called "arrogant" by Mike Bloomberg, "obnoxious" by Ed Koch, and accused of running a "racist" campaign by Al Sharpton. I've extracted three political and personal takeaways.

Reality Bites. "Confidence is the feeling you have before you know better" is something attributed to Mencken. My unvarnished optimism led me to go to political battle with D'Amato, Schumer, Bloomberg, Cuomo, and de Blasio. That takes either blind courage or merely poor shot selection, probably both.

While none of these races was unwinnable at the start, neither did I dig deep enough into the "analytics" before each contest. For example, after trailing Andrew Cuomo 2–1 in that pre-candidacy poll, I embrace the wishful thinking that Democratic voters will naturally come over to my full name over his last name.

Confidence is good. But confidence without analytics can be the difference between boldness and recklessness.

Money Shouts. "There are three things that matter in politics," power broker Mark Hanna reportedly said at the turn of the last century. "Money . . . and I can't think of the other two."

True, more important than money are the times and your location. That is, if you're a Republican running for the first time after Watergate or Hoover, you have a problem that money can't buy. Or if you're Ronald Reagan seeking a Harlem congressional seat or Obama in Wyoming, your communication skills will not be enough. But if it's a competitive race in a swing district or state, Hanna's on the money.

Bloomberg spends $92 a vote, an astonished *New York Times* writes after the election. Which is 100 times the amount per vote that Ken Livingstone spends the prior year to win the mayoralty of London. Bloomberg's war chest is more in one city than Richard Nixon had in 1972 in the whole country, more than Al Gore spent in 2000 to win a national nomination. (Years later, I encounter top Bloomberg campaign advisor Bill Cunningham on the street in the West 80s.

"It was unbelievable," he would recall. "We did everything we could think of. Price was no object.")

I raise $12.5 million and spend $16.6 million, including matching public funds, the most ever by far for a mayoral campaign in the country. After the election, I file a telephone directory–size book of nearly 10,000 donors with the Campaign Finance Board; Bloomberg's filing is effectively one name on one page—his own.

In 1972, I wrote *Who Runs Congress?* about how wealthy candidates will turn elections into auctions unless Congress and Court wake up. Then I enact a low-dollar, public-matching system in NYC to reduce that prospect, only to watch Bloomberg 30 years after my book swamp my candidacy with a tidal wave of money. Does God have a sense of humor? She does.

There are some very smart people—columnists George Will, David Brooks, and Rich Lowry come to mind—who cherry-pick some races where the bigger spender lost and conclude either that money's an overrated factor variable—implicitly disagreeing with Napoleon, who said that "God is on the side of big battalions"—and, in any event, constitutionally protected speech. (Of course, money is property; if it were just speech, then why do the words "here's $10,000 if you vote my way" send you to prison?) They assume away the role of money contrary to the opinion of about every candidate in the past half century who spends hours a day trolling for it. One wonders what these intellectuals know that those in the arena don't.

Or as my son overhead a fellow Cornell student saying in 2002, "First I'll make some money and then I'll get into politics and pull 'a Corzine'" (Wall Streeter Jon Corzine spent $60 million in 2000 to win a U.S. Senate seat in New Jersey.) When it comes to Bloomberg, I can relate to crooner Bing Crosby, who said of his gifted rival, "A Frank Sinatra comes along once every several generations. Why did it have to be mine?"

Personally Speaking. In the spirit of John McEnroe, who once told me that he learned more from the classic five-set 1980 Wimbledon finals that he lost to Borg than any match he won, my personal and/or political flaws are more instructive than any strengths that enabled me to go almost from Elmont to City Hall.

While everyone in high office has numerous friends and critics, anyone with a semblance of self-awareness knows the rap against each of us—and we all have them, *mas o menos*. In my case, it's that

I'm a bad listener, too clever by half, cocky, and arrogant. Indeed, the always-genteel Andrew Cuomo calls me "rude" and "inappropriate" in his autobiography, *All Things Possible.*

When my wife and the *New York Times,* in an editorial *endorsing* me no less, say that my "listening skills" need a lot of work, you have no choice but to confess error and plead for help. I now do recall how often I'd go into meetings and immediately try to steer opinion rather than to sharpen thinking by what the French call "mindful conversation." Whether reflecting a habit of advocacy or something worse, it's a personal and political liability.

As for being too clever by half, again I'm guilty as charged. I love language that grabs listeners because, like it or not, it's both second nature to me and what our modern media platforms demand. The reality, however, is that a "sound bite" on network TV in the Sixties averaged 40 seconds, and today it averages seven seconds in what Nader calls a "sound bark"—not to mention communicating in 140 characters.

Also, in a biological quirk, I think I was born lacking the gene for self-doubt (which the 2001 campaign helped cure). I understand why critics could consider my presentation as overconfident, egotistical, cocky. Indeed, when Jets quarterback Joe Namath famously "guaranteed" a victory over the heavily favored Colts in the 1969 Super Bowl—and then delivered—it became an iconic moment for New York sports fans . . . and for my forming political psychology. Bad choice. Only years later did I realize the crucial difference between a cocky underdog who prevails (think Truman) and a cocky favorite who seems too self-absorbed (LeBron taking "my talents to South Beach").

But arrogant? In a business that includes Koch, Cuomo, Giuliani, Bloomberg, The Donald? Allow me to plea bargain. When I ask about the label with Nader Raider Bob Fellmeth, he remembers me as "all do do do, not me, me, me." David Dinkins concludes, "Sure, you had the kind of confidence necessary to succeed in politics. But not arrogance." Perhaps Denny Farrell, who got to know me well over the course of the mayoral campaign, put it best: "You weren't arrogant. You just appeared to be arrogant."

Obviously, all public officials enjoy substantial egos, confidence, even arrogance, but the trick is how to harness it toward a policy goal beyond mere notoriety and how to deploy but not show it. For that, think of the way Reagan ran three times for president but sure didn't seem ambitious, and how Obama is incredibly competitive yet seems to glide around, a political Federer.

Weighing my flaws and skills over years as both advocate and politician, it appears that some of my strengths were my weaknesses, allowing me to make breakthroughs as an advocate but limiting myself as a pol. It's probably true I failed the have-a-beer test with some colleagues who regarded my bluntness, cockiness, "appearance of arrogance," background, and writerly approach off-putting. At times I found myself neither fish nor fowl, with politicians regarding me as an intellectual and intellectuals seeing me as a politician. At a 1999 cocktail party, Norman Mailer and I affably teased each other about our public roles. "Norman, for a writer, you were a pretty good politician in your 1965 mayoral race." He shot back, "Mark, for a politician running for mayor, you're a pretty good writer."

Whatever the reasons, however, I partly lost control of my narrative and let critics control my story. That, in a sense, is "a failure to communicate." If some people think one thing of you that doesn't jibe with your view of yourself, that's on you.

In other words, I'm more comfortable outside looking in, better at public advocacy than the game of politics. When I need to make some big decision, I find myself channeling Nader more than Cuomo/de Blasio because I can't fully embrace Leo Durocher's axiom of baseball and life: "Win any way you can as long as you can get away with it."

FIVE

WHAT IT'S LIKE—
NATIONAL POLITICS

Gary, Bill, John, Hillary . . . and Fidel

This is one Hart you won't leave in San Francisco.

—Senator Gary Hart to Democratic National Convention,
July 18, 1984

So, you think Cuomo's getting in?

—Fidel Castro to author, October 16, 1987,
dinner at Presidential Palace, Havana

IF YOU LOVE POLICY AND POLITICS, NOTHING—*NOTHING*
—matches the cocoonish intensity of a competitive presidential campaign. With decisions made on the fly and little time to game out alternatives, these are panoramic events where one speech, gaffe, or debate can spell the difference between the presidency and Palookaville . . . as I painfully discover trying to help my friend Gary Hart become president.

For one personal example: when Deni's water breaks in the afternoon of March 29, 1984, I'm hurtling around NYC in a motorcade with Gary. Pre–cell phones, texting, or pagers, she has to contact the Secret Service to get to our car to tell me to get the hell to the hospital. With my brain wired into a draft for the next morning's speech demanding that Walter Mondale return his "tainted PAC money," the words "Deni . . . delivery . . . hospital" all sound oddly familiar when the agent utters them. Then I hightail it to Lenox Hill Hospital on 77th Street.

GARY HART: PROPHET WITHOUT HONOR

Richard Nixon and Gary Hart are not alike, to say the least, but their final public images—Watergate and Donna Rice, respectively—have eclipsed nearly everything each had done before. But now I realize that Gary was eerily similar to a different presidential candidate a quarter century later—a cerebral, young, aloof, long-shot senator running on generational and policy change with an obvious disdain for the usual backslapping bonhomie. In most ways except two rather big ones—race and result—Hart was the Obama of 1984.

He is born in Ottawa, Kansas, to working-class parents who never get out of high school and who strictly adhere to a church forbidding congregants to dance or go to movies. At six, Gary signs his name "Professor Hart"; at 10, he declares he wants to be a minister, and he reads so many books that a school chart using stars as books "begins to look like the Milky Way."

Gary goes East and Ivy by entering Yale Divinity School because of his passion for philosophy and teaching. Campaigning in New Haven on Election Day 1960 for John Kennedy, however, he becomes infatuated with the president-elect's call to service. His civic religion now public service, Hart switches to Yale Law School and after graduation goes to work in the Justice Department of Robert Kennedy. Following a stint as a lawyer in Denver, he's recruited by the son of a minister running an uphill race for president, South Dakota's George McGovern, who later says that he was "attracted to Hart's churchly, almost geeky goodness, his mannerly Midwestern respect." Hart becomes his campaign manager in that defining candidacy.

At just 38, Hart parlays his experience, smarts, and Redford looks into a successful candidacy for a Colorado U.S. Senate seat only two years later. "Gary was different from the start," says Peter Gold, his first top legislative aide, "because of his insistence that we not view issues through the prism of traditional Democrats or Republicans. He was looking for a fresh, nonpartisan 'Hart' perspective based on what made sense, which he did on military reform, nuclear strategy, and industrial policy, to name a few. Once when I complimented him for some major legislation, he modestly shrugged and said, 'well, only a fraction of the Senate even tries to have a national impact.'"

Gold is my best friend and suggests to his boss that he involve me in any of his national efforts. "After I won reelection in 1980 when so many other progressive Democrats got wiped out in the Reagan landslide," Hart tells me in an interview in 2015, "I started hearing lots of people around the country say, 'You really should run for president.'" Ensconced in NYC, I get calls from time to time from Gary and his staff about framing and New York politics. Then with near-linear progression, the boy who read a lot of books grows into an intellectual presidential contender running, he declares in his February 1983 announcement, on "new ideas from a new generation of leaders." His evolving stump speech that year explains his rationale: "This nation has not passed its prime, its leaders have . . . This country cannot afford four more years of Reaganomics for the rich . . . It's not whether you turn left or right to elect a Democrat or Republican but whether to let this nation move into the future or slip backwards in the past."

Among other efforts, I become a one-man band pushing him to be the first major party candidate to refuse all special-interest PAC funds, the monkey wrench of democracy as I saw it in *Who Runs Congress?* After his finance team costs it out, he enthusiastically agrees to this "new idea" consistent with his rationale of challenging politics as usual. Still, we're almost disappointed when Hart's leading rival, former vice president and front-runner Walter Mondale, astutely agrees to the pledge, making our point but (apparently) mooting the issue.

Then comes a week with the biggest presidential upset since Truman-Dewey. It's the first month of 1984. The Eurythmics' "Sweet Dreams (Are Made of These)" is playing repeatedly on the radio as Gary's improbable dream starts coming into focus. Mondale wins the Iowa caucuses on January 24 by a huge 49 to 16 percent margin but Hart comes in second, "beating expectations," as defined by the wrong guesses of pundits who talk largely to themselves. The Mondale people seem nettled by a focus on the new guy and slip into an off-putting hubris that New Hampshire-ites, in the first primary the next month, famously dislike. "Somebody had to finish second," sniffs one Mondale strategist, while that campaign's pollster, Peter Hart, brags "we won the gold *and* the silver."

But they and most everyone miss a seismic shift among Democrats dismayed by Reagan's cowboy capitalism. Mondale has the money and machine but Hart has the message. And while Gary has been projecting his generational approach since he entered the Senate in 1975, Mondale reminds people of Churchill's complaint about pudding: "it lacks theme."

Gary's crowds in New Hampshire swell. At a traditional ax throwing contest on the Saturday before primary day, the plaid-shirted Hart buries his ax in a three-foot target 30 feet away. Commentators can't resist overdoing "axing" Mondale metaphors. A *Washington Post*-ABC poll released on Sunday has it 38 to 24 percent for Mondale, with Senator John Glenn fading. But mid-Tuesday afternoon, primary day, I start getting calls from semi-hysterical friends in all camps saying that *Hart is winning* by 10 in exit polls! I speak to his New York coordinator, John Connorton, a highly regarded Wall Street lawyer but political novice, who's uncharacteristically stammering in disbelief. "Can you imagine?" he says with wonder.

Gary wins 37 to 28 percent. Having gone almost overnight from inevitable to improbable, Mondale has to find the resolve to calmly absorb a potentially lethal loss and rally his troops for the next rounds in the South, then New York and Pennsylvania. "Sometimes a cold shower is good for you," says the ex–vice president unconvincingly that night, before finding his footing two days later: "There seeped into my campaign, and maybe even into my own mind, a kind of front-runner inevitability psychology that maybe people smelled, and that's gone now," he tells reporters with refreshing bluntness. "We're in for a long, tough fight."

The next night Gary is scheduled to come to a long-planned fundraiser hosted by ranking Democrats Howard and Lulette Samuels at their very tony duplex at 115 Central Park West. As Deni and I cab over, we pass by a ruptured street at 64th and CPW with loud hissing and a car precariously elevated some 25 feet in the air . . . took us a few gape-mouthed seconds to realize it's a shoot from some movie called *Ghostbusters*. But it sets the tone for the awesomeness of the evening.

On Monday the Samuels have 30 RSVPs. But Wednesday night, after the New Hampshire earthquake, 300 pour into their spacious living room dominated by a huge painting of Lulette's father, a former prime minister of France in the 1930s. "When Gary, Howard, and Lulette walk down our long staircase," recalls Bill Samuels, Howard's son, "people were going nuts. Everyone seemed to be at once thinking, 'This *is* the next president of the United States.'" Gary himself is impressed because he "rode up on the elevator with Joel Grey" and at the bold-faced names there who hadn't earlier returned calls. Hoarse, tired, *pumped up,* he mirrors their collective joy by concluding his 15 minutes of remarks with the crescendo, "We're going to win the nomination and then beat Reagan." If the room's energy could be converted to wattage, it'd light all of Ottawa, Kansas.

As we make a path for him through a wall of bodies on the way out, he asks, "Mark, can you help me with the New York primary in three weeks and then with national communications and policy?" Not a hard question for a Sixties Democrat who is a friend of a potential Kennedy of the Eighties. "Sure," I say casually (though inside I'm shouting the Eighties version of *OMG!*).

The next three weeks—and five months to the convention—are anything but casual.

In New York, we face a formidable lineup of Governor Mario Cuomo and nearly all state elected Democrats and organized labor. I move around with Gary and advise him on such New York customs as the heresy of milk with Nathan's hot dogs, which McGovern reportedly asked for, according to urban legend. Deni (pre-delivery) and I throw a modest fund-raiser for Gary at our apartment for 50 friends and family. "Mark's literary and strategic contributions have clearly earned a major posting," the candidate teases the crowd, "so we'll be holding open the Ugandan embassy for him" (this being shortly after the era of the murderous Idi Amin of that country).

Then a break: I get a tip that, despite Mondale's PAC pledge, labor unions close to him are instead funneling $400,000 into Mondale "delegate committees," including those in New York. Having overspent in early primaries attempting a knockout blow, it appears that his campaign is evading the federal $24 million primary spending cap. Gary green-lights a speech to expose Mondale's hypocrisy and reliance on old-time politics. Did the vice president and his top staff know about these funds? My job isn't to find excuses but to cast blame and let *them* find excuses.

The talk is set for a Midtown breakfast on the morning of March 30, four days before the primary. I'm reviewing the draft with him on the afternoon of the twenty-ninth when, as mentioned above, my wife goes into labor. I shift focus from delivering a speech to watching doctors delivering Jonah Frand Green, born healthy and beautiful at 2:30 a.m. By 6:30 a.m., mom and baby are fast asleep, whereas I am wide awake, brimming with adrenaline, ready to spend the next two hours in battle rather than in repose. Having warned Deni about such a possible situation, I slip out of the hospital and get to Gary just before he's introduced. "What the hell are you doing here?" he asks, smiling at my backward priorities. Hearing that everyone's in good shape, he snaps his towel one more time. "And what kind of name is Jonah? Wasn't he a bit of a whiner? But in the end, he did his job, right?"

He then takes the stage and lets it rip: "By denouncing PAC money at the front door while his campaign sweeps it in through the back door, the former vice president has failed the test of leadership—to say what he thinks and to do what he says. No president should enter the Oval Office with strings attached." With an un-Hart-like rhetorical flourish, he concludes, "Give the money back, Walter, just give the money back." It's my second-best moment of the day.

Five days later, the Hart campaign formally petitions the Federal Election Commission to investigate the Mondale delegate committees for possible violations of the spending cap. In late April Mondale agrees to disband these committees and urges them to return the labor funds.

Notwithstanding this successful battle, the Mondale campaign is winning the broader war in New York because it has the only real political infrastructure there—the governor, the Democratic Party, and Labor. Also, with far more money, he's clobbering us on air. Gary darts around the state for these weeks, making the same closing argument about "a new generation of leaders" on the Monday before the primary in Buffalo, in Albany, and to an outdoor rally of several hundred at NYU after being introduced by Carl Sagan.

At our suite in the always-tattered Roosevelt Hotel, Gary and 20 of us Tuesday night receive the returns. The group includes Connorton, the chief strategist Pat Caddell, then-assemblyman Jerry Nadler, Ellen Chesler, Dick Beattie, other local supporters. As expected based on weekend tracking polling, Mondale wins by 18 points. I tease Gary that he was 19 down in NYS when I joined his campaign three weeks before so "by my count, we just ran out of time." He manages a grin

(OK, more like a grimace) and turns aside my suggestion that we start using a "Give 'em hell Gary" line to show he can take a punch. Then the candidate explains to us that Pennsylvania, Illinois, New Jersey, and California will likely decide the nomination in a race where "there is now no clear front-runner." Except for the senator, we all hang until about 2 a.m., thrown off stride, still hopeful, and—as campaign junkies understand—unwilling to let go of the bonding that climaxes primary nights.

The day before the primary, however, Gary is looking beyond New York and feeling besieged by well-meaning longtime friends who all think they can just walk into his hotel suite and suggest what he should be saying. "My organization style is concentric circles, not a hierarchy. But I need a filter," he tells us. At a Midtown meeting with many of his top national and traveling aides, he explains his frustration and then adds, "Mark, can you consolidate the process so I'm not torn in different directions, especially before debates?" Media guru Pat Caddell is not happy with Hart's suggestion, angrily leaving the meeting and then slow-walking it to maintain his lead spot. Once the traveling campaign leaves New York, I don't so much filter as alternate with John Holum, a Washington lawyer and later head of the Arms Control and Disarmament Agency under President Clinton, as an on-the-road speechwriter and message enhancer, Hart's message already being as sharp as any in recent memory.

I'm away about a quarter of the time over the next three months flying around with Gary, press secretary Kathy Bushkin, aide Billy Shore, the press corps—and Warren Beatty. Warren is not only beyond famous but a real character, publicly mumbly, tactically brilliant, a sounding board for the candidate who, goes the staff refrain, "wishes he were Gary while Gary wishes he were Warren." Did I mention that whatever city we're in, Warren books the "presidential suite" in the town's biggest hotel where we'd all convene late night to polish off a speech or strategy for the next day?

Mondale rises to the occasion and asserts his natural strength with party super-delegates who committed to him before the first votes were cast. As significant, Mondale's campaign knows it has to knock Gary off his pinnacle of Ideas and Change. Mondale aide Bob Beckel (who would go on to be the oxymoronic Democrat on Fox Cable) comes up with a way: at the March 11 Atlanta debate, Mondale waits for Gary to go into his "new ideas" spiel and then delivers a well-rehearsed line, "Gary, when I hear you talk about your 'new ideas,'" he says looking directly at Hart, "I think of that [Wendy's] ad, 'Where's the beef?'"

The room erupts in laughter at a joke shrewdly constructed on tens of millions of dollars in previous advertising for that phrase. It becomes one of the best zingers in presidential debate history. That few-second exchange also shifts the media narrative to Gary's "authenticity." Articles start flowing about his "weirdness," his Kennedy-like moves, his family name change from Hartpence to Hart 30 years before, and even a birth certificate saying 1936 while Gary's official vitae says 1937 ("an inside family joke," he explains).

For a few weeks, "Who is Gary Hart?" seems to replace "Who is John Galt?" the message being, *Can we trust this upstart to be our president? If you lie about your age, you can lie about anything . . . good ol' Mondale.* With the ex–vice president slowly pulling away, I try to squeeze blood from the PAC stone and persuade the candidate to triumphantly announce "welcome to overtime" since we intend to challenge many of Mondale's super-delegates as "tainted" by dirty PAC money. With party rules not permitting such a challenge, this rhetorical gambit is a bluff but about all the leverage we have.

Then on June 25, Mondale and Hart have a summit at the elegant 69th and Park townhouse of Arthur Krim, the celebrated movie producer. Once Mondale wins Pennsylvania and New Jersey—the latter due to a 30-point swing after Hart jokes about New Jersey being a toxic waste dump—Mondale has enough delegates to become the presumptive nominee. That morning ten of us from both camps wait downstairs swapping war stories. When Gary arrives first, Krim asks him what he wants to drink. "Just lots of coffee," he says. "That's funny," responds the host, "I was told specifically you'd like tea with honey." "Well, that's been the problem of my campaign all along," the candidate half jokes.

For nearly two hours, the two vent, hug, and then mug for the 20 cameras outside capturing their agreement to stay positive and unite behind the eventual ticket. When reporters ask about their recent rancor, Gary responds with a line we had crafted if the opportunity presented itself. "Well, neither of us accused the other of witchcraft," a not-veiled reference to Bush's criticism of Reagan's "voodoo economics."

With personal hatchets buried, so is any challenge to "tainted" delegates." Gary is promised a major speaking slot at the convention.

It's not as momentous as the "Treaty of Fifth Avenue" between Nixon and Rockefeller ten blocks north and 24 years earlier, but it effectively ends the competitive phase of the contest.

A dozen staff join Gary and Lee Hart at the San Francisco convention three weeks later. We go as a runner-up with a story to tell: Mondale has captured the popular primary vote 38 to 36 percent, but Hart won more primaries and caucuses (17–15), including 10 of the final 11. A pre-convention Harris poll has Reagan ahead of Mondale 52 to 44 percent but Hart by only 49 to 48.

I tour that great city, hanging with political pals from New York and around the country, go to a benefit concert by Hart supporter Carole King (whose solemnly sweet "You've Got a Friend" strikes a chord with the candidate), and attend morning meetings in Warren's presidential suite at the St. Francis Hotel.*

Ted Sorensen and I work on Gary's speech, which is like when Chicago Bulls guard Stacey King declared that he and Michael Jordan once combined for 68 points, on a night when Jordan scored 66 and King 2. I count up the percent of the final draft speech that is Gary's, Ted's, mine. It's like 50–40–10, which is fine by me, given the classy company. (As if anyone else in the world cares.)

Speaking of speeches, Governor Cuomo gives a mesmerizing keynote address, offering a direct challenge to Reagan: "Mr. President, you ought to know that this nation is more a 'tale of two cities' than it is just a 'shining city on a hill.'" Weeks before, he asks me to make suggestions for his address, as he coyly does with apparently lots of others. I send him ideas. Watching enraptured and crying delegates on the floor with veteran journalist Jack Newfield, I ask Jack, a close ally of Cuomo's, if the governor uses any of his proposed language. "None," he replies. "I think I heard a preposition and verb tense that were mine," I say.

Other than Cuomo, the convention is largely remembered for Geraldine Ferraro's vice-presidential nod, Jesse Jackson's inspirational address, and Mondale's self-immolating comment that "Mr.

---

* One topic is the news that Natan Sharansky has died. We discuss what a heroic Refusenik he was and chat about some appropriately sorrowful language. "Could someone please double-check whether the story is true?" says the candidate. "We sure don't want to bury the guy if he's alive." We check with AP. The report is false! ("Mark Green, the Hart aide who stupidly told the world that Sharansky died, today did . . ." is a line I never have to read in later years, but it was a near thing.)

Reagan will raise your taxes and so will I. He won't tell you—I just did." But the week also reminds pols, donors, and journalists that, while Hart won't be in the general election, he's in a longer genera-tional election for the future of America. Cuomo's talk captures the hearts of progressive Democrats, but ideally Hart's future-oriented vision will win their minds. It's at his close that Sorensen appropri-ates Tony Bennett's line that Hart delivers as both a farewell and a wink: "This is one Hart you won't leave in San Francisco."

IT'S MARCH 1987 and I'm traveling alone with Hart in a limo to a fund-raising event at the LA home of Stanley Sheinbaum, a long-time friend, Democracy Project board member, and a Democratic poobah. I get to hear more of the private Hart from a relaxed candi-date than during the roller-coaster primary season three years before. How he grew up in a very repressed childhood, hated bragging about himself, admired how JFK "always looked so fresh and pressed—how did he do that?" and how "I really don't like being in a crowd."

"Gary," I tell him, "you've then chosen a hell of a line of work to be in." We laugh at the incongruity of someone with his introspective temperament succeeding in this most public of professions.

Then back home two months later, like on all Saturday nights, I trudge to the newsstand at 86th and First Avenue toward midnight on May 2, 1987, to buy the Sunday *Times* to get tomorrow's news today—and especially on this Saturday night to read E. J. Dionne's much-anticipated cover magazine profile of Hart. As of that moment, he's running 30 points ahead of all Democratic rivals for the 1988 nomination and double digits ahead of Vice President Bush. I'm slot-ted to be his New York State co-coordinator the next year.

I devour E. J.'s thoughtful, largely positive piece and, with a Pan-glossian glow, take a cab the next morning to a scheduled pro-Israel rally near the UN. As I climb onto stands put up on the west end of Dag Hammarskjold Plaza, a colleague asks if I heard the Hart news. "You mean the Dionne profile?" I say. "No, that he was caught sleep-ing with some woman in Washington." Knowing nothing more, my heart sinks (plunges is probably more accurate).

The *Miami Herald*'s story about Hart and Donna Rice, a 29-year-old model and actress—and his withdrawal five days later—are too familiar to detail here. Richard Ben Cramer's monumental *What It Takes* and more recently Matt Bai's *All the Truth Is Out* have chronicled this sad odyssey when, for the first time really, a major political figure is red-shirted from the political game for private misconduct.

According to Bai, the rules of journalism and politics now adjust to a brutal new vetting process by a generation of Woodward and Bernstein wannabes on the prowl for scandal, usually more personal than constitutional. (For those who missed Bai's book, Hart's now-famous statement that the media should "follow me" is not known by the *Herald* when it begins its stake-out, and the now-infamous *Monkey Business* photo with Donna Rice comes out two weeks after his candidacy ends.)

I'm scheduled to travel with Gary Tuesday in NYC to various events and meetings. It takes Sunday and Monday for me to absorb this stunning development and to be told that he's going ahead with his trip, intent on pushing back on the article and headlines. We meet up at 633 Third Avenue mid-morning and are escorted by a state trooper to the thirty-eighth floor and the offices of Governor Mario Cuomo. After some chit-chat, Mario cannot ignore the donkey in the room. "Don't worry, Gary, if this news had come out about a boring guy like me, my poll numbers would only increase!" says the governor, drawn to underdogs, which Gary is at this moment. The senator tries to explain away the incident as essentially untrue and ridiculous. No one mentions the insider pressure on Mario himself to run for president after his breakout '84 convention speech. The two go on to review some of the big issues likely to come up in 1988.

We then head to the Waldorf Astoria, where there will be an early test of the scandal's effect on his candidacy—a long-scheduled economic address to the American Association of Newspaper Editors. When Hart sees *NBC Nightly News'* network anchor Tom Brokaw in the audience, he thinks to himself, "Uh-oh, am I a bigger story than Iran-Contra?" which is then continuing to make headlines. In an interview in 2015, Gary admits, "Half of me was trying to rise above it but half was trying to figure out what the hell was going on since there was no precedent in American history."

He grits his way through a talk about his view of industrial policy, about how ITAs (individual training accounts) are better than picking winners and losers as a way of spurring economic growth. But given an audience thinking more about America's potential version of Christine Keeler and John Profumo than about ITAs, Gary addresses what's on everyone's mind: "Did I make a mistake by putting myself in circumstances that could be misconstrued? Of course I did. That goes without saying. Did I do anything immoral? I absolutely did not . . . [The *Miami Herald* published] a misleading and false story that hurt my family and other innocent people and reflected badly on my character."

Unfortunately for Gary, the first questioner standing up in the audience is Dick Capen, a staunch Republican and publisher of the *Miami Herald* (and later Bush 41's ambassador to Spain). I listen in agony, hardly imagining how Gary must feel. The issue is not the *Miami Herald,* says Capen, "it's Gary Hart's judgment. He's an announced candidate for president . . . who knows full well that womanizing had been an issue in his past." He goes on and on to a hushed audience—a live version of The *Herald* v. The Candidate.

Gary struggles to maintain his poise, asserting that the newspaper's amateur sleuthing hadn't watched the back door through which Rice and another couple had exited. But Tom Brokaw isn't buying it. When Tim Russert suggests to John Connorton in the back of the room that the only thing that will save Hart is an hour on *Meet the Press* the next Sunday, Brokaw growls, "He's finished. It will take him a million years to get over this." After several more questions on both Rice and the economy, Hart, staff, and supporters escape to a private adjacent room for a few minutes, and then he returns to the residence of Sydney Gruson, a longtime friend and *New York Times* editor.

That evening I join him at a Midtown fund-raiser that Bruce Wasserstein and I had spent considerable time organizing. Before Hart walks into a room of some 300 well-heeled but very curious donors (including one Donald Trump), Ted Sorensen, who's scheduled to introduce him, says to a cluster of us, "Well, to quote the great Richard Nixon, it's time to stonewall!" He gives a robust opening that not at all alludes to the news on everyone's mind.

The applause is restrained both before and after his prepared remarks, and then he adds some spontaneous and fiery comments of his own: "Anyone who wants to test my character is in for a surprise: I may bend but I don't break." But at our table, Donald Drapkin, a major finance person then closely associated with Ron Perelman, can't resist commenting on the tableau's dead-man-walking aspect. "Mark, you really know how to pick 'em, don't you?" I feign courage but Bruce's eye-rolling is closer to the truth.

My loyalty to Gary and dismay at how the episode is being treated like Watergate lead me to do a slew of media the next day defending him on TV and radio. I argue that if private sin is the test for public office, then America might have been denied the services of Alexander Hamilton, FDR, Eisenhower, Johnson, and Kennedy, and we'd be venerating Nixon, not King. When the devout Cal Thomas barks at me on CNN, "What could be worse than what Hart did?" I shout back, "Nuclear war!"

But resorts to history are swept aside by waves of salacious stories that drown the resolve of the candidate and his family. Two days later, at a boisterous scrum of reporters in New Hampshire, the *Washington Post's* Paul Taylor asks this question for the first time of a presidential candidate: "Senator, have you ever committed adultery?" Hart: "Uh, I don't have to answer that question." Afterward, Taylor lets the candidate know that his paper is researching a story about other women he's allegedly had affairs with. A forlorn Gary tells press aide Kevin Sweeney, "This isn't going to end, is it? . . . Let's go home." That day, he bends and then does break, flying back to Colorado to announce that he's "suspending" his campaign.

It's over, except for a sad reentry into the race in 1988 under the banner "Let the people decide."* Having given my all previously and assuming it to be impossible, I don't participate.

A month later, as he does with some others one by one, he takes me to lunch to apologize and add that (a) he didn't have sex with Rice, and (b) "You know, she's awfully bright, a Phi Beta Kappa who majored in history and philosophy."

Should his private misconduct have been publicly disqualifying? For one counter–Cal Thomas view, Rick Hertzberg writes in the *New Republic:* "The fact that a person will lie in the context of adultery proves nothing about his general propensity to lie . . . The point is that if Hart is a liar there must be one or two more lies among the

---

* Going on *Nightline* in September, Gary finally discusses his thoughts about the week of his withdrawal: "If the question is, in the 29 years of my marriage, including two public separations, have I been absolutely and totally faithful to my wife, I regret to say, the answer is no. But I also am never going to answer any specific questions about any individual . . . It isn't anyone else's business . . . I just want to say, to one very special young man and young woman [presumably his two grown children] out there, how sorry I am for letting them down and for many others like them."

many thousands of words he has spoken as a public man. Let them be produced." Although years later, Bai has a hard time getting Hart to reflect much on that fateful week, it's his wife, Lee, who goes there with the comment that "it's what he could have done for this country that I think bothers him to this very day." Gary responds: "Well, at the very least, George W. Bush wouldn't have been president and we wouldn't have invaded Iraq. And a lot of people would be alive today who are dead. You have to live with that, you know."

All the News Is Out in 2014 both blames Hart for his stupid rendezvous but also notes his brilliance, earnestness, and ability to see around corners. As a leading example, there's the bipartisan Hart-Rudman Commission Report of January 2001, which predicts a terrorist attack—"Americans will die on American soil, possibly in large numbers"—unless the new president creates a federal "homeland security" agency. President Bush and national security advisor Condoleezza Rice, however, refuse to even meet with them to discuss their findings.

Bai concludes his book: "[Hart is] perhaps the most visionary political mind of his generation . . . There's a way to describe a man who holds tightly to principle, whatever the cost. The word is character."

Years later, Gary himself addresses his fall from grace, if indirectly. His 2010 book, *The Thunder and the Sunshine,* uses Odysseus as a not-subtle analogy of searching for years for redemption. He writes, "Ultimate defeat should not overshadow successes along the way, and particularly successes that affect long-term outcomes." In 2015, Hart tells me that, since he never thought it inevitable that he'd be president, he's reconciled himself to his post-campaign life and is proud of the dozen books he's written and the fact that he's the only U.S. senator ever to earn a doctorate after his service in office.

Speaking of "successes along the way that affect long-term outcomes," there's this: he stays married to Lee for now over 50 years, and his "New Democrat" candidacy based on change helped spur and shape the very successful Clinton and Obama candidacies to come.

BILL CLINTON: THE SURVIVOR

My mother is picking me up at the West Palm Beach airport in December 1987 when a familiar face is walking toward us. I had only been introduced to Governor Bill Clinton the prior year by my law school roommate,

Sandy Berger. Looking impossibly young and ungubernatorial at 41, he says hello but I can see that my mother has no clue who he is. "Mrs. Green," the governor says, "do you know who your son is?" Well, my mother sure thinks she does and is wondering why this handsome young man is asking. "He's one of the leading Democratic thinkers and . . ." As he goes on for an uninterrupted half minute of almost believable blarney, I think, "First, this is some politician, and second, anyone who says that to my mom will have me as a fan for life." Both turn out to be true.

Concluding that he was not quite ready to run in 1988, Clinton starts moving around the country after Bush 41's win, preparing for a candidacy in '92. As noted above, he gives the keynote at our Democracy Project's "Retreat to Advance" in early 1989 and in 1990 anchors one of a series of Democracy Dinners at the hip West Side apartment of Realtor Lew Futterman, where he rubs elbows with high-end donors and continues spreading his word. There satirist (and senator-to-be) Al Franken, who's never met Clinton, goes up to him and asks, tongue-in-cheek: "So, exactly how many states are there?" Clinton earnestly explains 50 but then delves into the exact status of Samoa, Puerto Rico, and D.C. (Six years later, President Clinton calls Franken his favorite comedian and invites him to host the White House Correspondents Dinner.)

I see him working a fund-raiser at Tavern on the Green late one October night in 1991, pre–Gennifer Flowers, pre–Comeback Kid, pre-Elvis. Meaning he's not being swarmed by admirers so we have some quality time. As mentioned, he encourages me to organize a "Citizens Transition" book for whoever the 1992 winner might be. That's all I need. I then raise a few hundred thousand dollars to organize the Citizen's Transition Project and over the next year get Marion Wright Edelman, Henry Louis Gates Jr., Amory Lovins, Robert Reich, and Sandy Berger, among others, to contribute agency-by-agency critiques for the forty-second president.

This project becomes my sideline obsession, given my day job as the Consumer Affairs commissioner of New York City. Clinton has a politically and emotionally traumatic February and March—including discussions of his draft dodging, pot-smoking, and womanizing—ending up, amazingly, as the likeliest nominee entering the Connecticut primary on March 24.

At 11:15 that night, however, the phone rings in my apartment. "Mark, Harold Ickes here. The governor appears to have lost the primary to [Governor Jerry] Brown and we'll be coming to the city tomorrow morning." *Whoa.* As with Mondale-Hart in 1984, that means that New York—given the Empire State's delegates, media, and money—may again de facto anoint the nominee. "Got any ideas how we can start the New York campaign?" Having just sued H&R Block for its "tax anticipation loan" fraud, I do. "How about starting in front of an H&R Block exposing how Brown favors a flat tax, a regressive idea that our very progressive primary electorate won't like one bit?" We chat for about five minutes and the wheels are set in motion.

Ten hours later, I walk into a small Chinese laundry next to the H&R Block on 16th and First Avenue in Stuyvesant Town where Clinton aide George Stephanopoulos and I brief the governor on key talking points. He listens intently, takes some notes on the back of a copy of *New York Newsday* . . . and we exit five minutes later to face a large group of reporters and cameras. I introduce Clinton and he puts the wood to Brown, explaining how "Jerry's tax—his war-on-New-York-tax"—would hammer average families.*

Although early polls show him slightly trailing here, a city not known for warming to southern accents, New York takes to this sophisticated charmer. He stays on the flat-tax offensive and makes no flubs. Two weeks later, I attend an event at the 59th Street offices of the Jewish Community Relations Council where Brown is speaking to 200 leading Jewish New Yorkers. Audience members are grilling him about his willingness to consider Rev. Jesse Jackson, who admitted calling NYC "Hymietown" in a private conversation in 1984, among possible vice-presidential picks. "Don't worry, no matter who I choose, I'd be the president."

A voice in the back then shouts out, "What if you die?" Um. Er. The usually quick-thinking governor of California has no real answer. I bolt the room to join up with Clinton as he's walking across the rotunda of the Federal Building on Wall Street where he's about to give a speech at George Washington's statue, the very spot on which the first president was sworn in in 1789. I hurriedly tell him

---

* According to the liberal, nonpartisan Citizens for Tax Justice, Brown's flat tax would mean that the poorest fifth would see their taxes grow from 6.7 percent of their income to 26 percent. The richest 1 percent averaging income of $567,000 would see the percentage of earnings they pay in taxes fall by half.

about the exchange. He instantly figures out how this will net out among Jewish and black Democrats, who together total roughly half the primary state electorate. "Then he's lost New York," he says with undisguised pleasure, and walks out to commune with Washington.

Clinton wins New York handily with 41 percent (Paul Tsongas comes in second with 29 percent, Brown third at 26 percent), essentially locking up the nomination. He tells a staff member as they leave the city, "The two people I most owe my win to are Mark Green and Carol O'Cleireacain [a labor economist and the city's finance commissioner, who also prodded and briefed him on the flat-tax issue]."

I go back to my vocation as consumer commissioner and avocation of grinding out *Changing America: Blueprints for the New Administration*. Endorsements on the back cover of the 600-page book in November include Mario Cuomo, Bob Kerrey, Kevin Phillips— and Bill Clinton. After he wins the election, the president-elect is on a victory lap in late November and stops at the Fresh Meadows Shopping Center off the Long Island Expressway to thank the people of Queens. I'm in the crowd and get a shout-out. "Hey, Mark Green. Thanks! I read the whole thing!" I yell back "Thank *you!*" Now used to his expert ingratiation, however, I don't completely inhale his flattery. But still, I think to myself, *If any president-elect might read "the whole thing," it'd be this guy.*

The next month I'm in D.C. participating in the Clinton-Gore official transition project. I spend a week interviewing top appointees and managers of the Consumer Product Safety Commission in the far reaches of upper Northwest D.C. Because I represent the new president and at least appear to have sway over appointments and policies as the agency shifts from R to D, I enjoy a specific level of leverage that I've rarely enjoyed before or since. My team's report indeed does reshape the commission and leads to Anne Brown's appointment a year later as its effective chair. But lacking any interest in going to Washington, I politically prefer to stay in my sweet spot in NYC. Personally, I'm enormously happy to have played any tiny role in the rise of Clinton.

Over his two terms, we stay in periodic touch in private meetings—my favorite being in the Oval Office the day before Jonah's bar mitzvah when he also unsuccessfully tells Jenya she should go to Georgetown, not Cornell—and in public settings, like the final

White House dinner described in chapter 4 ("Mayor Clinton!"). On a Saturday morning just three months earlier, with Gore in a very tight race with Bush, I arrive at Antioch Baptist Church on 125th Street where President Clinton is just beginning to rally the faithful for his vice president. He spots me from the stage and adorably announces to the congregation, "I see another clergy of color, Rev. Green, is in the house. Let's find space for him." He's inspirational, convincing, smiling, as always. On our way out, however, amid the swirl of Secret Service and many well-wishers, he pulls me into his space and in a loud whisper says, "Mark, you've got to convince Al to use me more, not just in big cities." *Moi?*

Finally, on January 20, 2001, I'm proud to greet the former president and new Senator Clinton after their 36-minute flight on his blue-and-white 747, no longer Air Force One, when they land at JFK mid-afternoon. He walks slowly from the plane to a nearby hanger filled with several hundred supporters, as a few officials—Dinkins, Hillary, me—trail behind. She's completely composed, friendly, missing some early Senate votes because of the occasion, saying when I ask how she's doing, "I'm fine. He will be too."

"Thank you for coming out here in the cold weather and the cutting wind to welcome Citizen Clinton home," says the senator in her introduction. Then, in that very familiar slow drawl, as if savoring the magnitude of the moment, he briefly expresses pride in his terms and appreciation to the crowd. Then, nodding toward the senator, he adds that from now on "she would carry the family torch on behalf of the public."

Turns out we'd hear a lot from both in coming years.

JOHN KERRY: THE SECOND 9/11 ELECTION

The Kerry brothers and their pal David Thorne are returning to New Haven from a trip south in the early Sixties when John turns to David and says, "Let's drive through Washington." They steer into the national capital, by the Congress, the Justice Department, and then west on Pennsylvania Avenue by the White House. According to David, John looks up, beams and says, "I'm going to live there someday."

I meet John Kerry in 1982 through his sister Peggy, a well-known NYC activist, and Peter Yarrow, of Peter, Paul and Mary. He's running for lieutenant governor of Massachusetts after losing a controversial congressional race the decade before. A popular woman has just entered the contest and John's worried. "Just my luck," he frets at Peter's spacious West 67th Street apartment. But he goes on to win and then enjoy a spectacular career as a junior senator to the durable Ted Kennedy.

Over the years I'd see him occasionally as he's traveling around NYC to catch up on state and national politics.* I'm always interested to be with this classy war hero turned anti-war hero and am invariably impressed with his comprehensive knowledge and curiosity, notwithstanding an earnest long-windedness. (When Hart and I arrive at Sheinbaum's home for the 1987 fund-raiser mentioned above, each of several senators there are supposed to speak for a few minutes before the main attraction . . . yet Kerry goes on for 30 minutes!)

After Gore loses in 2000 and after 9/11, I'm not surprised to hear that this senator—the son of a foreign service officer who has served for 20 years on the Foreign Relations Committee—wants to run in 2004. In mid-2003 I join businessman Dennis Mehiel as the NYS co-chair and am all in, telling one commentator with glib enthusiasm, "He's as smart as Clinton, has the war record of JFK, the toughness of LBJ, and the hair of Reagan." Which is largely true . . . but it's Howard Dean who connects with Democrats yearning for a vocal anti-Iraq champion after the Bush-Cheney administration's failed policies.

At a summer 2003 party for Dean in East Hampton, near where he grew up, a hot-hot-hot and smiling candidate wonders why "you're not for me, given your views on the war. Come on, Green!" "Blame it on bad timing," I defensively explain, "since I got to be friends with John first." (Later, as restitution for my non-endorsement, Howard titles his 2004 campaign book *Winning Back America*, the name of my 1984 book on Reagan.)

In October, I escort John around a huge DNC fund-raising dinner at the Sheraton. His public game face—"Great to see you! Thanks for all your help"—privately dissolves from time to time. "Dean, Dean, all I hear is Dean," he mutters to himself. By early December 2003, at

---

* One morning in 1991, he says with annoyance, "What is it with Cuomo? I've called him three times and he never returns my call." I recall that comment especially because, at another meeting coincidentally on the same day, Senator Howard Metzenbaum, completely unaware of my earlier conversation with Kerry, asks, "How come I can't get Cuomo on the phone? I'm a United States senator!"

a California retreat of liberal Democrats, pollster Celinda Lake tells us, "At this point there's really no way Dean can lose the nomination," adding that Senator Hillary Clinton agrees with that assessment.

It's a bad time for Kerry. I recall having one of my only shouting matches with my brother, who had pledged to raise a significant amount for Kerry but who now tells me, "I just can't. No one wants to give to him!" Feeling for my candidate, I send several thousand New Yorkers a "Pre-Iowa E-Mail to Dispirited Kerry Supporters in NYS" in early January. It cites General Foch's famous exhortation at the Battle of the Marne in World War I and notes that "fifty years later in Vietnam a young lieutenant named John Kerry turned his speedboat into his attackers, surprising and subduing them. And today John Kerry is again fighting back. I'm proud to be with you in this campaign."

My purple prose aside, Kerry is literally and politically a fighter. He decides to basically live in Iowa and travel with his navy crewmen to validate his heroism and with bud Peter Yarrow singing at his side. While the numbers are daunting, Bob Shrum, his brilliant strategic advisor, thinks that Dean's 3-to-1 lead will dissolve once voters concentrate on who is most likely to beat Bush. He's vindicated when Kerry charms, speaks, and strums his way to a come-from-behind first-place finish in the caucuses, with Dean a distant third. And after the "Dean Scream" caucus night, John goes from strength to strength, chooses rival John Edwards as his VP nominee, and enters his convention as an even-money shot to be president.

As a delegate in Boston, I watch John on the culminating evening dramatically stride through the delegates (I'm with my son Jonah on the convention floor where he's "getting the shot" for a film he's shooting on the candidate). The senator opens his acceptance speech with a salute and "I'm John Kerry and I'm reporting for duty." That works but, the next month at the Republican Convention at Madison Square Garden, which I attend as credentialed media, I feel queasy as the entire Bush convention merges the War President and the City of 9/11. It's over the top, disgusting, exploitative . . . but effective.

Being neither on staff nor in the candidate's inner circle, that summer and fall I spend my effort in two areas: fund-raising, since NYC is largely an ATM machine presidentially, given the math of the Electoral College; and imploring the candidate and Kerry advisor John Marttila to plant their flag against Bush's war, notwithstanding the candidate's vote to authorize it in October 2002. In one small effort, I organize a meeting with John and a dozen New York policy intellectuals/opinion-leaders concerned about his shifting Iraq policy. (Recall his disastrous "I was against it before I was for it" formulation). In a two-hour blunt meeting at Al Franken's spacious Upper West Side home overlooking the Hudson, Fred Kaplan, Eric Alterman, and others grill him on his views and what he'd do as president. They and he are candid, smart, thorough, and, knowing both sides, feel better about each other when it's over.

Tasked with finding a prestigious location for a major planned September address on the war, I book Kerry into the new thousand-seat Kimmell Center at NYU, a half mile north of Ground Zero. When Marttila tells me the night before, "You're gonna be happy with this speech," I bring Jonah with me because, as I tell him, "I think tomorrow might become an historic moment if Kerry goes on to win."

John doesn't disappoint in his 47-minute address. To a packed house, he condemns Bush's "stubborn incompetence and colossal failures of judgment. If we do not change course, there is the prospect of a war with no end in sight." He finishes by explaining that if Bush or a new president begins to repair alliances, train Iraqi security forces, improve reconstruction, and ensure elections, we can "begin to withdraw U.S. forces starting next summer and realistically bring our troops home within the next four years."

Bush's lead throughout the fall shrinks after this address and three illuminating presidential debates that Kerry clearly wins. Then comes Friday, October 30.

First, I charter two buses, and at 6 a.m. from the lobby at the Graybar Building at 420 Lexington Avenue (an S. L. Green building), 100 Green supporters from 2001 set out for Cleveland, Ohio. Dulled by political inactivity in the deep-blue state of New York, we drive eight hours to spend three days going door to door in the state that will likely pick the winner for the other 49.

These three days are like summer camp that matters. We sleep in cheap motels and are briefed in how to talk Ohioan. Our teams of two (always a man and a woman) encounter mostly black families to urge them to vote and white families who question us about our "super liberal, flip-flopping" Democrat, reflecting the massive air attacks they watch nightly. I see dirty-tricks flyers distributed in minority communities about how those voters will be allowed to vote on

Wednesday so they can stay home Tuesday. And everyone's pumped to go to the final campaign rally with Kerry and Bruce Springsteen. But I miss "No Surrender" and "Promised Land" since I have to fly back that evening to get to a long-scheduled speaking commitment at a West Side high school the next morning.

Second, also on that Friday though a bit more consequentially, there occurs the greatest October Surprise in American presidential campaign history when bin Laden releases a videotape explaining why al-Qaeda attacked on 9/11 and how awful Bush is. The tape roils the campaigns. Both issue statements agreeing that we can't let terrorists affect America's presidential election. But John takes a calculated risk and goes further, regretting how Bush "outsourced the job [of capturing or killing bin Laden at Tora Bora] to Afghan war lords. I would never have done that. I think it was an enormous mistake and we are paying the price for it today." The Bush campaign harshly condemns Kerry for exploiting 9/11 (unlike, of course, their own 9/11 obsession at their convention).

No one can know for sure the impact of such a once-in-a-lifetime presidential variable. Does the tape hit swing voters in their patriotic gut—*We can't change our commander in chief mid-stream to satisfy this terrorist monster*—or in their brain—*The perpetrator of 9/11 is still at large because our bumbling commander in chief has not accomplished his mission?* Privately, Kerry supporters are nervous that, over the final decisive days, the issue of a country at war with evil again becomes the center of attention.

After voting, I fly to Boston election night to stay at the Westin Hotel with top staff and supporters. At 6:30 p.m., we're cautiously buoyant at a cocktail party because exit polls have John slightly ahead nationally and, more significantly, in Ohio. We then move to a larger ballroom to watch the returns. I recall two indelible images: Larry David, alone on a couch near a huge bay window looking glum, admittedly his natural visage, yet getting glummer as the night progresses. And Paul Rivera, a Kerry advisor (and later my New York attorney general campaign guru) assuring us on the half hour that the *exit* polling shows John winning Ohio and the presidency . . . while the TV monitors tabulating *actual* voters is showing Bush slowly pulling away in the Buckeye State.

As hundreds of strategists and lawyers crunch numbers searching for any hope and his campaign manager and running mate argue against any concession, the candidate—"who knows how to do math very fast," says Shrum—decides at 2 a.m. at his Louisburg Square townhouse to concede. He wakes at 7 a.m., starts scratching out a concession speech, and, despite winning 59 million votes, the most ever for a runner-up, calls Bush at 11:06 a.m. Then he goes to the majestic Faneuil Hall at Harvard where he had announced his candidacy and, his voice breaking, tells 500 supporters and his teary-eyed daughters, "We fought hard and I wish that things had turned out a little differently but in an American elections, there are no losers . . . because we all wake up as Americans."

Following custom, Kerry never publicly whines or explains. And, of course, he goes on to live not at the White House but largely on the secretary of state's plane in the second term of the man he put on the road to 1600 Pennsylvania Ave. by choosing him to give the 2004 convention keynote address. Privately, however, John confides to close friends that it was bin Laden's tape that stopped his momentum that final week and influenced—perhaps determined—the outcome.*

"LISTENING" TO HILLARY CLINTON

It's an early October night of the Hamptons Film Festival in 1998, a local event started by my cousin Stuart Suna to give that elite ZIP code even more cachet. After viewing some movies pre-release, Deni, Jenya, and I go over to Alec Baldwin's home, where he's on a panel with President Clinton, First Lady Hillary Clinton, and Democratic state chair Judith Hope, a friend of the Clintons from Arkansas. This being shortly after the Lewinsky scandal breaks, Hillary gets a huge welcoming applause from the 300 guests, exceeded only by the applause when she's done speaking. "Boy, they really like her here," says the president to Hope. "Yes they do, Mr. President." It was Judith who, at a White House Christmas party the prior December, was the first person to suggest to Hillary that she run for Moynihan's seat. "You really think so?" said a surprised Hillary.

---

* In fact, while Kerry was up by five just before the bin Laden tape in battleground states, a secret Mark Mellman poll the day before the election showed Kerry up by only one, a fall of four points in the post-tape few days.

In January 1999, Hillary is making due diligence calls to New York Democratic leaders, soliciting advice about her now-inevitable bid against Mayor Giuliani for the Moynihan seat. She reaches me mid-month while I'm making daily money calls for my 2001 mayoral bid. Given my frequent sparring with Rudy, she's especially interested in what he's like as an opponent. We review his strengths and weaknesses—his smarts and ferocity are obvious but less so his propensity to exaggerate to win any argument as well as his prosecutorial impulse to try to destroy opponents.

Then I go outside my lane to suggest a different route for her campaign. "Instead of a standard cheering, balloon-festooned announcement speech, which could contribute to the stereotype of you as a presumptuous big-foot, how about instead a more humble 'listening tour'?" Knowing her facility for actually listening in conversations and taking notes, I continue: "In fact, you *don't* know the state well, and it'll be an appealing way for you to learn from talkative, self-centered New York voters. Not to mention that if you screw up and mispronounce, say, 'How-sten Street' as 'Houston' Street, you can laugh it off as part of your learning curve."

The next month, on Moynihan's farm with the retiring senator, she launches her campaign with a "Listening Tour," and the phrase—perhaps also proposed by someone else, for all I know—enters the political lexicon. Truth is, the idea and words came to me because of a picture in my mind of Hillary sitting at some civic breakfast at the Roosevelt Hotel as petitioner after petitioner lined up to say or ask for something as Hillary patiently listened, nodded, and aide Huma Abedin took notes to follow up. "She has this great gift," Senator Alan Simpson (R-WY) once said to a friend of mine; "she's completely focused on you when you speak and no one else." She tells a journalist, "I try to give my full attention to the person I'm with." A listening tour for a listener.

She wins her contest easily after Rudy withdraws and then proves to be far more a diligent workhorse than showhorse in the Senate. After she handily wins reelection in 2006, talk of her presidential prospects gets serious.

I get a cell call the last week of December 2007, while on the beach with family in Florida, where my mother-in-law lives. "Mark, it's Hillary, you got a minute?" She's on with Neera Tanden, a ranking official in the Center for American Progress, the leading Democratic think tank in Washington, D.C. They ask if I'd be interested in co-chairing a new progressive transition project with John Podesta, the founder of CAP, for whoever becomes president in 2009—"like the one you did for Bill," says Hillary. Of course the answer is yes. Again via my Democracy Project, I spend half time for 15 months co-parenting an 800-page volume for a senator (a different one) who indeed does become president. We produce a great product, but it's a difficult delivery.

Podesta, CAP, and I host a two-day retreat at the Wye Planta-tion in South Carolina with many of the authors (I room with Peter Edelman) to learn from each other as we each develop our particular content. John and I share opening remarks: he provides a smart and panoramic view of our task based on his deep knowledge of federal policy both as President Clinton's last chief of staff and his work at CAP; I explain lessons learned from our '92 transition project for Bill Clinton and frame our mission historically. Mid-year, however, Podesta has the gall to resign our citizen's transition to become chair for the *actual* Obama-Biden transition to come (a good career move, I concede). After he exits, however, I clash frequently with his succes-sor as project co-chair, Michele Jolin, over who writes what agency chapter, deadlines, language, the introduction, that sort of thing. The problem is partly the different perspectives of a major institution in D.C. and me solo a distance away in NYC but also in part because, in hindsight, I'm too overbearing in my views of the best way to produce a transition book since I'd done one before.

Finally, after reasonable compromises brokered by both Podesta and CAP's Melody Barnes (later to be Obama's domestic policy advi-sor), *Change for America: A Progressive Blueprint for the 44th President* is published by Basic Books and sent to the president-elect as well as all his top appointees. Among its 60 writers are later Obama picks such as Elena Kagan, Jack Lew, Gene Sperling, Tom Donilan, Carol Browner, Harold Koh, and James Lee Witt—and Podesta in his sec-ond term.

On January 20, as I'm limping around from knee-replacement surgery and traveling with friends Ken and Katherine Lerer and John Sykes, Deni and I are among the million freezing, joyous attendees at the Obama inauguration. Wow, a black urban progressive intel-lectual in the Oval Office—with a mean jump shot, literary élan, and the cadence of both pulpit and street. I can still hardly believe it.

COMRADE CASTRO

My friend Smith Bagley, an heir to the R. J. Reynolds fortune and a major progressive philanthropist, calls in mid-1987 to ask if I'd join him and a small delegation on a four-day trip to Cuba to advance human rights there. We'd meet with public officials, dissidents, religious leaders—and President Castro. Though I'm no Cuba expert, I'm eager to go, learn, and, if nothing else, take a measure of this historic figure.

Our group of ten—including Smith's wife Elizabeth (later Clinton's ambassador to Portugal) and ex-Senator Fred Harris—leave Florida on a turbo prop on October 16, after a lot of screening by State Department and customs personnel, for the flight to Havana.

As we drive from the airport to our hotel, we are struck, as is everyone who's made this trek, by the aging infrastructure, spotty roads yet immaculate 1950s cars, captured in the popular mind by Francis Ford Coppola in *Godfather II*. We tour the city for two days under strict supervision, often with the very savvy Ricardo Alarcón, a Castro foreign minister and leading policy intellectual. We visit the Isle of Youth, some 50 kilometers south of the eastern tip of Cuba, where we enjoy a Q&A with an international delegation of high school students from Mozambique. I ask them if they'd ever heard of Stalin. No one had. Kennedy? No one had. Michael Jackson? Squeals of familiarity erupt. "Do you know him?" they pester me. "Do you have any of his tapes?" No and no, but I'm reminded that the global community is bound together more by culture than politics.

There's a drill that Castro famously deploys with all visiting delegations, and now it's our turn. We're told that we'll be meeting with him soon, very soon, and then hear nothing . . . until there's the expected middle-of-the-night call. "Mr. Green, would you please come to the lobby within 20 minutes where we'll assemble to be driven to the presidential palace?" At first groggy but then alert at this opportunity, we are driven a few minutes into the massive presidential palace, built in 1920 but still serving as Castro's ceremonial office. (It later becomes the Museum of the Revolution.) With little security, we're ushered into a spacious office with spare furniture and no wall art for what turns out to be the first of eight hours of meetings and meals over two days with *El Presidente*.

Sworn in as Consumer Affairs Commissioner, 1990.

Commissioner Green shutting down unlawful store, 1990. Credit: Dan Brinzac/NYPost.

Introducing Nelson Mandela to Jenya, with Mayor Giuliani, 1991.

Campaigning with Governor Clinton for president at H&R Block, NYC, 1992.

Protesting Joe Camel with a camel, 1995.

Announcing my Tuesday Nite Out initiative with Chrisopher Reeve, Jackie Mason, Alec Baldwin, Mayor Dinkins, and Colleen Dewhurst, 1992. Credit: Karen Winner

With Andrew and Mayor
Giuliani at our swearing-in,
January 1994.

As the presiding
officer, New York
City Council,
1994.

At 70th
Town Hall
meeting,
2000.

Sworn in for second term, 1997.

With Mayor Dinkins at his concession speech—that's Sharpton and Jackson behind him—the night that I also won for Public Advocate, 1993.

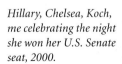

Hillary, Chelsea, Koch, me celebrating the night she won her U.S. Senate seat, 2000.

Announcing for Mayor with family and Bill Bratton in Brooklyn, April, 2001.

With Bill and Hillary Clinton at Unity Dinner, October, 2001, hosted by Jon Stewart.

Campaigning for Mayor, Puerto Rican Day Parade.

New York Post *front page from September 11, 2001, now hanging in 9/11 Museum.*

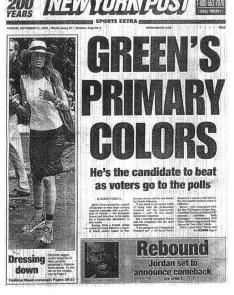

September 12, 2001, New York Times front page.

My family and me in a campaign van the night before November general election, 2001.

Concession speech election night, with Deni, family, supporters. Credit: N.Y. Daily News *Archive.*

With Arianna Huffington and Mary Matalin on Both Sides Now, *2012.*

Getting some editorial tips from grandkids Ava and Otis, 5 and 2, to whom this book is dedicated, 2015. Credit: Deni Frand

While he surely knows English, Castro, in his familiar fatigues and trending gray beard, greets each of us warmly in Spanish. He's well briefed, saying to me, "ah, the politician and writer." A female translator allows him time to better digest a comment or question before responding. He carries himself with the confident air of a successful revolutionary/prince/politician, seemingly knowledgeable about farming, finances, retail, trade, health, history—Cuba's and ours. Encyclopedic, dramatic, penetrating, humorous, *talkative*—he reminds me of Ralph, except this virtuoso is running a country and, 25 years ago to the day, almost started World War III during the 1962 Cuban Missile Crisis.

I decide to be blunt and jokey with him in an effort to provoke candor. After he brags how popular he is, I ask "why then do you not allow a handful of dissidents to print their small human rights pamphlets but imprison them instead?" His dismissive reply—"Why waste the paper?"—tells me that we're coming at this from very different directions. "When will you have free elections?" "Someday, when security concerns are gone." Then he turns the tables and quizzes us about American politics.

Asking about Cuomo, Hart, and the upcoming presidential campaign, Castro grows animated when I tell him that I know each well. "So, you think Cuomo's getting in? . . . Would Hart have been the favorite? . . . Does President Reagan perform well because he knows acting or he knows who he is?"

This is apparently a communist who hates America but loves Americans.

Beginning dinner on our second day of discussions, he says to me through his interpreter, "Did you see that your stock market fell 500 points yesterday?" I laugh. *"El Presidente,* you mean 50 points." Now he sees that he has me, and says gleefully in English, "No, *500 points!"* Indeed, this being before the Internet, we did not know on this day, October 19, that the stock exchange *had* lost 20 percent of its value, its worst day since the Crash of '29 . . . and I'm being told by the world's leading Leninist. We discuss what this might mean, then talk more about Cuban and American prisoners and the other big news of the week, the worldwide attention to the dramatic rescue of "Baby Jessica" from a well in her aunt's Texas backyard.

On our departure the next day, he continues our bantering and asks if I'll be running for office again soon [my Senate race being the year before] and, with the slightest of smiles, asks how he could help me. "Of course, please endorse my opponent." He gets a kick out of that probably anticipated answer, winking and laughing and extending his hand. Indeed, in my first Public Advocate race in 1993, one newspaper red-baits me as "Fidel's pal" based on a photo of him and me on my wall among 20 others.

Comrade Castro never endorses me or any opponent.

SIX

WHAT IT TAKES

12 Skills

You must know yourself and you must know the times.

—Benjamin Disraeli, on what it takes to succeed in politics

My right flank is weakening, my center collapsing. Situation excellent, I am attacking.

—Field Marshal Ferdinand Foch, before turning
the tide at the Battle of the Marne, 1917

TO BORROW THE TITLE OF RICHARD BEN CRAMER'S
epic political psychoanalysis, what *does* it take to win in polarized
politics and advocacy today?

Fortunately during our greatest crises, Washington, Lincoln, and
FDR all knew themselves and their times. In the modern era, political genius is rare but usually easy to spot. Harvard and Yale law
school classmates of both Barack Obama and Bill Clinton report
that they'd nudge each other and say, "That guy's gonna be president
someday." Asked at a TV audition how a modern outer-space alien
might sit, Mork-to-be Robin Williams immediately stood on his head
in a chair—and got the job. All of them were "naturals."

But for mere mortals, politics has become what Jefferson feared—
a business. That's the conclusion of Alan Ehrenhalt's *The United
States of Ambition*, a 1991 book on how professionalized our world
of politics has become. In my home state, most of our top officials

(Andrew Cuomo, Chuck Schumer, Kirsten Gillibrand, Bill de Blasio, Scott Stringer) were all kid pols who self-nominated to climb the greasy pole—and succeeded. Apparently, to prevail in a brutal Darwinian process requires, in Liam Neeson's signature line in *Taken,* "a very particular set of skills."

While public officials have mixed motives—power, service, money—there are still right and wrong ways to do it. So for all those thinking about entering the fray, below are 12 valuable skills/assets, followed by the false prophets of luck and lying. Though hardly Machiavelli's *The Prince,* consider these Mark's Rules based on examples both personal and historical.

If you score 10 or more out of 12, you're FDR and can go straight to a presidential library (Mount Rushmore's full). If you're a 7 to 9, I'd bet on you. But if you're a 4 or less, maybe Wall Street or the family business is preferable to this very high-risk/high-reward process. For politics is, quite literally, the ultimate winner-take-all profession. While being the second-best surgeon, Realtor, or retailer in your town will earn you much respect and wealth, coming in second in a political campaign in a state with 20 million is as good as coming in 20 millionth. Oscar losers aren't expected to go on stage to explain why they didn't win in concession speeches, a gauntlet that unsuccessful candidates must endure.

Here's how to come in first:*

1. Be Relentless. "If you do everything," Senate candidate Lyndon Johnson said, "you win." That means more events, more street campaigning, more fund-raising, more spy-versus-spy strategizing. A fellow Georgian who knew Stalin as a youth describes "his unquestionably greater energy, indefatigable capacity for hard work and . . . organization talent."

With the work ethic of Nader as my model and a deadline called The Election, I'd urge campaign staff to over-schedule me. I may not be able to affect the weather on Election Day or bin Laden's murderous intervention, but I sure as hell want to leave nothing on the table over things I can control. I started a tradition of campaigning all night before Election Day to symbolically convey my enthusiasm

---

* Suggestions involve traits, not tactics, not what percentage of the budget should go to social media versus field.

for service for all, including the midnight shift. And I'd treat every day as consumer commissioner and public advocate as a day lost unless I was as productive as possible, both to advance consumer justice and to enhance myself for whatever comes next.

There it is—that mix of idealism and selfishness that's embedded in every public person to varying degrees. So while I adore my family as much as anyone, I will do a half-dozen churches, pressers, brunches, receptions every Sunday for eight years while my talented rival Alan Hevesi is catching Jets and Mets games with his sons, a difference that cumulatively proves telling in our 2001 mayoral primary. Not that Alan was wrong or that I'm now proud of this truth, but "what it takes" is a level of immersion seen in *Jiro Dreams of Sushi* and *Whiplash*. Relentless drive is a level beyond standard ambition. It's Rafael Nadal, "who plays every point as if he were broke," according to Jimmy Connors. It's Lyndon Johnson, whose cousin said of him, "days meant nothing, nights meant nothing, weekdays, weekends, they meant nothing. He could not stand to lose, just couldn't stand it. He had to win, *had* to." It's Ted Williams swinging hundreds of thousands of times in front of mirrors until it becomes as natural as breathing. "The way the inevitable came to pass," said Justice Holmes, "was effort."

That means being in the moment nearly every moment . . . which we understand when it comes to driving, skiing, even baby-sitting, when even one mistake could be one too many. That includes a complete focus on *the* goal because, notes the Chinese proverb, "He who aims at two targets hits none." The essential golf skill, according to a popular book, is "Take. Dead. Aim." Which is why John Kennedy chose Lyndon Johnson for VP. His brother and key labor supporters opposed LBJ because he was no liberal and had said that JFK's father was a "Nazi sympathizer." But none of that mattered once Kennedy realized that the choice increased the chance of winning Texas electors and therefore the presidency.

After losing a congressional race in 1980, I visited Lorne Michaels—a brilliant, focused person pretending to be a laid-back Canadian—whom I got to know during the week that Nader hosted *SNL*. In an office with various memorabilia from his many shows, Lorne gave me this advice about what to do next: "Figure out what you want and then apply yourself to it almost without consideration of anything else." That apparently worked well for SNL graduates Eddie

Murphy, Martin Short . . . and, moving to local politics, Marty Markowitz, who served 22 years as a state senator while aching to become the borough president of Brooklyn. With that destination always in mind, he ignored other prospects until his time came in 2001, when he defeated a favored opponent and completed three terms, being the cheerleader who helped to turn that county into one of the coolest "cities" in the world. Then he plausibly considered running for mayor in 2013, given his popularity with both the Jewish and black communities, but he passed it up. After all, it wasn't *borough president.*

Relentless drive includes a level of anticipation essential to chess masters and generals. The best enumeration was the thinking of the great Chinese military tactician Sun Tzu: "If your enemy has superior strength, evade him. If your enemy is temperamental, seek to irritate him . . . The general who wins the battle makes many calculations in his temple before the battle is fought. The general who loses makes but few calculations beforehand." That is, think way ahead and put yourself in the other guy's shoes.

Last, a relentless drive means being insatiable. It's Arianna Huffington pushing herself and the *Huffington Post* to open yet more verticals and bureaus, Chuck Schumer continuing his Sunday press conference habit as he conquers the Senate, Bill Buckley knocking off his twenty-fourth book while on a two-week boating trip.

Where does this superhuman willfulness, focus, preparation, and insatiability come from? *Quien sabe?* Probably owes to unusual genetic wiring. But without it, the next 11 skills/traits probably won't suffice.

2. Always Optimistic/Never Defensive. What Teddy Roosevelt, Woodrow Wilson, Franklin Roosevelt, Ronald Reagan, Bill Clinton, and Barack Obama had in common was one parent who let them know they were beyond the moon and had to reach for the stars. In his book *The Defining Moment,* Jonathan Alter concludes that FDR "seemed to be missing the normal emotional equipment that produces worry" and traces it back to Freud: "A man who has been the indisputable favorite of his mother keeps for life the feelings of a conqueror. That confidence of success often induces real success." Adds Alter on FDR: "He was the first presidential candidate since his cousin Theodore to smile regularly and act as if he were enjoying himself."

A deep belief in yourself is a political essential because every candidacy is daily poised between a triumph and an embarrassment and no one's a prohibitive favorite in his/her first race.* Fifty reporters covering the 1948 presidential campaign were asked that summer whether Truman could win—not one thought so. When Roger Federer was 178–0 after winning the first two sets in majors and then won the first two sets against Jo-Wilfried Tsonga in the 2011 Wimbledon, no one gave the Frenchman any odds at all. Guess who won?

The lesson: there's almost no such thing as impossible odds. I won a primary as a laughable underdog in 1986 and lost a general election as a near-prohibitive favorite in fall of 2001—and it's not until later that it's clear why. "You never know," former representative Jack Brooks (D-TX) once told me, "when you're going to get caught wearing a blue shirt in a white-shirt year." (After winning 22 straight terms, Brooks lost in 1994.)

The irrepressible Lee Atwater memorably explained the best approach when you appear to be slipping or on the defensive: "Attack, attack, attack . . . if you're explaining, you're losing." The trick is how to turn an apparent defeat into a Dunkirk. Stories about a slush fund jeopardized Nixon's place on the ticket in 1952 until he figured out the right tone, images, and words in his Checkers Speech—end of story. After Governor Bill Clinton was nearly hooted down due to his too-long, boring, and well-lit introduction of nominee Mike Dukakis at the 1988 Atlanta convention, I watched him carefully as he then smiled and glad-handed his way around the arena's circular walkway. A couple days later, he went on *The Tonight Show* armed with an hourglass and plopped it on Carson's desk. Johnny laughed uproariously, and his flop went *poof.* Barack Obama lost badly in an ill-advised congressional race against incumbent Bobby Rush in 2000. Then he figured out what went wrong and ran for the U.S. Senate, against the advice of consigliore David Axelrod. He ended up doing pretty well for himself.

3. Maintain Flawless Discipline. If you "can resist anything except temptation," in the words of Oscar Wilde, you shouldn't go into politics. Or as the fictitious Frank Underwood tells his wife who lost

---

* Those who lost very early races include Lincoln (House; Senate, twice), Teddy Roosevelt (mayor), FDR (Senate), LBJ (Senate), Bill Clinton (House), George H. W. Bush (Senate, twice), George W. Bush (House), Barack Obama (House), Daniel Patrick Moynihan (city council president), and Rudy Giuliani (mayor). It appears that an early loss is a near prerequisite for the presidency if not other high offices.

her temper in public on *House of Cards,* "courage is knowing when to shut up when the stakes are so high." For in public life, you're only as strong as your worst moment, your stupidest mistake that can be incessantly advertised so a voter can't think of you without thinking of *that.*

In this era of cell phone videographers and political trackers, ask Virginia's George Allen about political discipline. He called an Indian-American tracker "macaca" at a 2006 event, one slur that knocked him out of contention for a presidential run *and* for two Senate seats. Or ask what Mitt Romney now thinks when the numeral *47* is uttered. "The clearest discoveries of virtue or vice in men" comes not from their great exploits, wrote Plutarch, the Greek biographer of Alexander, two millennia ago. "Sometimes a matter of less moment, an expression of a jest, informs us better."

The public is often waiting for that betraying moment. If a candidate gets intellectually bored saying the same thing ad nauseam or relishes spontaneity, he or she could be walking toward a land mine. John McCain couldn't resist parodying the Beach Boys hit by singing "bomb bomb bomb bomb bomb Iran" in 2007, which critics exploited as evidence of his knee-jerk militarism. It was also evidence of a candidate going way off message. Despite promising his staff to stop his favorite activity of wind surfing because of the "optics," an athletic John Kerry snuck out one afternoon from his Nantucket home when he thought no one else was on the beach; the eventual footage was incessantly shown in Bush ads about how he swayed with the wind.

When I run against a little known opponent for reelection as public advocate in 1997, I agree with advisors not to take the bait at a debate since I'm ahead by about 130 points. But after eight minutes of, in my view, his needling comments, I completely lapsed into my *Crossfire* habit and just verbally decked him. Contrast that with Al D'Amato who, if nothing else, was a political pro when we debated in 1986 and *I* was the one 130 points behind. Nothing I said in my kitchen sink of criticism provoked him to flinch or raise an eyebrow. Nothing. He just stared straight ahead rope-a-doping me, perhaps losing the debate on points but easily winning reelection.

After Barack Obama beat Hillary Clinton for the nomination in 2008, she gave a rousing convention speech for him. Watching her put aside many slights perceived by the Clinton camp, close friend Judith

Hope confided to Hillary after she left the podium, "I'm amazed at your capacity for political generosity." Replied the future Obama secretary of state and possibly Clinton 45, "Life is too short to stay in the bad places."

NYC comptroller Scott Stringer vowed after one election loss to hold no grudges, adding with a mischievous grin, "with, at most, three exceptions." That's good advice, but do I feel the rush of schadenfreude that State Senator Carl Kruger today sits in prison, District Attorney Joe Hynes is himself under criminal investigation, and the late Assemblyman Vito Lopez was ruined by sexual harassment charges? I claim immunity under the Stringer rule-of-three.

4. Use Memorable Language (i.e., Find Your Voice). When the CIA was having difficulty explaining its policy toward Cuba in early 1962, the agency's chief of covert operations, Richard Helms, instructed a flummoxed aide, "There are 500,000 words in the English language. Use them."

"A government of, by and for the people," . . . "a rendezvous with destiny," . . . "Ask *not* what your country can do for you," . . . "I have a dream," . . . "Mr. Gorbachev, tear down this wall." There's no formula to predict what precise emphasis or sequence of words will move audiences, but certainly the ability to draw vivid word images can promote political success. At the risk of oversimplification, there are three keys to language that soars and connects. It has to fit the occasion, be fresh, and convey an image or story that endures. Reagan could have said at the Brandenburg Gate, "This wall divides us"; Kennedy in his inaugural, "We should all contribute to public service"; and King at the Lincoln Memorial, "I have an agenda." But who would remember that?

Think of the creativity behind language we now take for granted. FDR doesn't just throw money at the British in its hour of peril but proposed what he calls "Lend Lease," which is like "lending a garden hose to your neighbor" when his home was on fire. Running against 73-year-old Bob Dole in 1996, the 49-year-old presidential incumbent couldn't comment directly on their age discrepancy. Instead Clinton aspires that his second term be "a bridge to the 21st century," which leads all to quietly wonder whether Dole can even last that long.

The language of politics especially includes imagery and stories that are "sticky." In their much-cited books and articles, behavioral psychologists George Lakoff and Drew Westin explain how politicians can create narratives that project who they really are. Historically such examples include Lincoln as the "Rail-Splitter," Kennedy's PT-109 tie clips, Lawton Chiles's boots as he walked Florida state, Joni Ernst's castration of pigs ("I'm going to Washington to make 'em squeal!"), Occupy Wall Street's "we are the 99 percent"—these all convincingly embody a candidate or cause.*

So find a voice. Especially with social media putting a premium on conveying your thoughts in under 140 characters, it's helpful to stand out with something distinctive, i.e., your brand. The late publisher Peter Workman was considered a marketing genius. When shaping my book *The Consumer Bible*, he told me to make it either the shortest such advice book or the longest: "But you must stand out either way." (The book is 652 pages.)

Whatever some may think of Nader's blunt righteousness, Buckley's polysyllabic high-browisms, and Trump's bullying and bragging, no one would doubt these different people each has a memorable voice. You know who they are.

5. Stay Calm! Calm is when Franklin Roosevelt, John Kennedy, and Lyndon Johnson all betray not a trace of anxiety to observers when, respectively, (a) they console the mayor of Chicago just shot at FDR's side in 1933, (b) receive the news in October 1962 that the Russian freighters carrying nuclear missiles to Cuba have turned back, and (c) oversee the transition of government from Parkland Hospital and Air Force One on November 22, 1963.

People want to know that a principal can handle controversies and concentrate on results because, according to New York Mets manager Terry Collins, "When the manager panics, everyone panics." On most days, a candidate will hear both terrific news and awful news that would clobber most people—or would lead a rational

---

*The problem, though, according to George Orwell's 1946 classic *Politics and the English Language*, is that "political language [can be] designed to make lies sound truthful and murder respectable, and to give an appearance of solidity to pure wind." Language can mislead as well as inspire. Consider "enhanced interrogation," "mission accomplished," and "death panels"—all had good runs until exposed as "pure wind" for only primed Fox viewers to inhale. Also, recall John Ford's timeless observation that "when the legend becomes fact, print the legend." Babe Ruth told friends that of course he never pointed to where he'd hit a home run in Wrigley Field in the 1932 World Series, "but if those bastards want to think I point to center field, let 'em."

human being to believe either that s/he can't lose or can't win . . . when in fact neither is almost ever true.

I grow up with an older brother repeating that "the Eleventh Commandment is—thou shalt not sweat." That's planted and grows in my formative mind. In high school, my on-field varsity baseball nonchalance earns me the nickname of "Sparky." That Sparky irony, however, helps me persevere on discovering with a month to go that my 1986 Senate primary opponent is outspending me 10 to 1 due to his inherited wealth, and drives me to deliver upbeat concession speeches over the years when the impulse, as Adlai Stevenson famously said, is just to cry.

Calmness can confound critics. It's pretty humorous how Barack Obama's "insufferable serenity"—his combination of Mr. Spock and Joe Friday—infuriates opponents. They disparage him as too aloof, disconnected, lacking an emotional register,* actually the very same things that were said about John Kennedy. ("As far as backslapping with the politicians," JFK told an interviewer, "I think I'd rather go somewhere with my familiars or sit alone somewhere and read a book.") After Bush 43's impetuous bring-it-on personality and presidency, Obama's steady-Eddie manner—whether dealing with a rumored terrorist attack at his 2009 inauguration or joking at the White House Correspondent's Dinner hours before the raid that killed bin Laden—seems far preferable.

6. A High IQ Is Good/A High EQ Essential. Teddy Roosevelt published 32 books, Woodrow Wilson was among the most noted historians of his era pre-presidency, and Daniel Patrick Moynihan was a leading sociologist pre-Senate. The brilliance of all three surely boosted their ascents.

One needn't be the smartest person in the room to succeed in politics, only "smart enough," as the often-ridiculed Eisenhower and Reagan surely were. Far more urgent than a big bandwidth is a superior EQ—for emotional quotient—the intuition of being able to interpret signals from your immediate environment. It is as easy to

---

* Four days before the 2008 general election at an NYC fund-raiser for the candidate, I ask Patrick Gaspard, a top Obama campaign aide, "Does your boss *ever* get angry?" Gaspard pauses awhile, then says to the audience, "Just once—when the *New Yorker* ran that cover with Michelle as an Angela Davis terrorist figure. We had to hold him back on that."

imagine playing tennis blindfolded as to believe a person can survive public life without being able to successfully read people and situations. It was said of Lincoln by his law partner that "he understood politics because he understood human nature." The best description of this kind of intelligence in the next century comes from the young John Maynard Keynes, observing British prime minister Henry Lloyd George at the Versailles Conference in 1919: "To see [him] watching the company, with six or seven senses not available to ordinary men, judging character, motive, and subconscious impulse, perceiving what each was thinking and even what each was going to say next, and compounding with telepathic instinct the argument or appeal best suited to the vanity, weakness, or self-interest of his immediate audience was to realize that the poor President would be playing blind man's bluff in that party."

The best modern approximation to Lloyd George has been, by common consent, Johnson. He often remarked that his father admonished him that "no man belonged in politics unless he could walk into a room of people and know at once who was for him and who against him." In his books on LBJ, especially *Master of the Senate*, Robert Caro described how he knew the price of every liberal and southern senator and then how to stitch them together into one coalition. This one a chairmanship, that one a cash donation, another a hint about VP—and he and aide Bobby Baker would be the tellers of this favor bank.

Another way to look at this is that Lloyd George and Johnson had great intuition. After analyzing many previous studies, researchers at Leeds University concluded that "an unarticulated, often unarticulatable, feeling—that something is right or wrong—is the brain drawing on past experiences and current external cues to make a decision; a process so rapid that the reaction is nearly subconscious." It's Bill Clinton's political fast-twitch muscles taking over when he makes a judgment call. Or in the movie *Premium Rush* when bike messenger Joseph Gordon-Levitt is speeding down NYC streets and a mental computer pops up on screen showing him making hundreds of calculations a second about the best route to take without running over anyone or being run over. Good time for good intuition.

7. Listen and Learn. If someone doesn't consider politics a "learning profession," Arthur Schlesinger Jr. reportedly said, they won't be very good at it. Society, issues, and popular opinion shift rapidly, and to stay a representative, you have to understand those you represent.

Listening isn't a slogan but an essential ingredient in the sauce of democracy. Lincoln famously spent hours personally meeting with petitioners during the Civil War in what he called his "public opinion baths." It was how he figured out that the country was not ready to emancipate the slaves in 1862 but, after a few victories on the battlefield, was on January 1, 1863. FDR got mixed grades as a listener, often using up time in meetings with long, funny stories. Still, as journalist Dorothy Thompson said, "Every pore in his body was an ear." Lyndon Johnson's father was apparently an axiom machine since his son also attributed this to him: "you ain't learning nuthin' while you're talking."

It's also essential that officials set aside time every day to learn and not merely respond to fire alarms. I recall how Nicholas Johnson, a former FCC commissioner under LBJ, asked me in the 1970s how much time I set aside a day to read. I guessed up to a couple of hours. "Not enough," he replied, and we settled on three hours as ideal. In this context, I find it reassuring that, after his wife and kids are asleep, President Obama reportedly surfs the Internet getting an unfiltered look into what people are saying and thinking. Isn't that sort of a modern Lincoln's "baths"?

In this category too go the previously discussed Hillary Clinton "listening tours" in 2000 and 2015/16.

8. Balance Ego and Empathy. The most common trait of politicians, says one psychologist, is the "impulse to dominance"—the belief that among 600,000 or 320 million citizens, respectively, s/he would be the best congressperson or president. That requires a large amount of confidence and optimism, as noted, but if it's too large, then a person can plunge over the cliff into narcissism if not solipsism, a place where others exist only for your enhancement. And extreme self-absorption is inconsistent with the public good of serving everyone. According to Craig Malkin, author of a book on the subject, the key is "to love yourself but not too much." Nader was getting at this in the chapter above when he said that avoiding excessive ego is essential since the public person is then wasting effort on appearance, position, and spin rather than bearing down on the substance and the goal.

Most close observers of Franklin Roosevelt agree that it was only his devastating infantile paralysis after 1921 that erased a youthful superciliousness and helped him understand people who needed help to survive. "There were two Franklin Roosevelts," writes Ted Morgan in his biography of FDR, "before and after polio."

Two with a terrible imbalance between ego and empathy were General Douglas MacArthur and Mayor Ed Koch. According to author David Halberstam, the former "was addicted to publicity and fame," and it was revealing that his most famous utterance was "*I* shall return" to the Philippines, not "we" shall return. Curiously, Koch's most well-known refrain was "How'm *I* doing?" He boasted to aides that his name appeared every day somewhere in the *New York Times* over his first term. Or as journalist Dan Janison of *Newsday* once wrote, Mayor Koch was always "unavoidable for comment." He'd fall asleep at meals with friends if the conversation veered away from him, and he took delight in being vindictive, once snapping at the young son of a councilman he was feuding with, "No one likes your father!"

After Koch chided Giuliani on our NY1 TV show for being "a nasty man," the title of his book on Rudy, I teased him about the irony of his title. "When was I ever nasty?" he asked, seriously curious. "When you bragged that you made city council president Carol Bellamy cry." "Well," responded Ed, his voice rising to a shriek, "she deserved it!" I felt like dropping my mic and flipping my bat. A few days after Koch's death, I joined a NY1 panel with Eliot Spitzer, Al D'Amato, and Carl McCall to comment on his career. I agreed that he was a good mayor in his first term, far less so his third, and that "he loved New York City and himself and wisely merged the two so it seemed as one." "Who did he love more?" inquired McCall. "We'll never know," I answered.

At the other end of the ego-empathy spectrum, there's Obama and Hillary Clinton. I first met Obama at an East Side apartment in 2007 while he was on a book tour for *The Audacity of Hope*. I was standing with Jonathan Alter, a journalist who knew him well. "Where are the sound bites and the me, me, me's?" I asked after hearing the author's subdued, substantive talk. Alter, who would go on to write the definitive book on Obama's first term in the White House, explained that his style is more issue-based than self-centered. Later out-of-context quotes about how he wanted to "slow the rise of the oceans" reflect not his personal megalomania, as Romney and others would tease—though he obviously has a monumental self-regard—but a far-reaching idealism. On the empathy scale, when Barack Obama unexpectedly said of Trayvon Martin that "if I had a son, he'd look like Trayvon," and then, Trayvon Martin "could have been me," it's hard to doubt the sincerity of the sentiment.

Hillary Clinton had the ego and guts to tee off on Senator Edmund Brooke at her 1969 commencement address at Wellesley and much later to run for the U.S. Senate, initially against hometown favorite Mayor Giuliani. But in a conversation with an associate of mine, she modestly described her anxiety in her first campaign for president at being the short woman on stages with so much testosterone. She never seemed to indulge in the did-you-see-me-on-TV mode that was like breathing to Koch. And from her student organizing to her legal aid work, efforts for the Children's Defense Fund, and adoration by staff, there's little doubt that her big heart is not a tactic but a trait.

9. Know When to Fold 'em. Asked what was the most essential skill for a general, George Washington replied, "To know when to retreat and dare to do it." (The general lost most of his battles during the Revolutionary War but not the last one.)

Basically, a smart politician will need to know when to insist on principle—Obama pushed for his health-care bill when Chief of Staff Rahm Emanuel predicted it would fail—and when to retreat, as Washington did for nearly all of the Revolutionary War until Yorktown. A stressed-out but savvy Andrew Cuomo understands this strategy when he drops out of his failing gubernatorial race in 2002 assuming he can come back another day, and does. When I'm falling behind Chuck Schumer in 1998 for the Democratic U.S. Senate nomination, some friends and family suggest that I consider dropping out and run instead for attorney general. But my personal approach about focus and odds make me stubbornly push onward. Years later, AG Eliot Spitzer says that if I had dropped down to his attorney general's race, he would have had a hard time competing.

Ditto the day that Ferrer demands that I fire two people because he thinks (incorrectly) that they organized the distribution of derisive literature about him and Sharpton. As discussed earlier, I refuse because I can't stomach publicly throwing two good, loyal, innocent people under the bus based on a losing candidate's pique and my political exigency. But is "stomach" the right consideration? Obama almost surely wasn't telling the truth when he went six years as president saying that he was "evolving" on marriage equality so as not to risk his presidency . . . until public sentiment caught up to his private belief. During the Ferrer fracas on the campaign's final weekend, Bill Clinton suggests that we figure out "some way to get past this until after Tuesday." He's politically right, of course. What's the point of sticking to Thursday's principles if by Tuesday night you'll be in no position to implement them? But at the time, we can't figure out a way to quell Ferrer's anger and bridge different goals—he cared mostly about saving face and protecting his base, I about winning the election.

10. Be Friendly, Funny if Possible. When asked early in his 1980 presidential run why he thought he could be president, George H. W. Bush replied without a pause, "Well, I've got a big family and lots of friends." In an era when it's good to be liked by billionaires with super PACs and by voters watching TV, it's ideal to be personable.

TR was immensely warm and entertaining (so long as you didn't get in his way) with a ready, explosive laugh. When he exclaimed "Bully!" it was not in the Chris Christie sense. FDR was like "opening a bottle of champagne," according to Churchill's apt metaphor. But at the level of sheer likability, Eisenhower was in a class by himself. There's a reason he won two landslides (though beating the Nazis helps). A modestly mannered Ike was a man without enemies.

Humor is wonderful if situational and doesn't take a bite out of anyone. In the modern era, Congressman Mo Udall (D-AZ) was an exemplar, as when he commented after losing a race for majority leader, in which some colleagues promised support but then voted against him in a secret ballot: "The difference between a cactus and a caucus is that in a cactus, the pricks are on the outside."

Speaking personally, I absorbed from my father the ingratiating impulse to be immediately jokey whenever I meet someone. My friend David Bender believes this instinctive kibitzing to be a Jewish defense mechanism, evolved over centuries of self-doubt and pogroms. When Danny Goldberg told me that his very discerning wife "really likes you," I immediately shot back, "You mean for a politician?" Danny later told me, "I love your New York shtick but can sure see why others wouldn't."

11. Have a Mentor. There are exceptions who rocket to high office without a major helping hand, but it's a lot easier if you have a mentor as a model and door-opener.

FDR had his fifth-cousin Teddy as an adored, obvious example. Then Eleanor became almost a second president because, unlike him, she could more easily move around absorbing and sharing intel. Of course, Andrew Cuomo had his father as a gubernatorial model and blocking back, and Bill had Hillary—and then Hillary, Bill. As Clinton confidant Bernie Nussbaum has said, he wouldn't have been president without her, nor she without him.

LBJ is perhaps the classic pol with mentors. Entering the House a big-eared freshman in 1937, he immediately attached himself to a fellow Texan, Speaker Sam Rayburn, who got him on the right committees and showed him the ropes. Once in the Senate, he did the same thing with the powerful Richard Russell of Georgia. These father figures plus his own savvy created a Senate majority leader in his *first term.*

For me, that would be Nader. Like so many Raiders reflecting on our years with him, I'm reminded of what Stephen Colbert said on Jon Stewart's final *Daily Show:* "We owe you because we learned from you. You were infuriatingly good at your job."

12. Raise Money. Then Raise More. Perhaps the most miserable feeling in politics is if you're indeed a superior candidate with a story to tell but lose because you run out of fuel in the last lap of the race. This is what spurred me to make those 30,000 phone calls to potential donors in my 2000–2001 mayoral campaign and what makes Chuck Schumer unbeatable. With the amounts essential to success rising geometrically after *Citizens United,* this skill becomes a ticket of entry to the game of politics. It was considered awesome when incumbent Richard Nixon outspent Senator George McGovern $60 million to $25 million in 1972. In 2016, it is expected each party's presidential nominee will end up raising well over $1 *billion.* Same trend lines, though involving lesser amounts, for House and Senate seats.

Raising the most money in a campaign does not guarantee victory. But raising the least means you have to hope to be among the fortunate 1 in 10 who wins nonetheless.

Skills 1 to 12 basically add up to *vitality* and *judgment*—the first you're born with, and the second you learn by a lifetime of mistakes.

So do you "want to be in the room where it happens," with the risk of perhaps giving concessions speeches in front of your weeping family, or choose the family business and wonder what might have been?

ON LUCK AND LYING

How'd you do? You running for office?

If you have a so-so score on the big 12 skills, there are two other routes to political advancement that are neither reliable nor sustainable.

One is *luck*—the hope that chance taps you on the shoulder. For all the quotes about it being "the residue of design" that benefits "the prepared mind," luck is still just fortuity. When it heavily rains upstate but not downstate on the day of my Democratic Senate primary on September 9, 1986, it depresses the more conservative upstate turnout for my opponent John Dyson and elevates the downstate liberal vote for me. But the law of averages says that such external variables even out over the course of a career. They did with me.

Knicks coach Red Holzman and President Kennedy were fatalists who understood luck and preparation. Holzman was once asked to explain a one-point loss and sensibly remarked that he'd either be regarded as brilliant or a bum only in hindsight once the final shot either went through the hoop or happened to bounce off the rim. Kennedy told his friend Ben Bradlee late in the 1960 presidential contest that after doing everything he could, he'd either win the presidency narrowly or go off to head a small college somewhere.

Relying on lying to win, however, exploits our evolutionary instinct to believe what we're told. As Sissela Bok explains in her book *Lying: Moral Choice in Public and Private Life,* imagine what life would be like if nothing could ever be believed.

Every person at some point in their life lies. No one frets little white lies ("Grandma, you look great!"). And then there are those acceptable "lies" politicians tell when everyone understands what's going on, like when a candidate quits a race to "spend more time with his family." Then there's something beyond the innocent but short of sinister/impeachable. Consider: for national security reasons, Eisenhower flatly lied about U2 flights over the Soviet Union in 1960, until Francis Gary Powers was shot down and captured; the Kennedy campaign denied that the candidate had Addison's disease throughout

1960 (he did); also, there were the early Clinton-Lewinsky denials, although presumably most people would lie about an extramarital affair.

May I cop to the one time I blew smoke?

I'm allergic to lying, even of the innocent kind, as family and friends will vouch. But when I was asked on a Sunday news program during my 1986 Senate race whether I ever smoked marijuana, in a blink I decided not to be the very first candidate in this pre–"I never inhaled" era to end his career on this routine private matter. "No," I heard someone with my voice say. "I grew up thinking myself an athlete and always avoided smoking anything. Those days are long past but my habit of not smoking hasn't." I'm amazed and chagrined at how easily I spoke those words, especially when staff later laughed about this denial from a boss who grew up culturally in the Sixties. (Yes, that was really the last time I did anything like that.)

Beyond the innocent and tactical, there's a Nixonian level of lying to help someone stave off what is perceived to be a disaster. (Lance Armstrong and steroids come to mind.) But should this become habitual, it forces the practitioner to always halt, however briefly, to calculate what s/he has previously said in order to fabricate consistency. However useful in the short run, the habit of lying on many small or some big things drains energy and means you're one slip-up away from self-immolation.

So—unless you're an especially entertaining reality-TV star with a hardcore racist following—skip it if you intend to be around for the long term.

THE RULE FOR ADVOCATES

What traits does it take to be an effective advocate?

I've met talented people who were great pols though not great advocates, and great advocates who were not great pols. There are very, very few who are both.

In politics, it's essential to figure out your leverage and use it. Bloomberg had money, Bush 43 and Cuomo 2 their last names, Obama and de Blasio their interracial stories. In advocacy, the sine qua non is a set of beliefs that you embody and project. While politicians necessarily compromise to get elected or bills enacted, advocates have a core moral principle that cannot be compromised away.

This is what Shaw meant by "unreasonable men" whose commitment and credibility draws followers, allies, media, funds. Think of Louis Brandeis a century ago exposing the railroad monopoly in New England. Or Gandhi: "His rejection of power enhanced his authority," wrote biographer Louis Fischer.

Who has leapt the chasm between inside pol and outside advocate? One is Robert Reich, who was an effective secretary of labor under President Clinton and candidate for governor of Massachusetts before losing a primary to a party regular. He then went on to become an even more influential public intellectual on economics. Going in the other direction is Ron Wyden, a leader of the Gray Panthers in Oregon in the 1980s when he won a House race and then a Senate seat. Civil rights heroes Andrew Young and John Lewis successfully made the conversion from cause to politician. Elizabeth Warren was a law school professor in 2008, ferociously devoted to fixing the bankruptcy system; then, due to a series of unusual events—like running for the Senate only when Republicans wouldn't allow her to head the Consumer Finance Protection Board—six years later she's a nationally renowned senator due to her smarts, drive, and voice.

Nader, of course, is a classic advocate: obstinate, idealistic, apolitical. He doesn't calibrate positions based on an electoral career and can't quite understand when others do. In mid-2014, he criticized George Miller (D-CA) over what Ralph argued was a weak push for a minimum wage increase. Said a Miller aide later to me, "He has no idea or concern about the politics of it and what we can and can't do."

"Unreasonable men" and women like Norman Thomas, Jeanette Rankin, Upton Sinclair, Ramsey Clark, Robert Reich, and Ralph Nader all seek office but end up being strong-willed and full-throated outsiders pressuring insiders to make law. They get presidential or mayoral pens at bill signings and the satisfaction of adding to the saga of democracy.

As for me, it turns out that I too am a better advocate than politician. Several years into electoral retirement, while writing books and hosting a radio show, I spot a longtime friend at a funeral. "I love the new Mark Green," says an astute Robert Zimmerman, a DNC official and businessman, "who turns out to be the old Mark Green who's found his inner Nader."

SEVEN

MEDIA POLITICS

From Buckley to Fox News to Air America

Popular Government, without popular information . . . is but a Prologue to a Farce or a Tragedy; or perhaps both.

—James Madison

If you tell a lie often enough, it becomes the truth.

—Unknown

Rhetoric is the principal thing. It precedes all thoughtful action.

—William F. Buckley Jr.

IT'S LATE OCTOBER 1979 AND I'VE BEEN INVITED TO GO *on Larry King's coast-to-coast radio show at midnight for three hours to talk about our third edition of* Who Runs Congress? *I know only what everyone does about King—he's an everyman who's curious, respectful, has no known ideology . . . and a very big audience much coveted by authors.*

I pull my motorcycle into an Arlington, Virginia, suburban complex of large glass buildings overlooking brightly lit parking areas with zero cars or people at this time of night. I go to the assigned, unmarked door at 11:30, enter the code I've been given, then hear nothing. OK, I'm early. Ten minutes later, I hit the code again; again nada. At ten of twelve, a bit more anxious, I buzz up but still hear and see nothing and nobody.

Then, approaching panic—"Did they cancel? Is it the wrong night?"—I buzz at 11:58 . . . and the door opens.

I take an elevator to the twelfth floor, am greeted by exactly no one, and shout out Larry's name. I hear his familiar, gravelly Brooklyn voice sand-papered by years in the Miami market. "Over here, Mark." I walk into a red-carpeted room where he sits like some wizardy Willy Wonka but instead of a Chocolate Factory there's a huge console of blinking lights and knobs. He waves me in, gives a quick hello, shushes me as he almost immediately announces into a mic, "Hello, America, this is Larry King of Mutual Broadcasting. I'm with Mark Green, Nader's right-hand man and author of a new edition of Who Runs Congress?, *the huge best-seller that tells us what's wrong with Washington and what you can do about it." He invites me to briefly summarize the book, asks for callers, takes a quick break, and then it's three hours of "Hello, Tulsa, you're on with Mark Green . . . Hello, San Diego, you're on with Mark Green . . . Hello, Chicago . . ."*

Now, I've done a fair amount of ad hoc radio and TV in the Seventies on various books and causes. But nothing has proven as vivid as the sense on King's show that I'm talking to the entire country one by one, each voice a different accent and attitude—this being well before the now-instantaneous interactivity of Twitter, Facebook, et al.—when King's giant control board is, in effect, the smartphones in our hands.

For years following, Larry has me periodically on his radio and TV programs and asks me to sit in for him on his CNN Larry King Live show on Super Tuesday, 1988, when I quiz a young-looking Al Gore on why he couldn't win outside his southern base. But that night in northern Virginia, I drive home at 3 a.m. along completely empty highways taking with me not a lifetime supply of chocolate but a lifelong ardor for this electronic platform.

EVERYONE QUOTES Shakespeare's "The first thing we do, let's kill all the lawyers," but in fact what revolutionaries and generals first do is seize broadcast stations because everyone—monarchs, presidents, even dictators—needs to win hearts and minds. When 100 disgruntled people protested Romania's communist leader Ceausescu, they died . . . but when 100,000 took to the streets, he did. As Thomas Jefferson famously put it, "If I had to choose between government without newspapers and newspapers without government, I wouldn't hesitate to choose the latter."

By the late 1970s, I also somehow come to the attention of Warren Steibel, the producer of Bill Buckley's *Firing Line* since its inception in 1966. It's the leading public affairs television show of the era starring the leading conservative of the era—a program and person who together become second only to Ronald Reagan in influencing the Left-Right tug-of-war over that half century. "Would you be interested in coming on in the role of Examiner for the last 15 minutes of a couple of shows we're taping next month?" He explains that they pay $750 per, which is a lot of money then to a Naderite, and adds that "although I'm a liberal, the show of course is guided by Bill's orientation and smarts but he's fair to all." That turns out to be true since the program, despite involving battles, "is like a Monty Python parody—everyone is so polite and genteel," according to Buckley biographer Sam Tanenhaus. The host does indeed combine personal civility, humor, big words, and a razor-sharp intelligence—or as he later tells me, "I'm quick but not deep."

Eager to match up against the country's leading conservative debater, I agree to these two shows. That begins a couple-decade run of nearly 100 shows either as examiner or guest, including his very last one in 1999 in the program's record-setting thirty-third year as a talk show with one host.

BUCKLEY WAS BORN to privilege and then defended it robustly for a lifetime.

The scion and namesake of an oil tycoon, William Francis Buckley Jr. had personal tutors and education in Europe along with his nine siblings. As a five-year-old, he petitioned his parents to get his father's middle name of "Frank" instead of the "sissy name" of Francis, but the young Buckley did pick up Senior's sarcastic dismissals of other opinions that didn't conform to the two major elements of their lives—Catholicism and Conservatism. If Nader was the son of Nathra and Winsted, Connecticut, Bill was the son of William and Sharon, Connecticut.

He admitted about his prep school days, "I could not understand; it seemed to me that anyone who was not an isolationist or a Catholic was simply stupid." In early 1940s England, this won him few friends. It was only at Yale that Buckley gained any sense of proportion and semi-tolerance. The school both challenged his reactionary views and taught him how to defend them. And it was at Yale that he sharpened his sparring style, eventually becoming the debate team's captain and making friends despite his brusque manner, which friends understood as efficiency rather than rudeness.

His scathing 1951 assault, *God and Man at Yale: The Superstitions of Academic Freedom,* won him national attention, if not critical acclaim, at just 25. Critics mostly panned his unsubtle argument that the Ivy League university had become a haven of godless collectivists that scorned traditional American values. But he gained admirers of his ilk and a big share of a marketplace that lacked many—indeed any—other entertaining conservatives.

A few years later, Buckley released *McCarthy and His Enemies,* a defense of the red-baiter—a personal friend of his—as an unsung patriot whose honor was wrongly maligned. Then in 1955, with support from donors and his father, Buckley founded *National Review,* a magazine of conservative thought that sought to inspire an intellectual counter-revolution. But when the *National Review* defended segregation—concluding that Caucasians were "for the time being . . . the advanced race"—it expanded his renown though not his reputation. (He later recanted.)

In 1965, the year of LBJ's Great Society, Buckley ran a quixotic yet highly publicized campaign for New York City mayor. When the press queried, "What would he do if he won?" he quipped, "demand a recount." More enduringly, the next year Buckley created *Firing Line.* There's been nothing quite like it before or since. For a full hour, he had an in-depth conversation with one major figure usually on one topic, such as programs on race relations with James Baldwin, capital punishment with Norman Mailer, welfare with Daniel Patrick Moynihan, arms control with Edward Teller, and economics with Milton Friedman.

During this period, he not only ran the *National Review* but also authored some 50 books—spy novels, autobiographies, books on music and sailing—and wrote 5,000 newspaper columns and articles. All of which laid the foundation of the conservative movement that would realign American politics.

Can you think of the Buckley of today? Neither can I.

THE DRILL IS ALWAYS the same. I arrive at the Midtown studio at 120 East 35th Street a half hour early to start reviewing my notes while in the makeup chair. Bill breezes into makeup ten minutes before taping, always "pleasantly disheveled" in the description of Gary Wills, with his treasured clipboard and pen in hand to play with his opening statement and possible questions on one sheet of paper. We'd briefly review the show's subject, sometimes chat about the news of the day, then quickly walk onto the set where I'd meet the guest and say hi to an audience of a couple dozen Catholic high school students sitting on pillows.

Opening to Bach's Brandenburg Concerto No. 2 in F Major, he introduces me always with some affectionate put-down, such as "Mark Green is an ardent and learned liberal wittily and informatively engaged in furthering the cause of the Devil." Then he interviews the guest, during which time I'm listening carefully since I have to play off something either of them say and not open myself to a put-down so erudite that I don't understand it. In my 15 minutes, I try to question unexamined premises, omitted counter-arguments, and slippery factoids while we periodically tease each other in the jocular way that respectful rivals do. So when he refers to my political losses and alleged socialist views, I volley back calling him "Mr. 13 percent" for his mayoral total and wonder whether his dictionary ended in 1850.

We're not friends but stay friendly, using each other as avatars of the opposition. He occasionally asks me to lunch to probe my take on issues, as a museum curator might examine a rare specimen. He invites me to a dinner at his elegant East Side mansion in the late '90s where I'm on the menu as 25 staff of the *National Review* quiz me for an hour on the upcoming national election and liberalism. In return, he accepts my invitation to be one of the four bold-faced names that year who sit for dinner and exchange with the major donors to the Democracy Project. But in what I can only describe as being "punked" by a performance artist, that evening he merely reads word for word from a forthcoming *New York Times* magazine article he'd written about his descent to the *Titanic*. The audience and I are understandably perplexed and disappointed.

But having reviewed hundreds of pages of our on-air conversations, I now can't find a cross word between us, despite his iconic Cheshire Cat grin that makes him always seem on the edge of eating his prey. Guest Ed Koch, however, is pretty contemptuous (no surprise there) and nuclear physicist (and Dr. Strangelove model) Edward Teller condescending (ditto). Three shows stand out in my memory.

First, in 1993 we do a program entitled "Resolved: Political Correctness Is a Menace and a Bore" with Buckley, Robert Bork, and Ira Glasser for the affirmative and Cornell West, Leon Botstein, and me for the negative. In an exchange still relevant, I figure out that PC is whatever is popular that your team disagrees with, though the Right has weaponized this tactic far more effectively.

The second was on March 30, 1981. After completing a taping, we look up on the overhead monitors to see that President Reagan, Bill's close ally and friend, has been shot. Everyone freezes. Bill only says, "I wonder what was bugging that guy" as he hurries away to get updated.

Finally, there's his 1,504th and last show on December 14, 1999. ("We lasted so long," Steibel explains to me, "because we made sure to be hosted by a South Carolina PBS station proud of the association, not a big-city station, which would consider us out of fashion some year.)" For this finale, he faces a panel comprising his successor Rich Lowry, fellow travelers Bill Kristol and Rick Brookhiser, and his three surviving Examiners—Jeff Greenfield, Michael Kinsley, and me (Al Lowenstein having died nearly two decades before). As we are getting seated before a special, invited audience, I think two things: *no women or minorities around; and, while some ungenerous critics impute to him a genteel anti-Semitism, all four Examiners over the life of the show are indeed Jewish, which probably traces to his regard for a group producing worthy intellectual adversaries.*

On this two-hour special, we watch as clips are shown of some of his most intriguing panelists—including Nixon, Reagan, Ali, Woody Allen, Bill Kunstler, Ken Galbraith, Mother Teresa, and Allen Ginsberg chanting an unhurried version of his Hare Krishna. We toss around the subject matter of the media in America, with all of us lauding the length and depth of *Firing Line* and Bill lamenting the medium's shortening of thought. He notes that while he used to get 15 to 17 minutes on the *Today* show, "now you've got to call a meeting of the Board if you go longer than 7 minutes." We speculate about how much briefer talk shows and public conversation could go, not then anticipating Twitter, Vine, or emojis. He asks me in particular if I "learned anything after nearly 100 appearances and what you might do now that you are going to be mayor of New York," and then seeks our general thoughts about the political divide in the country.

Kinsley: Many people are hypocrites. They want change but are [against] any particular change that upsets them.

Green: There is a schizophrenia. Ideologically the country is fairly conservative—big government is bad, keep our taxes low—congratulations, Bill, 33 years later. But then operationally people immediately turn around and say provide seniors with low-cost or free prescription drugs and have regulations so HMOs don't require my wife to leave a maternity ward after 48 hours. There is this clash between theory and operations.

Buckley: I think that is unquestionably true. It has been pointed out that the American people are against the welfare state but they want welfare for themselves, and that is a problem of insufficient knowledge.

Green: McGovern once said he knew he had lost in 1972 when he was in the supermarket and spoke to someone who denounced big government as they paid for their food with food stamps. He said to himself, "I'm gone."

Then it's time for Buckley to be gone. As this debonair polymath—author, publisher, sailor, harpsichordist, TV personality—comes to his closing remarks, it is touching and surprising to see tears well up in his eyes. He thanks Steibel because "without him nothing would have worked. So there it is, ladies and gentlemen. I wish you Godspeed . . . Please bear in mind all I have recommended in the last 30 years, tell your children and neighbors all those good things, say your prayers, stay healthy, and thanks for sticking with *Firing Line* all this time."

But, unfortunately, that does not turn out to be the last word.

Later that same day, Bill tapes a *Nightline* also about his final show and television career. Ted Koppel surprises him by airing the famous ABC clip from the poisonous Buckley-Vidal debate at the 1968 Republican Convention when Vidal calls him a "crypto-Nazi" and Bill, rising from his seat with eyes bulging, snarls, "Now listen, you queer, stop calling me a crypto-Nazi or I'll sock you in your goddamn face and you'll stay plastered." As I watch Buckley that night on *Nightline* watching the tape, he seems stunned. After that show, reports Tanenhaus, who's in the audience, "he made a beeline to me and said 'I thought that tape had been destroyed.'" He is obviously distressed since "it was the one time [on air] that he had lost his cool. He regretted it for a very long time."

I last see him at a cocktail party reception for him in early 2007 at George Plimpton's home. "How you doing, Bill?" I ask. "Decomposing" is all he says. He died February 27, 2008, at age 82.

CROSSFIRE, WISEGUYS, HARDBALL

Buckley would no doubt be mortified should his television legacy turn out to be not the leisurely, substantive *Firing Line* but instead that Buckley-Vidal exchange. According to at least the 2015 documentary *Best of Enemies,* that mud fight launches an era where hosts and guests bully, talk over, and growl at each other. An *SNL* parody of a then-popular *60 Minutes* segment—of Dan Aykroyd barking "Jane, you ignorant slut" at Jane Curtain—becomes the epitome of the genre.

Both traditions become part of my electronic experience. On the one hand, for much of the past 30 years, I end up as a regular panelist on programs that sometimes reflect the frisson of the Buckley-Vidal exchanges of 1968. Yet my own weekly *Both Sides Now* radio show starting in 2011 embraces the motto, "We exchange ideas, not insults . . . we sharpen differences or try to bridge them." Among our stable of conservatives is the same Rich Lowry, Bill's brilliant successor and co-participant on the last *Firing Line.*

Shortly after I start doing *Firing Line,* I get a call from Randy Douthit, one of the original producers of CNN at its start in 1980. He's seen me with Buckley and asks if I'd come on its new half-hour, weekday evening show *Crossfire.* I'm impressed that anyone would try a cable channel with news 24 hours a day and that they could do a 30-minute live news debate every night.

Two nights later, I'm driving far up Wisconsin Avenue NW to a shabby TV studio that was CNN's first one in D.C. After the briefest of orientations, I find it all doable so long as I stay poised and listen to guests intently even as co-host Pat Buchanan periodically interrupts me with something so reactionary that Molly Ivins would later famously say it sounded better in the original German.

The first guest is a former historian and second-term Republican congressman from Georgia, who easily parries my questions about President Reagan's economic ideas and stays unflappable and fluent throughout. *Guy has a future,* I think to myself of Newt Gingrich.

I sit in a dozen times a year when regular host Tom Braden—a former CIA operative and author of a book that became *Eight Is Enough* on TV—couldn't. *I'm Mark Green on the Left . . . and I'm Pat Buchanan on the Right. Welcome to* Crossfire. The pace is very different from *Firing Line,* with interruptions encouraged and speed essential because Pat is very quick-thinking and -talking. Ideologically, like Buckley, he too sees himself as an über-Catholic and conservative. But having been Nixon's hatchet man and a natural brawler—he was the author of the term "Silent Majority" and urged Nixon to burn the Watergate tapes—he displays little of Bill's suave persona. But he proves valuable training for later TV interviews and campaign debates, although a habit of sassy, curt replies can be off-putting to some voters and politicians.

I also periodically go on with columnist Robert Novak, a true Washington institution who is called "the Prince of Darkness" for his menacing, scowling, literally spitting manner on TV. But unlike Pat, who is nasty on and off air, Bob is a mensch when the red light is off—we maintain a friendly relationship for the rest of his life.

It's through *Crossfire* that I meet with many of the leading politicians on both sides of the aisle over the next two decades. Strangest is Rev. Pat Robertson during the 1988 presidential race. After I show a fair amount of skepticism on air about his prospects, he stares at me during a break and says, "Son, I *am* going to be president of the United States." And funniest is when *SNL*'s Al Franken and I do a bit at the 1988 Democratic Convention in Atlanta when we imitate a *Crossfire* segment where I spew liberal stuff, but, instead of fighting back as the supposed right-wing blowhard, he simply says, "Hmm, you're right . . . hey, good point," and figuratively lies down. It gets a good response, except from Ed (no relation to Ted) Turner, the channel's CEO, who tells us to cut it out because we're making fun of its franchise.

I'm rotating again as the regular liberal substitute with Kinsley—among the best essayists/editors of my generation. But he's more in the H. L. Mencken tradition of being a skeptic of everything rather than a robust progressive debater.

Which brings me to a major "sliding doors" moment in 1989. CNN has fired Braden because he really couldn't keep up with Pat.

On Thanksgiving Day, I take a call from Douthit who asks, "Would you like to be the permanent host 'on the Left'?" I express my surprise and delight but explain that would require either that I move my family back to Washington or I become a resident of NYC-Amtrak-D.C. "Can I think about it for a day?" "Sure."

But that evening he calls back. "Um, sorry Mark. I have to withdraw the offer. Pat simply won't go on with you every night. We'll be asking Kinsley and I'm sure he'll say yes." I'm stunned, both flattered and angry. Does Buchanan, who's hired talent, have that kind of line-up leverage? Turns out he does. Two days later, I decide to fly down uninvited to Atlanta to make Ed Turner explain the decision. Now he's the surprised one. He politely sees me and implies that while Pat does not have the right, he has the power, as the show's top dog, to in effect choose the person he goes up against nightly.

The choice of a replacement for Braden becomes a mini-controversy, with, for example, the leading liberal media watchdog group, FAIR—Fairness and Accuracy in Reporting—weighing in. FAIR's long been critical of how one-sided talk TV and radio are and is particularly upset that a political moderate like Kinsley—who had recently lauded Margaret Thatcher in a *Time* essay—is the choice. Jeff Cohen of FAIR later elaborates his view in an article and book: "Progressive leaders (and *Crossfire* producers) preferred Green, a Democratic activist and author of books critical of corporate power. [They believe] that Green—more combative and partisan than Kinsley—was feared by Buchanan because of his tough and uncompromising debating style . . . CNN sources said that Mr. Green was rejected because of Mr. Buchanan's personal contempt for him."

Though I occasionally come back on as Kinsley's substitute, never discussing the episode with Buchanan, I stay in NYC to keep on track to run and win and lose for political office. Pat stays on *Crossfire* until he leaves to run for president in 1992 and 1996, and ends up as the house conservative on MSNBC until his views on a less Caucasian America become untenable. The show goes through various iterations—with folks like James Carville, Geraldine Ferraro, Bill Press, and Mary Matalin rotating on and off. Then, in October 2004, Jon Stewart in effect TKOs the show when he says on the program that calling *Crossfire* a debate show "is like saying pro wrestling is a show about athletic competition . . . It's hurting America. Here is what I wanted to tell you guys: Stop. You have a responsibility to the public discourse and you fail miserably." CNN president Jonathan Klein cancels the program three months later, saying that he wants to move the network away from "head-butting debate shows."

It returns for a final try in late 2013 but is pulled for good a year later. I ask CNN president head Jeff Zucker what happened. "It was a good try but an old formula. The audience had moved on."

ONE AFTERNOON PREPARING for *Crossfire* in 1994, I take a call from journalist Chris Matthews suggesting that he had the energy, knowledge, and chops to be a good substitute panelist "on the left" as well. I'm convinced and pass along his idea . . . which proves to be not just self-serving but also true. His popular book *Hardball* and increasing TV appearances lead to his own show of the same name on MSNBC that I periodically appear on over the next decade.

One program I'm on stands out because it goes viral. He's quizzing a Kevin James (not the actor but head of some libertarian group) on President Bush's 2008 comment that Senator Barack Obama is an "appeaser" for suggesting that we talk to our enemies. James keeps bombastically and robotically equating Obama with British PM Neville Chamberlain, who negotiated badly with the Nazis in 1938. Then, 19 times over an agonizing three-plus minutes, Chris keeps asking James what Chamberlain *did*. But it becomes quickly clear that he has no idea.

For all this time, I see on the monitor that I'm on a split screen. So I limit myself to an amused look, knowing not to interrupt with my two cents because Chris is both destroying this guy and loving it. When James *finally* admits "I don't know," Chris triumphantly announces, "You don't know, thank you . . . Well, let's go to Mark Green, who knows something about history. Mark?" Feeling embarrassed for this guy, I say, "Kevin—when you're in a hole, stop digging." At over 600,000 hits, this becomes one of the most viewed *Hardball* clips ever.

Last, I appear every Tuesday evening for eight years on NY1's program *Wiseguys* with Koch and D'Amato. When asked in 2002 why I'm joining the show, I explain it's for diversity: "I'm the young guy with hair" . . . not to mention that Ed's more openly conservative stances as he ages make him largely indistinguishable from his close friend D'Amato.

When the program realized that it needed a more Democratic voice, they initially considered Mario Cuomo. Ed, who's had a tense relationship with Mario after their races against each other in 1977 for mayor and 1982 for governor, says, "It's fine with me if Al's OK with it." But D'Amato refuses, then grudgingly agrees to me. I enjoy the show, which attracts a sizable and influential audience and is hosted by the provocative Dominick Carter. When either of them attacks me, which is often, I know to stay poised and never return the ad hominem attacks that are a hallmark of Ed's debating style—I can only lose if I lose my temper responding to a three-term, now-80-something former mayor. And I love the 2-on-1 lineup, telling the many people who wonder about it, "It's only fair."

FOXY

During the spring of 2011, Harold Camping, an octogenarian preacher and Christian broadcaster, grabbed headlines for pinpointing a precise date for the Rapture—May 21, 2011. His followers quit their jobs and donated their savings to spread the word on thousands of billboards, while some even retreated into the mountains to await The Day. But when it passed and the Earth remained intact, a humbled Camping threw in the towel and announced that he would no longer be in the business of prophecy.

This is not a story that worries Fox Cable News. For while Camping finally acknowledged that the truth has consequences, the cable channel has rewritten *Love Story*'s famous Seventies axiom, "Fox means never having to say you're sorry."

I watch a lot of Fox's prime-time lineup for my nationally syndicated radio show *Both Sides Now.* My experience is that this "news" channel couldn't care less about its flood of false predictions and provable distortions night after night, month after month, year after . . . This is not a shocking revelation since its top star, Bill O'Reilly, is caught lying about his coverage of the Falklands War by David Corn and suffers no penalty since it's seen as, well, routine. And when Benghazi, Lois Lerner, Fast and Furious, the Obamacare website, and the tape about Planned Parenthood fall well short of being "Obama's Watergate," they just either triple-down (1,100 segments on Benghazi) or move on to the next *Breaking News!* without breaking a sweat. *What about this old tape of Rev. Wright's worst sermons (implying that*

Obama heard and approved of them)! What about this (outlier) of a poll showing him again plummeting (apparently toward zero based on all their prior outlier polls)!

As for "low-information/low education" viewers holding Fox accountable, they are understandably bewildered by a blizzard of professionally crafted graphics, snark, hyperbole, lies, and rehearsed indignation. Nor is their audience very motivated to fact-check something since they're only too happy to hear validation of their biases. *I knew climate change was a hoax!* One 2003 poll showed that 50 percent more Fox viewers thought that the United States had found weapons of mass destruction in Iraq than NBC, CNN, or ABC viewers.

Two of my Fox experiences back this up. O'Reilly apparently thinks that he can trap this liberal Jew with the question of whether I'm as much against allowing a menorah in a public square as a crèche. "Of course," I answer since both violate the First Amendment's church-state separation. But since that answer doesn't advance his "narrative," the next night O'Reilly laments on air something like "while Mark Green seems like a good guy, he was wrong to oppose a nativity scene yet allow a Menorah." I e-mail his producer to ask for a retraction since that is only 180 degrees off what I said and believe. He writes back, "Well, you and Bill have a different interpretation of what you said." Like misinterpreting a "yes" as a "no"?

A month after the Newtown shootings, producers at both O'Reilly and Hannity call within minutes of each other to ask me to come on that night because I'd written that if Megan's Law requires sex offenders to publicly register their addresses, why not homes with registered firearms since pedophiles and guns can both do harm? I go on Hannity armed for his familiar tactics. First comes the loaded rhetorical question: "Mark, do you really think sex offenders and gun owners are the same?" I decide to go with candor, plus ask one of my own: "Of course not, since one person has engaged in illegal conduct and the other possesses a lawful weapon. But since *either* can result in great harm, like in Sandy Hook, wouldn't you want to know as a parent if your child is living next door to an Adam Lanza with access to a gun?"

He wouldn't answer my hypothetical as I had his, instead opting for personalization and falsehood. "Mark, do you own or have you ever used a gun?" "No, but what does that have to do with the policy we're discussing? I've never gone over Niagara Falls in a barrel but I know it's dangerous." Then he wonders if I know that George Washington once said that gun ownership was not just a right, but something akin to a sacrament. "Rifles and pistols are equally indispensable . . . They deserve a place of honor with all that's good." I admit that I didn't know the general said that, perhaps because he hadn't. (The editor of the *Papers of George Washington* project at the University of Virginia has called that quote "either a complete fabrication or a case of misattribution.")

But should something become too factually untenable even for them—i.e., Romney didn't win the election, Shirley Sherrod wasn't a "racist"—the channel can always retreat behind its impregnable wall of being "Fair and Balanced." To prove their balance, Fox will put on some little-known "Democratic Strategist" who then imitates a local pick-up squad in the Fifties playing the Harlem Globetrotters while O'Reilly and Hannity say something outrageous and then ask Karl Rove, Sarah Palin, or John Bolton if they agree. "Bill, you're right . . ."

I was surprised and amused when Roger Ailes himself, the founder of Fox, said to me at a social event—Peter Johnson Jr.'s Christmas party in 2003—"Mark, we really are fair and balanced." I thought to myself, *Wow! He's so on message, so shamelessly assuming that saying makes it so, that he's trying to persuade* ME. "Roger, really? You must know I don't buy the slogan." But I'm almost awed by someone who seems to believe that repetition creates reality.

So why not just accept that a cable channel reaching only 3 million average prime-time viewers in a country of 320 million is the price we pay for a First Amendment? Because Fox matters. A lot. For at least two reasons.

First, the conservative movement started going off the rails in the mid-1990s with the explosion of right-wing talk radio and Fox. That's when Murdoch and Ailes revved up their perpetual-motion machine of grievance and fury at liberals, minorities, and "elites." Journalist Jen Senko wondered how her friendly, popular, non-partisan Democratic father began turning into a snarling winger hating "the radical left" late that decade. She made a documentary called *The Brainwashing of My Dad,* which traced his transformation to long daily commutes to and from work when he would only listen to the vivid, vicious polemics of Bob Grant, Mark Levin, and Limbaugh, without any contrary voice, something Senko concluded was happening to millions of dads, uncles, aunts, etc. Her film concluded that talk radio involves one person talking almost as if to one other person, creating an intimate bond where "the thinking is done for you." There's no scientifically provable cause-and-effect here one way or the other, only that is was when the center in America started disappearing and the Republican Party began to have a fringe at the top.

Second, it's now why the GOP can't readily repair itself. Like an abusive spouse you can't live with or without, Fox both provides national Republicans with a bridge to their base yet at the same time deepens the extremism that undermines a party trying to win the presidency. It's why minutes on Fox are regarded by Republican presidential contenders as the surest way to talk to the basest of the base. It's why grown-ups who know better, like Mitt Romney and John Boehner in 2012, would say only that they take President Obama "at his word" that he was an American citizen.

It's hard to overstate Fox's outsized influence on American politics and on the ongoing progressive-conservative clash. Consider what happened that fraught election night of November 2, 2000. George W. Bush's first cousin, John Ellis, manned Fox's decision desk, checking in frequently throughout the day with his cousins and the Florida governor, Jeb Bush. It fell to Ellis to make the calls of the states for Fox. Fox initially called Florida for Al Gore, then retracted that and, at Ellis's direction, at 2 a.m. called Florida for his cousin. Ellis excitedly told his staff, "Jebbie says we got it!" He later gushed to a reporter, "It was just the three of us guys handing the phone back and forth—me with the numbers, one of them a governor, the other the president-elect. Now, that was cool." Declaring Bush the winner led Gore to concede in a phone call to the governor but, when the vote tightened, Gore retracted his concession and appeared to be a sore loser for the duration of the recount.

Dismissing criticism of bias, Fox defenders usually simply repeat that "MSNBC is the liberal Fox." Upon hearing this on one *Both Sides Now* program, the normally unflappable Arianna Huffington loses it: "But they just make stuff *up!*" To be sure, MSNBC is liberal and Fox conservative, which can affect their choice of whom to host prime-time and what to emphasize. But Rachel Maddow, Lawrence O'Donnell, and Chris Matthews would rather stab themselves in the eye than repeat something on air they know to be false, plus each of them relishes opportunities for serious conservatives to come on to debate, not to be patsies. Nor does MSNBC, as Fox does, in effect e-mail political talking points most mornings to its talent and staff. And Phil Griffin of MSNBC is not a former political operative like Ailes—the man who gave us "the New Nixon" and the Willie Horton ad.

A more credible critique comes from Frank Rich who, in an insightful *New York* magazine article, argues why liberals over-respond to Fox, given its parlous numbers nationally (albeit far more than MSNBC and CNN though far less than NPR). Rich is right to observe that, since Fox's debut, the GOP has lost the presidential popular vote four of five times, in part because their eventual nominee was yanked to the right before trying to "Etch-A-Sketch" himself in the general election. And speaking of different audiences, while O'Reilly's favorability numbers are nationally underwater, he's popular enough with his crowd to reign as the number-one cable talk show and to make best-sellers out of such tripe as *Killing Who-ever.*

In sum, Fox is far better at inflaming its base than electing presidents. Best understanding Fox's role as the modern incarnation of Neil Postman's classic *Amusing Ourselves to Death,* David Frum calls it the "conservative entertainment complex."

THE CRASH OF AIR AMERICA

I'm watching a Jets game in mid-December 2006 with my brother. "So what are you doing now?" Steve asks to catch up shortly after my loss to Andrew Cuomo in the Democratic attorney general primary.

"Well, I'm settling back into the Democracy Project and sitting in for a couple weeks as the host of my friend David Bender's Air America radio show. I've been a frequent guest and think it'll be fun."

"How's Air America going?"

"Not great. It's just filed for Chapter 11 reorganization because its costs outran its model and they're looking for a buyer to try to turn it around."

"Maybe I'll buy it."

Whoa! What? "Steve, you know bricks-and-mortar real estate, not a talent-driven media firm. Are you kidding?"

Turns out he isn't. Having taken S. L. Green Realty Corp. from a one-room office in the Franklin Building at the corner of 58th and Madison in 1981 into the largest owner of commercial buildings in

Manhattan with a market cap of $12 billion, he's apparently looking for a next thing and, to cite Google, "feeling lucky." Three months and a lot of due diligence later, he signs a letter of intent to buy Air America out of bankruptcy for $4.25 million—to which Rush Limbaugh scoffs, "$4.25 million? I have that in my checking account"—and installs me as its president.

IT WAS BAD ENOUGH that by the early 2000s right-wing talk radio controlled 90 percent of all radio talk; that probably 90 percent of media property owners were wealthy Republicans; and that Fox's Fleet Street graphics and propaganda were dominating cable TV. Yet at the same time, conservatives were winning the argument that The Media was dominated by the Left. This conclusion might be true if Stephen Colbert was being literal when he famously joked that "reality has a liberal bias." Otherwise, it required this herculean suspension of disbelief, best described in Eric Alterman's influential book, *What Liberal Media?:* that Rupert Murdoch, the *Wall Street Journal,* Rush Limbaugh, and Fox News were media also-rans; that NBC/ABC/CBS/NPR were left-wing equivalents of Beck/Savage/Levin (have they ever actually listened to Brian Lehrer, Leonard Lopate, and Terry Gross?); and that the Sunday shows don't over-book Republican officials ("Get me McCain!").

For one example, Joe Scarborough goes on a rant around Halloween 2015—on MSNBC no less—repeating and repeating to guest Mark Halperin that "nearly all the anchors and Sunday hosts are liberals—even Cronkite was a *liberal.*" He spits out the word like *communist.* Then I realize that, even if his definition of liberal is a bit elastic—Huntley and Brinkley? Scott Palley?—he's missing the point, *viz.* that while everyone in the media has private beliefs, the question is whether they tilt the news that way. I doubt even Scarborough thinks that *liberal* Cronkite did. The true test of a good reporter, anchor—or scholar—is not whether they're liberal or conservative but whether they're intelligent, open-minded, science-based, factual. With those salient criteria, no wonder that most reporters and professors vote for, say, Kerry over Bush. That's not prejudice, just the marketplace that conservatives usually embrace choosing who writes and teaches.

Yet by "working the refs," in Alterman's useful phrase, a Brent Bozell and Bernard Goldberg create entire careers portraying their audience as victims. GOP presidential contenders win points and applause whenever they ridicule a question as coming from "the liberal mainstream media."

In this context, I'm eager to join the fray as president of Air America.

After President Reagan's FCC ends the Fairness Doctrine in 1986, there are no rules requiring balance for a federal licensee using the public airwaves. So the private sector model of ads, ratings—and program directors at Clear Channel, Sinclair Broadcasting, and Salem Broadcasting—then could determine what Americans learn from a platform that 250 million listen to at some point in the year. That's not far off from allowing GE to own I-95 and then permitting it to profile all Muslims or Mexicans driving from NYC to D.C.

In early 2003 wealthy Chicago Democrats Sheldon and Anita Drobney start talking with radio entrepreneur Jonathan Sinton about putting together a liberal network to challenge the near-monopoly on the Right. Although the Drobneys lack the deep pockets and temperament needed for such a huge enterprise, the idea, at least on paper, has political and perhaps commercial appeal, especially approaching the 2004 election year. It organically grows into a consortium of funders, talent, celebrities, and some radio hands who in mid-March announce with fanfare to a downtown Manhattan audience of 400—I'm among them—the plan to start Air America Radio later that month. Yoko Ono and Tim Robbins are there; so are the earliest talent—Al Franken, Rachel Maddow, Marc Maron, Janeane Garafalo, Randi Rhodes, Mark Riley, Laura Flanders, and Sam Seder. CEO Mark Walsh, a digital entrepreneur and Internet advisor to the DNC, sends all into a frenzy when he announces, "We will stop the bile being shoved down the throats of radio listeners by the Right Wing!"

The plan is audacious: to create not a program but a network of 18 hours of programming a day to run on leased or owned stations around the country. And the publicity for the launch is enormous, alone worth millions of dollars, with the media relishing a promised fight within its own industry. Features appear in nearly all major publications and outlets, cresting with a favorable *New York Times* magazine cover story centered on Franken.

Then at noon, March 31, 2004, at the WLIB 1190 studios on the 14th floor at 34th and Park, it begins. "This is Al Franken speaking to you from 30,000 feet under Dick Cheney's bunker and *this* is Air America Radio . . . We have watched the right wing take over the Congress, White House, and courts and, as insidiously, the airwaves. We need a great watchdog to track them and, until one comes along, I'll have to do." Michael Moore swings by for an interview, adding his cachet and cred.

It turns out that its first day is its best day.

An HBO documentary *Left of the Dial* depicts the swirl of high expectations, nervous talent, bustling staff, and money men reviewing their spreadsheets . . . and then the dawning of the sickening reality that the original funder, Evan Cohen, a slick-talking 30-something out of Guam, is a con artist who promised $30 million and misses by about 95 percent. When payroll checks start bouncing and the number-two and number-three stations in Chicago and LA drop the programming two weeks later, long faces replace the early ebullience. In an interview for this book, Walsh recalls a late-night meeting of investors, talent, and top managers right after the *Drudge Report* gleefully announces the bounced checks to staff and stations. He reports to the group that the company's bank account, which is supposed to have $15 million in it, has double digits. As in $50. Franken cuts to the chase: "Does this mean we're fucked?"

Looking back now, the Air America story really has three major elements: talent, ads, and money.

First, Air America certainly had the talent to survive and succeed:

Al Franken. A very thoughtful person despite his on-air goofy persona, Franken was a success at *SNL,* a best-selling author of books defrocking Limbaugh and O'Reilly, and a committed liberal when Sinton approaches him about joining the nascent network. Al is understandably skeptical about leaving his flourishing career for this leap of faith. (Ed Asner is approached about a show; "I'm an actor," he replies.) Franken and his wife Franny spend several hours with, among others, David Bender, the original political director of Air America, as they review the potential and pitfalls as well as Franken's long-term interest in a Minnesota Senate seat.

Once Al's in, however, he's all in. At the start, he is the face of the franchise, displaying the authentic humor and work ethic that have characterized his *SNL,* radio, writing, and Senate careers. In markets where he's on a comparable signal, he equals or bests Limbaugh's numbers. (Today, what's funny is how studiously unfunny he is as a steadily rising influence in the Senate.)

Rachel Maddow was a bartender with enough self-confidence to think she could excel when a local radio station runs a contest to be a talk-show host. She enters, wins, learns on air, and becomes an early hire for Air America. Bouncing around between different shows and times, she starts on *Unfiltered* with Lizz Winstead (one of the founders of *The Daily Show*) and rap star Chuck D. Despite being insanely relegated for a time to the 5 to 6 a.m. slot, she becomes the shooting star at Air America and then at MSNBC because she's a "brainful of joy," according to Winstead.

When I become her "boss," as she affectionately refers to me, I watch her unique "prep" before a show: starting religiously about five hours pre-air, she takes over a large area of office floor space to lay out multiple copies of her planned two-hour program—oddly, she prefers scripts that she writes to taking calls—and then barely looks up as she keeps rewriting and learning her material. When in 2008 she asks to be excused from the first hour of her daily radio show to be on a new MSNBC panel program headed by David Gregory called *1600 Pennsylvania Avenue*, I can't just let her out of her contractual obligation. But I also want to do everything feasible to accommodate this popular trooper. I meet with MSNBC's Phil Griffin and 15 of our and their producers at their offices to figure out a simulcast of her on the panel's first hour, which becomes the first hour of her show. (The show doesn't last long at MSNBC, but she sure does.)

Marc Maron. A comic genius with the potential to be the next Imus because of his creative, manic mind, we don't get along well for most of our time together—he treats me like a "suit" . . . until a night that Deni and I catch his raw, painfully honest stand-up in the Village. He sees me, and after that I'm a human rather than merely management. In his years at Air America, however, he's jerked around, moved around, fired, and rehired. But toward the end of my tenure, a coveted slot opens up from 3 to 6 drive-time. While several real talents compete for it, I push for him, but the new owner chooses a very capable lawyer/talk-show host, Ron Kuby, instead. Maron then exits for the final time. (He's obviously gone on to enormous success with a popular podcast out of his garage, *WTF with Marc Maron*.)

These hosts and others have the skills to excel and compete on any station, except for the dual hurdles of "No Buy" lists and weak signals.

Commercial radio is driven by ads, yet the gatekeepers who place them—at companies and ad agencies—are largely older guys not much interested in outspoken progressive views. An ABC Radio Network memo of December 25, 2006, for example, is headlined (caps in original): "**FOR IMMEDIATE ATTENTION** AIR AMERICA BLACKOUT" and explains that 100 ABC advertisers insist that "NONE of their commercials air during AIR AMERICA programming." Among advertisers listed are Bank of America, ExxonMobil, FedEx, General Electric, McDonald's, Microsoft, Walmart, and the U.S. Navy.

Ironically, six years later when Limbaugh calls student Sandra Fluke a "slut," many corporate advertisers pull ads from *all* talk shows—right and left—out of concern over audience backlash. Revenue for talk radio, including Rush, falls significantly.

And the economics of distribution becomes a dead weight. Big signals in big cities cover a large area while stations with smaller signals reach fewer people and are "in the glove compartment," according to an industry joke about where they appear on the dial. With owners like Murdoch buying big signals at the start and then sustaining losses while programs find their audience, Air America has no such deep pockets and long runways.

When Cohen is forced out, he sells the company to Piquant, an investment group led by the earnest Douglas Kreeger, part of the Durst real estate family. He and others raise enough to stop checks from bouncing, cover health insurance, and keep the hobbled entity going. This group in turn sells to technology investor Rob Glaser of Seattle, founder of RealNetworks, who keeps it solvent—with ACLU honcho and music impresario Danny Goldberg as its president—until it files for Chapter 11 in the fall of 2006.

Steve buys it to challenge himself in a new venue while I want to get back in the fight, albeit in the new arena of media management. The good news is that the staff and interested parties are relieved to see the network stay afloat with what appears to be a stable team—Steve financially and me programmatically. But the bad news is that we are neither billionaires nor radio professionals and what is needed, now in hindsight, is a tandem combining a Murdoch with patient capital (which isn't Steve) and a radio magician like Mel Karmazin, who founded Sirius (which isn't me).

The restart though—again—is fun and promising. We throw a launch party at my downtown loft for 150 industry leaders curious whether we could pull off this post–Chapter 11 rescue and to hear from President Clinton, who comes and speaks. He's on message: "If anyone can make this work, it's Steve and Mark . . . and it has to work. I can't tell you how frustrating it was as president to know that large areas of the country would only learn about my policies from Limbaugh and his allies without hearing from our side." Here's my message that evening: "Our goal is to be profitable and influential, and it can't be one without the other."

I get Mayor Bloomberg to be the first guest on my weekend show *7 Days in America*. He jokes, "Who would have thought we'd be here with you as the media guy and me as the politician?" We announce "Air America 2.0" when a dozen of the biggest progressive names are interviewed on air by our talent—like Senator Obama, both Clintons, Senator Kerry, Nader, Reich, Sorensen, etc. I spend quality time on talent, staff, media . . . but the bulk of my time is spent on reaching out to hundreds of potential investors, corporations, unions, and ad agencies in a largely futile search for gold.

We successfully shrink overhead from $13 million to $9 million annualized, as talent contracts are halved. But while Chapter 11 is designed to allow a person or firm time to restructure to survive, it also casts a pall that scares investors away. "Once bitten, twice shy" is how Sinton describes it in *Left of the Dial*. My time as Air America president begins to feel eerily like my time as Ramsey's campaign manager in the summer of 1976, beginning with high hopes while the news only gets worse and worse.

Affiliates fall from 90 to 66, as our weekly affiliate reports would regularly show stations flipping to sports or Hispanic programming, the two hot spots of radio. When Franken departs as planned to run back in Minnesota, Randi Rhodes becomes our highest-rated host. That's a problem. Although someone with real on-air skills, she's also a very insecure and angry person who screams at staff, at me, at everyone. That can be tolerated in a business of driven prima donnas, but then two unusual things happen. One morning we're informed by her agent that she's been mugged in front of her residence and shoved to the ground, breaking her front teeth. Except it turns out that she was seen exiting a bar and falling down. She recovers and returns to air. Then late afternoon April 3, 2008, I'm sent an online video of Randi calling Geraldine Ferraro and Hillary Clinton "fucking whores" at an Air America–sponsored event for our station 960 AM in San Francisco.

My first reaction is disbelief, immediately followed by "looks like we're gonna be losing our most popular talent." Several days follow of back-and-forth between her and me, on *Larry King Live,* online, in the *Huffington Post.* She portrays herself as an Alfred Dreyfus being unjustly punished for her free speech; in my view, she has a right to say whatever she wants but not the right to a guaranteed job at a media company with standards—and while it may be hard to draw lines, surely she's crossed them at 120 mph. She's then suspended, refuses to apologize, jumps to another network, is later picked up by Premiere, and, with her affiliates dwindling, eventually departs radio altogether in mid-2014.

The "whore" controversy is transpiring just as Charlie Kireker, a wealthy, progressive businessman from Vermont and among the earliest investors, comes forward offering to buy the company at a steep discount from Steve, who jumps at the chance because of its financial descent. Charlie, on the other hand, has the dream of wedding his political values to a media platform. He too tries everything he can think of—including giving a show to the ill-suited Montel Williams—until January 21, 2010, when he and I walk into a room of very grim-faced staff to announce that he's that day filing for Chapter 7. It's over. It turns out to be a memorably bad week for progressives also watching Scott Brown win Ted Kennedy's Massachusetts Senate seat and the Supreme Court announce the *Citizens United* decision. A conservative trifecta.

I'm constantly asked, why did Air America fail while right-wing talk succeeds? The simplest answer may be the most accurate: "It died stillborn," in Senator Franken's view, and never recovered from the death spiral that Evan Cohen sent it into.

Alan Colmes, a successful radio host and ex-occasional sidekick to Hannity, thinks that "because conservatives were so entrenched on heritage stations, the progressives on Air America were relegated to smaller, less powerful signals, underperforming signals that could not compete with their more established counterparts, certainly not without lots of promotion and time to develop, both of which were denied in most cases."

Paul Farhi, the *Washington Post*'s media critic, says "there's a liberal tendency toward inclusiveness and reflectiveness—both deadly qualities in a medium [described as] 'The World Wrestling Federation of Ideas.'" Danny Goldberg gives credit to wealthy conservative investors "who understood that talk radio goes directly into the brain of passengers in cars, unlike even cable TV when a viewer might be getting a beer or dinner. So they spent heavily while a George Soros chose not to get involved."

In my version of Fantasy Radio, *if* Evan Cohen had combined Charlie Kireker's integrity and money with Mark Walsh's digital smarts—who said at the launch that "Air America should not be radio with an Internet component but Internet streaming with a radio component"—and *if* there had been no "No Buy" lists, then Air America's talent would likely have found their audience.

Instead, we're left with two realities. The first is that progressives lost a rare opportunity to occupy a prized public space in an important medium. Failing means that it'll probably be years before anyone else tries, although the evolution of radio might produce a different and far-lower-cost model, as happened with television—so rather than stations selling audiences to advertisers, they instead aggregate and distribute content edgier than NPR to mobile devices and online for fee-paying listeners. Or some version of a revived Fairness Doctrine might be enacted based on the analysis of media-watchers John Nichols and Robert McChensey, who surveyed the precipitous decline in working journalists in the digital age where ads follow algorithms: "Journalism is a classic 'public good.' Something society needs and people want but market forces are now incapable of generating in sufficient quality or quantity. The institution should be understood the way we understand universal public education, military defense, public health, and transportation infrastructure."

The second reality is that the Air America experiment produced at least three spectacular legatees—Al Franken, Rachel Maddow, and Marc Maron—and surviving it are current liberal radio talents like Thom Hartmann, Ed Schultz, and Stephanie Miller. The continuing legacy of right-wing talk is that there are still vast swatches of the country that swallow their extremism whole. That creates an irrational, intemperate Republican base that in turn produces a Trump and sabotages governance. They reap market shares of 10 percent but not presidential elections requiring 50 percent plus one.

Be careful what you wish for.

HURRICANE HUFFINGTON

An eager, poised, attractive woman comes up to me and Deni at the 2000 Democratic National Convention in Los Angeles explaining her "Counter-Convention" across the street to expand the debate beyond just whatever Gore is saying—would we come? We do, enjoy it, and that begins my ongoing relationship with Arianna Huffington, a force of nature best captured by comedian Tracey Ullman. Her impersonation of Arianna—multi-tasking, dictating, writing, calling, editing while getting ready for bed—is more Huffington than Huffington.

Bill Moyers thinks she's one of the smartest people he ever met while a critic calls her the "most upwardly mobile Greek since Icarus."

Born in Greece in 1950, Arianna Stassinopoulos often spends her time as a child alone reading and has to be nudged by her parents to make friends. While a teen in Greece, she spots a photograph of Cambridge University in a magazine that set stars in her eyes. Arianna applies and, somewhat miraculously for a Hellenic no-name, talks and earns her way in. Once there, she brushes up against her peers' classism. (She errs in front of her classmates by referring to horseback riding. "What other kind of riding would there be?" they laughed. "*Donkey* riding?") She takes care not to present herself as the conservative she then was but instead as ideologically elastic, a habit that resurfaced and remained decades later.

Freshly out of school, her anti-feminist book *The Female Woman* is an enormous success, soon translated into 11 languages. In the coming years, she writes a slew more books, some on the need for politics to be injected with spirituality as well as two well-received biographies of Maria Callas and Picasso. While promoting her Callas tome, she lands and stays in New York and meets Michael Huffington, an oil and gas heir. Within a year, they marry and together begin plotting a political career that would, they hope, lead to the White House.

They get as far as a congressional seat in 1993, which brings her into Newt Gingrich's orbit. Although then openly conservative, she urges fellow Republicans to fight poverty and bridge inequality as part of the "core of true conservatism." But she becomes increasingly dismayed with their obsessive focus on slashing the budgets of programs for the poor. She begins building friendships with people to her left, like Franken. A decade and a half before Occupy Wall Street, Huffington writes about "two nations"—the widening gap between the haves and the have-nots.

After her husband's narrow defeat in a 1994 Senate race against Diane Feinstein and their subsequent divorce, she starts to aim her barbs at the Right. What matters, she stresses, is not the Left-Right divide but the Rich-Poor one. The same woman who as a young conservative became the first female head of the Cambridge Union debating society decamps for Los Angeles and takes up liberal causes, making yet a new circle of friends.

What follows is a far-fetched, brief run for governor against Arnold Schwarzenegger in a 2003 special election.

That fall Deni and I are visiting our friends Katherine and Ken Lerer at their Utah ski home when Kenny asks what I'd think about a liberal version of the *Drudge Report* run by Arianna. "That's a great, big idea—and she has the energy, brains, and contacts to pull it off, if anyone can." Kenny then includes me in an original stable of several dozen bold-faced names who will write unpaid blogs to attract eyeballs and hires Arianna to be the content Zen Master as he figures out financing. After being called the *Lerer-Huffington Post* for a day, the modest Lerer takes his name off the masthead. Two years later, it expands to eight verticals and passes *Drudge* in uniques (separate monthly readers) with 6 million. By 2016, it has 90 verticals (Politics, Media, Parenting, Gay Voices, etc.), eight bureaus around the world (France, Australia, Greece, etc.), and over 100 million uniques. I now write a featured column every Monday based on the radio show that she and I create in 2011.

As Air America is going down, Arianna and I are at the Bedford, New York, wedding of the Lerers' son Benjamin (later to go on to found *Thrillist*). I explain what's happening to Air America since she, Ron Reagan, and I have a weekly program on it. "Instead of a program with three like-minded people which lacks tension," I explain, as a couple hundred guests gyrate to "Dancing in the Streets," "how about we start a free-standing weekend show with me as moderator, you as the liberal, and we find a non-crazy conservative woman as the conservative? We can call it *Both Sides Now.* With all talk radio being largely male, and hard-right or occasionally left, we'd stand out."

She pauses, thinks for a moment, says, "Sounds great! Yes!" and extends her hand to shake on it. That both starts our show—we quickly settle on an enthusiastic Mary Matalin as the conservative— and tells me a lot about how super-smart entrepreneurs operate. Two years later, she has to bow out because of her staggering corporate responsibilities at the *Huffington Post,* especially after it's bought by AOL for $315 million. In her place, we create rotating panels of some of the best political talkers anywhere on air—Shrum, Alter, Reagan, Corn, Joe Conason, Gara Lamarche; also, Matalin, Lowry, Frum, Ron Christie, Charles Cooke, and for a while Erick Erickson. It's still on 200 stations five years later because it proves to be easier to air one interesting weekend program than an entire 24/7 network.

EIGHT

ECONOMY AND DEMOCRACY

The Fringe Fourth vs. the New Progressive Majority

I like the dreams of the future better than the history of the past.

—Thomas Jefferson

We're not perfect. But they're nuts.

—Former Democratic Rep. Barney Frank, on Republicans

Facts do not cease to exist because they are ignored.

—Aldous Huxley

FOUR POLITICAL ERAS

It was irrational exuberance when Bill Rusher, publisher of the *National Review,* predicted shortly after Ronald Reagan's decisive 1980 election that "liberalism is dead" and when Karl Rove looked forward to a "permanent Republican majority" after George W. Bush's reelection in 2004.

Political realignments that produce definable eras are exceedingly rare in American history, usually following such upheavals as the Industrial Revolution, the Great Depression, and Sixties turmoil that shifted the White South from the D to R columns. And they are usually discernible only retrospectively, like realizing we're in a recession only after it's started, and out of one only after it's over. As John Kenneth Galbraith wrote of Black Monday, October 29, 1929, "The end had come but it was not yet in sight."

There have been three earlier eras over the past century. First came the *Progressive Era* of 1902 to 1920, from Teddy Roosevelt through William Howard Taft to Woodrow Wilson, when muckraking journalists amplified a public demand to balance the rights of business and workers. Groundbreaking laws against unsafe food and drugs, industrial monopolies, campaign finance abuses, plus the seeds of environmentalism started to define a new form of regulated capitalism—"liberty plus groceries" was the phrase of liberal Texas congressman Maury Maverick then—which is largely with us still.

The Great Depression, occurring on the watch of Herbert Hoover, did the reputation of the food relief hero of World War I no favors and launched the *New Deal Era* of 1933 to 1968. It includes the two terms of the Republican Eisenhower, who was careful not to start wars or end Social Security. No TR or FDR, Ike was more a caretaker than an era-maker. But the shared democratic values of Roosevelt, Truman, Kennedy, and Johnson over these years saw the creation of the civil rights architecture and modern regulatory state, both now ratified by history.

Then the dislocations of this lengthy era—starting with FDR's unprecedented public solutions to market failures and concluding with the blunder of Vietnam, end of Jim Crow, and epic domestic protests—were skillfully if cynically mashed together by Richard Nixon and Ronald Reagan into a new *Backlash Era*. This coherent conservative period from 1968 to 1992 clearly emerges from the "positive polarization" memos of Pat Buchanan and Kevin Phillips, the multiple political crimes of Watergate, and Reagan's ability to cheerfully shift trillions of dollars from middle-class families to the wealthy yet stay popular.

These Republican electoral successes, however, were not built on improving average Americans' quality of life but rather by feeding their fears about student radicals, welfare cheats, Black Panthers, communists, you name it. The GOP assault encountered less resistance than might have been expected when the three greatest leaders of the opposition—John Kennedy, Martin Luther King Jr., and Robert Kennedy—were killed.

This combination of convincing hobgoblins, a lost war, political assassinations, Nixon's tactical prowess, and Reagan's personal
charm proved to be an electoral elixir. Net-net, this *Backlash Era* saw
a shift of perhaps six to eight points to the Right, largely the defection
of so-called Reagan Democrats—white Catholics whose parents had
been FDR Democrats—plus white southerners.

Looking back, it may seem unfair but it's also undeniable that
the turmoil of the Sixties turned much of the public against those
liberals who, surely in retrospect, were vindicated in their opposition
to that war, Jim Crow, and sexism. Consider how in the fall of 1972 a
public poll showed that Nixon was more trusted than McGovern by
52 to 25 percent. But unlike a Jefferson, Lincoln, TR, or FDR, whose
humanity and accomplishments are still revered, Nixon—whom
Barry Goldwater called "the most dishonest man I ever met"—will
be justly remembered as a corrupt bigot who resigned in disgrace.
Nixon's administration was so pervasively malevolent that it's easy to
forget that his original vice president, Spiro Agnew, quit rather than
fight charges of bribery.

As for Reagan, he was certainly neither corrupt nor merely an
actor, though acting was perhaps his core asset as a president. "I
don't know how you do this job," he once said, "unless you *are* an
actor." Liberal condescension aside, he was smart enough to succeed
in every profession he attempted. But the three defining experiences
of his youth—as a heroic lifeguard, a radio baseball announcer re-
creating games from wire reports, an actor trained to convince audiences—created a habit of confidently making stuff up to save the
day.

Any objective reader of Lou Cannon's definitive biography,
President Reagan: Role of a Lifetime, or close observer of his early
career and presidency would be surprised by the "Reaganolatry" of
today. His daughter Patti was dismayed when her parents made up
an elaborate story to cover up the fact that she was conceived out of
wedlock—"they weave bizarre, incredulous tales and stick by them
with fierce determination"; Speaker Tip O'Neill was confounded and
then angered by Reagan's uninformed anecdotage from 3 × 5 cards
in private congressional meetings; and, speaking personally, President Reagan inspired me to write two books using his own words to
document his convenient presidential dissembling—*Reagan's Reign
of Error* I and II.

How can we today reconcile his obvious intelligence and public warmth with his private emotional distance and lifelong reliance on magical stories? I asked his son and my friend, Ron Reagan, that question on a *Both Sides Now* show. "Ah, that's the mystery of it," he replied.

Combining charm and policy, Reagan indeed *was* the nicest guy who began the modern tilt toward extreme inequality by transferring trillions to the wealthiest citizens, ignored the exploding AIDS crisis until there were 20,000 dead, announced his 1980 candidacy discussing "states' rights" from Philadelphia, Mississippi (known only as the place where the KKK killed Chaney, Goodman, and Schwerner), watched complacently as 29 aides were indicted or convicted of corruption (26 more than Clinton and Obama combined), tripled the national debt while railing against federal spending, sent 241 marines into an ill-defined mission in Lebanon where they were killed in a terror attack—a Benghazi × 60—and engaged in what was the illegal act of transferring arms to Iran. Reagan skated by impeachment only by ultimately acknowledging that he really, *really* believed it when he denied under oath knowing about the arms-for-hostages deal. In his version of "it depends on what your definition of 'lie' is," he told a special counsel, "My heart and my best intentions tell me that's true [i.e., he didn't approve the deal], but the facts and the evidence tell me it's not."

Because of Nixon's pathologies and Reagan's lightness of being, there appears to be little remaining from their reactive, reactionary era except for Nixon's opening to China and, some would argue, the collapse of the Soviet Union. (The RNC thinks so; China does not.) What else? Surely not the fortieth president's unsustainable military spending, tax cuts creating record deficits, incarceration of a generation of black youth for nonviolent drug offenses, or supply-side economics that his own budget director admitted was a "Trojan horse" to hide upward wealth redistribution.

Since homilies don't make history, he is probably the most overrated president in the past century. When it comes to laying a foundation stone for a new America, Reagan is the God Who Failed. And Reaganism without Reagan—witness the struggles of Bush 41 and 43 and brother intending to be 45—is not a winning formula for this century.

Which raises two key questions: While no one thinks that we are in the midst of a sharp political realignment, are we already in a slow-motion one? Republicans won five of six presidential popular votes from 1968 to 1988 while Democrats have won five of six since then. Will trends continue or interrupt this momentum?

It was Clinton's bad luck to be elected, as he shared with aides, "a liberal president in a conservative era." Still, his two terms in office slowed and stopped the Nixon-Reagan *Backlash Era*—an historic achievement. Clinton's southern roots and outsized political skills—and tactical shifts on welfare and crime—enabled him to blunt standard Republican attacks on "tax and spend" liberalism. And his budget surpluses and job creation showed that Democrats could successfully deliver on the top voter concern.

Of course, George W. Bush's two terms chronologically interrupted any emerging *New Progressive Era*. But while an electoral winner, Bush 43 was a Fluke Who Failed.

It was truly aberrational to lose the popular vote to Al Gore by a half million nationally in 2000 yet win the presidency by 537 votes in the decisive state of Florida. This margin owed itself to the almost unimaginable conjunctive events of ill-designed butterfly ballots, a gubernatorial brother purging thousands of eligible African Americans and Latinos from voter rolls, Gore's legal misjudgment in seeking to cherry-pick counties rather than recount them all, and five Republican Supreme Court justices chosen largely by the candidate's two heroes, Reagan and father Bush.

This is not to argue that Bush didn't constitutionally win the White House, only that—since Gore would have won if everyone who went to vote that day in Florida voted as they intended—it was a victory without a mandate. What could the mandate have been—better-designed ballots? As for his narrow margin in Ohio and three-point national popular win over Kerry in 2004, it followed 9/11, a potentially realigning event. That calamity understandably frightened wavering voters and elevated terrorism to a top concern, not to mention that bin Laden's well-timed video on the Friday before the Tuesday election in 2004 reminded everyone of the threat out there, which, as noted, Kerry privately mused may have tipped that election.

It's hard to deny, however, that his presidency was an historic failure—it resulted in a Great Recession, wiping out $14 trillion of wealth; the conversion of record surpluses to record deficits; ignoring CIA director George Tenet's urgent warning at a July 10, 2001, meeting with NSC chair Condi Rice that bin Laden was planning "spectacular attacks . . . in the coming weeks or months against the United States homeland"; a disastrous and pointless war, the Katrina incompetence, as well as a POTUS so inarticulate as to be barely able to frame a case or get through a complicated press conference. The Senate Intelligence Committee's 6,000-page report on CIA torture, which included horrific interrogation tactics endorsed by Bush-Cheney, was a painful reminder of this dark decade in which our leaders seemed to momentarily lose their minds. No surprise that Bush 43 ended his presidency with a 34 percent favorable rating. As his speechwriter David Frum candidly reflected, "it wasn't a successful presidency and that's a painful thing."

Then comes Obama, as implausible a president as any in our history, who, to use his comic self-description, is a skinny black guy with the middle name Hussein, no less. The key point is not his two majority wins with 53 percent and then 51 percent of the popular vote, remarkable though that is. Rather, beyond merely holding conservatives even, as Clinton had done, he also goes on the offensive to, more often than not, prevail over implacable foes.

How does that happen? Better than being lucky or good is being both.

Unlike Mondale facing Reagan in 1984, Obama in 2008 surfs waves of discontent over Bush's economy and war. At the same time, there are his huge multi-dimensional gifts. Objectively, he and Clinton were probably the smartest presidents since Wilson; Obama as literate and eloquent a president as any since Lincoln. He is only a slightly less capable "great communicator" than Roosevelt and Reagan; among the wittiest at a podium, as his matchless White House Correspondent's Dinners show; and, befitting his dozen years as a law professor, almost as deft answering questions at press conferences as Kennedy (if a bit long-winded).

In a world of numerous armed conflicts and in polarized America, there are worse things than a president radiating "insufferable equanimity." The reality is that his black-white story from mellow Hawaii to the halls of Harvard and then to the mean streets of Chicago produces something unique. Doubters in 2008 arguing that he "lacks experience" miss the larger truth that his diverse *life* is his experience, allowing him to deal with all different races, classes, and issues. It takes someone pretty unique to leap from the Illinois state senate to the U.S. presidency in four years.

Obviously Obama has made many mistakes over the course of two terms, even serious ones—drawing a "red line" against the use of chemical weapons in Syria which would "change my calculus" (what changed was his mind when he realized that Congress wouldn't approve of an attack and instead he—with Putin's help—removed the chemical weapons diplomatically); jumping prematurely into a racially fraught local law enforcement controversy involving Skip Gates by calling a police officer's action "stupid"; being inattentive to a deadly management failure at the Veterans Administration; screwing up the initial Affordable Care Act website. (I don't count the attack on Gadhafi in Libya here because he and his secretary of state chose to avoid the imminent genocide of 800,000 residents of Benghazi with NATO-led air strikes and no loss of American lives, at the admitted cost of subsequent turmoil there.) And the knock that he's too "aloof" is one many congressional Democrats believe, as does *Meet the Press*'s Chuck Todd in his critical assessment, *The Stranger: Barack Obama in the White House.*

Although there's no Vietnam, Watergate, Iraq, or Great Recession on this list—nothing really close—the level of viciousness against Obama, partly though not exclusively because of race, reached unprecedented levels. Democratic leaders didn't much like Reagan or Bush 43 but also didn't demand to see their birth certificates, or say that they didn't love America or even want to protect it. Indeed, as Obama largely brushed off these ad hominem insults and largely enacted his agenda, this poise seemed only to humiliate and unhinge conservatives even more. "Disappointment and opposition inflame the minds of men," wrote an insightful Hamilton, "and attach them still more to their mistakes." Their anger reached a sort of apogee during the debate over the Iran Nuclear Accord when opponents used language usually reserved for World War II totalitarian enemies. From Inaugural eve when Senator Mitchell got his caucus to agree to oppose everything the president proposed even if it had been a Republican idea, they might as well have chanted at the end of every day's session, in the spirit of Roman senator Cato the Elder, *"Obama delenda est!"*

If he has been too aloof, one is reminded of General Ulysses S. Grant's indulgence for whiskey, which led Lincoln to suggest sending "a barrel of it to my other generals" if it made them fight as well. By 2016, it's clear that this is what a very successful presidency looks like, perhaps even one anchoring a new political era. No personal scandals, no indictments of major officials, no economic collapse, no invasions of the wrong country. Just a presidential educator in chief using his intellect, eloquence, and persistence to change the national conversation, and often national policy, on topics such as criminal justice, race, diplomacy and war, LGBT rights, climate change, immigration reform, and, perhaps most significantly, middle-out economic growth rather than trickle-down economics.

Then there are Obama's significant achievements:

- The Recovery Act helped end the Great Recession and spurred some 70 months of steady economic growth, reducing unemployment from 10 percent to 5 percent.
- The Affordable Care Act, enacted and upheld, insured some 20 million in its first six years of existence.
- The American auto industry was rescued—and Detroit as well.
- Dodd-Frank Wall Street Reform was enacted.
- Almost all U.S. combat troops were withdrawn from two unpopular Middle Eastern wars, while a third was avoided despite some popular hysteria.
- LGBT rights were historically expanded by legislative and judicial action.
- Diplomatic relations with Cuba were restored after 50 years.
- Progress was made on climate change with stricter auto fuel-efficiency standards, proposed EPA reductions on carbon from coal-fired plants, and initial agreement with China and India to pursue long-term mutual reductions of greenhouse gases.
- An immigration executive order reduced massive deportations (now pending in court).
- Bin Laden was found and killed, as Obama promised to do in 2008, "even if in Pakistan."
- A national conversation began on over-incarceration and disparate racial penalties for criminal conduct.

- The 2009 Credit Reporting Act and Tobacco Regulation Act were passed, respectively saving $20 billion annually and tens of thousands of lives.
- The Iranian nuclear deal was signed that freezes Iran's nuclear capacity for 15 years and moves America away from a military-first approach to a diplomacy-first one.
- After announcing that network neutrality—which forces Internet providers to treat traffic equally instead of giving giant businesses a leg up—was his top FCC priority, the Commission voted to regulate broadband Internet like a utility.

All this was accomplished while facing not an obstructionist like Senator Strom Thurmond, as Johnson did, but rather 45 Strom Thurmonds wielding the filibuster on just about everything for six years. "Barack Obama sought the presidency hoping to be the Democrats' Reagan," in the view of *Atlantic* author Peter Beinart, "a president who changed America's ideological trajectory. And he has."

In response to this proven record, not one Republican political leader or public intellectual has publicly acknowledged the reality that President Obama is far more likely to end up on historians' lists as among the top ten presidents than in the worst ten along with George W. Bush. Presumably, some will safely admit this in the early years of the next Democratic POTUS, just as they lauded Clinton 42 when compared to the awful Obama. Call it what you will—GOP lockstep partyology, political correctness, denialism—Obama-phobes can't utter the truth now for fear of losing fees, subscribers, donations, positions, ads, or TV appearances. These furious "Lost Causists" are reminiscent of the wealthy businessmen in Peter Arno's famous *New Yorker* cartoon "going to the Trans Lux to hiss Roosevelt."

Clinton's and Obama's combined electoral and policy successes have launched a new fourth age over the past century. But if those successes relied largely on their immense personal talents—Al Franken told me that "these two guys make all the rest of us look bad"—then perhaps there won't be a continuing liberal revival because there aren't many like Bubba and Barack. So irrespective of who's nominated in 2016 and 2020, what are the larger trend lines and fault lines of this and the next decade that might extend or end this nascent *New Progressive Era?*

TRENDING . . .

When I was at Cornell, I took a seminar with the famous political theorist Hannah Arendt, who would tell us that "a graph may imply where the next dot will appear but that doesn't mean it will."

Predictions are hard, especially about the future. Let us recall analysts at the turn of the last century worrying that if projected population growth continued, our cities might sink in poop from those proliferating horse-drawn carriages. We invented our way out of that (helping our streets but not so much our air). Thirty years ago, many thought that immigration to the Sunbelt would mean a Republican lock on the Electoral College. Didn't happen.

But if trends are not immutable, neither are they irrelevant. Here are several observable trends or tremors likely to influence whether this new era endures:

Demographics and Politics. What may have otherwise been a mere routine Census Bureau report from May 17, 2012—the anniversary of *Brown v. Board of Education*—instead heralded the emergence of a different America: for the first time in the country's history, whites were a minority of the roughly 4 million births in the United States in the period of July 2010 through July 2011.

California is especially worrying for Republicans. In 1994 Republican governor Pete Wilson pushed an initiative that would deny public services to undocumented immigrants and their children. It passed, by 59 to 41 percent. But after years of wrangling and publicity, the anti-immigrant initiative was eventually declared unconstitutional . . . though not before starting the implosion of the California Republican Party, launching pad for Ronald Reagan. Before Wilson's war on immigrants, the GOP had carried the electorally rich state in six of seven previous elections. Since then, only one Republican has won a statewide senatorial, presidential, or gubernatorial vote in more than two decades—the one-of-a-kind Arnold Schwarzenegger.

It's a transformation that isn't limited to Latinos, an umbrella term that includes origins in dozens of countries. Asian Americans are now the fastest-growing racial cohort in the nation and the largest share of new arrivals in the United States. They've gone from voting 31 percent Democratic in 1992 to 73 percent in 2012, based largely on perceived Republican insensitivity to minorities in general.

While the white share of the electorate in 1992 was nearly 90 percent, it will likely fall to less than 70 percent in 2016. In only a quarter century, this fact alone has meant a net shift of about 12 points to Democrats since Bill Clinton won the White House by five points. For example, with one-fifth of its population Hispanic, Colorado, once seemingly homogenously white and reliably Republican, is now a swing state; Nevada was largely unwinnable for Democrats for decades but now leans Democratic. Donald Trump's harsh nativist slanders have certainly deepened an inclination that already saw Obama beat Romney 73 to 27 percent among Latinos, although that trend won't continue indefinitely if newly eligible voters don't actually vote as often as non-Hispanics. Pat Buchanan's nightmare that his country wouldn't remain a "White Nation" has become a near certainty, ironically because of so many "dreamers"—by 2043, according to demographers. That may be when America becomes California. *Advantage: Democrats.*

Millennials Now Outnumber Boomers. "Each new generation is a new people," wrote Tocqueville in the nineteenth century. Now the biggest generation ever at 75.3 million, surpassing boomers in 2015, Millennials (born after 1980) are also the most diverse American adults in history. Surveys confirm that they can't see why marijuana is illegal, were years ahead of the Supreme Court in believing that it's absurd to deny LGBT citizens the right to marry, think undocumented immigrants should have a pathway to citizenship, and are just barely fonder of capitalism than socialism.

Though skeptical of both parties, bottom line: they support the Democratic Party by much wider margins—55 to 36 percent—than other generations. In 2011, Pew found that while the oldest Americans supported repealing health-care reform by 29 percentage points, Millennials favored expanding it by 17 points. They were also 25 points more likely than those 65 and older to approve of Occupy Wall Street. As the Pew report put it, "Millennials, at least so far, hold 'baked in' support for a more activist government."

The Republican response to the sweeping transformations of the Obama era almost ensures that Millennials won't be easily delivered to the GOP anytime soon. When the U.S. Supreme Court affirmed a constitutional right to marriage on the heels of the previous day's affirmation of the Affordable Care Act, presidential candidate Ted (the human hyperbole) Cruz counted it among "some of the darkest 24 hours in our nation's history," a statement that doesn't resonate with a generation whose friends include all sexual persuasions. If they stick with their earliest affections—as young voters did with FDR after the Thirties and with Reagan after the Eighties—they may prove to be the pig-through-the-python after signing on with Obama by a 2-to-1 margin. ***Advantage: Democrats.***

Unmarried Women. In the summer of 2014, Jenny Spencer was a 26-year-old unmarried lab technician living in North Carolina, "not especially political," she said. But she became energized to support Democratic Senator Kay Hagan's reelection campaign because of the state's lurch to the right that came with a new Republican governor who threatened women's health clinics by mandating that they match hospital standards, forcing most to close under the pretense of safety.

Hagan lost but Spencer is the future.

True, if a young woman is ardently pro-life, she'll likely vote for a Republican candidate. But every state and region of the country is rife with women like Jenny who have particular economic and health-care needs and feel threatened by lawmakers who seem to value the health of microscopic potential humans over actual adult women. Nor do they much appreciate being called "murderers" when exercising their constitutional right to choose to end a pregnancy. Single women, with or without children, now number 55 million, and they're growing by nearly a million a year.

Democratic leaders uniformly support equal wage and essential health services—and in 2016 may nominate a woman for president. The other party, stampeded by a doctored tape from a far-right organization, threatened to shut down the United States government to defund Planned Parenthood for spending 3 percent of its budget on constitutionally protected abortion while participating in lawful fetal tissue research. Republicans even voted against the reauthorization of the Violence Against Women Act. So it was no surprise that in 2012 the gender gap favored Obama by 11 percentage points.

Single women have unique challenges in getting to the polls. Working long hours and caring for their kids, they're also more likely to be renters or move frequently. Harder to reach, they're less likely to vote. When they are reached, however, they can make all the difference. They helped avert a Republican takeover of the Senate in 2012. In Virginia's 2013 governor race, the GOP's far-right nominee pressed for the shuttering of women's clinics and invasive mandatory ultrasounds before abortions. Democrat Terry McAuliffe pulled out a two-point win after he carried the unmarried women's vote by a staggering 43 points. *Advantage: Democrats.*

"Losing Our Religion"? From 2007 to 2014, the number of Americans identifying as Christians dropped from 78 to 70 percent and the number of those who were unaffiliated with religion—the "nones"—rose from 16 percent to nearly 23 percent. More Americans now identify with no religion, surpassing all other affiliations but evangelicals.

Religion in America might be waning, but the Religious Right that helped sweep Ronald Reagan into office still holds sway in Republican politics. A leading 2008 presidential candidate who won eight states, Mike Huckabee, said that while he respected the High Court, "The Supreme Court is only that—the supreme of the courts. It is not the Supreme Being. It cannot overrule God." In a similar appeal to the divine, Kentucky marriage clerk Kim Davis couldn't overrule the Supreme Court—turns out that in a country with a secular Constitution and a tradition of separation of church and state, the law holds sway.

At the national level, however, Republicans face a landscape very unlike a mere dozen years ago when George W. Bush won reelection in part on the coattails of several statewide anti-marriage referenda. According to a 2015 *NBC News/Wall Street Journal* poll, Americans are more comfortable with a gay president than a born-again president. Among the youngest Millennials (aged 18 to 25), the trend is even more dramatic—36 percent are affiliated with no religion; again, nearly one-third report that they have left their church in part because of the anti-gay teachings of the religion they grew up with.

Of course, there are religious Democrats and Republican atheists. But data shows that, overall, the more religious a person, the more likely s/he is a Republican: almost half of weekly churchgoers vote for Republicans, while just over a third vote for Democrats. Whatever the effect on America spiritually, the effect politically seems clear. *Advantage: Democrats.*

Senior Insecurity. At 16 percent of the electorate in presidential elections—often swelling to around a fifth in midterms—seniors are the smallest *age* cohort but a bigger *voting* bloc than either African Americans or Hispanics. It's fast growing, too, as boomers age.

They're a force not only in number of voters but also in number of volunteers, with plenty of free time and, for most, without the worry of work, thanks to Social Security and Medicare.

In 2004, the day after John Kerry conceded defeat, Bush 43 served the country notice that his election earned him a mandate and that it meant something: "I earned capital in this campaign, political capital, and now I intend to spend it." But like his youth, Bush misspent his mandate in a quickly doomed drive to privatize Social Security.

Undaunted, eight years later, the GOP was at it again with the plan of congressman and VP nominee Paul Ryan—now Speaker—to voucher-ize Medicare, a plan that Democrats said would effectively end the program. Yet the GOP won the senior vote in 2012 as focus groups simply did not believe a politician would be so foolish to offer an alternative like that. Republicans seemed more successful in (falsely) accusing Democrats of pilfering funds from Medicare to subsidize Obamacare than Democrats were in pinning the tail on the elephant for embracing radical Ryanomics.

Although seniors now slightly lean Republican by a narrow 47 to 43 percent, Democrats seem well-positioned to shift older voters their way. First, though it's conventional wisdom that people become more conservative as they age, they also "become" more female because of a disparity in gender survival rates: the Census reports that for every 100 women at age 75, there are 80.2 men; by age 85, that falls to 58.3. While a majority of older men see government programs as perpetuating dependency, women by wide margins look upon them as a "hand up, not a hand out" (Bill Clinton's adage). The gender gap carries through generations.

Second, it was clearly Republican Bush 43 who cratered the economy and pensions, and Democrats who not only founded Social Security and Medicare but also now want to protect both against deficit hawks urging higher retirement ages and, again, privatization. Faced with these aims, some progressive Democrats, led by Senators Sherrod Brown (D-OH) and Elizabeth Warren (D-MA), are pushing to expand these programs since a majority of Americans now retire without pensions and with less than $5,000 saved in the bank. Although David Frum argues that older people in this slower-growth century are increasingly frantic about "retirement security," progressives should not lose the retirement security debate to the party that has long wanted to end, privatize, or block grant it (as in "block that grant!"). ***Advantage: Lean Democrats.***

Can Labor Come Back? "Democracy cannot work," observed Senator Robert Wagner (D-NY), "unless it is honored in the factory as well as the polling booth." With passage of his National Labor Relations Act in 1935, the government created the legal right to collectively bargain and form a union. But a decade later, the same Congress elected in 1946 that brought us Joe McCarthy and Richard Nixon also took aim at the New Deal and the NLRA. The Taft-Hartley Act, passed over Harry Truman's veto, ate away at unions' powers and led to the growth of right-to-work states, which now encompass half the country. After the narrow failure of Labor Law Reform in 1978 and the firing of striking air traffic controllers in 1981 by President Reagan, corporations have enjoyed nearly carte blanche to dominate and decimate unions. The historical result is clear: while 1 in 4 workers in the private sector were unionized in 1973, today it's 1 in 16.

Americans of today might not remember the battles of the 1930s, but the simmering war against unions over subsequent decades—with lawyers in pinstripes at the NLRB replacing goons with clubs—has had expensive consequences: economically, unions press for higher wages, so weakened unions contribute to income inequality, as the IMF concedes; politically, fewer union members means fewer volunteers and donations to Democrats. In the 2010 elections, when the Tea Party took the House, seven of the top ten outside groups gave money to the GOP. The remaining three—National Education Association; Service Employees International Union; Association of Federal, State, County, and Municipal Employees—were unions.

This decline creates the mistaken assumption that modern, post-industrial workers in cubicles are resistant to unions. For decades Canadian and U.S. union membership rates were both around 30 percent. But while Canada's unionization process and rates have stayed relatively constant, business and Republican leaders in the United States made unionization more difficult by law—most prominently, Governor Scott Walker in Wisconsin. Can Labor slow or reverse this politically driven trend? On the one hand, a Gallup Poll in mid-2015 showed a 5 percentage point rise over the prior year in approval of organized labor, from 53 to 58 percent, its highest point since 2008. But with a Republican Congress, companies threatening to move facilities to South Korea or South America, and public sector organizing threatened in the Supreme Court case of *Friedrichs v. California Teachers Association*, this variable seems unlikely to change in the near term. ***Advantage: Republicans.***

Two final, consequential trends involve the comparative strengths of our two parties. In a politically binary country, if one declines, it boosts the other.

CHICKEN LITTLE REPUBLICANS

In May 2011 at the Le Roy High School in western New York, one teenage girl collapsed, displaying Tourette-like symptoms of involuntary twitching and uncontrolled verbal outbursts. Shortly thereafter, another five girls fell similarly ill, then 15. When all organic or infectious causes were ruled out, neurologists finally concluded they had been afflicted by "mass psychogenic illness"—commonly called mass hysteria—caused by "significant life stressors" that converted severe mental stress into physical manifestations.

Pathological mental contagions are not unknown in America. When religious and community leaders in 1692 thought certain women were bewitched, over 150 of them were imprisoned and 19 hanged. Slave ownership in the South greatly enriched plantation owners yet depressed the wages of all white workers, who nonetheless were convinced to fight and die in 1861 for this "heritage"—and a century later, southern officials actually shut down public schools rather than integrate them. The problem of economic bubbles—from tulips in 1600s Netherlands to mortgage-backed securities in 2007—involves multitudes failing to see the obvious because of greed or fear. Surely there were communist agitators in the Twenties and Fifties, some committed to violence, but Attorney General Mitchell Palmer and Senator Joseph McCarthy stampeded the public into condoning massive violations of civil liberties. Throughout those decades, being gay was regarded as a sickness justifying being lobotomized, imprisoned, even castrated.

In this vein of craziness, a *majority* of today's Republican Party in polls recently believed that the American president is not an American, that Islam should be outlawed in the United States, that there were WMDs in Iraq, that we should spend $300+ billion to round up and ship 11 million "illegals" out of the country, that Benghazi is worse than Watergate, that global warming is a hoax, that waterboarding can be justified, and that it's OK to disenfranchise millions of eligible voters because .00000001 of those who vote may have engaged in voter impersonation. Thirty-seven percent of white southerners say they'd still join the Confederacy in a Civil War and 43 percent can imagine conditions that would justify a military coup against the United States government. While 99 percent of the world's nations, a unanimous UN Security Council, the U.S. commander in chief, and the pope favored the Iranian nuclear deal that would freeze or even end its ability to build a nuclear bomb, only 3 percent of Republicans did in a national poll and zero percent of 300 Republican Members of Congress. Not one.

Should independents and Democrats respond to such views with satire or psychoanalysis? Bill Maher, shortly before Pope Francis visited the United States in late 2015, joked that "29 percent of Republicans think the pope is a Muslim who's coming here to have an anchor baby." More seriously, a GOP gripped by a form of intellectual hysteria seems to validate theologian and ethicist Reinhold Niebuhr's conclusion that people in groups are often more immoral than when acting alone.

Do I demonize Republicans? No more than they do themselves when they occasionally stray into candor. Shortly after President Obama's 2012 reelection, Louisiana governor Bobby Jindal said that Republicans shouldn't continue to be "the stupid party." Yet there are a flood of examples—throughout this book and in the appendix—supporting the nuts-stupidity thesis of Barney Frank and Bobby Jindal. Frank Rich wrote a classic essay explaining how they are now a party of "nullifers and nihilists," tethered to a South still nursing emotional wounds from 150 years ago. Republican used to be seen as the adults in the room—think Jim Baker and George Schultz—but are now more like Thelma and Louise sharing their exuberant victimhood as they joyfully accelerate the convertible over the cliff.

This is when self-described "centrists" or journalists on deadline indignantly or lazily resort to the false equivalence of, well, *both sides do it*. But they don't. American Enterprise Institute scholars Norman Ornstein and Thomas Mann in their book *It's Even Worse Than It Looks*—and E. J. Dionne in *Why the Right Went Wrong* in 2016—argue that America is gripped by "asymmetrical polarization" because the GOP has become an "insurgent outlier . . . unpersuaded by conventional understanding of facts, evidence, and science." For one example, 82 percent of consistent liberals say they believe in compromise, according to Pew Research, but only 32 percent of consistent conservatives do. In a 2006 Fox News poll, Democrats by 50 percent to 40 percent concluded that they hoped Bush would fail—for a +10 percent; but a 2014 ORC poll asking Republicans if they wanted Obama to fail found that they did by 73 to 14 percent—for a +59 percent. Again, who are the public Democratic equivalents of 9/11 Truthers, climate deniers, white militiamen, and conspiratorialists of the Jade Helm species? Where are the entire books full of Carter's or Clinton's or Obama's "reigns of error"?

There aren't any. So conservative stalwarts then cherry-pick any counter-example to be able to get on a slippery slope and fill time in a quick radio debate or Twitter exchange. This involves a frantic search for at least one black swan—no matter how trivial, unrepresentative, or irrelevant—to "prove" that all swans are black. A GOPer accused of racial intolerance? *Remember when Bob Byrd was in the Klan in the 1920s?* To low-information voters eager to grab onto anything to maintain their conservative world view, anecdotage defeats data.

William Buckley Jr., the intellectual father of conservatism, famously exiled Robert Welch and his Birchers from his Republican Party with a 5,000-word screed in 1962 because calling Eisenhower a communist was a bit much. Who are the Buckleys of today calling out the "crazies" of the Republican Party, a word both Obama and McCain have used to describe them? Is the belief that Obama is ineligible to be president any less insane than believing Ike a communist? If twentieth-century Republican greats like TR and Ike—both of whom passionately supported public works for the public good—were to return today, is there any serious doubt that they'd feel more at home in the party of Obama than the party of Limbaugh?

For years, the prevalence of such GOP wing nuts, like sex in Victorian England, has been privately understood though not publicly discussed by the party, while the ethic of journalism was "must be evenhanded." Then came Trump, the shocking though not surprising child of right-wing talk radio and the "conservative entertainment complex," a talented combination of (Howard) Beale, Bulworth, and Bunker. When he began dominating the GOP nomination contest starting in the summer of 2015, it was clear that the party's base had grown into the insatiable blood-sucking plant in *Little Shop of Horrors* ("Feed me, Seymour!").

For example, while at one time Senator Marco Rubio endorsed a path to citizenship and Senator John McCain supported reasonable solutions to global warming, they quickly retreated rather than risk excommunication from the Church of Conservatism. As pulpit preachers say, "It's the congregation that writes the sermon."

Other western European countries also have significant percentages of their populations who are racist and xenophobic, producing political leaders like a Jean-Marie Le Pen and Enoch Powell. The best available data puts this at 25 percent of France, 23 percent of Denmark, 22 percent of Great Britain, 20 percent of Austria. We're not immune. America too now appears to have a Fringe Fourth—statistically over half the current Republican base—who at one time will support extremists like Trump, Cruz, or Carson and want to impeach Obama because . . . well, just because. This significant extremist minority in America may not be enough to elect a president but is still a monkey wrench in the machinery of a democracy designed to make progress hard to pursue and easy to block.

Democracy knows how to get rid of bad politicians. They can be defeated or prosecuted. But how do you get rid of a bad electorate that religiously ignores "facts, logic or reason"?* When, as Mel Brooks put it in *The History of the World* as King Louis IV, "the people are revolting"? What happens "to an elite whose followers withdraw their assent?" asks David Frum in *The Atlantic* about the cavernous gap between the GOP establishment and radical base. "Does it self-examine? Or does it take refuge in denial? Does it change or try to prevent change?"

Probably it just waits.

The time line of the rise and fall of modern conservatism is fairly clear, though the reasons for its decline less so.

---

* Unintentionally agreeing with this conclusion is Stephen Hayes, a credentialed neoconservative and *Fox News* regular, who complained that the half of his party with a favorable view of Trump at one point were immune to "facts, logic or reason." Precisely. Presumably, Hayes's lamented half won't alter their reasoning or values should their bullying billionaire somehow fall short of the White House. Will Hayes then acknowledge their deficiencies?

Buckley founded *National Review* in 1955 to resuscitate a comatose conservative movement after 20 years of the New Deal. Two of
his early principles were white supremacy and segregation (which he
later renounced) and McCarthyism (which he didn't). Then Goldwater's nomination in 1964 showed that conservative activists had
seized control of the party at the grassroots. He lost but his 4 million volunteers didn't seem fazed, returning home to continue their
proselytizing. The Watts, Newark, and Detroit race riots of '65 to '68
soured many whites about, in their view, a government helping people who didn't seem to appreciate it. Then Nixon and Reagan rode
this backlash to their victories.

It was Falwell, Gingrich, Fox, and Limbaugh in the mid-1990s,
however, who really launched the new conservative extremism. In the
1980s, Rev. Jerry Falwell's Moral Majority figured out how to connect
Christian clergy and flocks to the Republican Party—if it worked for
Martin Luther King Jr., why not Pat Robertson? Then Speaker Newt
Gingrich, fresh off his stunning takeover of the House in 1994, moved
to consolidate his gains with his strategic Contract with America and
memoranda urging his team to always use words like "traitors, pathetic, corrupt, weak, anti-family, anti-flag" to describe liberals. This
irredentist, doctrinaire approach became the template for two other
Nineties phenomena—a fledging cable news organization founded
by the deep pockets of Rupert Murdoch and a singular radio talent
named Rush Limbaugh. These no-apologies conservatives were looking to be anti-something following the fall of communism and economic successes of Kennedy and Clinton.

They found it in Barack Hussein Obama, who seemed to be
everything they despised—an urban black liberal, product of elite
Eastern education, and a child of both Alinsky-like street organizing
and Rev. Jeremiah Wright's liberation theology. It was only when
Obama became president that a Tea Party erupted and grew. So from
Buckley to Goldwater to Nixon/Reagan to Gingrich to Limbaugh
and the Tea Party—with Fox News providing the indispensable distribution system—the GOP literally became, in what was considered
a laugh line when Reagan said it, a "party of the far right and the
farther right."

But what really explains this group-think of anger and intolerance? In my view, it's the result of a volatile mix of first philosophy,
second psychology, and third unreality.

The foundational philosophy of limited government is not per se irrational. Government can be either too big and intrusive—see eighteenth-century monarchies and East Germany pre-unification—or too small to meet great challenges—see America in the late Twenties. But the constant refrain of so-called "constitutional conservatives" elevating "states' rights" and the Tenth Amendment ignores history. It was Federalists who in 1787 overthrew the state-based Articles of Confederation hamstringing our fledging government and whose thinking, starting with George Washington and Alexander Hamilton, dominated American politics for decades. It was Federalists like Lincoln who defeated the "confederation" of southern states on behalf of one indivisible nation. And it was the federal government that broke the back of Jim Crow. While disagreements over exactly what should be done at the margins by states or D.C. will continue, the war over a strong federal government essentially ended in 1865 and 1965 despite Texas governor Gregg Abbott's proposed nine—*nine*—constitutional amendments to allow states to overrule the Supreme Court and federal law in a new push for nullification.

Similarly, the economic philosophy of laissez-faire may be a reasonable way to generate wealth but has obvious flaws with allocation and "externalities." The great free-market thinkers of the eighteenth and nineteenth centuries—Locke, Burke, Hume—felt comfortable describing how economic contracts productively bind people together but not how a social contract can also elevate people and communities. Yet Social Darwinism hypnotized generations of Republican policy makers into pretending that low tax rates on the rich were ultimately in the interest of workers, which was quite a convenient approach for the party's biggest donors. In a world linked by war, climate, trade, and currencies, a libertarian/states' rights model that in effect asks "What would Wyoming do?" is not a very useful guide today.

The psychological basis of modern conservatism has recently been illuminated by a new school of behavioralists, especially Jonathan Haidt in *The Righteous Mind: Why Good People Are Divided by Politics and Religion*. The Republican phenomenon of conclusions-leading-to-"facts" rather than the reverse may have biological origins. Haidt and others are showing that people may be wired at birth to lean toward either authoritarian structures out of fear—the church, military, talk radio—or tolerance and open-minded debate. As for whether the anger of white working-class men owes to race or economics, the answer is both. While most Republicans are not racists, most racists are Republicans, often those men whose income had been flat for decades and who are the biggest job losers as American manufacturing shrinks. It has not proven difficult for talented talkers—from Wallace to Nixon to Reagan to Trump—to convince them to turn against those on the next lower rung of the ladder: minorities and welfare recipients.

Last, GOP leaders exist in evidence-free zones as they embrace any policy that may enable them hold onto power. They're not so much liars as delusionists, according to Dostoevsky's observation that "lying to ourselves is more deeply ingrained than lying to others."

But what happens when catechism collides with reality? When Kansas actually slashed taxes according to the Republican catechism and it produced not large surpluses but ruinous deficits? When Clinton's tax hikes led to record growth while Bush's tax cuts led to a near economic collapse? When a party belittled the Stimulus and Affordable Care Act as "wasteful . . . job-killers" and then employment steadily grew? When the United States launched a preemptive military attack in Iraq based on falsehoods that it was supposed to be a "cakewalk" but that produced 30,000 American casualties? It's like the mayor in *Jaws* who assures everyone on the beach that there's no shark . . . until swimmers are dragged down by something with a big fin and teeth.

Another reality confronting conservatives is that many of their political villains are either gone or defanged. Buckley told his biographer that "the conservative movement lost its raison d'être with the end of Communism and never got it back." With per capita crime way down, gays marrying, bipartisan support for drug reform rather than *Reefer Madness,* and federal deficits shrinking, it's getting harder to panic voters. ISIS is scary but, causing fewer deaths than white supremacists and anti-abortion killers, not confused with a nuclear U.S.S.R.

The result of all these developments? A movement and party in a rut that they're digging deeper.

Since "facts are stubborn things" (said both Lenin and Reagan), here are the facts: Obama became the first Democrat since FDR to win two national popular vote majorities. Democrats now outnumber Republicans by 48 to 39 percent. The GOP has an overall popularity of minus 28 percentage points—32 to 60 percent unfavorable, according to the Pew Research Center—its worst showing since 1992, when Pew began asking the question. In 2014 and 2015, self-described conservatives fell from 37 to 33 percent and self-described liberals rose from 23 to 27 percent, meaning that this ideological gap shrank by half. A majority of Americans see Republicans as more extreme and Democrats as "more concerned about people like me." True, the Congress for now is Republican because of low-turnout mid-term elections and gerrymandering based on the 2010 Census and (fortuitously for the Republicans) "shellacking" of Democrats that year, which favored the House GOP for the entire rest of the decade. The next Census and decade-determining election, however, will occur in 2020, which (fortuitously for the Democrats) will reflect the new demographic math and will have ballots likely headed by an incumbent Democratic president.

After Romney's defeat, the GOP tried to learn from all this evidence, especially since their membership had been assured that Romney would beat "the anointed one" (Hannity's nightly reference to the elected president). RNC chair Reince Priebus announced a political autopsy to determine what went wrong and how to do better. His report in March 2013 did in fact sensibly hint at growing the base by being more inclusive and less intolerant. That lasted about a week before the nativist wing of the party started to brand as apostasy anything other than the ol' time anti-immigrant religion, notwithstanding the fact that there's been no net immigration from Mexico for several years.

To their credit, some conservative intellectuals haven't given up hope. So-called "Reformicons" like Reihan Salam, Ramesh Ponnuru, and David Frum are searching for smarter approaches beyond simply anti-Obama-ism. But this isn't an easy assignment for a movement that fundamentally doesn't believe in public sector solutions and can't let go of looking to the "free market" as the answer to everything. No wonder Frum worries that "a generation of young Americans has been lost to our party."

When asked about actual alternatives to the much-despised Stimulus, Obamacare, Iran nuclear deal, and Obama ISIS policy, the answer from GOP leaders was and is, in effect, "We'll get back to you on that." The wait for a winning GOP governing agenda is like watching a shell game on Broadway in front of a marquee for *Waiting for Godot*. For the Republicans' problem is not merely that they're anti-government but—based on the obstructionism of the 113th and 114th Congresses—anti-governance, anti-science, anti-math.

The most probable near-term response, therefore, is the conservative default position over the past couple of decades due to demands of the faithful—just keep defending the Grand *Old* Positions. According to a much-heralded book in 2015, *The Conservative Heart*, American Enterprise Institute president Albert C. Brooks argues that the GOP's policies and analyses are fine, but its rhetoric had to be more welcoming. Like breaking up millions of immigrant families but doing it with a smile? Reminding blue-collar workers that they should be grateful to a party for making labor pay a higher share of taxes than capital? More likely will be a continuation of the sneering tone that now flourishes on the Right. This has obvious appeal to conservative pols and pundits who, lacking hard evidence, understand the great legal axiom that "when facts are on the other side, pound the law; when the law is on the other side, pound the facts; when both are on the other side, pound the table."

After years of debating Buckley, Buchanan, Novak, and others on talk TV and radio and hearing their table-pounding favorites, I've summarized the best verbal sleights-of-hand in "The Book of GOP Twistifications" (see appendix). All rest on three foundations. They prey on credulous, uninformed people who want their beliefs reinforced, not challenged. They rely on the misdirection of changing the subject when they can't change minds. And they reflect J. P. Morgan's profound insight that "a man always has two reasons for doing anything. A good reason and the real reason."

Hence the sine qua non of euphemism. So when conservatives historically *said* "property rights," they *meant* slavery; when they *said* "states' rights," they *meant* segregation; when they *said* "property values," they *meant* housing segregation. And today when they *say* "money is speech," they *mean* it's fine for their billionaires to buy democracy; when they *say* Voter ID, they *mean* denying minorities the right to vote; when they *say* "over-regulation," they *mean* that big business should write the rules of the consumer marketplace; when they *say* "religious liberty," they *mean* that everyone's entitled to comply with Kentucky marriage clerk Kim Davis's religion. "When

I use a word," said a scornful Humpty Dumpty, "it means just what I choose it to mean—neither more nor less."

Mind you, I feel some professional sympathy for conservative colleagues who must wake up each morning wondering what crazy thing they'll be called on to defend—Cliven Bundy and *Duck Dynasty* bigotry; why Obama's 5 percent unemployment rate is worse than Bush's 10 percent (at its peak after he left); why Arctic ice isn't melting. I also feel sympathy for candidates asked questions to which there is no serious answer, as they immediately have to sort through these 14 rhetorical tricks, or twistifications, to facilitate an escape if not turn the tables. It takes talent not to sound like an idiot when you imply that Mexicans are rapists, that possible terrorists should get guns while denouncing Obama as weak on terrorism, that a ten-year-old girl impregnated by her stepfather should have the baby, that the president's Iran policy will again send Jews "to the ovens." (The last two are from Mike Huckabee.)

Then there's the possibility that the GOP hasn't hit "rock bottom," in the phrase of not-to-be-Speaker Kevin McCarthy after a Tea Party revolt in late 2015. It could go lower, and die from self-inflicted wounds, which happened to the California GOP after Governor Pete Wilson's anti-immigration Prop 187, or splinter into something different that's far short of a national majority. What happens when blue-collar employees/middle-class voters realize that wealthy businessmen in boardrooms are laughing at how their $40,000-a-year workers have been conned into being foot soldiers fighting for lower taxes for their $14-million-a-year bosses? If white working class workers should come to realize who's not on their side economically, just as white southerners eventually realized who wasn't on their side racially in the '60s, the jig's up for the GOP. British economic historian Edwin Cannan understood a century ago that "however lucky Error may be for a time, Truth keeps the bank and wins in the long run."

Today's GOP, riven by its corporate donors and culturally fundamentalist base—is essentially a philosophy of freedom fronting for a big business agenda. Whether it survives depends on who wins the struggle for its soul—purist radicals like Erick W. Erickson who don't seem to care about winning elections or more open-minded realists like Frum.

My guess: it'll take two more presidential losses for the Republican Party to resist the one-note of always sounding hyperbolic and apocalyptic, always whining that they lost only because their nominee wasn't right wing, always rhetorically yearning to go back to some idyllic moment in 1785 when a states' rights credo misgoverned America. Instead, the political lithosphere of 2016 involves two shifting tectonic plates, a GOP plate lurching to the right and the rest of America moving left, with likely disruptive results in November 2016. *Advantage Democrats.*

DEMOCRATS: THE GOVERNMENT IS *US*

Which brings us to a final trend—the other party. Democrats can either extend the new progressive majority by building a program of prosperity and democracy or end it by fulfilling Robert Frost's observation that "a liberal is a man too broadminded to take his own side in a quarrel."

Unlike grief, overcoming Frost's hurtful jab entails only a three-stage process.

Stage 1: Get Back on Offense. Since wars aren't won by Dunkirks but by Normandys, Democrats need to bluntly call out conservatives when they say stupid stuff. Why should Republicans have all the fun as they colorfully and relentlessly go after their opposition? It was slightly hilarious when they slandered Obama every which way for seven years and then freaked out when he accurately observed that GOP hardliners were aligning with Iranian hardliners (see Senator Tom Cotton's letter from 47 senators to the Ayatollah). Democrats' general gentility helps explain why Elizabeth Warren became so enormously popular and Bernie Sanders drew record crowds—people want bold leaders who can clearly frame a case, not just legislative incrementalists. Among the best *New Yorker* cartoons from the 1960s was a well-dressed protestor holding up a sign that read: "a little less bombing please."

Vivid conservative attacks require vivid progressive counterattacks. Those who want to abolish Obamacare, it should be said, would in effect be imposing death sentences on the estimated 19,000 lives now saved annually because of expanded health insurance . . . and these deaths would be literal, not like rhetorical "death taxes" and "death panels." The NRA and its kept politicians are in effect pulling the trigger on thousands of guns deaths annually by opposing every single idea to reduce gun violence, even though the Second Amendment in the *Heller* decision allows reasonable regulation. Based on recent evidence, one party proposes solutions while the other side largely just kvetches, as if fulfilling the Gypsy aphorism, "The dogs bark but the caravan moves on."

While Bush 43 solemnly announced that government had "to err on the side of life" when trying to revive the comatose Terri Schiavo in 2005, his party is today "erring on the side of the death" of not one person but millions by putting its collective heads in the sand of climate denial. And no politician should be able to get away with pretending to want to help the middle class by doing everything possible to sabotage unions that shrink the wage gap.

Jon Stewart's rants against "bullshit-ocracy—if you smell something, say something"—made him our Mark Twain. Other than Elizabeth Warren, there's one sitting senator with Stewartian skills if he chose to become a satirical, factual bullshit detector—Al Franken. (When I tell Franken in 2015 how sincerely and thoughtfully he comes across in the media and why he should be doing more on national TV after his decisive reelection win, he replies, "Thanks. What happens in interviews is that I can't memorize and recite talking points. Can't do it. So I say what I think.")

Stage 2: Don't Forget the Grassroots. When Labor Secretary Frances Perkins pushed FDR on labor reforms, the sympathetic politician in chief famously said, "Fine—now make me do it." And labor organizers did. Anti-war protestors and civil rights advocates organized locally, marched in big numbers, and changed the country. Even a movement that numerically failed—there are no Occupy Wall Street congresspersons—completely shifted the axis of debate over income and wealth inequality in America after they occupied public spaces to gain public attention.

More recently, #BlackLivesMatter, #Fightfor15, J Street, and 350 .com—and groups such as the Center for American Progress, MoveOn, Campaign for America's Future, Media Matters, Netroots Nation, Progressive Change Campaign, and Democracy Alliance—are influentially pressuring public officials on race, the minimum wage, the Iran nuclear deal, and climate change. "Revolutions, like houses," concludes Gloria Steinem, "are built from the bottom up."

Consider the minimum wage and gay rights. "Did you see the *Times* editorial today coming out for a $15 minimum?" Nader asks me with amazement the last week of 2015. "The blasphemy of yesterday becomes the commonplace of today when a few thousand fast-food workers in brand-name companies take to the streets. That's the value of civic protest."

Intensity can create a majority—and then policy. Writes David Cole in the *Nation* of marriage equality: "That change came about not through the whim of five justices but through the painstaking work of thousands of people across the country committed to an idea of equality, and willing to fight for it in state legislatures and courts, on state referendums, in their churches and their communities. And that is just how constitutional law has generally evolved in our society: through the persistent struggle of groups of committed citizens."

The core idea was Cicero's in ancient Rome: his definition of freedom was "participation in power."

Stage 3: Democrats Must Expose the Oxymoron That You Can Love Your Country Yet Hate Its Democratically Elected Government. It's a shame that "trust in government"—which is often the instrument of liberal change—plummeted after the illiberal calamities of Vietnam and Watergate. One of the most radical, un-American things any president has ever said came from Reagan at his inaugural—"Government is not the solution to our problem, government IS the problem." That formulation ran counter to two centuries of progress as democratic government, however imperfectly, has battled crime, pollution, racism, an economic depression, dangerous products, infant mortality, wildfires, floods, and extreme economic inequality. Were those problems caused by government? Should they have waited for private sector solutions? The answer, in effect, was provided by Benjamin Franklin at the start of our democracy and Jean Tirole two centuries later: Franklin: "Private property is a creature of society and is subject to the calls of that society, whenever its necessities shall require it." Reflecting that wisdom, the Nobel Committee in 2014 awarded French economist Tirole its economics prize for showing that, since markets often fail, "government regulation of such markets could produce better outcomes for society."

According to Machiavelli, enacting something new is far harder than stopping something bad because of a political version of the

Second Law of Thermodynamics, commonly called inertia—objects
at rest stay at rest. Those benefiting from the status quo are wary of
disturbing it for some possible future benefit for others. But if the
anti-government slur goes unanswered, it becomes accepted. That
creates a "vicious cycle," according to the always-trenchant Barney
Frank, when "people understandably are disappointed that government doesn't work and then elect candidates who don't *want* it to
work." Too many economically stressed Americans embrace a version
of that Tea Party senior who supposedly said "tell the government to
keep its hands off my Medicare." The only way to break this fever is
for Democrats to actually use the four-letter word "government"—or
"democracy" or "life-saving programs"—in order to remind voters
that the issue isn't the *size* of government but the *side* it's on . . . that
is, the side of people needing protection from hunger, illness, poverty,
discrimination, and poor education.

"Let us never forget," FDR simply and powerfully said, "that government is ourselves and not an alien power over us."

It's hard to make reasoned arguments to a biased political jury, as
I experienced in the 1978 Consumer Protection Agency fight, when
emotionally charged slogans like *big government, overregulation,* and
federal overreaching rhetorically overpowered earnest progressive
proposals. The key is to convert ideological abstractions into people and families. Who does the public turn to when a GM defective
car ignition switch kills 104 and Volkswagen rigs emissions tests, or
when a town, oil rig, or mine explodes—witness West Texas, BP's oil
rig in the Gulf, and the Upper Branch Mine in West Virginia? Doesn't
every parent appreciate the reduction in smoking, crib deaths, auto
fatalities, and infant mortality brought about via the instrument of
democracy called government? Aren't even libertarians thankful that
a federal bureaucrat, Dr. Frances Kelsey at the FDA, in 1962 stopped
the importation of the drug thalidomide, sparing thousands of families the horror of limbless children?

That decade saw a series of major books exposing social ills
and illuminating smart government solutions—*Silent Spring, The
Feminine Mystique, The Other America, Unsafe at Any Speed.* Three
decades later, a month after the Oklahoma City bombing by an anti-
government fanatic targeted and killed scores of federal civil servants,
President Clinton told an audience I was in at the Rockefeller Estate in
Westchester, "I'll never again use the words 'government bureaucrat'

as a pejorative." Five decades later, President Obama explained in a series of four speeches—starting with his commencement address at the University of Michigan in 2010 and ending with his remarks at the fiftieth anniversary of the Selma march—how often conservative Cassandras were disproven when government acted successfully to save lives, spur economic growth, and advance rights. He grounded these talks on Lincoln's memorable observation that "the legitimate object of government is to do for a community of people whatever they need to be done but cannot do in their individual capacities."

When it came to government, Obama argued that Lincoln's framework was far superior to Reagan's. The new forty-fifth president has to elaborate how the federalism versus "states' rights" argument—from Washington to Obama—has been litigated. Based on the very creation of America, we can't go back to our future.

WHAT'S THE SUM of all trends above?

As the Enlightenment supplanted monarchy, Lincoln's cause defeated Calhoun's, and LBJ pushed aside mentor Richard Russell on Jim Crow, the jury of history is now returning a verdict in the progressive-conservative contest because the former simply has the better case. A new progressive era that began slowly with Clinton and grew with Obama will likely continue due to the march of demography, majority support for progressive values, the GOP lurch into fringeland, and comparisons of the Clinton-Obama and Bush 43 administrations. Consequently, (a) the Democratic nominee in 2016 is a strong favorite to win by about the same four- to seven-point margin as Obama's two victories and (b) Democrats are even money on retaking the Senate, and perhaps the House by 2022, post-Census and reapportionment. Of course, there could be some disruptive event— a personal scandal, economic calamity, voter suppression that tips a swing state, $3 billion super-PAC expenditure—that reshuffles presumptions, as Watergate did for 1976.

Or the Republicans could again play its go-to Fear Card—as Senator McCarthy did in the '50s, Nixon and Reagan did against Reds and Blacks in the '60s and '80s, and as the GOP did in 2014 when they made it seem as if Ebola and migrating Central American children were threatening to sweep across America. (By the way, every person who contracted Ebola in the United States recovered, and no one else has gotten it here, due to federal policy and facilities.)

It's impossible to know whether the next sky-is-falling alarm will be sounded over race, refugees, a new very, very bad Planned Parenthood video . . . or, probably, the most recent or imminent ISIS-related death. But while jihadism is a serious, fearsome threat, it's not equal to the challenge from fascism and communism, nor is it an "existential . . . civilizational struggle"—as if there are two comparable, contending sides with Sharia law threatening to supplant our Constitution. The only surprise in October 2016 will be if there's *not* an October Surprise exploiting terrorism (of the international and not domestic variety).

But looking at America through a wider lens, trends are more certain than terrorism, economic collapse, or even the perversion of democracy by money. A rising new progressive era—the century's fourth—will likely continue because Americans in a high-turnout election are not about to turn over their country to the amalgam of nativists, billionaires, and theocrats in a modern era prizing human rights, science, and diplomacy. An ascending majority of minorities, Millennials, and women—totaling 83 percent of the electorate—who in the past two presidential elections preferred the level-headed progressivism of a Barack Obama won't leap into the lap of a party that thought Donald Trump was a plausible president.

To help ensure this result and make it worthwhile, however, requires a positive prgressive program rooted in Sixties principles—an Economy for All, Democracy for All, Climate for All, and Racial Justice.

I. AN ECONOMY FOR ALL: CLOSE THE PAY GAP

America has two civic religions: our *democracy* presumes equal justice under law since everyone, theoretically at least, is entitled to the same one vote in an election and due process in court; our *economy*, to the contrary, assumes unequal financial returns in order to spur effort and innovation. But while there's never been an agreed-upon level of inequality that's desirable or intolerable, clearly there's some extreme that, to use a term from substantive due process, "shocks the conscience." A CEO-worker pay ratio of 30:1 in the 1950s didn't become controversial. What about now that it's 300:1? What about

ExxonMobil and Walmart CEOs whose compensation per *hour* has recently been greater than their average workers' per *year?* What level brings us to the Calcutta-ization of America?

Disparities of wealth in the Gilded Age and the Roaring Twenties produced significant political upheavals in the Progressive and New Deal eras that tempered some of the excesses of unbridled capitalism. In recent decades, excessive inequality/immobility was not a first-order issue and usually associated only with left-wing scholars and activists. Until Occupy Wall Street in 2011. Now even most Republican presidential candidates acknowledge that inequality is a significant problem and their standard rhetorical rebuttals—"class war," "the politics of envy," "takers vs. makers"—have largely disappeared. The reason: it's untenable for politicians to ignore a wage and wealth gap that voters live every day:

- 93 percent of income gains since the Great Recession ended have gone to the top 1 percent, the remaining 7 percent to everyone else.
- The top 1 percent controlled 22 percent of all income in 1929, 10 percent in 1960, and 22 percent in 2012.
- The 85 richest billionaires on the planet have as much money as the 3.5 billion poorest; in the United States, just 47 individuals own more wealth than 160 million people, i.e., all those below a median wealth level of $58,000.
- Between 1940 and 1970, average CEO pay stayed below $1 million (in 2000 dollars), but from 1978 to 2013, it rose 937 percent to $15.2 million for the top 350 companies, as compared to gains in worker compensation over this period of 10.2 percent.
- Between 1945 and 1973, U.S. workers' productivity rose 96 percent and they received a 94 percent increase in their wages. But between 1973 and 2011, while workers' productivity grew 80 percent, they saw only a 10 percent increase in their wages.

Based on the best available evidence, inequality and immobility is greater in the United States than in any other democracy in the developed world. In our increasingly winner-take-all economy, millions of average families are trying to run up a descending escalator and looking for a second job as their bosses are buying their third houses.

How did this happen? Partly it's the result of international trade patterns where very-low-wage countries attract jobs away from high-wage countries—and partly because of technology breakthroughs that pay extraordinary sums to pioneers (which includes only a few of the super-rich). But trade and technology also affect American competitors who do not suffer from such growing gaps. So we're left with an obvious truth: extreme inequality is not inevitable but intentional, the result of policies drafted by the American business elite for themselves. Or as the influential twentieth-century economist Karl Polanyi put it, presumably enjoying the irony, "Laissez faire is planned."

When the housing bubble burst in 2007–08 and the country went on to lose $14 trillion over two years, no less a priest of capitalism than former Fed chairman Alan Greenspan expressed shock that markets didn't behave as he had thought. The old paradigm that giving more money to the rich helps the middle class, that higher deficits invariably mean higher interest rates, that spending on transfer payments depresses economic growth have been exposed as little more than "intellectual malfeasance," according to Paul Krugman. Instead, a new school of thought not only rejects the assumed trade-off between growth and equality—starting with Thomas Piketty's *Capital in the 21st Century*—but also establishes that less inequality produces more jobs and growth. The reason should be self-evident: companies hire when consumer demand signals there are markets to be supplied, not because a few top executives are plied with more after-tax income that they largely bank but because workers have more income to spend. The S&P Capital Report from August 2015 "sees a narrowing of the income gap as beneficial to the economy."

Conservative economists and politicians are struggling to react to this new paradigm and world. Resorting to theories discredited by Hoover and Bush 43—and even explicitly denounced by Pope Francis—is a losing argument. While the GOP is seen as the party of the rich and big business—with its 2012 presidential nominee seemingly sent by central casting for this purpose—65 percent of all Americans, including a majority of Republicans, believe the economic system is rigged, according to the Pew Research Center. Then there's this devastating comparison: growth and employment rates over the past 56 years—half during Democratic administrations and half Republican—show that they're 50 percent greater under the Democrats.*

Given these numbers, it's hard to imagine that the progressive party in 2016 can lose the economic argument to a party still paying homage to reducing taxes on the rich, still seeking to privatize Social Security, and having presided over a recession that led to a loss of $14 trillion, 8 million jobs, and 6 million homes. But since voters look ahead, it's essential that Democrats don't merely win arguments about the past but also own the future. Here are several approaches based on the framework, as expressed by Senator Dick Durbin, that "everyone's better off when everyone's better off."

They won't be enacted in the next president's first year or even term but will surely never be enacted unless there are candidates who propose and explain them:

Taxes. The Code needs a complete overhaul since corporations accounted for 40 percent of all revenue four decades ago but only 10 percent now. Top rates can rise to the 50 percent accepted in Great Britain and France—where CEOs with after-tax earnings of only $5 million a year appear as motivated as those earning $25 million in the United States; the income of hedge fund managers should be taxed at the same rates as the rest of us; capital gains rates should be less than income rates only for long-term investments; and unpatriotic corporations should stop seeking "inversions" abroad to escape taxes at home.

Infrastructure. No one would let their house crumble while living in it nor should our country tolerate an infrastructure gap that makes our economy less productive. The answer is a modest gas tax, while prices are historically low, that both parties simultaneously agree to. Perhaps a second-term

---

* The average GDP growth rates under Democratic presidents over a 54 year span (1961 to 2015) was 3.68 percent—and under Republican presidents 2.67 percent—for a 40 percent differential. Each party governed for 27 years over this period. This analysis omits the first two quarters of each president's first term because that president obviously wasn't responsible on January 21 for the economic performance that he inherited. Six months or two quarters seemed a reasonable interim period since a new president's budget would only have been enacted by then.

president can explain to car owners why pennies per gallon with gas at 20-year-lows can enable them and their families to avoid dangerous roads and bridges.

Financial Transaction Tax. This would both limit the kind of speculative trading that contributed to the financial meltdown in 2008 and, at say one-tenth of 1 percent of all stock trades, would generate $66 billion a year. Wrote one advocate, "While average Americans pay up to a 10 percent sales tax on shoes, investors pay a zero sales tax on financial purchases . . . The FTT is easy to administer and difficult to evade [since] clearing houses already review all trades and serve as collection agencies for transaction fees."

Profit-sharing. The New York Stock Exchange once estimated that if American business broadened participation in ownership and management across the board, productivity would surge an incredible 20 percent in a single year. At least one presidential candidate in 2016 agrees. Hillary Clinton's approach: a tax credit if profit-sharing payments are above existing wages and benefits.

Minimum Wage. The British call it a "Living Wage." It will be going up there to about the equivalent of $15 an hour by the end of this decade, and conservative PM David Cameron has warned that there will be stiff fines to "unscrupulous employers who underpay their staff." Indeed, in the United States, states with significant minimum wage increases have not seen jobs lost to neighboring states without such raises. A higher minimum wage rewards work and stimulates the economy.

Say on Pay. Laws won't put a ceiling on pay but can require disclosure so workers, shareholders, and policy makers can understand how the game is fixed by executives who appoint pals to boards who then increase their pay package . . . to keep up with everyone else, of course. The SEC should carefully police a new rule, to go into effect for public companies in 2017, requiring that top managers disclose their pay and compare it to the median compensation of their employees.

Family Security. China understands that early childhood development produces a healthier and more productive people: investing in pre-K education, early child care, family leave, paid leave, and workplace flexibility. All legislation should include a "Children's Impact Statement" that assesses how it affects the lives of kids.

Retirement Security. With most Americans retiring with $50,000 in savings or less, it's essential to develop plans to expand retirement accounts, such as a federal Government Retirement Account, not slash "entitlements," as the Ryan-led GOP proposes.

Even before such public policies are considered and adopted, market reactions are mitigating some of the worst attributes of "America, Inc." For example, the costs of what I named the "corpocracy," discussed above, became so glaring that resources today are flowing less to wasteful middle management and more to smaller start-ups with the promise that some may be the next Google or Amazon; indeed, Google was smart enough to spin off "Alphabet" before its bureaucracy strangled its creativity. Turns out that, beyond a certain scale, bigger *isn't* better.

But macroeconomically, the magical theory that tax cuts pay for themselves got its chance when economist Arthur Laffer's napkin combined with Reagan's popularity. It didn't work. Here's what's on the progressive napkin: *Fact: Democrats produce 40 percent more growth.*

II. A DEMOCRACY FOR ALL: IT'S "WE THE PEOPLE" NOT "WE THE CORPORATIONS"

Question: Why is it that large popular majorities for a more progressive tax code, gun background checks, path to citizenship, systemic campaign finance, and reduction in global warming do not result in legislation? *Answer:* The circuit-breakers of big money, voter suppression, plus anti-democratic rules like gerrymandering and the filibuster blunt majority rule. The mindless explanation that both-parties-do-it cannot begin to exonerate "gridlock." Rather, it's the intentional result of a corporate elite that creates a system to enhance their wealth and then uses that financial clout to control our political democracy as well. But while it's one thing for corporate money to purchase a CEO or another company, it's quite another to purchase politicians.

The *Washington Post* calls it the "New American Oligarchy." According to Bill Moyers, we are thisclose to losing a system "of, by and for the people," still the best definition of a democracy. How, in fact, do you know if democracy is disappearing? Is it still a democracy—or is it the proverbial frog slowly boiling to death degree by degree—when:

- 0.1 percent of Americans who contribute over $1,000 to campaigns have far more political influence than the other 99.9 percent;
- only 160 families—overwhelmingly white and in finance and energy—contributed half of all the campaign funds as of late 2015; at the same time, $4 out of every $5 raised on behalf of GOP presidential candidates went to "independent" super-PACs;
- the United States is number 31 of 34 Western nations in voter turnout, with a 36 percent rate in 2014 being the lowest in 72 years;
- strings-attached PAC money goes 7 to 1 for incumbents, and 95 percent of them win;
- Thelma Mitchell, a 93-year-old black cleaning woman who'd worked at the Tennessee State Capitol for 30 years and had been voting for decades, was turned away in 2012 because of a state Voter ID law. Seems she lacked a birth certificate since she had not been born in a hospital but through a midwife. "I was so mad," she said after a clerk refused her plea . . . all this to stop alleged "voter impersonation" that occurred possibly 31 times out of a billion votes cast, according to a study out of Loyola University.

The reality is that our campaign funding system has barely improved from the Gilded Age of a century ago when, according to a commentator in that era, "Standard Oil did everything to the Pennsylvania legislature except refine it." But as with race and climate change, conservatives address this problem by denying this problem. As one very smart conservative explained on *Both Sides Now:* "No, I'm not bothered by 160 families having more power than 100 million families; after all, newspapers spend money on editorial endorsements but we don't regulate that!" *(OK, but there's this First Amendment explicitly referring to "the freedom . . . of the press.")* "Money can corrupt candidates but not money going to 'independent' super PACs" *(ignoring that candidates will easily find out pre- post-election who enabled them to win or lose. "Hey, Bob, thanks for that $5 million!")*

Sophistic arguments can't wish away the undeniable costs of our pay-to-play political system. True, the biggest spender doesn't win every time, just 90 percent of the time; fund-raising is a "time thief," usually consuming over half a candidate's waking hours; it ups the ante of entry, which prices out the "silent casualties" of the money game; and, of course, special interests are not philanthropies but rather give money to make money because the returns are reliable. Who bites the hand that funds them?

Majorities of 75 to 80 percent favor major reforms of the campaign process and reversing the 2010 *Citizens United* decision that allows unlimited funds in elections, contrary to the 1974 post-Watergate limits. Indeed, Occupiers and Tea Partiers, at least philosophically, agree that it's a bad thing when elites buy elections and candidates, and judges too, in judicial elections.

How did we get to this extreme point? Sandra Day O'Connor's husband and the power of metaphor. The multiple anomalies of 2000 that put George W. Bush in line to nominate justices took another bizarre turn when Justice O'Connor's husband got Alzheimer's and she decided to leave the bench to take care of him . . . which opened a seat for the hard-hard-right Samuel Alito. Then right-wing plaintiffs combined two absurd metaphors into a *reductio ad absurdum:* i.e., corporations are "people" and money is "speech"—and so therefore corporations are individuals who can't be limited in what they can spend on elections. Some arguments are so stupid that only brilliant lawyers trained to argue anything could come up with a theory on why the rich should be able have even more political influence, as if their lack of enough was a problem to solve. This theory has inspired mockery at progressive rallies: "If corporations are people, can I marry one, ideally Apple?" And: "I'll believe corporations are people when Texas executes one."

But while liberals could mock the illogic, the Right had five justices who were searching for a way to empower the powerful. The result: the 5–4 *Citizens United* decision and a process that will lead to two billionaires facing off for senator, governor, president—by which time the frog and democracy will be cooked. Since that decision is probably the worst since *Plessy* v. *Ferguson,* it evokes Professor Charles Black's comment that in the 1896 case, "the curves of callousness and stupidity intersect at their respective maxima."

At the same time, Republicans have noticed that when there are turnouts of over 50 percent of eligible voters, as in presidential election years, Democrats often prevail; but when it's under 40 percent, in off-year elections, the GOP does. This reality has created a no-brainer for them: increasingly lose elections or win by making it harder for Democratic constituency groups to vote. This is surely nasty but not stupid: one survey of the 50 million registered but non-voting Americans saw them break 59–24 percent for Obama over Romney.

Because the GOP prefers the second option, 33 states—including all of the Old South—have versions of Voter ID laws or related schemes to reduce Democratic turnout, even though it's already a crime to impersonate someone else at voting places. A Government Accountability Office study found that Voter ID laws reduced voting by 2–3 percent in Tennessee and Kansas in their last elections.

Can anything be done about political crimes of this magnitude?

Some things can't change, like the 1787 Connecticut Compromise allowing two senators per state to ensure that all 13 states agreed to the Constitution . . . although then the largest state (Virginia) had 11 times the population of the smallest (Delaware) while today California is 70 times the size of Wyoming. Having paid this extortionate price to create a strong federal union, at the least America should now try to rebalance our democracy rather than worsen our tilt toward rural and moneyed interests. Here's a *MoneyOut/VotersIn* plan to restore our democracy the next time there's a political scandal that provokes the public to pressure Congress:

> **Enact universal voter registration** at age 18 based on data
> already in Social Security computers, which can then spit
> out a letter every ten years to avoid extra trips and fees
> for Voter ID. Several states, like California and Oregon,
> are doing this for everyone who gets a driver's license.

Combining all such secure databases, the number of eligible voters could swell by over 30 million. But since so many of new voters would come from beneficiaries of social welfare programs, ardent conservatives will have to conjure up more alibis and euphemisms (see Twistifications appendix) to explain why they're against expanding the franchise in a way that could increase Democratic voters. One *Both Sides Now* panelist already explained that "we don't want to make it *too* easy to vote."

Enact a low-dollar matching system based on the successful NYC model so that people who contribute up to $100, when matched 6 to 1 with public funds and aggregated together, can enable unwealthy candidates to be competitive.

Enact a cap on candidate or super-PAC spending per campaign. If we limit the decibel level of sound speakers in political rallies in neighborhoods, why not the decibel level of money—since it's property, not speech—to avoid others from being drowned out?

An executive order should require all federal contractors to disclose how much they spend on campaigns and to whom, including money that goes to secret super PACs even if disguised as charities, and the SEC should require this disclosure of all registered companies. The IRS should stop the sham of allowing such nonprofits to spend funds on politics, not "social welfare" as the law requires.

Merge Veterans Day and Election Day in early November to create one national holiday called "Democracy Day" to make it easier to vote and honor veterans who fought and died defending their democracy.

Prevent gerrymandering: Instead of politicians choosing their voters, states should use non-partisan commissions—as California does—to draw congressional lines.

Limit filibusters: Since the combination of two-senators-per-state plus the filibuster means that 10 percent of the population could veto 90 percent, there should be limits on the number that can be filed annually by the majority party and cloture should be reduced from 60 to 55 votes.

Grant ex-felons voting rights: Allow 5 million ex-felons who have paid their debt to society to vote.

Create instant runoff voting: Instead of a round two of voting and acrimony, electronic allocation of first, second, and third choices on election night can easily determine who won between the eventual top two contenders.

Three irrational Supreme Court decisions need to be revisited and reversed to save our democracy, ideally sometime after Justice Scalia's death, when a Democratic successor effectively closes the book on the most conservative court since the 1920s.

Citizens United is in part based on Justice Kennedy's now-discredited ex cathedra assertion that independent spending "does not give rise to corruption or the appearance of corruption." In reality, it's cringe-worthy to watch Republican presidential candidates eagerly audition for the $890 million in political spending promised by the Koch brothers and also pretend that ex-staff to a candidate "independently" runs his/her super PACs. Already, Kennedy admitted five years later that he erred by concluding that greater disclosure—which Congress refused to enact—could remedy any problems his decision created. Will that now persuade him to change his vote in a future test case? Or will a post-Scalia majority return to America's prior two-century-long understanding that speech is something done by actual human beings and not largely by billionaires and corporations?

Let's step back to look at the history behind this sophistry: while Pericles in his funeral oration in 430 BC for the Athenian war dead said democracy works "because its administration is in the hands not of a few but of the whole people," and James Madison in *The Federalist Papers* wrote that a democratic government is "not [for] the rich more than the poor," the Roberts/Kennedy court has figured they know better. When it comes to democracy, the approach of these jurists impeaches Darwin's theory that evolution is supposed to improve the species.

Michael Waldman, previously of the Democracy Project and Green-Dyson campaign and now head of the prestigious Brennan Center at NYU Law School, said in a speech to his leadership and membership in 2015, "We won't rest until we add *Citizens United* to *Plessy* and *Lochner* on the ash heap of history." Whether that's done by a constitutional amendment, which is hard to imagine at this time, or by a different Court lineup under a new Democratic president—which is likely and which even the pro–*Citizens United* counsel, the famed Floyd Abrams, agrees would probably reverse the decision—that "democracy-perverting decision will not stand."

The *Shelby County* decision weakened the historic 1965 Voting Rights Act when Chief Justice Roberts, who lectures eloquently against judicial activism, decided to ignore a *unanimous* U.S. Senate vote to strike down the crucial provision requiring mostly states in the old Confederate South to "pre-clear" voting changes that could diminish minority voting. This justice from Virginia claimed that the South was now no more likely to discriminate against minority voters than other regions—and then watched Alabama post-*Shelby* try to eliminate DMVs in black counties where residents would go to get IDs.

Last, the Court approved an Indiana Voter ID provision because the state asserted a nonexistent problem of voter impersonation. Since that decision, Justice Stevens recanted his vote and lower court judge Richard Posner, one of the most prominent conservative jurists in the country, regretted his lower court decision because these laws "are widely regarded as a means to voter suppression."*

Voters rarely regard a Democracy Agenda as a top-tier goal. Too procedural, too abstract. But if 0.1 percent of wealthy people continue to be the gatekeepers of our political system, there can be no real solutions to the linked evils of inequality and oligarchy since the latter creates the former. That is, to paraphrase James Carville's immortal observation, it's *still* "about *the economy and the democracy*, stupid."

---

*Consider this priority: while most conservatives demand that longtime, lawful voters affirmatively prove who they are before exercising their fundamental right to vote, they also refuse to impose a similar requirement for those on the Terror Watch List before obtaining a gun. It's actually jaw-dropping that a party eager to project strength against America's enemies would favor potential terrorists over eligible voters.

A *Money Out/VotersIn* program is the precondition of enacting an economic program appealing to disaffected workers and moving us toward the classic definition of democracy by revolutionary patriot James Otis, "a government of all over all."

III. RACIAL JUSTICE: TIME FOR WHITES TO PUT *THEIR* SKIN IN THE GAME

In 1903, W.E.B. Du Bois wrote that "the problem of the 20th Century is the problem of the color line." Notwithstanding such upheavals as *Brown* v. *Board* and civil rights laws, he could have said it again at the turn of the next century. When a 13-year-old black youth in Alex Kotlowitz's *There Are No Children Here* was asked what he wanted to be as an adult, the child earnestly replied, "*If* I grow up, I want to be a bus driver." And the poisoning of Flint, Michigan, appears to be a clear case of environmental racism.

The issue of race and justice, however, may be shifting in the early twenty-first century. Of course there's been a black president, who alone hasn't erased racial differences but certainly makes it harder for white supremacists to pretend to superiority. Then there's been an extraordinary body of literature about recent black history and experience—from Ta-Nehisi Coates, Isabel Wilkerson, Michelle Alexander, Charles Blow, Bryan Stevenson—that illuminates why racial healing now requires that whites put *their* skin in the game.

This won't be easy. Nixon gave away the game when he said on tape, "You have to face the fact that the whole problem is really the blacks. The key is to devise a system that recognizes this while not appearing to." He pioneered the trick of persuading white working-class voters to associate government with minorities and then vote against their own interests out of fear of The Other. Getting white politicians to make white voters understand how they've been misled will fly in the face of both Hume's and Haidt's centuries-apart analyses that deep-seated intuition can override reason.

But there's been a new element in our unending racial conflict: technology recording lethal events—from Rodney King to Tamir Rice—that came as a shock to many whites. Videos and body cameras are now showing the world that far too many cops—not all or most, but many—are violent, racist, or lie to cover up an incident . . . or use insulting, racist language of the kind documented in my lawsuit over police misconduct in the mid-1990s. There is also a bipartisan push, including Rand Paul, Newt Gingrich, and Barack Obama, to embrace second chances rather than three-strikes-and-you're-out— i.e., to de-incarcerate prisons of low-level, nonviolent, often young black and Latino offenders because of cost and humanity. Bill Clinton has acknowledged that his 1994 crime bill "overshot the mark" in its punishment provisions. And #BlackLivesMatter—a descendant of the Sixties civil rights movement—has sprung up after recorded instances of violence against unarmed black citizens to demand responses from major politicians and police departments.

Today's "color line" is drawn by those who angrily deny they're racists yet always find ways to blame the victim. Keeping minorities down now are not the Bull O'Connors of Alabama but the Bill O'Reillys of Fox News who assert that there's no such thing as white privilege, who argue that blame goes to "the breakdown of the black family" while ignoring policies that lead to that breakdown. (Let's imagine how he'd react if someone said "Irish family" problems.) He goes on to accuse #BlackLivesMatter as being a "hate group" responsible for police deaths. (O'Reilly himself was criticized for repeatedly calling abortion doctor George Tiller a "murderer"—"Tiller the Baby Killer" was his choice of words—until a "pro-life" fanatic shot him to death in 1998). O'Reilly and followers invariably embrace a white victimology in which the majority of Americans are the ones discriminated against, as the sneaky use of the phrase "reverse racism" implies. They are aided by what Ta-Nehisi Coates calls the "Gospel of Giuliani," which harps on "black-on-black crime." Since nearly all crime is intra-racial, this is like "shooting a man and then shaming him for bleeding." As intended, this framework misleads people to focus on what's supposedly wrong with African Americans rather than on what's wrong with America.

O'Reilly and Giuliani have high-class help. Chief Justice John Roberts wrote in an affirmative action case that "the way to stop discrimination on the basis of race is to stop discriminating on the basis of race." That apparent truism conveniently presumes an America color-blind toward all and ignores that one race and not the other has endured slavery, legal segregation, and bird whistles. When I asked Bill Buckley in 1995 and his successor at National Review, Rich Lowry, in 2015 the same question—"Is there institutional racism?"—both said "no." Bernard Goldberg of Fox News assures us that "racism is on its last legs." All of which is true if you don't count employment, income, wealth, mortgages, housing segregation, voting, prison, jury selection, access to lawyers, health care, and life expectancy.

- The typical white family is 20 times wealthier than the typical black family, and the minority unemployment rate is twice that of the white rate.
- Fifty years after the creation of the Department of Housing and Urban Development, according to a *New York Times* editorial, "economic isolation is actually growing worse across the country, as more minority families find themselves trapped in high-poverty neighborhoods without decent housing, schools or jobs, and with few avenues of escape."
- A study at the University of Kansas showed that police stopped black drivers for minor violations, like expired license plate stickers and failure to signal, twice as often as white drivers—"investigative stops" that can lead to tragedies like Sandra Bland's arrest and death.
- The "justice" system incarcerated black youth six times longer than white youth for the same offenses, and black children are two and a half times as likely as white children to be held in custody before their trials.
- The *New York Times* editorial refers to them as "The Missing Black Men"—the 1.5 million who have disappeared from society due to incarceration and excess rates of death from violence, bad health, and crime. Like a real-life version of the TV show *The Leftovers*.
- Studies show that blacks are twice as likely to be preemptorily knocked off juries in capital cases.

Given this history, a Racial Justice agenda should pursue these goals:

Mandatory minimums should be avoided. Instead, give clemency to first-time offenders having/selling small amounts of drugs, and provide education, including access to college courses, for inmates.

Police training should clearly explain (a) why the "code of silence" covering up criminal police misconduct is a crime and (b) why street cops should first attempt de-escalation and mitigation techniques in potentially dangerous situations.

Stricter gun laws are essential since there have been more gun-related deaths in the United States in the past 50 years years than all American deaths in all our wars combined, more per *day* on average than all jihadist-related deaths in the last *decade*. Essential and popular reforms, given the 80 percent majorities for them, include universal background checks, bans on warlike assault rifles, and "smart guns" encouraged by federal and state procurement agencies purchasing weapons. The argument that stricter gun safety laws are futile since criminals ignore them is also an argument against laws about murder and speeding. Indeed, speaking of cars, while deaths from cars and guns were about 50,000 and 30,000 respectively a half century ago, this year gun deaths will exceed car deaths because of auto safety regulation. If "well-regulated" cars and roads have reduced injury and death by 80 percent since the key 1966 laws, why not "well-regulated" guns, to use the second amendment phrase? The way to stop a bad man with a gun is to make it harder for him to obtain one.

A new **Kerner Commission**—like the one established a half century ago—could expose institutional racism and publicize solutions.

It's unclear whether videoed shootings and #BlackLivesMatter is a moment or a movement. Already, there's pushback from some, including FBI director James Comey, that body cameras might discourage police from doing their jobs. But "their jobs" must include accountability for being the only public servants provided lethal force to use at their discretion without real-time supervision.

IV. CLIMATE: BECAUSE THERE'S NO PLANET B

A century ago, famed environmentalist John Muir implored us to "keep close to Nature's heart." If so, here's what our environmental stethoscope is diagnosing: Greenland melting away, predictions that the Persian Gulf will be uninhabitable by humans by 2100, food supplies threatened, coral reef ecosystems dying, New Delhi's 2015 heat wave melting pavements and killing thousands, the Pentagon counting climate change as a national security threat, half of wildlife species lost in just the past 40 years, arctic ice at record lows as oceans are expected to rise between 2.5 and 6.5 feet by the next century, 3.7 million Americans living within just feet of high tide as Miami residents wake up wondering why there's ocean water sloshing down their streets, and Superstorm Sandy—with hurricane winds accelerated by warmer oceans—slamming the New York region in 2012 with $100 billion in destruction, the worst natural disaster in my city's history.

While this global emergency is accepted by the UN and 190 countries, it's met by derision and yawns from Republicans. Despite global heat records nearly year after year, they retreat to a myriad of excuses to explain why they're not rushing to take action since, after all, "they're not scientists." Instead they take their cues from the 3 percent of scientists who are not sure and from "experts" like columnist George Will who reassure us there's no crisis. Or they rely on the dismissive conclusions of the Heartland Institute, a Chicago-based think tank that's bankrolled by the Koch brothers. One of the original thinkers behind the institute was the brains behind a 1998 editorial—"Five Lies About Tobacco"—that reassuringly declared that moderate cigarette smoking has "few, if any, adverse health effects."

Mitch McConnell, the Senate GOP leader from coal giant Kentucky, blithely disregards climate change and its dangers. "For everybody who thinks it's warming," McConnell says, "I can find somebody who thinks it isn't." No, he can't—not to mention how odd it is that the GOP hates the federal debt we're passing on to our grandchildren but not the soiled planet they're inheriting.

Faced with this growing threat, Republicans and Democrats finally joined together to pass far-reaching legislation. They agreed to a joint amicus brief to urge the Supreme Court to uphold the EPA's Carbon Reduction Plan, which has already shrunk carbon emissions by 17 percent and seeks to make it 40 percent by 2040. A broad, popular coalition also got Congress to finally enact sweeping proposals to (a) cut carbon emissions by a "carbon rebate" that taxes carbon but then rebates the funds back to rate payers; (b) end tax breaks for oil and gas producers; (c) tightly regulate shale oil; (d) install half a billion solar panels by 2020; and (e) generate enough from carbon-free renewable green energy to power every home in the country. This breakthrough occurred when Republicans finally admitted the scientific near unanimity and when President Obama got China and India, the two other big carbon emitters, to start a process of joint reductions of man-made gases. This breakthrough agreement was ratified at the Paris Climate Summit in December 2015.

Just kidding. The part about China and India is true. But what *did* happen was that the Senate's Environment Committee chairman, Jim Inhofe, brought a snowball to the Senate floor to disprove global warming. It was an embarrassing spectacle, but one where he had some company. In Florida, the terms "climate change" and "global warming" have been banned by the state's environmental protection department from e-mails and reports—talk about politically incorrect! A few months later, when the pope released an encyclical condemning global warming, Republicans, including Catholic candidates for the White House, like Jeb Bush, essentially told His Holiness to stick to his day job.

What can explain such public ignorance? Could it be that Republicans reliably fill their coffers from oil and gas companies, from which came both the party's last president and vice president? Their argument that climate-mitigating efforts will hurt the economy is frivolous—true, it will hurt coal mining jobs, which are costly both to workers and the world and which should attract carbon fee funds as adjustment assistance. But that's dwarfed by the estimate of Robert Pollin of 2.7 million new green jobs, American jobs that can't be exported. Or was it the talk radio zeitgeist that makes science-based policy politically incorrect? "I normally don't pat myself on the back," said Rush Limbaugh in 2010, "but today global warming has the concern of 30 percent of the American people [*sic*] and years ago it was over 50 percent. That's because somebody spoke up day in and day out and said, 'This is a hoax, this is BS.' That somebody was *me*."

Limbaugh, McConnell, and Inhofe may reflect and reinforce the Fringe Fourth but not most Americans: two-thirds of us—and 88 percent of Democrats—say they'd be more likely to vote for candidates who campaign on addressing climate change. A Democratic presidential candidate running on the proposals above would be doing something politically smart and environmentally essential. Washington's Democratic governor, Jay Inslee, explained the challenge: "We're the first generation to feel the impact of climate change and the last generation that can do something about it."

USA, USA, USA

Progress isn't a destination but a process that has enabled America to conquer fascism, communism, space, polio, and de jure racism, and dramatically reduce car deaths, seniors in poverty, and infant mortality. All this because of a people believing more in progress than stasis—Bernstein's "bright, infinite future"—rather than Buckley's devotion to thwarting progress.

Two journalists expressed best why change may be hard but never unimaginable. "No one knows enough to be a pessimist," wrote Norman Cousins, a mantra I often share with family and colleagues when facing stiff odds. Looking at the world through this lens in 2008 was Rick Hertzberg of the *New Yorker:* "A generation ago, few people anywhere imagined that they would witness the dissolution of Soviet totalitarianism or the inauguration of Nelson Mandela as President of a multiracial South African democracy, or the transformation of China into a fearsome engine of capitalist commerce. Nor did Americans of an age to remember Selma and Montgomery imagine that they would live to see an African-American elected President of the United States."

The country watched this same evolution from unimaginable to inevitable play out in June 2015 when a 21-year-old white supremacist who loved guns and the Confederate flag went on a murderous spree at the Emanuel AME Church in Charleston, South Carolina. It was a grotesque echo of lynchings and shootings in the South of past centuries. But this time proved different.

For seven days in June, the world witnessed the families of victims forgiving a hateful young man in an act of generosity that struck people of all faiths and races. A mixed-race president channeled their grace on race into a soaring eulogy. And South Carolina politicians who the day before would as likely have questioned the Rebel flag as the American flag did something nearly unthinkable. Governor Nikki Haley and Senators Lindsey Graham and Tim Scott said "no" to a hateful symbol of slavery and segregation.

The South Carolina Confederate flag was first raised over its Capitol Dome on April 11, 1961, both to commemorate the beginning of the Civil War, which started in that state exactly 100 years before, and also to defy the new Kennedy administration's pledge to expand civil rights.

On the morning of July 10, 2015, 8,000 people, all linked by memory or history in a chain of oppression, watched as a gray-uniformed honor guard of five black and two white state troopers solemnly approached the Confederate flag at 10:10. As it began to be lowered, a spontaneous chant began, from a few at first and then nearly all, that grew louder and louder until it was effectively heard by millions of Americans through the national media there. It was an old, familiar refrain that, on this day, seemed to have an altered meaning—not so much a pride in our past but Jefferson's "dreams for our future": *USA, USA, USA.*

Patriotism—famously called "the last refuge of scoundrels" by Dr. Johnson—has often been confused with mere jingoism, the super-patriotism of "love it or leave it" and "go back to your country." But since that includes everyone other than Native Americans, there is a more tolerant, humane, and welcoming patriotic tradition in America.

The author of the 1892 Pledge of Allegiance, Francis Bellamy, was a leading Christian socialist who also sought a more egalitarian version of America and came up with "one nation, indivisible, with liberty and justice for all." ("Under God" was added in the 1950s.) Senator Carl Schurz (D-NY) in 1899 updated the standard toast of "My country right or wrong" to "My country—if right, to be kept right, and if wrong, to be set right." In 1903 Katharine Lee Bates, poet and professor of English at Wellesley, wanted to both describe the beauty of the country and renounce imperialism and greed. So she wrote "America the Beautiful," ending with "and crown thy good with *brotherhood*, from sea to shining sea." In this tradition came Barack Obama, who at Selma in May 2015 saw our patriotism as rooted in "we the people," especially those who fought for and even died for the right to vote. "That's what it means to love America . . . That's what it means when we say America is exceptional."

Like the competing definitions of patriotism, history is a constant race between hope and hate, democracy and privilege, optimism and cynicism. On that bright summer day in South Carolina, hope, democracy, and optimism prevailed. The Rebel flag took only 30 seconds to travel its 30-foot descent. Then it was neatly folded and taken away to the South Carolina Confederate Relic Room and Military Museum by Leroy Smith, the African American director of the state's Department of Public Safety.

Throughout, the crowd gathered outside continued their chant: *USA, USA, USA.*

APPENDIX

THE BOOK OF GOP "TWISTIFICATIONS"

SO YOU'RE TIRED OF YELLING AT GOP DEBATE MODERATORS or want to shut down your Foxified uncle?

Since it's not easy for faithful conservatives to convincingly answer questions about climate science, gun violence, and mass deportation, among many others, they often resort to 14 rhetorical tricks to sway credulous audiences—tricks I spotted from my years debating Bill Buckley, Pat Buchanan, and now some of the smartest conservatives on my weekly nationally syndicated radio show.

To see these "twistifications" in action—Jefferson's word for saying things that are convincing falsehoods—I refer you to any speech by Ted Cruz, tweet by Erick W. Erickson, radio show of Rush Limbaugh, or cable hour of Hannity/O'Reilly. (Readers wired to say "both sides do it" in a game of false equivalence to sound thoughtful, as noted in text, sadly are just not paying careful attention.)

Underscoring all that follows is the projection of implacable confidence. In the words of the immortal British axiom, "perhaps wrong but never in doubt."

1. Black Swans. When data and common sense are to the contrary, just emphasize one outlier and ignore voluminous contrary examples. Pretend that the aberrational is typical. To argue that Obama really isn't smart, Sean Hannity several dozen times cites when Obama once mispronounced "corpsmen" as corps-men, not cores-men. To prove that Hillary is a confirmed liar, find that time Hillary thought she was under sniper fire landing at an airport in Bosnia. This method could "prove" that Ted Williams was an awful hitter by showing you video of his only three-strikeout game in a .341 lifetime career.

2. Lie, Brazenly. All candidates "lie" to some extent, though most instances are harmless puffery that nearly all voters discount. But then there are repeated untruths that poison debate. It's all GOP presidential contenders asserting that Obamacare is a job-killer when jobs increased every year since enactment. It's Donald Trump asserting that "83%" of white victims were killed by African Americans (it's in the teens) all while he invariably adds phrases that seduce the faithful—"frankly . . . in all candor . . . believe me . . . OK? . . . right?" It's the Bush 43 aide telling journalist Ron Suskind that "we create our own reality." The Niagara of repeated GOP lies reveals a new post-truth world that earnest fact-checkers apparently cannot deter and that democracy has not yet adjusted to.

3. Hyperbole. Mark Twain called them "stretchers"—when there's a germ of truth in a comparison that's far more dissimilar than alike. Hence all those times critics simply label any controversy as "Obama's Katrina, Obama's Watergate, Obama's Munich." Or use a loaded adjective—the best early example being Gingrich's 1996 memo urging GOP candidates to always use words like "traitor, pathetic, corrupt" to describe Democrats. The best current example: if there's any international problem that Obama doesn't think warrants risking World War III, just call him "feckless" or "weak." Q.E.D.!

4. Deny, Deny, Deny. In the play *Chicago,* a wife walks in on her husband *in flagrante* as he keeps calmly saying "what woman?" until the liaison hurriedly dresses and leaves . . . and the wife starts to question her memory. In real life, it's Jeb Bush insisting that his brother "kept us safe" because W spoke patriotically into a bullhorn *while standing on the rubble of 9/11.* So no matter how obviously Voter ID state laws suppress hundreds of thousands of eligible minority voters and U.S. deficits don't turn us into Greece, just assume that the Japanese axiom is correct: "After six months, no one remembers."

5. Politically Correct! This is a close relative to 1–4 above. What if your opinion is unpopular because it's both false and stupid—like Mexicans are rapists, the climate is cool. Why bother admitting error when you can ignore evidence by decrying censorship, which enables you to never have to respond to the core problem. While Republicans are the ones to denounce PC, notice how none of them ever criticize the NRA or laud 5 percent unemployment? Here the world champion was Ben Carson: You don't agree that Jews with guns could have deterred the Holocaust? You're just being *politically correct!*

6. Reverse Language and Speak Quickly. Lincoln said audiences should be careful with slick talkers who confuse "a horse chestnut and a chestnut horse." Today that kind of word play is skillfully deployed by conservatives who ignore "racism" but harp on "reverse racism." Chief Justice Roberts, as noted in the text, said in a key voting rights opinion that the way to end discrimination is to end discrimination, which smoothly equated centuries of oppression of African Americans with centuries of dominance by white Americans. Or if you have an antifeminist organization, call it the Susan B. Anthony group. If you can't convert 'em, confuse 'em.

7. Shameless Hypocrisy. There aren't many human search engines in Republican debate audiences. So when Karl Rove of the Bush Great Recession attacks Obama's economic record, Fox News runs segment after segment about Obama playing golf on vacation (Bush and Reagan took off 300 percent more time), Paul Ryan votes against paid family leave but insists he'd only become Speaker if he could be with his kids on weekends, these politicians don't flinch when their words completely contradict their actions.

8. *Ergo Hoc Propter Hoc.* There's a joke about an old man sweeping leaves in DuPont Circle to keep away the elephants. "But there are no elephants here," comes the reply. "See!" he says. If there's little evidence to support some prejudice, a surefire way to convince reactionary listeners is just to list problems and then say a version of "on Obama's watch!" If inequality, illegal immigrants, and an exploding Middle East precede the forty-fourth president, ignore those realities and blame him. Assume most people lack any sense of consequence.

9. Fear Itself. As noted in the text, our evolution includes a brain clump called the amygdala so we can flee or fight when in danger. This primitive impulse was essential to cavemen and is to modern cavemen like Ted Cruz who brilliantly confuse the patriotic with the apocalyptic ("the world's on fire!"). He theatrically asserts that an Iran nuclear deal that slows or stops a nuclear Iran—agreed to by nearly all the nations on earth—actually guarantees that Iran will somehow build and use nuclear weapons against Israel and America. Not to be outdone, Marco Rubio brags that he bought a gun to stop ISIS if they attack his family. This tactic works best when it instills not merely fear, according to the *New Yorker*'s David Remnick, but "perpetual fear."

10. Next Faux Scandal. "It's always something," said Gilda Radner's character Roseanne Roseannadanna. Should some controversy be resolved against your team—say, Barack has released his birth certificate and Michelle in fact did not spend $200 million traveling to the South Pacific—just quickly move on to some new allegation to feed the conservative perpetual grievance machine. If it's late year, the "War on Christmas"—when America's 7 percent nonbelievers supposedly bully the 80 percent Christian population—will do nicely. Or if you have no obvious policy difference with Obama on, say, Syria and ISIS, then attack his refusal to use the words "Islamic terrorism" which equates the substantive and the superficial. See: Benghazi-gate and Emailgate.

11. Change the Subject with a Rhetorical Question. Here's a nearly infallible misdirection: if you're cornered on having to defend something insane—such as a Gestapo-like registry of Muslims or helping billionaires spend more millions in secret campaign gifts, have this arrow in your quiver: "What about Obama's IRS that was governed by an enemies list? What about Mayor Richard Daley throwing the election to Kennedy with graveyard votes in 1960? What about Obamacare's website?" Because relevance and proportionality are not required, the opportunities are truly endless.

12. Snark Attack. The King of Snark is Erick Erickson, a very popular radio host/tweeter on the Right. To take one example: he ardently embraces a Second Amendment with the words "well-regulated." But since it's impossible to square that belief with the lethal statistics on gun-related deaths in the U.S., here were some of his 50 tweets the week in December when 14 were killed in San Bernardino, four at a Planned Parenthood Clinic, and Obama attended the Climate Summit in Paris: he displayed a *New York Times* editorial on gun control with supposed bullet holes . . . "I expect the President will demand we all put solar panels on our roofs to stop ISIS" . . . "Wonder where *Rolling Stone* will get glam shot of shooters for next cover." *Reductio ad absurdums* are fun to read.

13. Attack "The Media" or "Elites." Blame the messenger who won't answer back. If CBS reports that there are 50 times more gun deaths per capita in America than Germany, why would O'Reilly bother denying the truth when he can smirk and say, "Well, what do you expect from the *lame-stream media?*" Or dismiss Obama's call for more college education by saying, as Rick Santorum did in 2012, "What a snob!" VP and felon Spiro Agnew launched this *Them vs. Us* meme in the modern era. George Wallace and Sarah Palin are still its champs.

14. Hitler! Last, if nothing else is available, there's always a comparison to the Führer himself. Although Newt Gingrich nearly cornered this market, it still has some political utility when less-skilled speakers try it. At least you know for a certainty that the target will not deny it by asserting "I am not Hitler!" Works every time.

It's now almost impossible to pin down quick-witted GOP contenders deploying these tricks. But before throwing up your hands, eventually there will be a general election when a Democratic nominee will have a pulpit to expose that "truth has a liberal bias" and a media more willing to use their BS detectors. Eventually, the best hope for a remedy to these artful devices is Benjamin Franklin's observation that "when truth and error have fair play, the former is always an overmatch for the latter."

ACKNOWLEDGMENTS

NO BOOK IS AN ISLAND, AS JOHN DONNE DIDN'T WRITE but could have.

Bright, Infinite Future wouldn't exist without the patience, editing, love, and support of those who know me best—Deni, Jonah, Jenya, and Steve. Since my wife Deni is a thread through the book, not to mention my life, you simply need to know that when I asked her after finishing an earlier book, "Would you like a dedication?" she answered, "No, I want an apology."

This book also wouldn't exist without Elisabeth Dyssegaard's confidence in me and brilliant editing of me, including her belief in the truth that "the eraser's more important than the paper." I'm also enormously lucky to have the best writer/researcher/fact checker I've ever encountered, Douglas Grant, as well as my agents David Kuhn and Lauren Sharp for finding me the perfect harbor and encouraging me throughout.

I'm very grateful to Jonathan Alter, Wayne Barrett, David Bender, Joan Claybrook, Danny Goldberg, Ken Lerer, John Richard, Bob Shrum, John Siegel, Jerry Skurnick, and Michael Waldman for reading all or parts of the book to red flag mistakes of fact, content, or tone. However bad readers might think this book is, trust me, it would have been worse without them.

I also greatly appreciate the time taken by those 75 people who gave interviews to remind me of events over the decades covered by this book, which has been the equivalent of crowd-sourcing to this memoirist. So have been my 200 shows on air with my *Both Sides Now* colleagues, left and right, whom I've learned volumes from every week for five years. I hope in turn they and readers can learn from this volume.

—*Mark Green*

NOTES

INTRODUCTION: THE PROGRESSIVE-CONSERVATIVE CLASH

4 **"Liberal" and "progressive":** For useful discussion of these labels, see Paul Waldman, *Being Right Is Not Enough: What Progressives Must Learn from Conservative Success* (Hoboken, NJ: Wiley, 2006), 10–11.

6 **Liberalism:** For a useful exegesis of liberalism, see Paul Starr, *Freedom's Power: The History and Promise of Liberalism* (New York: Basic Books, 2008).

7 **"cap over the wall":** Clifton A. Leonhardt, "'Cap Over Wall' Joined Political Lexicon," *New York Times*, February 19, 1996, http://www.nytimes.com/1996/02/19/opinion/l-cap-over-wall-joined-political-lexicon-055735.html.

CHAPTER 1: THE SIXTIES

13 **number of births:** Todd Gitlin, *The Sixties: Years of Hope, Days of Rage* (New York: Bantam, 1993).

13 **More babies are born:** Neil A. Wynn, Historical Dictionary of the Roosevelt-Truman Years (New York: Scarecrow Press, 2008), 51.

14 **Armey once blustered:** Todd Gitlin, The Bulldozer and the Big Tent: Blind Republicans, Lame Democrats and the Recovery of American Ideals (New York: Wiley, 2007), 239.

14 **Hayden on reach of Sixties:** Tom Hayden, *The Long Sixties: From 1960 to Barack Obama* (New York: Paradigm, 2009), 5.

17 **creator of *Family Ties*:** Bruce Weber, "Gary David Goldberg, Television Writer and Creator of 'Family Ties,' Dies at 68," *New York Times*, June 24, 2013, http://www.nytimes.com/2013/06/25/arts/television/gary-david-goldberg-creator-of-family-ties-dies-at-68.html.

21 **"cussers and doubters":** "LBJ Raps Cussers, Doubters," *Daytona Beach Morning Journal*, June 28, 1967.

28 **"Why not? Get her on the phone":** Taylor Branch, "How Kennedy Won the Black Vote: A Call to Coretta Scott King Brought Groundswell of Support," *Los Angeles Times*, December 15, 1988, http://articles.latimes.com/1988-12-15/news/vw-329_1_coretta-king/2.

28 **"confronted primarily with a moral issue"**: Adam Clymer, "When Presidential Words Led to Swift Action," *New York Times,* June 8, 2013, http://www.nytimes.com/2013/06/09/us/remembering-two-seminal-kennedy-speeches.html?pagewanted=all.

29 **"two societies"**: John Herbers, "Panel On Civil Disorders Calls for Drastic Action to Avoid 2-Society Nation," *New York Times,* February 29, 1969, http://www.nytimes.com/learning/general/onthisday/big/0229.html.

29 **Ho Chi Minh at Versailles**: A. Scott Berg, *Wilson* (New York: G.P. Putman, 2013), 528.

29 **"within five years"**: Rick Perlstein, *Nixonland: The Rise of a President and the Fracturing of America* (New York: Scribner, 2008), 102.

31 **with thinly veiled threats:** Jean Fritz, "Remember the Lady," *New York Times,* June 7, 1987, http://www.nytimes.com/1987/06/07/books/remember-the-lady.html.

31 **Sanger was indicted**: Gloria Feldt, "Margaret Sanger's Obscentity," *New York Times,* October 15, 2006, http://www.nytimes.com/2006/10/15/opinion/nyregionopinions/15CIfeldt.html.

31 **"menace to society"**: "Margaret Sanger Is Dead at 82; Led Campaign for Birth Control," *New York Times,* September 7, 1966.

31 **excessive expectations are attached**: Cathy Booth Thomas, "The Pill That Unleashed Sex," *Time,* March 31, 2003, http://content.time.com/time/specials/packages/article/0,28804,1977881_1977891,00.html.

31 **an end to poverty:** Elaine Tyler May, "Promises the Pill Could Never Keep," *New York Times,* April 24, 2010.

31 **opposition is unlike anything**: Marlene LeGates, *In Their Time: A History of Feminism in Western Society* (New York: Routledge, 2001).

32 **One student interested in exploring**: Fred M. Hechinger, "Women 'Educated' Out of Careers," *New York Times,* March 6, 1963.

32 **"Some people think"**: "Angry Battler for Her Sex," *Life,* November 1, 1963, https://books.google.com/books?id=VlIEAAAAMBAJ.

32 **"weekend of lip service"**: Betty Friedan, "Demanding Full Equality," *Time,* March 31, 2003, http://content.time.com/time/specials/packages/article/0,28804,1977881_1977891_1978447,00.html.

32 **"In my growing up years"**: Gloria Steinem, interview by the author, December 2, 2014.

32 **"It was the first time"**: Ibid.

33 **"We assumed that it was such simple justice"**: Ibid.

33 **It started with fire ants:** Elizabeth Kolbert, "Human Nature," *New Yorker,* May 28, 2007, http://www.newyorker.com/magazine/2007/05/28/human-nature.

34 **"The Desolate Year"**: "Rachel Carson Dies of Cancer; 'Silent Spring' Author Was 56," *New York Times,* April 15, 1964, https://www.nytimes.com/books/97/10/05/reviews/carson-obit.html.

34 **sees the weather conspire:** Jane E. Brody, "Millions Plagued by Air Irritants," *New York Times,* November 26, 1966, http://timesmachine.nytimes.com/timesmachine/1966/11/26/issue.html.

34 **Cuyahoga River in Ohio catches fire:** Michael Scott, "Cuyahoga River Fire 40 Years Ago Ignited an Ongoing Cleanup Campaign," *Cleveland Plain Dealer,* June 22, 2009, http://www.cleveland.com/science/index.ssf/2009/06/cuyahoga_river_fire_40_years_a.html.

34 **first-ever Earth Day:** Gladwin Hill, "Activity Ranges from Oratory to Leg-islation," *New York Times,* April 23, 1970, http://timesmachine.nytimes.com/timesmachine/1970/04/23/issue.html.

34 **"reason Earth Day worked":** Keith Schneider, "Gaylord A. Nelson, Founder of Earth Day, Is Dead at 89," *New York Times,* July 4, 2005, http://www.ny times.com/2005/07/04/politics/gaylord-a-nelson-founder-of-earth-day-is -dead-at-89.html.

35 **"Just keep me out of trouble":** Elizabeth Drew, "Nostalgia for Nixon?" *Washington Post,* June 9, 2007, http://www.washingtonpost.com/wp-dyn/content/article/2007/06/08/AR2007060802260.html.

35 **no other mass movement:** John McCormick, *Reclaiming Paradise: The Global Environmental Movement* (Bloomington: Indiana University Press, 1989), vii.

35 **sewed together his safety net:** A.W. Gaffney, "The Hundred Years' War for Healthcare Reform," *In These Times,* March 25, 2010, http://inthesetimes .com/article/15098/the_hundred_years_war_for_healthcare_reform.

36 **AMA's best friends in Congress:** Julian Zelinzer, *The Fierce Urgency of Now: Lyndon Johnson, Congress and the Battle for the Great Society* (New York: Penguin Press, 2015), 191.

36 **advertise the healthful effect:** Catherine Gourley, *Media Wizards: A Behind-the-Scenes Look at Media Manipulations* (New York: 21st Century, 1999), 51.

36 **biggest drop in smoking in 20 years:** Mike Strobbe, "Historic Smoking Report Marks 50th Anniversary," *USA Today,* January 5, 2014, http://www.usatoday.com/story/money/business/2014/01/05/historic-smoking-re port-marks-50th-anniversary/4318233/.

37 **smoking dips 3.5 percent:** Thomas R. Marshall, "The 1964 Surgeon General's Report and Americans' Beliefs about Smoking," *Journal of the History of Medicine and Allied Sciences* 2, no. 70 (2015): 250–278, http://jhmas.oxford journals.org/content/70/2/250.short?rss=1.

37 **lives have been saved:** Alexandra Sifferlin, "Thank You, Surgeon General: Tobacco Control Has Saved 8 Million Lives," *Time,* January 7, 2014, http://healthland.time.com/2014/01/07/thank-you-surgeon-general-tobacco-con trol-has-saved-8-million-lives/.

37 **"lights and rights":** "The Inheritor," *Time,* January 7, 1967, http://content .time.com/time/subscriber/article/0,33009,843150,00.html.

37 **"it relaxes you, makes you forget":** Gene Johnson, "As Pot Goes Proper, A History of Weed," Associated Press, December 6, 2012, http://www.nydaily news.com/news/national/pot-proper-history-weed-article-1.1214613.

38 **Senate hearings publicize its horrors:** Perlstein, *Nixonland,* 73.

38 **"sell slavery to the young":** "State of the Union Address," January 17, 1968, Washington D.C., Speeches, Lyndon Johnson Presidential Library.

38 **marijuana arrests jump tenfold:** Richard C. Schroeder, *The Politics of Drugs: An American Dilemma* (New York: Congressional Quarterly Press, 1980), 16.

38 **remained on the books:** *David E. Newton, Marijuana: A Reference Handbook* (Denver, CO: ABC-CLIO, 2013), 66.

38 **95 percent of addicts in Vietnam:** Alix Spiegel, "What Vietnam Taught Us About Breaking Bad Habits," NPR, January 2, 2012, http://www.npr .org/sections/health-shots/2012/01/02/144431794/what-vietnam-taught-us -about-breaking-bad-habits.

38 **"We understood that drugs":** Dan Baum, *Smoke and Mirrors: The War on Drugs and the Politics of Failure* (Boston: Back Bay Books, 1997).

38 **"Pot Peace Prosperity—Vote McGovern"**: Perlstein, *Nixonland,* 713.

38 **"The key is to devise a system"**: "Haldeman Diary Shows Nixon Was Wary of Blacks and Jews," *New York Times,* May 18, 1994, http://www.nytimes.com/1994/05/18/us/haldeman-diary-shows-nixon-was-wary-of-blacks-and-jews.html.

38 **reduced in 28 states**: George Galster, *Reality and Research: Social Science and U.S. Urban Policy Since 1960* (Lanham, MD: Urban Institute Press, 1996), 158.

38 *High Times* **starts appearing**: Seth Stevenson, "Gnarly Birthday, High Times!" *Slate,* October 15, 2014, http://www.slate.com/articles/arts/culture box/2014/10/the_40th_anniversary_of_high_times_a_pot_magazine_in _the_era_of_legal_marijuana.html.

38 **According to Governor David Paterson**: Madison Gray, "A Brief History of New York's Rockefeller Drug Laws," *Time,* April 2, 2009, http://content.time.com/time/nation/article/0,8599,1888864,00.html.

39 **gays in America**: Mark Jenkins, "At Stonewall and in Salt Lake, Gays at the Barricades," NPR, June 18, 2010, http://www.npr.org/templates/story/story.php?storyId=127839207.

39 **Quincy Troupe wrote in the late 1940s**: Stuart Timmons, Bo Young, and Will Roscoe, *The Trouble with Harry Hay: Founder of the Modern Gay Movement* (New York: White Crane Books, 2012), xiv.

39 **Things begin to change**: Dudley Clendinen, "Harry Hay, 90, Early Proponent of Gay Rights, Is Dead," *New York Times,* October 25, 2002, http://www.nytimes.com/2002/10/25/obituaries/25HAY.html.

39 **"The average homosexual, if there be such"**: Dylan Stableford, "'The Homosexuals': Mike Wallace's Controversial 1967 CBS Report Gets Second Viewing Online," *Yahoo News,* April 10, 2012, http://news.yahoo.com/blogs/cutline/homosexuals-mike-wallace-controversial-1967-cbs-report-gets-170733217.html.

40 **"And it was fantastic"**: American Experience: Stonewall Uprising, directed by Kate Davis and David Heilbroner (2010), film.

40 **In a seminal *Village Voice* piece**: Lucian Truscott IV, "Gay Power Comes to Sheridan Square," *Village Voice,* July 3, 1969, http://www.pbs.org/wgbh/americanexperience/features/primary-resources/stonewall-village-voice/.

CHAPTER 2: NADER

44 **"I took it seriously"**: Justin Martin, *Nader: Spoiler, Crusader, Icon* (New York: Perseus, 2002), 5.

45 **"From day one"**: Ralph Nader, interview by the author, March 12, 2015.

48 **"He was unflappable"**: Martin, *Nader,* 47.

48 **puts under oath James Roche**: Stan Luger, *Corporate Power, American Democracy and the Automobile Industry* (New York: Cambridge, 1999), 70.

49 **"in fairness to Ralph"**: Paul Ingrassia, "How the Corvair's Rise and Fall Changed America Forever," Reuters, May 9, 2002, http://blogs.reuters.com/great-debate/2012/05/09/how-the-corvairs-rise-and-fall-changed-america-forever/.

49 **"scale of priorities"**: Nancy Bowem, *Ralph Nader: Man with a Mission* (Brookfield, CT: Twenty First Century Books, 2002), 45.

50 **"You might call it my obsession"**: Nader, interview with author, March 12, 2015.

51 **"only did 20 percent"**: Robert F. Buckhorn, *Nader: The People's Lawyer* (Upper Saddle River, NJ: Prentice Hall, 1972), 97.

51 **Nader Raiders like *McClure's*:** based on Doris Kearns Goodwin, *The Bully Pulpit: Teddy Roosevelt, William Howard Taft, and the Golden Age of Journalism* (New York: Simon and Schuster, 2013), xii.

52 **"crime in the suites":** Ralph Nader, "White Collar Crime: America's Crime without Criminals," *New York Times,* May 19, 1985, http://www.nytimes.com/1985/05/19/business/white-collar-fraud-america-s-crime-without-criminals.html.

54 **extremists "like Ralph Nader":** Jacob S. Hacker and Paul Pierson, *Winner-Take-All Politics: How Washington Made the Rich Richer and Turned Its Back on the Middle Class* (New York: Simon & Schuster, 2010), 117.

56 **Nader and Green articles:** Nader, "A Citizens Guide to the Consumer Economy," *New York Review of Books,* September 2, 1971; Green and Moore, "Winter's Discontent: Market Failure and Consumer Welfare," *Yale Law Journal,* April, 1973, 903.

62 **"If there were one thing":** James Lardner, "Bad News Bearers," *Washington Post,* March 22, 1982, http://www.washingtonpost.com/archive/lifestyle/1982/03/22/bad-news-bearers/81577ef7-a5ce-4792-b9e8-3ff86de20744/.

63 **shocked and thrilled:** Eileen Shanahan, "Nader Asserts Monopolies Mulct the Public of Billions, Report Charges Political Power Aids Giants in Blocking Antitrust Suits," *New York Times,* June 6, 1971, A1.

63 **There is a big reaction:** *The Closed Enterprise System: Ralph Nader's Study Group Report on Antitrust Enforcement* (New York: Grossman Publishers, 1972).

68 **"His wild mane":** Hays Gorey, *Nader and the Everyman* (New York: Putman, 1975), 88.

69 **"The gentlemen who run":** Robert F. Buckhorn, *Nader: the People's Lawyer* (New York: Prentice Hall, 1972), 127.

70 **While reviews are positive:** John Kenneth Galbraith, "Like Jackals Feeding on the Body Politic," *New York Times,* May 18, 1975.

70 **asked about Nader:** Buckhorn, *Nader,* 137.

70 **hear a president:** "Remarks at the 100th Anniversary of the Los Angeles County Bar Association," May 4, 1978, Los Angeles, California, Jimmy Carter papers.

70 **"minimum fee schedules":** *Golfarb* v. *Virginia State Bar.* U.S. Supreme Court, 16 June 1975.

71 **"Nader's Biggest Raid":** "Nader's Biggest Raid," *Time,* July 31, 1972, http://content.time.com/time/subscriber/article/0,33009,877927,00.html.

73 **"believe in a division of labor":** Roberta Ann Johnson, *The Struggle against Corruption: A Comparative Study* (New York: Palgrave Macmillan, 2004), 26.

73 **"It may still be one":** Hays Gorey, *Nader and the Power of the Everyman* (New York: Grosset & Dunlap, 1985), 253.

73 **"good deal of meat":** "Nader's Criticism 'Valid'—Mansfield," *Sarasota Herald-Tribune,* October 5, 1972.

73 **Bollier on *Who Runs Congress?*:** David Bollier, *Citizen Action and Other Big Ideas: A History of Ralph Nader and the Modern Consumer Movement* (Washington, D.C.: Center for the Study of Responsive Law, 1989), 25.

75 ***Wall Street Journal* runs a front-page piece:** Robert Merry and Albert Hunt, "Business Lobby Gains More Power as It Rides Antigovernment Tide," *Wall Street Journal,* May 17, 1978.

78   **"both sides of my mouth"**: Cheryl Lavin, "Nader: The Dragon Slayer Still Breathing Fire," *Chicago Tribune*, July 13, 1986, http://articles.chicagotribune.com/1986-07-13/features/8602190959_1_ralph-nader-prepaid-ticket-candy-bar/2.

79   **"come at them with a national outcry"**: Marc Fisher, "Ralph Nader's Paradise Lost," *Washington Post*, July 23, 1989, https://www.washingtonpost.com/archive/lifestyle/magazine/1989/07/23/ralph-naders-paradise-lost/7b384962-f600-455b-b3c1-fd4401407e6d/.

79   **from companies to consumers**: Ralph Nader, "California Voters Acted to Save $100 Billion," *Huffington Post*, November 15, 2013, http://www.huffingtonpost.com/ralph-nader/california-prop-103_b_4282587.html.

80   **well-known CNN and *LA Times* commentator**: Jon Healey, "Sen. Bernie Sanders Positions Self to Be Next Ralph Nader," *Los Angeles Times*, September 15, 2014, http://www.latimes.com/opinion/opinion-la/la-ol-bernie-sanders-president-independent-hillary-clinton-ralph-nader-20140915-story.html.

80   **Schneider on Nader:** Marlene Cimons, "Nader's Raiders 20 Years Later," *Los Angeles Times*, October 27, 1989, http://articles.latimes.com/1989-10-27/news/vw-778_1_nader-s-raiders/2.

80   **"thought he had his day"**: Matthew Purdy, "Congress' Loss Is Nader's Gain," *Philadelphia Inquirer*, February 10, 1989, http://articles.philly.com/1989-02-10/news/26152231_1_ralph-nader-nader-s-raiders-meat-and-poultry-safety.

80   **"four-person strikes forces"**: Nader, interview by the author, March 12, 2015.

80   **"My problem is that I'm bolder"**: Ibid.

81   **"invasion from Mars"**: Martin, *Nader*, 226.

81   **New Hampshire primary ballot:** Ibid., 229.

81   **21 state ballots:** 1996 Official Presidential General Election Results, http://www.fec.gov/96fed/geresult.htm.

82   **raises an unexpected $8 million:** Martin, *Nader*, 260.

82   **"joy and justice!"**: "Nader Rally Refrain: If Bush Equals Gore, Why Not?" *New York Times*, October 15, 2000, http://www.nytimes.com/2000/10/15/politics/15NADE.html.

82   **"borders on the wicked"**: *An Unreasonable Man*, directed by Henriette Mantel (2007, Genius Entertainment), film.

82   **"He cost us the election"**: James Dao, "Angry Democrats, Fearing Nader Cost Them Presidential Race, Threaten to Retaliate," *New York Times*, November 9, 2000, http://www.nytimes.com/2000/11/09/us/2000-elections-green-party-angry-democrats-fearing-nader-cost-them-presidential.html.

87   **"you're more driven"**: Nader, interview by the author, March 12, 2015.

90   **"nervous if things go wrong"**: Justin Martin, Nader: Spoiler, Crusader, Icon (New York: Perseus, 2002), 155.

91   **"a man without parallel"**: Gorey, *Nader and the Power of the Everyman*, 153.

91   **"Ralph is living proof"**: Michael Kinsley, "Saint Ralph," *Washington Post*, November 21, 1985, http://www.washingtonpost.com/archive/politics/1985/11/21/saint-ralph/019823dd-a4c7-4e57-897f-a96bfc0d570a/.

92   **"talent and technique"**: Dotson Rader, "Inside the Actors Studio Host James Lipton on His Favorite Interview and Pimping in Paris," *Parade*, May 28, 2013, http://parade.com/17599/dotsonrader/inside-the-actors-studio-host-james-lipton-on-his-favorite-interview-and-pimping-in-paris/.

CHAPTER 3: THE ADVOCATE

95   **President Clinton on public advocate:** William J. Clinton, "Remarks on Kick Butts Day in Brooklyn, New York," April 15, 1997. Outline by Gerhard Peters and John T. Woolley, The American Presidency Project, http://www.presidency.ucsb.edu/ws/?pid=53996.

98   **the term "corpocracy":** Eric Gelman, "Corporate Bloat," *Businessweek,* September 9, 1985, 92F.

98   *Fortune* **lauds:** Michael Kinsley, "A New Kind of Naderism," *Fortune,* September 16, 1985, 193.

100   **three blocks north:** Dennis Hevesi, "New Consumer Chief Faults R.J. Reynolds on Its 'Camel' Ads," *New York Times,* February 21, 1990.

101   **traces back to 1831:** Mark Green and Laurel Eisner, "The Public Advocate for New York City: An Analysis of the Country's Only Elected Ombudsman," *New York Law School Law Review* vol. 42 (1998).

109   **"They would view":** Sydney Schanberg, "Food (Still) Costs More in Poor Districts," *Newsday,* May 29, 1991.

110   **under the leadership:** Jonathan P. Hicks, "Mayor Gives Final Approval for East Harlem Supermarket," *New York Times,* August 2, 1995, http://www.nytimes.com/1995/08/02/nyregion/mayor-gives-final-approval-for-east-harlem-supermarket.html.

112   **take the lead:** Trish Hall, "How Fat? Burger King to Post Answers," *New York Times,* August 8, 1991, http://www.nytimes.com/1991/08/08/nyregion/how-fat-burger-king-to-post-answers.html.

112   **"Kosher coalition":** Leonard Sloane, "Fighting Price Gouging on Passover Foods," *New York Times,* April 11, 1992, http://www.nytimes.com/1992/04/11/news/fighting-price-gouging-on-passover-foods.html.

116   **"de-fund the Public Advocate's office":** Peter Vallone, *My Life in New York Politics: From Hell Gate to City Hall* (New York: Chaucer Press, 2005), 211.

117   **Giuliani's charter commission:** Dan Barry, "A Mayor's Like-Minded Charter Panel," *New York Times,* June 17, 1999.

117   **"I can't imagine":** Barry, "A Mayor's Like-Minded Charter Panel."

118   **"Never be a bully":** Rudy Giuliani, *Leadership* (New York: Miramax, 2005), 267.

118   **"loyalty tests":** Michael Powell and Russ Buettner, "In Matters Big and Small, Crossing Giuliani Had Price," *New York Times,* January 22, 2008.

119   **"mayoral brutality":** Jim Dwyer, "Red Light Row Leaves Rudy Seeing Red," *New York Daily News,* September 14, 1997.

123   **backs us up:** "Laxity on Police Abuses," *New York Times,* September 18, 1999.

123   **spotted on the red carpet:** Kevin Flynn, "Safir Faces Criticism After Oscar Trip," *New York Times,* March 23, 1999.

124   **"wasn't an altar boy":** Eric Lipton, "Giuliani Cites Criminal Past of Slain Man," *New York Times,* March 20, 2001.

124   **sue the mayor:** Thomas J. Lueck, "Mayor May Face Inquiry in Dorismond Case," *New York Times,* November 22, 2000.

126   **It's all run:** Selwyn Raab, "He Runs Trash Hauling with Silence and Pastry," *New York Times,* February 20, 1993, http://www.nytimes.com/1993/02/20/nyregion/he-runs-trash-hauling-with-silence-and-pastry.html.

127   **Mayor "Eliot Ness":** Selwyn Raab, "Giuliani Has a Plan to Battle Mafia Grip on Trash Hauling," *New York Times,* November 30, 1995, http://www.nytimes

.com/1996/06/19/nyregion/trash-haulers-face-new-list-of-charges-about
-fees.html.

CHAPTER 4: WHAT IT'S LIKE—
NEW YORK POLITICS

131 **"they lie more":** Evan Thomas, *Robert Kennedy: His Life* (New York: Simon & Schuster, 2000), 297.

132 **"restore order and respect":** Richard Nixon, "Address Accepting the Presidential Nomination at the Republican National Convention," speech, August 8, 1968, Miami Beach, Florida. Online by Gerhard Peters and John T. Woolley, The American Presidency Project, http://www.presidency.ucsb.edu/ws/?pid=25968.

133 **The opponent is Lee Alexander:** Lawrence Van Gelder, "Lee Alexander, 69, Mayor Whose Career Ended in Jail," *New York Times,* December 27, 1996, http://www.nytimes.com/1996/12/27/nyregion/lee-alexander-69-mayor-whose-career-ended-in-jail.html.

134 **spokesman for Attica inmates:** Robert McG. Thomas Jr., "Herbert Blyden, 61, Speaker for Inmates in Attica Revolt," *New York Times,* September 24, 1997, http://www.nytimes.com/1997/09/24/nyregion/herbert-blyden-61-speaker-for-inmates-in-attica-revolt.html.

134 **Ramsey's idea of limiting:** "Al and Ramsey and Abe; But Bess Is No One's Woman," *New York,* May 27, 1974, 13.

134 **contribute a total:** Steven R. Weisman, "Clark Says He's Raised $500,000 in Spite of Limit," *New York Times,* October 19, 1974.

134 **Javits has accepted $15,000:** Michael Kramer, "Will Javits Beat Javits?" *New York,* October 28, 1974, 42.

136 **running guns for the IRA:** Jack Holland, "Paul O'Dwyer Always Fought the Good Fight," *Irish Echo,* February 16, 2011, http://irishecho.com/2011/02/a-view-north-paul-odwyer-always-fought-the-good-fight-2/.

136 **writes a story:** Frank Lynn, "Moynihan Backing Off Senate Bid; Crangle 'Out on Limb,'" *New York Times,* June 4, 1976.

136 **On June 11:** Maurice Carroll, "Moynihan Enters U.S. Senate Race," *New York Times,* June 11, 1976.

138 **raises a recent** Times **series:** Seymour Hersh, "The Contrasting Lives of Sidney R. Korshak," *New York Times,* June 27, 1976.

139 **unforced error:** "Mrs. Abzug Won't Back Moynihan If He Wins Primary," *New York Times,* August 29, 1976, 43.

141 **Lowenstein shot:** Rudy Max, "A Tale of Two Greens," *Washington Post,* April 13, 1980.

143 **won't be a candidate:** Frank Lynn, "Ferraro Bars Senate Race in '86," *New York Times,* December 12, 1985, http://www.nytimes.com/1985/12/12/nyregion/ferraro-bars-senate-race-in-86.html.

144 **exposed-pipes office:** Bennett Roth, "Dyson-Green Contest a Contrast in Political Funding," *Sunday Times Union,* August 31, 1986.

144 **"listen to the organ grinder":** David Egner, "Green, Dyson, Senate Hopefuls, Clash in Debate," *Schenectady Gazette,* August 12, 1986, 30.

146 **"millions of reasons":** Jennifer Peltz, "Hank Morris, Political Consultant, Sentenced For Pension Fund Scheme," *Huffington Post,* February 17, 2011, http://www.huffingtonpost.com/2011/02/17/hank-morris-political-con_n_824769.html.

147 **"one of most vituperative political debates":** Frank Lynn, "Green and Dyson Exchange Accusions," *New York Times,* August 20, 1986.

147 **Dyson's financial portfolio:** Fred Dicker, "Dyson: Gov Inspired My Sale of South Africa Stock," *New York Post,* September 3, 1986.

148 **big front-page picture:** Frank Lynn, "Mark Green Beats Dyson in Primary," *New York Times,* September 10, 1986.

148 **back to earth:** "Mayor Commends D'Amato as Being 'Superb Senator,'" *New York Times,* September 11, 1986, 1.

149 **"anything short of killing Javits":** "Around City Hall," *New Yorker,* September 22, 1980, 132.

149 **cocaine derivative in Washington Heights:** "Crack Operation Lawmakers Learn the Drug World's Ways," *Philadelphia Inquirer,* July 11, 1986, http://articles.philly.com/1986-07-11/news/26099097_1_federal-drug-agent-drug-users-dealer.

149 **enforces an illegal scheme:** Murray Waas, "The Soul of a New Machine Politician," *New Republic,* March 10, 1986, http://www.newrepublic.com/article/politics/105039/the-soul-new-machine-politician.

149 **"return your phone calls":** Phillip M. Stern, *Still the Best Congress Money Can Buy* (New York: Regnery Gateway, 1992), 90.

150 **$13 million war chest:** Howard Kurtz, "New York City Support Wanes for Beleaguered Senator D'Amato," *Washington Post,* September 27, 1989.

151 **"there was a nonaggression pact":** Michael Oreskes, "The Election: New Voting Patterns and a Look at '88," *New York Times,* November 6, 1986.

152 **"obviously distraught":** "Ex-Opponent Asks Senate Ethics Panel for D'Amato Inquiry," *New York Times,* July 18, 1989, http://www.nytimes.com/1989/07/18/us/ex-opponent-asks-senate-ethics-panel-for-d-amato-inquiry.html

152 **Ethics Committee releases its ten-page report:** Helen Dewar, "Ethics Panel Criticizes D'Amato for Letting Brother Use Office," *Washington Post,* August 3, 1991, http://www.washingtonpost.com/archive/politics/1991/08/03/ethics-panel-criticizes-damato-for-letting-brother-use-office/e5474cef-ee95-4f42-ab91-1f82cf07402a.

152 **"completely exonerated":** Lindsey Gruson, "Senate Panel Finds No Evidence to Warrant Action on D'Amato," *New York Times,* August 3, 1991, A1.

153 **In a reversal:** Elissa Gootman, "Old Rivals in Court, with Nary a Cross Word," *New York Times,* June 17, 2003.

154 **who chooses words carefully:** Celestine Bohlen, "Cuomo Calls for 'New Era of Harmony,'" *New York Times,* September 5, 1989, http://www.nytimes.com/1989/09/05/nyregion/cuomo-calls-for-new-era-of-harmony.html.

155 **"Mayors come and go":** Francis X. Clines, "Dinkins Ends the Campaign on Note of Gratitude," *New York Times,* November 3, 1993, http://www.nytimes.com/1993/11/03/nyregion/the-1993-elections-the-incumbent-dinkins-ends-the-campaign-on-note-of-gratitude.html.

156 **Fritz Schwartz on Green:** Joe Conason, "Mark Green's Poll Inspiring Campaign for Public Advocate," *New York Observer,* March 22, 1993, 1.

157 **"the voluble Mr. Green":** "Mark Green for Public Advocate," *New York Times,* October 26, 1993.

158 **Michael Tomasky writes:** Michael Tomasky, "Campaign Wishes," *New York,* April 15, 1996, 30.

160 **Dole annoys Chuck:** Emily Heil, "Chuck Schumer and That 'Most Dangerous Place in Washington' Joke," *Washington Post,* April 1, 2015, https://www

.washingtonpost.com/news/reliable-source/wp/2015/04/01/chuck-schumer
-and-that-most-dangerous-place-joke/.

161   **"fumes of fame":** Marc Humbert, "Ferraro Loses New York Senate Bid,"
Washington Post, September 16, 1998, http://www.washingtonpost.com/wp
-srv/politics/campaigns/keyraces98/stories/apny091698.htm.

161   **political weirdness:** James Bennet, "Clinton Moves from School to Fund-
raiser," *New York Times,* April 16, 1997, http://www.nytimes.com/1997/04/16
/nyregion/in-brooklyn-clinton-moves-from-school-to-fund-raiser.html.

162   **"era of D'Amato is over":** Blaine Harden, "New York's Veteran 'Senator
Pothole' Gets Run Over by Schumer," *Washington Post,* November 4, 1998,
https://www.washingtonpost.com/wp-srv/politics/campaigns/keyraces98
/stories/ny110498.htm.

167   ***Buckley* v. *Valeo:*** Amy Handlin, *Dirty Deals?: An Encyclopedia of Lobbying,
Political Influence, and Corruption* (New York: ABC-CLIO, 2014), 189.

169   **"wide reputation":** Wayne Barrett, "The Early Line," *Village Voice,* April 1,
2000, http://www.villagevoice.com/news/the-early-line-6417841.

170   **what a coincidence:** Leslie Maitland, "D'Amato Cited in Another Brief
Filed by Green," *New York Times,* December 14, 1989, http://www.nytimes
.com/1989/12/14/nyregion/d-amato-cited-in-another-brief-filed-by-green
.html.

171   **tells the *New Yorker:*** Elizabeth Kolbert, "How to Succeed," *New Yorker,* December 20, 1999, 40.

171   **"How does a New York politician":** Bob Herbert, "Trouble for Ferrer," *New
York Times,* May 14, 2001, http://www.nytimes.com/2001/05/14/opinion/in
-america-trouble-for-ferrer.html.

171   **wedding vows:** Greg Gittrich and Corky Siemaszko, "Rev. Al Sports New
'Do': Sleeker Sharpton, Wife Renew '80 Marital Vows," New York Daily News,
August 27, 2001

172   **"4 Democrats Spar Cordially":** Adam Nagourney, "4 Democrats Spar Cordially In Mayor Race," *New York Times,* May 7, 2001, http://www.nytimes
.com/2001/05/07/nyregion/4-democrats-spar-cordially-in-mayor-race.html.

172   **Sharpton then disingenuously:** Adam Nagourney, "Ferrer Refuses Endorsement Linked to Race," *New York Times,* May 10, 2001, http://www.nytimes
.com/2001/05/10/nyregion/ferrer-refuses-endorsement-linked-to-race.html.

173   **1199 Hospital Workers:** Juan Gonzalez, "How 1199 Cast Vote for Ferrer,"
New York Daily News, September 6, 2001, http://www.nydailynews.com
/archives/news/1199-cast-vote-ferrer-article-1.933594.

173   **wine-splashed dinner:** Steven Greenhouse, "Labor Divided House in
Mayoral Fight," *New York Times,* September 4, 2001, http://www.nytimes
.com/2001/09/04/nyregion/labor-a-divided-house-in-mayoral-race-each
-democrat-has-a-union-s-support.html.

174   **Atta is having dinner:** "The Night Before Terror," *Portland Press Herald,* October 5, 2001, http://www.pressherald.com/2011/08/25/september-11-port
land-maine-chronology-fbi-mohamed-atta-abdulaziz-alomari.

180   **phone interview:** Michael Cooper and Adam Nagourney, "Green Says He'd
Top Giuliani in a Crisis," *New York Times,* October 2, 2001, http://www.ny
times.com/2001/10/02/nyregion/green-says-he-d-top-giuliani-in-a-crisis
.html.

181   **"moral prestige":** James Traub, "No-Fun City," *New York Times Magazine,*
November 4, 2001, http://www.nytimes.com/2001/11/04/magazine/no-fun
-city.html?pagewanted=all.

181 **"this and that":** Robert Hardt Jr., "Mario Goes for Green," *New York Post,* October 9, 2001, http://nypost.com/2001/10/09/mario-goes-for-green/.

181 **"a mother hiccups":** Jonathan P. Hicks and Randal C. Archibald, "Green Presses Attack Tactics, Accusing Rival of Inconstancy," *New York Times,* October 7, 2001, http://www.nytimes.com/2001/10/07/nyregion/green-presses -attack-tactics-accusing-rival-of-inconstancy.html.

182 **tough, negative ad:** Robert Hardt Jr., "Dems' Runoff Getting 'Ugly'—With One Day to Go, Charges of Racism Fly Amid Dueling Ads," *New York Post,* October 10, 2001, http://nypost.com/2001/10/10/dems-runoff-getting-ugly -with-one-day-to-go-charges-of-racism-fly-amid-dueling-ads/.

182 **"They lynch you":** Michael Cooper and Randal C. Archibald, "Runoff Campaign Turns Strange as Candidates Trade Charges," *New York Times,* October 10, 2001, http://www.nytimes.com/2001/10/16/nyregion/political-memo-he ated-race-revisited-amid-claims-of-racism.html.

182 **"stay out of Harlem":** Peter Noel, "Mark Green, You Can't Hide," *Village Voice,* October 16, 2001 http://www.villagevoice.com/news/mark-green-you -cant-hide-6396685.

182 **"That ad is defensible":** Adam Nagourney, "Heated Race Revisited, Amid Claims of Racism," *New York Times,* October 16, 2001, http://www.nytimes .com/2001/10/16/nyregion/political-memo-heated-race-revisited-amid -claims-of-racism.html.

187 **"emphasizing not politics":** Eliot Spitzer, interview by the author, March 10, 2015.

187 **"appeal to both":** Arnie Sergura, interview by the author, May 12, 2015.

188 **"too independent":** Dominick Carter, interview by the author, May 13, 2015.

188 **"That's fine":** Michael Saul, "Billionaire Says Tax Returns Are His Business," *New York Daily News,* November 1, 2001, http://www.nydailynews .com/archives/news/billionaire-tax-returns-business-article-1.926163.

188 **Purnick on Bloomberg:** "For Bloomberg, Ambition vs. Caution," *New York Times,* January. 28, 2016, A29. See also *Mike Bloomberg: Money, Power, Politics* (New York: PublicAffairs, 2010).

189 **"give him a hug":** Jules Witcover, "Support of Guiliani Put Bloomberg on Top," *Baltimore Sun,* November 9, 2001, http://articles.baltimoresun.com /2001-11-09/news/0111090109_1_rudy-giuliani-giuliani-endorsement-garth.

190 **racial anthrax:** Joyce Shelby, "Rev. Al Warns Green: Black Nod's in Doubt," *New York Daily News,* November 4, 2001 http://www.nydailynews.com /archives/news/rev-al-warns-green-black-nod-doubt-article-1.934339.

190 **headlines start appearing:** Mark Stamey, "Bitter Rev. Al Says Green Played 'Race Card' to Beat Ferrer," *New York Post,* October 14, 2001, http:// nypost.com/2001/10/14/bitter-rev-al-says-green-played-the-race-card-to -beat-ferrer/.

190 **"Sharpton and, to his credit":** Elizabeth Kolbert, "How to Succeed," *New Yorker,* December 20, 1999, 44.

191 **provocative lead:** Larry Cohler-Esses, "Sharton-Ferrer Flyper Flap: Green campaign did it, 3 Dem Sources Charge," *New York Daily News,* October 30, 2001, http://www.nydailynews.com/archives/news/sharpton-ferrer-flyer -flap-green-campaign-3-dem-sources-charge-article-1.922719.

192 **At the dinner:** Michael Cooper, "Unity Dinner for Green Is Anything But, with Ferrer Absent," *New York Times,* November 3, 2001, http://www.ny times.com/2001/11/03/nyregion/unity-dinner-for-green-is-anything-but -with-ferrer-absent.html.

195 **Gracious Tone:** Joel Siegel, "Green Takes Gracious Tone," *New York Daily News*, December 13, 2001, http://www.nydailynews.com/archives/news/green-takes-gracious-tone-article-1.923517. See also Adam Nagourney, "Avoiding 'Should Have,' Green Looks Back at Race," *New York Times*, December 13, 2001, D4.

196 **Dismayed journalists:** Michael Tomasky, "Carpe Dems," *New York* magazine, November 19, 2001, http://nymag.com/news/articles/bloomberg/tomasky.htm.

196 **"walk on eggshells":** Joyce Purnick, "The Race Card and When to Fold," *New York Times*, November 12, 2001, http://www.nytimes.com/2001/11/12/nyregion/metro-matters-the-race-card-and-knowing-when-to-fold.html.

196 **"white sheets and a hood":** Clyde Haberman, "Sharpton Loses the Ring But Never the Spotlight," *New York Times*, January 23, 2002, http://www.nytimes.com/2002/01/23/nyregion/nyc-sharpton-loses-the-ring-but-never-the-spotlight.html.

198 **skeptical *New York Times*:** "A Primary Choice: Mark Green," *New York Times*, September 2, 2001, http://www.nytimes.com/2001/09/02/opinion/a-primary-choice-mark-green.html.

198 **Smith on Green loss**: Chris Smith, "Not Mike," *New York* magazine, October 20, 2011.

198 **"one other thing":** Ray Kelly, *Vigilance: My Life Serving America and Protecting its Empire City* (New York: Hachette Books, 2015).

199 **McGovern reportedly replied:** Katie Glueck, "Mondale: McGovern Funny, Idealistic," *Politico*, October 21, 2012, http://www.politico.com/story/2012/10/mondale-recalls-mcgoverns-humor-ideals-082686.

199 ***The New York Post* writes:** Richard Perez-Pena, "McCall Criticizes Cuomo for 'Divisive' Comment," *New York Times*, November 17, 2001, http://www.nytimes.com/2001/11/17/nyregion/mccall-criticizes-cuomo-for-a-divisive-comment.html.

199 **proudly informs:** Tom Robbins, "The Hidden Persuaders," *Village Voice*, October 16, 2001, http://www.villagevoice.com/news/the-hidden-persuaders-6396683.

200 **contributed $50,000:** Benjamin Smith, "Bloomberg Donates $50,000 to Group Linked to Fulani," *New York Sun*, July 17, 2002, http://culteducation.com/group/1076-new-alliance-party/15182-bloomberg-donates-50000-to-group-linked-to-fulani-.html.

200 **"So what!":** Joyce Purnick, *Bloomberg: Money, Power, Politics* (New York: Public Affairs, 2010), 114.

200 **"that racial contract":** Ricahrd Perez-Pena, "McCall Criticizews Cuomo for 'Divisive' Comment," *New York Times*, November 17, 2001, http://www.nytimes.com/2001/11/17/nyregion/mccall-criticizes-cuomo-for-a-divisive-comment.html.

200 **"racialized and ridiculed":** Wayne Barrett, "Getting Greened," *Village Voice*, September 11–18, 2002.

201 **Biden memorably says:** "Biden: Rudy's Sentences Consist of 'A Noun, a Verb and 9/11,'" *Huffington Post*, http://www.huffingtonpost.com/2007/10/30/biden-rudys-sentences-con_n_70509.html.

201 **flicker of irony:** Celeste Katz, Chauncey Alcorn, and Larry McShane, "Al Sharpton Rips Giuliani Over Obama Comments, Says 'Rudy Needs a Hug,'" *New York Daily News*, February 22, 2015, http://www.nydailynews.com/news/politics/al-sharpton-rips-giuliani-obama-comments-article-1.2123984.

201 **"What's Next for Green":** Dean E. Murphy and Michael Cooper, "What's Next for Green? Politics (and a Beard) May Be Out," *New York Times*, December 3, 2001, http://www.nytimes.com/2001/12/03/nyregion/what-s-next -for-green-politics-and-a-beard-may-be-out.html.

206 **"a nesting place":** "Cuomo vs. Green," *New York Times*, August 27, 2006, http://www.nytimes.com/2006/08/27/opinion/nyregionopinions/CIattyge nl.html.

206 **"maybe 10 phone calls":** Patrick Healy, "In Son's Race, Father Sees Cuomo Comeback," *New York Times*, October 31, 2006, http://www.nytimes.com /2006/10/31/nyregion/31mario.html?n=Top%2FReference%2FTimes%20 Topics%2FSubjects%2FO%2FOrganized%20Labor&_r=0.

209 **"look into this again":** Ben Smith, "New Probe into Green's '01 Mayor Campaign," *New York Daily News*, June 22, 2006, http://www.nydailynews.com /archives/news/new-probe-green-01-mayor-campaign-article-1.636062.

209 **letter exonerating me:** Michael Brick, "Investigation into '01 Race Exonerates Green," *New York Times*, July 22, 2006, http://www.nytimes.com/2006 /07/22/nyregion/22green.html?pagewanted=print.

210 **under criminal investigation:** Damon Winter, "Notes Found in Review of Police Work Could Exonerate 2 Convicted in Killing," *New York Times*, April 8, 2014, http://www.nytimes.com/2014/04/09/nyregion/notes-found-as-bro oklyn-detectives-work-is-reviewed-could-exonerate-two-convicted-of-mur der.html; Josh Saul, "Fishy-Funds Probers Closing in on Hynes," *New York Post*, October 19, 2015, 2.

210 **selfish about-face:** Michael Barbaro and Tim Arango, "Bloomberg Said to test a Term-Limit Reversal," *New York Times*, August 22, 2008, http://www .nytimes.com/2008/08/23/nyregion/23bloomberg.html.

211 **exclusive interview:** Jonathan P. Hicks, "Put Off by Term-Limits Fight, Green Ponders Another Run for Public Advocate," *New York Times*, December 7, 2008, http://www.nytimes.com/2008/12/08/nyregion/08green.html.

212 **"most corrupt":** Annie Karni, "Bill de Blasio Sought Campaign Contributions from Landlord He Once Blasted as 'One of the Most Corrupt' in City: Sources," *New York Daily News*, September 7, 2009, http://www.ny dailynews.com/news/election/de-blasio-sought-money-corrupt-landlord -sources-article-1.1448450.

214 **astonished *New York Times*:** Michael Cooper, "At $92.60 a Vote, Bloomberg Shatters n Election Record," *New York Times*, December 4, 2001, http://www .nytimes.com/2001/12/04/nyregion/at-92.60-a-vote-bloomberg-shatters-an -election-record.html.

CHAPTER 5: WHAT IT'S LIKE—NATIONAL POLITICS

221 **"somebody had to":** Kurt Andersen, "Going for a Knockout," *Time*, March 5, 1984, http://content.time.com/time/subscriber/article/0,33009,952336,00 .html.

222 **buries his ax:** Matt Bai, "How Gary Hart's Downfall Forever Changed American Politics," *New York Times*, September 18, 2014.

223 **Hart on Mondale's PAC:** "Hart Draws Some Blood," *Newsweek*, May 7, 1984.

224 **Hart's rallies in NYC, with Sagan:** Maureen Dowd, "New Yorkers to Vote Today in Primary," *New York Times*, April 3, 1984, http://www.nytimes.com /1984/04/03/nyregion/new-yorkers-to-vote-today-in-primary-hart.html.

226 **Have a summit:** Bernard Weinraub, "Mondale and Hart, With Smiles, Say Only Target is Reagan," *New York Times*, June 26, 1984, http://www.nytimes.com/1984/06/27/us/mondale-and-hart-with-smiles-say-only-target-now-is-reagan.html.

228 **farewell and a wink:** "Excerpts from Hart Speech to Convention Exhorting party for Campaign," *New York Times*, July 19, 1984.

229 **"Did I ... ?"** Robin Toner, "Hart, Conceding Error, Says He Did Nothing Immoral," *New York Times*, May 6, 1987, http://www.nytimes.com/1987/05/06/us/hart-conceding-error-says-he-did-nothing-immoral.html.

232 **"Let them be produced":** Hendrik Hertzberg, *Politics: Observations and Arguments, 1966–2004* (New York: Penguin, 2004), 171.

234 **Clinton on Brown's flat tax:** Evans and Novak, "Brown's Flat Tax Can Cost Him NY," *New York Post*, March 27, 1992, 23.

236 **Clinton and Gore:** For more on the tense situation between the two, see Robert Shrum, *No Excuses: Concessions of a Serial Campaigner* (New York: Simon & Schuster, 2007), 366.

236 **Clinton lands at JFK:** Vincent Morris, Dan Mangan, "Bill's Slow Ride Out on Ex-Prez Flight," *New York Post*, January 21, 2001.

239 **John doesn't disappoint:** Michael Tackett, "Bush's Handling of the War Emerges as A Central Issue," *Chicago Tribune*, September 21, 2004.

240 **"outsourced the job":** Richard W. Stevenson and Jodi Wilgoren, "Candidates Give Tough Response to the al Qaeda Tape," *New York Times*, October 30, 2004.

241 **Kerry's concession:** For the best summary of Kerry's last day as a candidate, see chapter seven of Shrum, *No Excuses*.

CHAPTER 6: WHAT IT TAKES

250 **produces worry:** Jonathan Alter, *The Defining Moment: FDR's Hundred Days and the Triumph of Hope* (New York: Simon and Schuster, 2005), 23.

251 **"Attack, attack, attack":** Todd Gitlin, *The Bulldozer and the Big Tent: Blind Republicans, Lame Democrats and the Recovery of American Ideals* (Hoboken, NJ: Wiley and Sons, 2007), 102.

254 **"let 'em":** Larry Getlen, "Journalist Debunks Babe Ruth's Legendary 'Called Shot,'" *New York Post*, February 1, 2014, http://nypost.com/2014/02/01/chicago-journalist-debunks-babe-ruths-called-shot/.

257 **"public opinion baths":** Stephen Wynalda, *366 Days in Abraham Lincoln's Presidency: The Private, Political, and Military Decisions of America's Greatest President* (New York: Skyhorse Publishing, 2014), 171.

257 **"learning nuthin'":** Robert Caro, *Master of the Senate: The Years of Lyndon Johnson* (New York: Vintage, 2002), 569.

258 **"unavoidable for comment":** Dan Janison, "Ed Koch Wasn't Always What He Seemed," *Newsday*, February 1, 2013, http://www.newsday.com/long-island/columnists/dan-janison/ed-koch-wasn-t-always-what-he-seemed-1.4547518.

259 **"look like Trayvon":** Byron Tau, "Obama: 'If I Had a Son, He'd Look Like Trayvon,'" *Politico*, March 23, 2012, http://www.politico.com/blogs/politico44/2012/03/obama-if-i-had-a-son-hed-look-like-trayvon-118439.

259 **"could have been me":** Tom Cohen, "Obama: 'Trayvon Martin Could Have Been Me,'" CNN, July 19, 2013, http://www.cnn.com/2013/07/19/politics/obama-zimmerman/.

259 **"know when to retreat and dare to do it"**: "Great Leaders Know When to Retreat," *Financial Times,* November 15, 2010, http://www.ft.com/cms/s/0 /ee27af48-eb57-11df-b482-00144feab49a.html#axzz3lSfynI7P.

260 **The EQ of Henry Lloyd George**: A. Scott Berg, *Wilson* (New York: G. P. Putnam's Sons, 2013), 524–525.

261 **Clinton confidant Bernie Nussbaum**: Rebecca Trasister, "The Best Thing Hillary Could Do for Her Campaign? Drop Bill," *New Republic,* May 7, 2015, http://www.newrepublic.com/article/121733/best-thing-hillary-could -do-her-campaign-drop-bill.

264 **Gray Panthers in Oregon**: Jeff Mapes, "Wyden's Political Apprenticeship with the Gray Panthers," *Oregonian/Oregon Live,* July 24, 2013, http://www .oregonlive.com/mapes/index.ssf/2013/07/wydens_political_apprenticeshi .html.

CHAPTER 7: MEDIA POLITICS

267 **Buckley on Green**: William F. Buckley Jr.: *On the Firing Line: The Public Life of Our Public Figures* (New York: Random House, 1989), 172–175.

267 **prep school days**: John B. Judis, *William F. Buckley, Jr.: Patron Saint of the Conservatives* (New York: Simon & Schuster, 2001), 36.

271 **"been destroyed"**: J. R. Jones, "The Real Buckley-Vidal Debate Happened on the Page," *Chicago Reader,* August 5, 2015.

271 **Buckley on Green**: Buckley, *On the Firing Line,* 172–175.

276 **segments on Benghazi**: Hannah Groch-Begley and Rob Savillo, "Report: Fox's Benghazi Obsession By the Numbers," *Media Matters for America,* September 16, 2014.

277 **One 2003 poll**: David Brock, *The Republican Noise Machine: Right-wing Media and How It Corrupts Democracy* (New York: Crown Publishing, 2004), 334.

278 **"complete fabrication"**: Steve Rendall, "George Washington on Guns . . . According to Sean Hannity," *FAIR,* January 9, 2013.

279 **"Jebbie says..."**: Jill Lepore, "Bad News," *New Yorker,* January 20, 2014.

280 **Rich is right**: Frank Rich, "Stop Beating a Dead Fox," *New York,* January 26, 2014.

281 **"working the refs"**: Eric Alterman, "What Liberal Media?" *The Nation,* February 6, 2003.

282 **Taking Over Air America**: Matt Flamm, "Air America Goes Green," *Crain's New York Business,* March 19, 2007, 3.

284 **"brainful of joy"**: Lizz Winstead, *Lizz Free or Die: Essays* (New York: Riverhead Books, 2012), 255.

288 **"a liberal tendency"**: Paul Farhi, "With O'Reilly Joining Peers on Radio, Liberals Are Being Left Out of the Mix," *Los Angeles Times,* May 17, 2002.

288 **"public good"**: John Nichols and Robert W. McChesney, "How to Save Journalism," *The Nation,* January 7, 2010.

289 **"since Icarus"**: Lauren Collins, "The Oracle," *New Yorker,* October 13, 2008.

CHAPTER 8: ECONOMY AND DEMOCRACY

293 **irrational exuberance**: William A. Rusher, "Liberalism: Dead Or Alive?," *Ludington Daily News,* April 22, 1987, 4.

295 **Reagan as actor**: See Sean Wilentz, *The Age of Reagan: A History, 1974–2008* (New York: HarperCollins, 2008).

298	**tactics endorsed**: Mark Mazzetti, "Panel Faults C.I.A. Over Brutality and Deceit in Terrorism Interrogations," *New York Times,* December 9, 2014, http://www.nytimes.com/2014/12/10/world/senate-intelligence-committee-cia-torture-report.html.

298	**Bush's low polls**: Megan Thee-Brenan, "Poll Finds Disapproval of Bush Unwavering," *New York Times,* January 16, 2009, http://www.nytimes.com/2009/01/17/us/politics/17poll.html.

298	**July 10, 2001, meeting:** See *The Spymasters,* Showtime, 2015.

300	**Obama's successful presidency**: For the three best books on this man and his presidency, see: David Axelrod's *Believer: My Forty Years in Politics* (2015), Jonathan Alter's *The Center Holds: Obama and His Enemies* (2013), and David Remnick's *The Bridge: The Life and Rise of Barack Obama* (2010).

301	**Not one Republican:** An exception appeared as this book went to print: David Brooks, "I Miss Barack Obama," *New York Times,* February 9, 2016.

302	**Census Bureau report:** Sabrina Tavernise, "Whites Account for Under Half of Births in U.S.," *New York Times,* May 17, 2012, http://www.nytimes.com/2012/05/17/us/whites-account-for-under-half-of-births-in-us.html.

302	**deny public services:** Roxanna Kopetman, "Politics, Activism, Families: How Prop. 187 Is Still Felt 20 Years Later," *Orange County Register,* October 31, 2014, http://www.ocregister.com/articles/california-640388-prop-state.html.

302	**fastest-growing racial cohort**: Anna Brown, "U.S. Hispanic and Asian Populations Growing, But for Different Reasons," Pew Research, June 26, 2014, http://www.pewresearch.org/fact-tank/2014/06/26/u-s-hispanic-and-asian-populations-growing-but-for-different-reasons/.

303	**white share of the electorate:** Chris Cillizza and Jon Cohen, "President Obama and the White Vote? No Problem," *Washington Post,* November 8, 2012, http://www.washingtonpost.com/news/the-fix/wp/2012/11/08/president-obama-and-the-white-vote-no-problem/.

303	**seemingly homogenously white:** Jack Healy, "A Drive for Swing State Votes Has Colorado's Latinos Listening," *New York Times,* May 26, 2015, http://www.nytimes.com/2015/05/27/us/republicans-seek-to-bridge-gap-with-latinos-in-colorado-and-beyond.html.

304	**"not especially political":** Jackie Calmes, "To Hold Senate, Democrats Rely on Single Women," *New York Times,* July 3, 2014, http://www.nytimes.com/2014/07/03/us/single-women-midterm-elections.html.

304	**now number 55 million:** Mara Liasson, "All the Single Ladies: 5 Takeaways About Unmarried Female Voters," *New York Times,* May 5, 2014, http://www.npr.org/2014/05/05/308955525/all-the-single-ladies-5-takeaways-about-unmarried-women-voters.

305	**identifying as Christians dropped:** Nate Cohn, "Big Drop in Share of Americans Calling Themselves Christians," *New York Times,* May 12, 2015, http://www.nytimes.com/2015/05/12/upshot/big-drop-in-share-of-americans-calling-themselves-christian.html.

305	**"cannot overrule God":** Ashley Killough, "Mike Huckabee: The Supreme Court Can't Overrule God," CNN, April 29, 2015.

305	**more comfortable with a gay president:** Trudy Ring, "Poll: Americans Prefer Gay President to Evangelical or Tea Partier," *Advocate,* May 6, 2015, http://www.advocate.com/politics/2015/05/06/poll-americans-prefer-gay-president-evangelical-or-tea-partier.

305 **trend is even more dramatic:** Michael Lipka, "Millennials Are Increasingly Driving Growth of 'Nones,'" Pew Center Research, May 12, 2015, http://www.pewresearch.org/fact-tank/2015/05/12/millennials-increasingly-are-driving-growth-of-nones/.

305 **left their church:** Jaweed Kaleem, "One Third of Millennials Who Left Their Religion Did It Because of Anti-Gay Policies: Survey," *Huffington Post*, February 26, 2014, http://www.huffingtonpost.com/2014/02/26/millennials-gay-unaffiliated-church-religion_n_4856094.html.

306 **"capital in this campaign, political capital":** Richard W. Stevenson, "Confident Bush Outlines Ambitious Plan for Second Term," *New York Times*, November 5, 2004, http://www.nytimes.com/2004/11/05/politics/campaign/confident-bush-outlines-ambitious-plan-for-2nd-term.html.

306 **would be so foolish:** Rachel Maddow, "Why Focus Groups' Incredulity Matters" (blog), MSNBC, July 9, 2012, http://www.msnbc.com/rachel-maddow-show/why-focus-groups-incredulity-matters.

306 **David Frum argues that:** David Frum, "The Republican Advantage Among Older Voters Won't Last," *Atlantic*, May 14, 2014, http://www.theatlantic.com/politics/archive/2014/05/the-republican-advantage-among-older-voters-wont-last/370851/.

307 **"Democracy cannot work":** David Moberg, "America's 200-Year-Long Battle for Workplace Democracy," *In These Times*, September 3, 2015, http://inthesetimes.com/article/15546/americas_200_year_long_battle_for_workplace_democracy.

307 **slow but steady decline:** Steven Greenhouse, "Union Membership in U.S. Fell to a 70-Year Low Last Year," *New York Times*, January 21, 2011, http://www.nytimes.com/2011/01/22/business/22union.html.

307 **IMF concedes:** Michael Hitzik, "IMF Agrees: Decline of Union Power Has Increased Income Inequality," *Los Angeles Times*, March 25, 2015, http://www.latimes.com/business/hiltzik/la-fi-mh-imf-agrees-loss-of-union-power-20150325-column.html.

307 **highest point since 2008:** Lydia Saad, "Americans' Support for Labor Unions Continues to Recover," Gallup, August 17, 2015, http://www.gallup.com/poll/184622/americans-support-labor-unions-continues-recover.aspx.

308 **threatened public sector organizing:** Garrett Epps, "The End of Public-Employee Unions?" *Atlantic*, February 20, 2015, http://www.theatlantic.com/politics/archive/2015/02/the-end-of-public-employee-unions/385690/.

308 **western New York:** Susan Dominus, "What Happened to the Girls in Le Roy," *New York Times Magazine*, March 7, 2012, http://www.nytimes.com/2012/03/11/magazine/teenage-girls-twitching-le-roy.html.

309 **Frank Rich wrote a classic essay:** *Whitewash, New York*, May 5, 2013, http://nymag.com/news/frank-rich/republicans-civil-rights-2013-5/.

309 **American Enterprise Institute scholars:** Thomas E. Mann and Norman Ornstein, *It's Even Worse Than It Looks: How the American Constitutional System Collided with the New Politics of Extremism* (New York: Basic Books, 2013), xxiv.

310 **82 percent of consistent liberals:** Norman Ornstein, "Yes, Polarization Is Asymmetric—and Conservatives Are Worse," *Atlantic*, June 19, 2014, http://www.theatlantic.com/politics/archive/2014/06/yes-polarization-is-asymmetric-and-conservatives-are-worse/373044/.

315   **Lowry on conservatism:** George Packer, "The Fall of Conservatism," *New Yorker*, May 22, 2008, http://www.newyorker.com/magazine/2008/05/26/the-fall-of-conservatism.

315   **worst showing since 1992:** Paul Singer, "Poll: Republican Party Approval Ratings Lowest in Decades," *USA Today*, July 24, 2015, http://onpolitics.usatoday.com/2015/07/24/poll-republican-party-approval-ratings-lowest-in-decades/.

315   **gap shrank by half:** "Liberals Make Big Comeback in 2015," *Wall Street Journal*, June 7, 2015, http://blogs.wsj.com/washwire/2015/06/07/liberals-make-big-comeback-in-2015-poll-analysis-finds/.

315   **"concerned about people like me":** Aaron Blake, "Poll: Republicans Seen as More Extreme, Democrats as More Bipartisan," *Washington Post*, January 27, 2014, http://www.washingtonpost.com/news/post-politics/wp/2014/01/27/poll-republicans-seen-as-more-extreme-democrats-as-more-bipartisan/.

315   **report in March 2013:** Thomas B. Edsall, "The Republican Autopsy Report," *New York Times*, March 20, 2013, http://opinionator.blogs.nytimes.com/2013/03/20/the-republican-autopsy-report/?_r=0.

315   **"lost to our party":** David Frum, *Comeback: Conservatism That Can Win Again* (New York: Broadway Books, 2007), 2.

316   **much-heralded book in 2015:** N. Gregory Mankiw, "The Conservative Heart, by Arthur C. Brooks," *New York Times*, July 28, 2015, http://www.nytimes.com/2015/08/02/books/review/the-conservative-heart-by-arthur-c-brooks.html.

317   **send Jews "to the ovens":** Jennifer Shutt, "Mike Huckabee: Obama Marching Israelis 'To the Door of the Oven,'" *Politico*, July 26, 2015, http://www.politico.com/story/2015/07/mike-huckabee-iranian-nuclear-deal-120636.

317   **the jig's up:** For example, see this comment: "'The Republican Party has never done anything for the working man like me, even though we've voted Republican for years,' said Leo Martin, a 62-year-old machinist," quoted in Patrick Healy and Jonathan Martin, "Republicans Fearing a Lasting Split as Class Divisions Erupt," *New York Times*, January 10, 2016. Generally, see Thomas Frank, *What's the Matter with Kansas? How Conservatives Won the Heart of America* (New York: Henry Holt, 2004).

318   **freaked out:** Jordan Fabian, "Obama Defends Comparing GOP to Iran Hardliners," *The Hill*, August 7, 2015, http://thehill.com/homenews/administration/250542-obama-doubles-down-on-comparing-gop-to-iranian-hardliners.

318   **19,000 lives now saved:** Harold Pollack, Bill Gardner, and Timothy Jost, "Valuing Medicaid," *American Prospect*, July 26, 2015.

318   **"warrior spirit":** See Paul Waldman, *Being Right Is Not Enough: What Progressives Must Learn from Conservative Success* (Hoboken, NJ: Wiley, 2006), 19.

318   **Republican gains in states:** Alec MacGillis, "Who Turned my Blue State Red?" *New York Times Sunday Review*, November 22, 2015, 4.

320   **of marriage equality:** David Cole, "The Roberts Court Tunes In to Democracy, For Once," *The Nation*, July 2, 2015, http://www.thenation.com/article/the-roberts-court-tunes-in-to-democracy-for-once/.

320   **"better outcomes for society":** Binyamin Appelbaum, "Jean Tirole Wins Nobel in Economics for Work on Regulation," *New York Times*, October 13, 2014, http://www.nytimes.com/2014/10/14/business/jean-tirole-wins-nobel-prize-in-economics.html.

321 **"hands off my Medicare":** Timothy Noah, "The Medicare-Isn't-Government Meme," *Slate*, August 5, 2009, http://www.slate.com/articles/news_and_po litics/prescriptions/2009/08/the_medicareisntgovernment_meme.html.

321 **sparing thousands of families:** Robert D. McFadden, "Frances Oldham Kelsey, Who Saved U.S. Babies from Thalidomide, Dies at 101," *New York Times*, August 7, 2015, http://www.nytimes.com/2015/08/08/science/frances -oldham-kelsey-fda-doctor-who-exposed-danger-of-thalidomide-dies-at -101.html.

324 **93 percent of income gains:** "Top 1% Got 93% of Income Growth as Rich-Poor Gap Widened," *Bloomberg*, October 2, 2012, http://www.bloomberg .com/news/articles/2012-10-02/top-1-got-93-of-income-growth-as-rich-po or-gap-widened.

324 **85 richest billionaires:** Graeme Wearden, "Oxfam: 85 Richest People as Wealthy as Poorest Half of the World," *Guardian*, January 20, 2014.

324 **just 47 individuals:** Paul Buchheit, "5 Facts About How America Rigged for a Massive Wealth Transfer to the Rich," *Alternet*, November 4, 2014, http://www.alternet.org/economy/5-facts-about-how-america-rig ged-massive-wealth-transfer-rich.

324 **rose 937 percent:** Bryce Covert, "CEOS Earn Nearly 300 Times What Their Workers Make," Think Progress, June 12, 2014, http://thinkprogress.org /economy/2014/06/12/3448115/ceo-worker-pay-ratio/.

324 **productivity rose 96 percent:** Dean Paton, "Poverty Is Not Inevitable: What We Can Do Now to Turn Things Around," Bill Moyers.com, August 29, 2014, http://billmoyers.com/2014/08/29/poverty-is-not-inevitable-what -we-can-do-now-to-turn-things-around/.

325 **$14 trillion over two years:** Mark Gongloff, "The Financial Crisis Cost More Than $14 Trillion: Dallas Fed Study," *Huffington Post*, July 30, 2013, http://www.huffingtonpost.com/2013/07/30/financial-crisis-cost-fed-study _n_3676118.html.

326 **Progressive economic program generally**: See George Stiglitz, *The Great Divide: Unequal Societies and What We Can Do About Them* (2013); Robert B. Reich, *Saving Capitalism: For the Many, Not the Few* (2015); Jeff Madrick, *Seven Bad Ideas: How Mainstream Economists have Damaged America and the World* (2015); Paul Krugman, "Is Vast Inequality Necessary?" *New York Times*, January 15, 2016, A31; Patricia Cohen, "Raising Taxes on the Wealthiest Would Pay for Candidates' Bold Plans," *New York Times*, October 17, 2015, B1; Harold Myerson, "Why Democrats Need to Take Sides" *American Prospect*, July/August 2015, 18.

326 **Financial trading tax:** Editorial, "The Need for a Financial Trading Tax," *New York Times*, January 28, 2016, A26.

327 **Wrote one advocate:** Paul Buchheit, "Infuriating Facts About Our Disappearing Middle-Class Wealth," Common Dreams, November 3, 2014, http://www.commondreams.org/views/2014/11/03/infuriating-facts-about -our-disappearing-middle-class-wealth.

327 **Profit-sharing:** Dan Merica, "Hillary Clinton to Propose 15% Tax Credit for Profit Sharing," CNN, July 16, 2015, http://www.cnn.com/2015/07/16 /politics/hillary-clinton-tax-credit-profit-sharing/.

327 **there will be stiff fines:** Andrew Sparrow, "'National Living Wage' Dodgers Face Higher Penalties," *Guardian*, August 31, 2015, http://www.theguardian .com/society/2015/sep/01/national-living-wage-dodgers-face-higher-penal ties.

328 **"are not frills":** Barack Obama, "Remarks by President Obama at the White House Summit on Working Families," June 23, 2014, Washington D.C.

328 **Guaranteed retirement accounts:** Teresa Ghilarducci and Hamilton James, "A Smarter Plan for Retirement," *New York Times,* January 1, 2016.

329 **only 160 families:** Nicholas Confessore, Sarah Cohen, and Karen Yourish, "Small Pool of Rich Donors Dominates Election Giving," *New York Times,* August 1, 2015, http://www.nytimes.com/2015/08/02/us/small-pool-of-rich-donors-dominates-election-giving.html.

329 **the lowest in 72 years:** "The Worst Voter Turnout in 72 Years," *New York Times,* November 11, 2014, http://www.nytimes.com/2014/11/12/opinion/the-worst-voter-turnout-in-72-years.html.

329 **study out of Loyola:** Justin Levitt, "A Comprehensive Investigation of Voter Impersonation Finds 31 Credible Incidents Out of One Billion Ballots Cast," *Washington Post,* August 6, 2014, http://www.washingtonpost.com/news/wonkblog/wp/2014/08/06/a-comprehensive-investigation-of-voter-impersonation-finds-31-credible-incidents-out-of-one-billion-ballots-cast/.

329 **"except refine it":** Henry Demarest Lloyd, "Story of a Great Monopoly," *Atlantic,* March 1881, http://www.theatlantic.com/ideastour/markets-morals/lloyd-full.html.

333 **eagerly audition:** Nicholas Confessore, "Koch Brothers' Budget of $889 Million for 2016 Is on Par with Both Parties' Spending," *New York Times,* January 26, 2015, http://www.nytimes.com/2015/01/27/us/politics/kochs-plan-to-spend-900-million-on-2016-campaign.html.

333 **Justice Kennedy expresses regret:** Paul Blumenthal, "Anthony Kennedy's Citizens United Disclosure Salve 'Not Working,'" Huffington Post, November 2, 2015.

333 **Kennedy, Scalia and Citizens United:** See Brennan Center Report, "Six 5-4 Roberts Court Decisions have Transformed Role of Money in Elections," January 13, 2016.

334 **"I want to be a bus driver":** Samuel G. Freedman, "The Other America," *Los Angeles Times,* March 3, 1991, http://articles.latimes.com/1991-03-03/books/bk-241_1_alex-kotlowitz.

335 **Nixon on blacks:** "The Long Dog Whistle," *The Nation,* November 9, 2015, 8.

336 **Bipartisan push on justice reform:** Michael Shear, "Obama Calls for Less Prison and More Fairness in Sentencing Laws," *New York Times,* November 3, 2015.

336 **20 times wealthier:** "About Gun Violence," Brady Campaign, http://www.bradycampaign.org/about-gun-violence.

336 **"Tiller the Baby Killer":** Gabriel Winant, "O'Reilly's Campaign Against Murdered Doctor," Salon, Mar

336 **"Gospel of Giuliani":** Ta-Nehisi Coates, "The Gospel of Rudy Giuliani," Atlantic, November 24, 2014.

337 **white family is 20 times wealthier:** Dave Gilson, "Chart: the Typical White Family is 20 Times Wealthier than the Typical Black Family," *Mother Jones,* October 2, 2014, http://www.motherjones.com/mojo/2014/10/income-inequality-race-wealth-income.

337 **"few avenues of escape":** The Editorial Board, "The Architecture of Segregation," *New York Times,* September 5, 2015, http://www.nytimes.com/2015/09/06/opinion/sunday/the-architecture-of-segregation.html;

337 **study at the University of Kansas:** Jaeah Lee, "Driving While Black Has Actually Gotten More Dangerous in the Last 15 Years," *Mother Jones,* April 15,

2015, http://www.motherjones.com/kevin-drum/2015/04/north-carolina-tr
affic-stops.

337 **"justice" system:** "Criminal Justice Fact Sheet," NAACP, http://www.naacp
.org/pages/criminal-justice-fact-sheet.

337 **"Missing Black Men":** Editorial, "The Methodology: 1.5 Million Missing
Black Men," *New York Times,* April 20, 2015.

338 **Comey and body cameras:** "Ferguson Effect: Political Lies About Police Brutality," *New York Times,* October 27, 2015, A26.

339 **heat wave melting pavements:** Vivek Nemana, "At least 800 Have Died
in a Heat Wave That Has Melted Roads in India," *Business Insider,* May
26, 2015, http://www.businessinsider.com/afp-india-heatwave-kills-800-as
-capitals-roads-melt-2015-5.

339 **half of wildlife lost:** Damian Carrington, "Earth Has Lost Half of Its
Wildlife in the Past 40 Years, Says WWF," *Guardian,* September 30, 2014,
http://www.theguardian.com/environment/2014/sep/29/earth-lost-50-wild
life-in-40-years-wwf.

339 **6.5 feet by the next century:** "Sea Level Rise," *National Geographic,* http://
ocean.nationalgeographic.com/ocean/critical-issues-sea-level-rise/.

339 **within just feet of high tide:** Justin Gillis, "Rising Sea Levels Seen as Threat
to Coastal U.S.," *New York Times,* March 13, 2012, http://www.nytimes
.com/2012/03/14/science/earth/study-rising-sea-levels-a-risk-to-coastal
-states.html.

339 **"Five Lies About Tobacco":** Joseph Blast, "Five Lies About Tobacco," Heartland Institute, July 1998, https://www.heartland.org/policy-documents/july
-1998-five-lies-about-tobacco-tobacco-bill-wasnt-about-kids.

339 **"For everybody who thinks it's warming":** Igor Bobic, "Mitch McConnell
Shrugs Off Climate Change: 'Each Side Has Their Scientists,'" *Huffington
Post,* August 20, 2014, http://www.huffingtonpost.com/2014/08/20/mitch
-mcconnell-climate-change_n_5694575.html.

340 **In Florida, the terms "climate change":** Tristram Korten, "In Florida, Officials Ban Term 'Climate Change,'" *Miami Herald,* March 8, 2015, http://
www.miamiherald.com/news/state/florida/article12983720.html.

340 **more likely to vote:** Coral Davenport and Marjorie Connelly, "Most Republicans Say They Back Climate Action, Poll Finds," *New York Times,* January
30, 2015, http://www.nytimes.com/2015/01/31/us/politics/most-americans
-support-government-action-on-climate-change-poll-finds.html.

339 **Carbon tax:** Editorial, "Proof that a Price on Carbon Works," *New York
Times,* January 29, 2016, A26.

340 **"We're the first generation":** Thomas Friedman, "Memorial Day 2050,"
New York Times, May 24, 2014, http://www.nytimes.com/2014/05/25/opin
ion/sunday/friedman-memorial-day-2050.html.

340 **"few people anywhere imagined":** Hendrik Hertzberg, "Obama Wins," *New
Yorker,* November 17, 2008.

341 *USA, USA, USA:* Richard Fausset and Alan Blinder, "Era Ends As South Carolina Lowers Confederate Flag," *New York Times,* July 10, 2015.

INDEX

ABOUT THE AUTHOR

MARK GREEN GREW UP ON LONG ISLAND AND GRADU-
ated from Cornell University and Harvard Law School, where he was
editor in chief of *The Harvard Civil Rights–Civil Liberties Law Review*.
He was a public interest lawyer, working with Ralph Nader from 1970
to 1980, ultimately as director of Public Citizen's Congress Watch. He
founded and ran The Democracy Project in NYC from 1981 to 2014.

Green served for 11 years in citywide offices, first as the Commissioner of Consumer Affairs under Mayor David Dinkins (1990
to 1993), then as the twice-elected Public Advocate (1993 and 1997),
the #2 citywide official, before narrowly losing the mayoralty to Michael Bloomberg in 2001. He was a regular panelist on *Firing Line*
with William F. Buckley Jr. and on CNN's *Crossfire* and also taught at
NYU School of Law and College of Arts and Sciences (2002 to 2007).

He was the last president of Air America Radio and currently
hosts the nationally syndicated weekend radio program, *Both Sides
Now* (BothSidesRadio.com) and writes a weekly column for the *Huffington Post* (@markjgreen). His #1 best-selling *Who Runs Congress?*
is the largest-selling book ever on the U.S. Congress. *Bright, Infinite
Future* is his twenty-third book.